Child Neglect

Best Practice in Working with Children Series

The titles in the Best Practice in Working with Children series are written for the multi-agency professionals working to promote children's welfare and protect them from harm. Each book in the series draws on current research into what works best for children, providing practical, realistic suggestions as to how practitioners in social work, health and education can work together to promote the resilience and safety of the children in their care.

of related interest

Engaging with Fathers
Practice Issues for Health and Social Care
Brigid Daniel and Julie Taylor
ISBN 1 85302 794 4

Assessing and Promoting Resilience in Vulnerable Children
Three Volume set:
1: The Early Years
2: The School Years
3: Adolescence
Brigid Daniel and Sally Wassell
ISBN 1 84310 045 2

Child Development for Child Care and Protection Workers
Brigid Daniel, Sally Wassell and Robbie Gilligan
ISBN 1 85302 633 6

Supporting Parents
Messages from Research
David Quinton
ISBN 1 84310 210 2

The Developing World of the Child
Edited by Jane Aldgate, David Jones, Wendy Rose and Carole Jeffery
ISBN 1 84310 244 7

Assessing Children's Needs and Circumstances
The Impact of the Assessment Framework
Hedy Cleaver and Steve Walker with Pamela Meadows
ISBN 1 84310 159 9

Child Protection Work
Beyond the Rhetoric
Helen Buckley
ISBN 1 84310 075 4

Prevention and Coping in Child and Family Care
Mothers in adversity coping with child care
Michael Sheppard with Mirka Gröhn
ISBN 1 84310 193 9

Child Neglect

Practice Issues for Health and Social Care

Edited by Julie Taylor and Brigid Daniel

Foreword by Olive Stevenson

Jessica Kingsley Publishers
London and Philadelphia

Table 11.1 is adapted from World Health Organization (2003) *International Classification of Diseases* (10th edition), with permission from WHO.

First published in 2005
by Jessica Kingsley Publishers
116 Pentonville Road
London N1 9JB, UK
and
400 Market Street, Suite 400
Philadelphia, PA 19106, USA

www.jkp.com

Library of Congress Cataloging in Publication Data
Child neglect : practice issues for health and social care / [edited by] Julie Taylor and Brigid Daniel ; foreword by Olive Stevenson.
    p. cm.
    Includes bibliographical references and index.
    ISBN 1-84310-160-2 (pbk.)
    1. Child abuse--Prevention. 2. Social work with children. 3. Child mental health services.
4. Children--Health risk assessment. I. Taylor, Julie, 1961- II. Daniel, Brigid, 1959-
    HV6626.5.C4965 2004
    362.76--dc22

                                                    2004010047

British Library Cataloguing in Publication Data
A CIP catalogue record for this book is available from the British Library

ISBN-13: 978 1 84310 160 4
ISBN-10: 1 84310 160 2

Printed and Bound in Great Britain by
Athenaeum Press, Gateshead, Tyne and Wear

Contents

List of Tables

List of Figures

Foreword

I was particularly pleased to be asked to contribute a foreword to this book because of my long-standing interest in the topic of neglected children and their families. For nearly a decade, there has been increasing recognition in the UK that we have often been ineffective in addressing the needs of children neglected within their own families. We have become more aware of the grave and long-lasting impact of various kinds of neglect upon children's development. The more obvious evidence of physical neglect has long been recognized. However, less clear-cut signs, such as when children do not receive adequate stimulation, protective discipline or reliable health care, were not until recently fully incorporated into assessments of risk in the child protection context. This book is timely. It incorporates a good deal of research and practitioner experience which has become available since my own work on neglect was published in 1998.

Since 1997, there have been, and are likely to be, very important developments in policy and practice which affect, directly or indirectly, the issue of neglect. Some of these have been initiated by government in England. It is not yet clear how, and in what ways, these policies will influence comparable services in Northern Ireland, Scotland and Wales, but it is highly likely that they will have some impact.

In relation to neglect, probably the single most important change in the last five years has been the acceptance that children who are neglected must be seen as being on a continuum of severity and that service responses must be developed accordingly. This marks a shift towards greater involvement in preventative strategies to support families at early stages. Thus, the 'Sure Start' projects in England began modestly but have been widely extended. They have been designed to address problems of child rearing in the pre-school years, for example, by identifying and helping families who might be described as 'incipiently neglectful', for whatever reason. These projects look very promising.

However, the separation of the projects from mainstream social services, whatever its merits, does not encourage 'joined up' thinking between the agencies about family policies. Despite earlier guidance from the English Department of Health (Department of Health 1995) it took the Climbié catastrophe to force into the open the fact that neglected children, even those who should be legally regarded as 'children in need', often needed the key of formal registration as children at risk of abuse to be turned before services were made available to them. Lord Laming identified this in the Climbié report (Lord Laming 2003) as a critical issue, to the point of proposing the abolition of the child protection register as a procedural stage. The Green Paper *Every Child Matters* (Chief Secretary to the Treasury 2003), whilst not unequivocally upholding this Laming recommendation, proposes a local comprehensive data base, using national standards, for all children, on which early warnings of concern would be flagged up by practitioners. However, it accepts that 'it would be a matter of professional judgement whether the combination of two or more flags of minor concern warranted some form of action' (p.53). For neglected children, the effectiveness of such a data base in mobilizing appropriate action will be crucially dependent on the understanding of practitioners of the actual or potential harm caused to children by all forms of neglect. This is usually not only about 'events' or 'incidents', it is about awareness of neglectful 'processes'.

Although not specific to issues of neglect, the English Green Paper has exceedingly important proposals which, if successfully implemented, could have a positive impact on such families. The proposal to bring together, at local level, services to children and families with education services offers an opportunity to integrate the education and social care of children with special needs, whether in special or mainstream schools. Many neglected children fall into this category. For more than a decade in England, there has been relentless pressure on schools to improve educational standards and to meet national standards of performance. Whilst in many ways highly desirable, these policies have left some neglected children 'out in the cold'; more especially those in mainstream schools, who may have been marginalized or excluded. The structural proposals in the Green Paper offer hope of improvement. They do not guarantee it.

The stress in the Green Paper on the benefit of multidisciplinary teams offers hope of better assessment and more effective intervention in work with neglected children and their families. However, my fear is that the sheer scale of the proposed structural changes at national, local and office levels may blow us into a whirlwind of busy-ness and distract us from the reflective consideration of the best ways to help these particularly vulnerable children. We are now at the point when we have valuable research, knowledge and experience to serve the children and their families better than heretofore. The solid material in this book should be used to move us forward professionally. It is much to be welcomed.

Olive Stevenson, University of Nottingham

Chapter One

Introduction to Issues for Health and Social Care in Neglect

Brigid Daniel

Introduction

Neglect is now recognized as leading to significantly poor outcomes for children in the short and long term. It is also known to co-exist with other forms of abuse and adversity. At the same time, the child protection system struggles to find an appropriate response to neglect which is often chronic and associated with poverty and material deprivation. In part, we suggest, this is because neglect exemplifies some of the wider tensions within the current system.

We consider that the case has been made that neglect is harmful to children and therefore we do not give extensive coverage in this book to delineating the effects on children (Dubowitz *et al.* 1993; Gaudin 1993; Stevenson 1998a). We also recognize that practitioners are concerned about the well-being of children who are neglected and, on the whole, do not need to be persuaded that neglect can be harmful. However, practitioners still lack a coherent set of effective responses and therefore the aim of this book is to draw together theoretical and research-based information to help improve practice on behalf of children who are neglected. We also suggest that effective responses to neglect can provide a model for developing more effective protection and support for all children who are considered to be in need of support and in need of protection. If we can find a way to respond effectively to neglect, then we can get it right for all children.

We begin with a broad overview of issues of context, definition and recognition of neglect. We go on to consider the complexity of the complementary roles and responsibilities of different agencies and disciplines. We then cover specific issues that are known to be of particular relevance to neglect before we broaden out again into consideration of the evidence about what works with neglect. In the final chapter we bring all the practice suggestions together and cluster them into themes.

Where we have used case studies, all names and indentifying details have been changed to protect identities. Names, when used are pseudonyms.

Contemporary child protection

Neglected children are, clearly, simultaneously in need and at risk, with the risks flowing both directly from the unmet needs and indirectly from the dangers associated with lack of care and supervision. They, therefore, sit right in the middle of the artificial divide in our system that encourages labelling of children as 'in need' or 'at risk'. This was evident from the findings of the audit of practice that formed part of the Scottish review of child protection (Scottish Executive 2002a). One hundred and eighty-eight cases were selected for audit based on a sample that drew from the range of care and protection concerns including all children that health visitors had concerns about and those referred by education services because of child protection concerns. Cases included children subject to child protection investigations and children on the child protection register. In total 91 were on the child protection register, 31 under the category of physical neglect. However, when all the information was collated about the children it was evident that at least 85 (45%) were experiencing neglect. The significance of this finding lies in the fact that many of these children had not been subject to formal child protection proceedings.

For some years now, there has been fierce debate about the efficacy and appropriateness of a child protection system that is preoccupied with the investigation of, and establishment of risk to the child (Parton 1995). It is argued that this preoccupation with risk creates a narrow portal into the ranges of support and resources on offer to families. It also means that human and material resources are poured into the investigation and establishment of risk at the expense of the provision of support to families who need, and often repeatedly ask for, help. The development of the Assessment Framework was a direct response to this dilemma and was meant to signal a move to delivery of services based upon need (including the need for protection) rather than risk (Department of Health 2000). At the same time, though, our understanding of the direct and indirect risks associated with neglect have been sharpened, and indeed there is some concern that the Assessment Framework does not encourage sufficient attention to risk. Just as we now have a much greater understanding of the needs of children, we have a greater appreciation of the kind of nurturing environment that is optimal for child development and what best supports parents in being able to provide it. We are also developing a sophisticated language of child rights that locates children not only as members of families, but also as members of society who are entitled to protection and services in their own right. With all these competing strands in contemporary child care and protection it is not surprising that individual practitioners may have difficulty in finding an appropriate response to child neglect which they, sadly, encounter all too often in their work.

Definitions

It is interesting that, although we now have a considerable body of evidence about child development, and the milieu in which healthy emotional and physical development can be promoted, we struggle to formulate a clear definition to describe the absence of such a milieu. Perhaps it is inevitable that operational definitions of neglect cannot keep pace with growing expectations, as our understanding of children's needs expands. Stevenson has suggested that it is all too easy to become preoccupied with pinning down a precise definition of neglect which can deflect from purposeful action (1998a). As she observes, practitioners usually know a neglected child when they see one, and, we would argue, would be able to describe the factors which led them to that view. We would suggest, however, that anxieties about how best to respond can affect practitioners' ability to define neglect. Thus, the general population can objectively look at a child who is hungry, tired and dirty and say 'that child is neglected'. However, practitioners are often catapulted straight into asking 'is this a situation in which I can, and should, legitimately intervene?' Uncertainty about how best to act can then leak back to create uncertainty about whether the child really is neglected.

Three other issues add to the complexity of defining neglect. The first is whether the focus should be upon physical or emotional aspects. Even the official definitions used within the UK differ in this regard. In Scotland the category is 'physical neglect' and gives prominence to physical care: this 'occurs when a child's essential needs are not met and this is likely to cause impairment to physical health and development. Such needs include food, clothing, cleanliness, shelter and warmth' (Scottish Executive 2000). English guidance, on the other hand, describes neglect as: 'the persistent failure to meet a child's basic physical and/or psychological needs' (Department of Health, Home Office and Department for Education and Employment 2000).

In Chapter Four Minty discusses this issue in considerable detail and proposes that, whilst emotional neglect can occur even when physical needs are met, physical neglect always has some emotional impact on the child. He provides a typology for distinguishing between abuse and neglect and whether either are emotional or physical neglect. The message from this chapter is that it is dangerous to assume that physically neglected children are 'dirty but happy'. Equally, emotional neglect may have a physical impact. Glaser's (2002) comprehensive review chillingly describes the physiological effects of early emotional deprivation upon the developing brain. Humans have evolved so that early brain development is shaped by expected patterns of social interaction related to attachment behaviour. If these are absent then brain connections can be directly affected.

The second issue relates to whether neglect is best captured by describing parental lack of care and the circumstances within which the child is living, or whether the focus should be upon the impact on the child. In Chapter Five Horwath describes her research which revealed different social work team cultures: some teams focused on incidents of neglect whilst others focused on the impact upon the child. In Chapter Eight Srivastava *et al.* suggest that intervention is often too late if practitioners wait until serious harm to the child is evident. As Glaser and Prior (2002) assert, if a definition of neglect depended on harm to the child it would not be possible to intervene to prevent harm before it occurs or becomes too serious. Of course any manifestations of harm in a child must be taken seriously and responded to. But we are clear that the establishment of neglect should not depend on the presence of obvious damage to the child. Such a position would only compound the tendency for reactive and crisis-led intervention rather than preventive approaches and early intervention. What this does mean, though, is that practitioners need the knowledge and confidence to frame an articulate case that a child is likely to be harmed if their situation does not improve.

The third issue coalesces around matters of intent. In many countries the neglect of a child is a criminal offence and as such implies some parental culpability. But prosecutions and convictions for neglect are low. This raises questions about how comfortable we are in using the criminal justice system to pursue parents who neglect their children. Usually individual judgements are made about cases on the basis of very unclear criteria. This is also the case within the civil rather than criminal arena where, as Buckley describes in Chapter Seven, decisions are often linked with judgements about caregiver performance and the extent to which parents 'acknowledge culpability'. The majority of people want to be good parents (Gaudin 1993). Practitioners, therefore, often feel sympathy with parents who are struggling with a range of personal and social adversities and are not 'deliberately' neglecting their children (Stevenson 1998a). This is neatly summarized by Glaser:

> There is a linguistic and conceptual dilemma between a wish and need to protect children from harm, and a reluctance to label or blame caregivers who hold a primary role and responsibility in the child's life. (2002, p.700)

Golden, Samuels and Southall suggest that it has been very unhelpful to link neglect and abuse in language and legislation (2003). They suggest that a distinction should be made between neglect as a 'non-deliberate failure to provide the child's needs' and 'deprivational abuse' as the 'deliberate or malicious failure to supply the needs of a child...' (p.105).

Our position is that the establishment of intent is not necessary to determine that neglect is occurring, nor is it necessary as a precursor to a decision that protective intervention is needed. It is, however, essential in reaching a decision about the nature of that intervention and the extent to which legal authority will be required to back it up.

Dubowitz *et al.* (1993) has proposed a very useful all-encompassing definition that allows for different levels of causality to be addressed: 'neglect occurs when a basic need of a child is not met, regardless of the cause'. Our view is that it is never appropriate to rely on the label 'neglect'. It must always be accompanied by careful delineation of the circumstances within which the child is living, the current and likely future physical and emotional impact and an analysis of the parental context. It is equally important that researchers set out what definition they are using. As Gough explains in Chapter Three, the kind of research that is carried out into neglect will be shaped by the definition that is used.

Noticing the neglected child

Despite increased public awareness of abuse and neglect in recent years children are still unlikely to seek help directly from statutory agencies. Children who are neglected are particularly unlikely to seek help in their own right. For example, between 2000 and 2001 ChildLine Scotland received 4330 new calls specifically about abuse and neglect, of which only 1% were about neglect, as opposed to 54% about physical abuse (Scottish Executive 2002b). And yet the figures for categories of registration on the child protection register for 2000 show that 33.8% were for physical neglect and 33.7% for physical injury.

Children who are neglected are, therefore, highly dependent on others to identify and respond to their needs for support and protection. Of course there must be efforts put into ensuring that our systems are more child-friendly. However, because of the effects of child neglect it is always likely that such children are going to need to be reached out to by concerned adults. These may be other members of their family and neighbours so practitioners must take referrals from the community seriously.

One of the recurrent manifestations of neglect is that children do not gain access to universal services. Neglected children are not taken to vital health and dental appointments, treatment regimes are not complied with and they miss school or are consistently late. Therefore, health and education professionals must also play a crucial role in seeing and responding to neglect. As stated above, neglect exemplifies many of the tensions that run through the child protection system and nowhere are tensions more obvious than in the negotiations between agencies about protective responsibilities. Chapters Six, Seven and Eight explore the relationships between agencies in considerable detail.

Much is made of the importance of agencies sharing information. But sharing information is not sufficient; agencies have to be clear what they are expecting of each other and they must also decide what to do about the information they receive. Stevenson explores these issues in Chapter Six, arguing that each agency has to be clear about its own role and expertise. Agencies must then be clear about what they are communicating (Reder and Duncan 2003).

Sometimes there is simple confusion about what constitutes a 'referral'. In many cases when other professionals refer a child to social services the more or less explicit statement is 'we are worried about this child'. This message, though, tends to be heard as 'you must do something about this child'. The social service response to this is often 'you have not convinced us that this is bad enough to warrant state intervention' which is, in turn, heard as 'we are not as worried as you, you are over-reacting'. Other agencies' referrals to social work also often contain the implicit or explicit expectation that children will be removed from home. The discussion then can be catapulted into a debate about whether a threshold has been reached for removal rather than a threshold for recognizing that to a greater or lesser extent this child's welfare is being compromised. A joint inspectorate report in England found reluctance by some agencies, including schools, to refer child welfare concerns to police and social services and found that there were serious concerns:

- about the thresholds that social services were applying
- that social services were not able to provide an adequate response to situations which did not involve a high risk of serious harm to children and young people
- that social services did not provide sufficient guidance, advice and support when they raised concerns about the welfare of children.

(Department of Health 2002)

We suggest that it is important to separate the agreement about the level of concern from the decision about what action to take. There need to be mechanisms that allow for social work services to hear the concerns of others without fears of being swamped with demands.

Further, if other agencies are to be encouraged to engage with the statutory child care and protection system, as represented by police and social work, then they have to see some benefit to it. In other words there has to be a general perception that involvement of these agencies leads to better outcomes for children. Unfortunately, all too often this is not apparent. Children who are considered not to be at great immediate risk are perceived to be filtered out of any route to resources, whilst the families of children deemed to be at risk are catapulted into a bewildering arena of investigation, case conferences and possibly court appearances, culminating in a very limited choice of interventions. Buckley (Chapter Seven) describes her research in Ireland that illustrated how difficult it can be for other agencies to obtain resources for a neglected child when they have to access them via a child protection referral system. A cornerstone of health visiting practice, for example, is to build a working relationship with parents and to offer support. Social workers can be quick to criticize health visitor reluctance to make child protection referrals for fear of compromising their 'working relationship' with parents, but all too often child protection investigations are very heavy-handed and inefficient ways to obtain extra support for families. In Chapter Eight Srivastava *et al.* describe the implementation of an agreed joint referral and assessment protocol between social services and health visitors that aims to minimize such interagency disagreements.

Assessment

The importance of assessment is stressed throughout this book. All too often the process of assessment is leapfrogged and expensive resources are poured into neglect situations on the basis of scant information about what has been previously tried and what may work (Daniel 2002; Scottish Executive 2002a). A range of frameworks is available to guide assessment (Department of Health 2000; Iwaniec 1995; Stone 1993; Srivastava *et al.* 2003). We provide further frameworks for the assessment of neglect; Appendix One contains a framework that was devised in conjunction with a number of local authorities in Scotland and in Chapter Five Horwath provides a framework based on research in Ireland. These can be used in conjunction with each other and with other frameworks. Throughout the book the authors provide pointers about factors that need to be taken into account in a range of specific circumstances. Here we stress, though, four key areas that we consider to be essential for effective intervention in neglect but which are not always covered properly:

1. factors associated with neglect

2. risks to, and needs of, children

3. chronology and past history and patterns within cases

4. parental ability and motivation to change.

Factors associated with neglect

In this book we explore a range of factors that can be associated with neglect. Different chapters address different ecological levels and it is important that, in all cases, comprehensive assessment addresses each of these levels.

In Chapter Two Spencer and Baldwin set out the social context within which neglect thrives and starkly remind us of our social responsibility towards children. They describe the ways in which society can be held to be both directly and indirectly responsible for neglect and make suggestions for change. This is a crucial starting point for a book about neglect. They argue that many parents in the UK are expected to bring up their children in the context of unreasonably scant resources. Although practitioners working with individual children and families can never be expected to right all the wrongs of society, they do have a responsibility to take account of that context when assessing needs and risks in individual families. This means that they must be careful to assess the impact of the social and economic factors on families and take account of them in their work. But they are also in a strong position to document the impact of policies on communities and to ensure that this is made known to local policy makers, and beyond.

At a different ecological level, several chapters focus on the parental characteristics and parent–child relationships associated with neglect. It is still the case that both research and practice with neglect tend to focus on mothers (Scourfield 2003; Swift 1995). Over the years an extensive array of characteristics associated with being 'neglectful' have been attributed to mothers, including factors such as:

- less able to plan
- less able to control impulses
- less confident about the future
- less equipped with a sense of workmanship
- psychological and psychosomatic symptoms
- lower intelligence
- high anomie
- difficulty with managing money
- lack of emotional maturity
- physical and emotional exhaustion
- depression
- lack of knowledge of children's needs
- difficulty with meeting dependency needs of children
- large number of children
- difficulty with relationships with own mothers and with partners
- isolation from informal and formal helping networks
- less social embeddedness
- poor socioeconomic circumstances
- high levels of stress.

(Coohey 1995; Crittenden 1996; Giovannoni and Becerra 1979;
Mayall and Norgard 1983; Polansky et al. 1981; Thompson 1995)

Many of these factors are associated with disadvantaged economic and social circumstances, yet may be focused on as individual inadequacies.

Chapter Fifteen looks at what is known about the fathers of children who are neglected and shows that there has been very little research into this area. In Chapter Fourteen Turney explores the extent to which neglect is constructed as an absence of mothering. Rather than focusing on the specific characteristics of mothers, Turney concentrates on exploring the concept of caring and the extent to which it has been associated only with mothers. She examines the complexity of the caring relationship and the ways in which it can break down. A similar theme is drawn upon by Dent and Cocker in Chapter Nine which reviews the lessons from situations when children have died (or nearly died) as a result of neglect. The authors consider the extent to which relationships with children can be influenced by parents' own attachment histories. Together these chapters highlight the importance of assessing attachment relationships, those of the child in question, and also the attachment histories of all significant male and female adult figures.

In Chapter Eleven Watson and Taylor pick up again on the theme of attachment in their analysis of the potential association between very low birth weight and neglect. They suggest that the factors associated with very low birth weight overlap with those associated with premature birth. Low birth weight can increase the risk of attachment difficulties and of neglect. The complex ongoing health needs of these children can also render them vulnerable to problems if parents struggle to meet their medical requirements. All of this must be carefully assessed at the birth of such a tiny baby. In a similar vein, Wright, in Chapter Ten, provides guidance for professionals on how to assess when a child's failure to thrive may be indicative of neglect. These chapters highlight the importance of looking at health issues through a social-emotional lens.

In Chapter Twelve Walker and Glasgow consider drug misuse, one of the major factors associated with neglect. They set out a detailed framework for assessment, stressing that the primary focus must be on the impact of the drug misuse upon the child. They highlight the importance of constructive engagement with the family and establishing an effective working relationship. This is an important theme for this book because many parents whose children have been referred for neglect will have difficulties in establishing working relationships and professionals need to develop effective methods of engaging families in the process of assessment (McCarrick, Over and Wood 2001). Parents are also likely to have low self-esteem and self-efficacy and to believe that:

- they do not have the ability to change
- no one else will be able to help them to change.

(Crittenden 1996; Daniel 1999)

Such attributions can be very discouraging for professionals unless they are recognized and assessed as part of the presenting problem.

In Chapter Thirteen Kennedy and Wonnacott draw our attention to the extent of unrecognized emotional and physical neglect of disabled children. They point to the serious lack of evidence about the neglect of disabled children. This is doubly unfortunate because some disabled children have acquired their impairment as a direct result of early chronic neglect. The vast majority of disabled children should be known to health professionals in some capacity and the health professionals, therefore, have a significant responsibility to gauge the extent to which their physical and emotional needs are being met. There can, for example, be a tendency to attribute symptoms of distress in disabled children to their impairment. As with all children, a full and accurate assessment of needs, risks, strengths and abilities is essential.

Risks and needs

It is our view that there should not be a divide between the assessment of need and risk. Risks to children's development and safety are present when their needs for nurturing and protection are not met. Although the Department of Health framework is a comprehensive overview of needs, it is less detailed in its attention to risk. It is important that practitioners consider specifically issues of risk (Department of Health 2000). As Chapter Nine shows, children can, and do, die as a direct or indirect result of neglect.

The Alaska checklist (cited in Gaudin 1993) is a helpful starting point for the assessment of risk. It includes:

- previous referrals for neglect
- number of previous out-of-home placements
- caretaker neglected as a child
- single caretaker in home at time of referral
- caretaker history of drug/alcohol abuse
- age of youngest caretaker at time of referral
- number of children in the home
- caretaker involved in primarily negative social relationships
- motivation for change on part of caretaker.

When assessing risk in cases of neglect it is important, also, to consider:

- possible impairment of brain development during the very early years

- intellectual delay resulting from poor cognitive stimulation and educational problems

- health problems due to poor nutrition and care and untreated illness

- danger of accidents because of lack of supervision.

When looking at the needs of children we would stress the importance of considering the developmental stage of the child and, in particular, the importance of carrying out a careful assessment of attachment relationships and of potential areas of strength and resilience (Daniel and Wassell 2002a; Daniel, Wassell and Gilligan 1999; Howe *et al.* 1999).

Chronology and patterns

We had particular concerns about practitioners failing to obtain background information, treating information discretely so that a threshold of concern was not reached, intervening without the guide of an assessment and missing warning signs. (Reder and Duncan 1999, p.138)

Teachers, social workers and health visitors will all be familiar with the large size of some of the files on children who are referred for neglect. These children are often in large family groupings and may have experienced a number of family separations and reconstitutions. It is absolutely essential that all practitioners take the time to go back through *all* the files contained within their agency on the child and family members when carrying out an assessment. It is a false economy of time to omit this basic task. It has to be the responsibility of each agency to ensure that there is a mechanism to collate all significant events in the child's life over time and that information within that agency is fully considered and shared in full with other agencies rather than passed across in a piecemeal fashion:

- In education there may be educational psychology files, guidance files, pupil records and child protection notes.

- In social work there may be criminal justice workers'/probation files on adults in the household, social work assistant notes, home care records, children and families files, family centre files, files on siblings who have been fostered or adopted, files in different local authorities.

- In health there may be GP files, health visitor records, hospital notes (accident and emergency, inpatient, clinics) and psychiatric files.

- Police in different areas may hold information about adults who have moved areas.

- Housing departments in different areas may have files about previous evictions.

- Voluntary agencies may have information about tackling substance abuse programmes.

An examination of the chronology provides invaluable information about the child's experience to date. It can also reveal patterns of behaviour and patterns of response to previous intervention. This data will help with the assessment of the following area.

Ability and motivation to change

All too often extensive resources are poured into neglect situations without an initial or ongoing assessment of whether parents are able to change or are sufficiently motivated to change. Jones (2000b) suggests six dimensions of parental capacity and stresses that parental ability on each of these needs to be assessed and linked with the developmental needs of the child:

- basic care

- ensuring safety

- emotional warmth

- stimulation

- guidance and boundaries

- stability.

For example, if it is going to take a parent six months to learn how to sterilize a bottle properly then that is too slow for an infant. If it takes two years to learn how to supervise a toddler safely, then that is also too slow. The way in which parents have responded to previous interventions can provide useful information about capacity to change. In Chapter Twelve Walker and Glasgow suggest that if a good working relationship is established with parents it provides a mechanism whereby capacity to change can be assessed more effectively.

Serious case reviews and inquiries into child deaths (see Chapter Nine) show that practitioners can be beguiled into believing that parents are willing to change, when they are in fact showing 'apparent compliance' (Reder and Duncan 1999). Horwath and Morrison (2001) have developed a very helpful framework to help with assessing motivation that we would recommend to help with this aspect of assessment. It uses the dimensions of effort and commitment to give four categories:

1. genuine commitment, in which there is high effort and high commitment

2. tokenism, where there is commitment, but low effort

3. compliance imitation or approval seeking, where there is high effort but low commitment

4. dissent or avoidance where there is low effort and low commitment.

Art of assessment

As is evidenced by the chapters in this book, neglect can be analysed from different ecological levels. All the information from all the different agencies involved and from all ecological levels must be brought together. The art of assessment lies in analyzing the interaction between different layers of factors. For example, as illustrated in Figure 1.1, when a parent believes that he or she cannot change and that no one else can help, they are less likely to make use of community resources, professional intervention may be less effective and social problems may have a significant impact upon parenting.

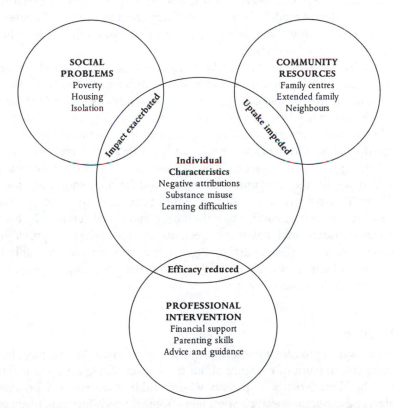

Figure 1.1 The art of assessment lies in analyzing the interaction between individual characteristics and wider factors

Intervention

Each chapter provides suggestions for intervention and they range from pointers for work with individual children and their families through to broader social reforms that would help to prevent the conditions within which neglect can flourish. Spencer and Baldwin (Chapter Two) provide a helpful diagram that illustrates the dimension of provision that is required, from early prevention and family support for the majority, through to intensive therapeutic help for the minority. Turney (Chapter Fourteen) emphasizes that there are no 'quick fixes' in working with neglect. She suggests the concept of 'managed dependency' to capture the fact that longer-term support is often necessary (Daniel 1999). It is also important to pay attention to whether intervention is actually improving the child's life. There is some evidence that direct, therapeutic work with children may lead to the best outcomes (Gaudin 1993). We suggest that it will be particularly helpful to focus on nurturing children's resilience as it is this that is most likely to be undermined by the experience of neglect (Daniel and Wassell 2002a, 2002b, 2002c).

It is quite clear that intervention is not the responsibility of social work alone and different models for service delivery are suggested. In Chapter Ten Wright describes how a multidisciplinary team can work effectively to help a child who is failing to thrive.

In Chapter Sixteen Macdonald brings together the research evidence about 'what works' with neglect and evaluates different methods of intervention. Unfortunately, as she highlights, there is a paucity of such evidence and far more research is needed, especially about what helps neglected children.

In Chapter Seventeen we draw together all the practice suggestions and suggestions about different agency roles and provide a framework for intervention. We suggest that, for practice to be effective, all agencies must accept a joint responsibility for the recognition of neglect and for improving outcomes for children. This will require a shift in language so that the child protection 'system' is not seen as confined to the police and social services. Instead all agencies, statutory and voluntary, need to see themselves as providing a 'protective network' (Daniel 2004). Protective networks would not only help neglected children, they could also help children who are being abused, or who are vulnerable in any other way.

Evidence

Our aim was to produce a book that was evidence-based. We do, now, have a considerable amount of evidence about the impact of neglect upon children, about the characteristics of parents whose children are referred because of neglect and about the social circumstances from which children are likely to be referred. There are, however, some specific areas where evidence is woefully lacking, for example there is little evidence that explores issues of diversity and culture and neglect. We know that social workers, in particular, can struggle to formulate effective responses when they are anxious about differentiating between different cultural norms and 'good enough' parenting. We have little evidence about what works once neglect has been identified. There are some promising indications of the kind of approaches that might be effective (see Chapter Sixteen), but there is need for far more research into how services and resources can best be deployed and which approaches lead to the best long-term outcomes for children.

Finally, as emerges from a number of chapters, practice wisdom, professional skill and the ability to develop good working relationships are of vital importance. Without these qualities, practitioners will not be able to put the evidence they have into practice in order to improve the lives of neglected children.

Chapter Two

Economic, Cultural and Social Contexts of Neglect

Nick Spencer and Norma Baldwin

Introduction

This chapter is based on the concept that the development and well-being of children is not simply the responsibility of individual parents and families but of societies as a whole. Societies, through social, economic and educational policies, can be supportive or neglectful of children, providing an environment and climate in which the capacity of families to care for their children is either strengthened or undermined. Social and economic policy decisions may enhance or impede the ability of parents to undertake the difficult task of child rearing. This societal responsibility still receives insufficient attention in the debates related to child care and child abuse and neglect. Research and policy have largely been driven by explanations based on the failings of individual families and their psychological functioning and structures. It is worthy of note that societies with the least child and family friendly policies such as the USA and the UK are those in which the greatest attention is given to individual parental responsibility for child care and least attention to societal responsibility. When children are neglected to the point of harm, or where harm becomes likely, the focus of professionals will be on their immediate circumstances and their interactions with carers.

We are not suggesting that the causes of neglect are purely structural, nor that the eradication of poverty and material disadvantage will ensure an end to neglect. We are suggesting however that the wide context of neglect – the numerous influences on the situations in which it is most likely to occur – needs to be understood holistically.

Children's experience of growing up will be influenced by the circumstances, beliefs, attitudes and relationships of parents and carers, which in turn will be influenced by the wider economic and social context. Parents and carers will be the mediators of these wider influences. We argue that realistic understandings of these inter-relationships need to underpin policy and practice.

Effective strategies to combat the problem of neglect will be concerned with a continuum of services from universal and preventive through to individualized and intensive. Their planned interconnections will be crucial.

The chapter starts with an ecological perspective, using the UN Convention on the Rights of the Child as the reference against which societal provision for children should be judged. We stress the corrosive influence of poverty and social exclusion on family functioning and child well-being and the ways in which societal attitudes to children are reflected in the way children are treated in their own families.

We then review some of the empirical data and theoretical debates related to the links between child neglect and societal factors such as levels of child poverty. We explore the economic and material resources needed for healthy child rearing, the influence of social resources such as neighbourhood supports and networks and the impact on parenting of cultural and societal attitudes to children. Changing family structures, particularly the increase in marital breakdown and in lone parent families, have been implicated, as possible causal factors, in neglectful parenting. These changing structures have economic and social drivers and do not arise simply because individual attitudes to parenting and marriage change. We will explore these influences as part of our illustration of the societal influences on child rearing.

Next we examine the mechanisms and pathways through which societal level factors influence child rearing and the capacity of families to provide a supportive environment for their children. The roles of labour market wages, child care, and educational provision in this process will be explored with particular reference to the UK. We also look at the role of social exclusion, stigmatization and racism as mechanisms by which the child rearing capacity of individual families may be undermined.

Clearly, when any child is neglected, vital components of the caring and safeguarding role of parenting have broken down. We examine the relationship between political and economic factors and parenting, to demonstrate the influence of societal level factors on parenting styles and approaches. Great emphasis has been laid on parental psychological dysfunction in research and practice in relation to child neglect. However, parental mental health problems such as depression and anti-social conduct and attitudes are strongly socially patterned, suggesting that research findings which link parental psychological dysfunction with child neglect may reflect one of the pathways by which social factors exert their effects on child rearing. Research has also focused on the potential for intergenerational transmission of child rearing practices and psychological functioning (Newcombe and Locke 2001; Sidebotham, Golding and The ALSPAC Study Team 2001). We use empirical evidence from longitudinal studies to demonstrate how these intergenerational effects are influenced by poverty and poor social circumstances.

The chapter concludes with a discussion of the policy and practice implications of our analysis, with particular attention to the UK. We argue that social, economic and educational policies are key components of measures to reduce neglect and enable families to provide 'good enough' child care. Universal provision will need to underpin strategic local plans of a range of preventive and ameliorative supports and services across health, education and social work.

The ecological perspective on neglect – the role of societies in relation to neglect

The UN Convention on the Rights of the Child (United Nations 1989) places responsibility on participating states to protect the rights of children by ensuring that: they are protected from injury and abuse (Articles 19, 33, 34, 35, 36 and 37); have adequate shelter (Article 27) and nutrition (Articles 24 and 27); have the right to optimal development and survival (Article 6) and the right to benefit from social security (Article 26). The key message of the Convention is that societies through their economic, social and cultural policies have a direct responsibility for the protection of children and the promotion of their welfare. Societies and their governments determine the social, economic and, to some extent, the cultural context in which parenting and child rearing takes place. The Convention makes it clear that societies as well as families and parents are capable of neglecting children.

Societies can neglect children through a number of mechanisms. They can directly endanger their well-being by failing to provide shelter and adequate resources for health care, education and nourishment, by failing to respect their rights as citizens, by incarcerating children in adult prisons and by denying their rights to cultural and religious freedom. The level of acceptance of children and respect for their rights within a society has a major effect on how children are regarded, how they are protected and how they are reared within families.

Indirect societal neglect occurs when child rearing and parenting are adversely affected by economic policies and societal attitudes. Within highly sophisticated consumer societies, such as the UK, low income and poverty within households have a powerful and corrosive influence on family functioning and children are particularly vulnerable to its effects. Families and children are constantly under pressure to consume, generating debt and conflict when there are limited resources. Low income imposes restrictions on essential purchases such as clothing (Gordon 2000) and food (Dowler, Turner and Dobson 2001) and directly affects parenting and child rearing styles (Taylor, Spencer and Baldwin 2000; Tuck 2000). Racism, for example through institutional practices such as detaining asylum seekers and preventing children from attending local schools, or by covert or overt prejudice and discrimination, can act to exclude children from society, potentially harming their well-being and development. These indirect influences have a pervasive effect on day-to-day functioning within families. Racism, bullying and exclusion cause tension and stress in everyday life for children and adults in black and minority ethnic groups (Atkar *et al.* 2000; Krieger *et al.* 1993; Seale and Mkandla 2000) limiting choice and essential freedom of movement.

Social exclusion, stigmatization and racism

Social exclusion, stigmatization and racism are experienced at the individual and household level but they are frequently driven by societal factors such as economic and educational pathways and a society's human rights legislation and record of enforcement. Children may experience social exclusion through lack of material resources and as a result of their social circumstances. This can take the form of exclusion from services, from social activities and from forms of leisure and entertainment taken for granted by their peers (Howard *et al.* 2001). Black and minority ethnic children also experience social exclusion through racism. This is often compounded by poverty, as these families are more likely to be poor – for example, in the UK, 60% of Pakistani and Bangladeshi families are in the lowest fifth of the income distribution (Platt 2002). Children of disabled parents or who are disabled themselves may suffer a similar form of double jeopardy. In the UK, they are amongst the poorest of the poor (Gordon, Parker and Loughran 2000), at the same time as being likely to experience exclusion because of their disability. Economic, social and practical demands on families coping with disabilities may be major sources of stress. Stigmatization of the poor has a long history in the USA and Europe. The cumulative effect of these influences over time has been shown to mould personal characteristics of children, to erode interpersonal relationships within families, and to undermine 'good enough' parenting (Spencer *et al.* 2001).

Poor people, particularly those living in readily identifiable disadvantaged areas, continue to feel stigmatized and excluded from access to goods and services (Howard *et al.* 2001). Children are stigmatized by lack of the 'right' designer clothing or because they are dependent on free school meals. As a consequence of their experience of marginalization, there is evidence that poor children have low expectations for their life now and in the future (Shropshire and Middleton 1999), a perception that is amply justified by research findings from longitudinal studies (Hobcraft 1998, 2003; Sacker, Schoon and Bartley 2002).

Thus, although most child rearing takes place within families and child neglect occurs within families, societies provide the economic, social and cultural context in which families care for their children and so are implicated in neglect, whether directly or indirectly.

Empirical data and theoretical debates on the links between child neglect and societal factors

Sidebotham (Sidebotham and The ALSPAC Study Team 2000) identifies a paradigm shift towards an ecological understanding of child maltreatment. He argues that this has arisen as a result of the recognition that child maltreatment is multiply determined by forces at work in the individual, in the family and in the community and culture. This model goes beyond the psychodynamic model, explicitly to include the contribution of society to the phenomenon of child abuse and neglect.

Consistent with the ecological model, registered child abuse and neglect, as well as other sorts of harm, are strongly correlated with poverty and low income (Baldwin and Spencer 1993; Creighton 1992; Thoburn, Wilding and Watson 2000; Tuck 2000). Of all the various forms of child maltreatment, neglect is most strongly correlated with low socioeconomic status (Sedlack and Broadhurst 1996; Tuck 2000). A recent study (Sidebotham et al. 2002), based on the Avon Longitudinal Study of Parents and Children, reported a seven times greater risk of registered child abuse if the family lived in rented accommodation (a reliable income marker in the UK). Twenty-eight per cent of the registrations were for neglect. Thoburn et al. (2000), in a study of 712 children under eight from 555 families, referred because of concerns about neglect or emotional abuse, acknowledge the link between poor material conditions, problematic and stressful social circumstances and neglect and maltreatment. Fifty-seven per cent of their sample had no wage earner in the household; 59% lived in over-crowded housing conditions; 10% had had 5 or more house moves in the previous five years. Forty-seven per cent of households were headed by a lone parent; 26% of parents and 24% of children had a disability or long-term/serious illness. Fifty-six per cent of respondent parents reported high levels of emotional stress.

Macdonald (2001) quotes a study by Sedlak and Broadhurst (1996) which showed that over half the cases of demonstrable harm recorded in the USA were cases of neglect and that the rate of neglect was increasing more quickly than that of physical abuse. She makes the related point that 'Neglect is a frequently defining characteristic of the context in which physical abuse takes place' (p.65). In the UK, inquiries such as that of Lord Laming into the death of Victoria Climbié, have shown the role of neglect alongside serious physical harm in a small number of very extreme cases (Lord Laming 2003). Cases of such extreme cruelty and neglect are fortunately very rare, but general concerns about increasing levels of neglect are substantial. Golden et al. (2003) in making a distinction between neglect and what they call deprivational abuse (deliberate deprivation of food and care) argue that severe neglect 'almost always results from the impoverished circumstances and life stresses affecting the family' (p.106). They go on to assert that 'the mother's time, energy and thoughts are concentrated elsewhere in an effort to cope; in this respect the neglected child is part of the family and "shares" its distress and deprivation' (p.106). Fortunately a majority of families living in extremely disadvantaged circumstances do manage to provide safe, nurturing and loving environments for children. Our argument is that it is very much harder to do so in disadvantage.

Policy and practice need to prioritize universal provision which supports healthy child rearing whilst also supporting initiatives which will build resilient, nurturing families and increase social capital and supports for child rearing in communities. This approach recognizes the interconnections of harmful influences and can avoid problems which arise from attempts to categorize and target specialist services in ways which may fragment and stigmatize. For example, increasing concern about the parenting capacities of people who abuse drugs and alcohol is leading to specialist provision. This needs to be planned and co-ordinated with mainstream provision to promote children's well-being. In the same way, services to reduce and respond to neglect need to be in the mainstream of child-centred services, concerned with each child's needs over time.

The powerful association of child neglect with poverty and low income suggests that rich societies with high levels of child poverty associated with their economic and social policies are increasing the probability of child neglect within families. Indeed, it has been argued that on a global level societal neglect is a common problem, resulting from unethical inequalities in health care and social support, associated with poverty (Golden *et al.* 2003). In 1999, the UK and the USA had very high child poverty rates (the proportion of households with children with incomes less than 50% of the national median income) – 19.8% and 22.4% respectively – compared with other rich nations such as Sweden (2.6%) and Belgium (4.4%) (UNICEF 2000). Although some progress has been made in Britain towards the eradication of child poverty, the rate remains high by European standards. The different rates are a direct reflection of the level of economic protection provided for children. Figure 2.1 shows the impact of different tax and credit transfer policies on child poverty rates among lone parents in selected rich nations.

Child poverty rates are most closely linked to the percentage of lone parent households in a country, the proportion of households with no working adult and the proportion of households in which the main breadwinner earns less than two thirds of the national average income (UNICEF 2000). The UK has high proportions of all three of these factors. UNICEF (2000) estimate that it would only take 0.48% of Gross National Product (GNP) to close the poverty gap in the UK, indicating that current UK child poverty rates are not the result of historical accident but of economic and social policy priorities and decisions.

High child poverty rates mean that there are many children living in families with material resources insufficient to enable them to participate fully

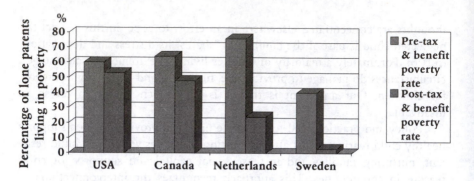

Figure 2.1 Effects of tax and benefits on low income. Source: Ross, Scot and Kelly (1996).

in the life of society. The activities in which children can participate are restricted; for example, poor families report that they cannot afford to send their children on school trips and outings with friends (Cohen *et al.* 1992). The Poverty and Social Exclusion Survey (Gordon 2000), using a consensus method to define monetary levels of absolute poverty (unable to afford essentials for daily living) and overall poverty (unable to afford to do the things that most people in the society take for granted), defined a weekly household income level of £227 for a British couple with two children in 1999 to avoid absolute poverty and a level of £301 to avoid overall poverty. Benefit levels on which so many families with children depend are inadequate to ensure that families avoid these levels.

Demographic changes affecting particularly rich nations have profoundly changed the lives of many children. Increasing rates of births to single mothers and higher prevalence of separation, divorce and reconstituted families (Howard *et al.* 2001) affect economic and social opportunities, place demands on child rearing practices and affect levels of stress. As indicated above, children of lone parents are more likely to be poor (Howard *et al.* 2001) and there is a body of research suggesting that these children are more vulnerable to neglect. However, a detailed study of children's emotional and behavioural well-being (McMunn *et al.* 2001) indicated that the high prevalence of psychological morbidity among children of lone parents is a consequence of socio-ecoomic factors. In the UK, it is teenage girls who are the age group most likely to have a birth outside marriage and to be the sole parent on the birth certificate (NCH Action for Children 2000). The increase in lone parents and single motherhood, seen particularly in the UK and the USA, has been explained by changes in individual behaviour, prompted by welfare benefits available to young mothers (Murray *et al.* 1990). However, there is evidence that limited career opportunities, poor educational attainment and economic influences may underlie the high levels of teenage births in some countries (Spencer 1994, 2002). Thus, these demographic changes cannot be characterized simply as cultural shifts or individual moral choices, but must also be seen as reflections of economic and social conditions. Their role in influencing circumstances for children needs to be recognized as one factor in complex, multidimensional processes and dynamics.

Pathways through which societal level factors influence child rearing

The discussion so far indicates the importance of societal level influences on child rearing and on the potential for child neglect. However, in order to inform practice and policy changes that may promote positive child rearing, we need to explore some of the mechanisms and pathways by which societies influence child rearing.

Employment and labour markets

Employment and labour market policies, particularly as they relate to women, are key mechanisms affecting the economic stability of families and their ability to participate fully in the life of their societies. Worklessness appears to have a corrosive effect on family functioning within high pressure consumer societies (Howard *et al.* 2001). In the UK in 1999, 19.6% of households with children had no working adult (UNICEF 2000). In some districts in the most deprived areas of the UK in the late 1990s, more than half the households with children had no working adult. Black and ethnic minority families are over-represented in this group (Platt 2002). Many of these households had been without work for long periods (Howard *et al.* 2001). Not only are individual families socially excluded by worklessness but whole neighbourhoods become blighted with increasing levels of crime, drug abuse and deteriorating services.

Being in employment in some countries does not ensure economic security. Almost one fifth of UK households with children in which at least one adult was working in 1999 had earnings less than two thirds of the national median income (UNICEF 2000). Households in which a woman is the main earner are most susceptible to low income (Howard *et al.* 2001). One of the most powerful indicators of societal differences in economic stability for families and children is the level of wages for women at work (Bradbury and Jantti 1999). Compared with the Scandinavian countries and other Northern European countries, the UK and the USA have low levels of wages and poor job security.

Thus, the extent to which societies protect families from economic hardship is likely to have a direct effect on child rearing.

Benefits relating to child rearing

Financial and other support given to parents during pregnancy and the early years of the child's life is a powerful indicator of the commitment of a society to the welfare of its children. Pregnancy is a critical time in which adequate levels of nutrition and freedom from stress are important. Maternity benefits can contribute to ensuring that the nutrition and well-being of expectant mothers is protected. In the UK, maternity benefits are set too low to ensure that all women can afford an adequate diet (Maternity Alliance 2001). Poor women dependent on income support or Job Seeker's Allowance would have to spend 40% of their income on food to eat the kind of diet recommended by health professionals (Maternity Alliance 2001). Young pregnant women are the most disadvantaged due to restricted benefits for those aged 16–24 and no separate benefits for those aged under 16 years. Maternity benefits in some other European countries are set at levels adequate to purchase a healthy diet in pregnancy.

Without adequate safeguards, childbirth can precipitate poverty; for example, in the UK, for one in three people, the birth of a child results in a drop down the income distribution graph by a fifth or more, and for 10–15%, it results in poverty (Howard *et al.* 2001). Some European countries, notably the Scandinavian countries, the Netherlands and France, protect new mothers with child benefits sufficient to ensure an adequate income during early child rearing. Paid parental leave is another pathway through which societies can assist parents and diminish the probability of child neglect. Parental leave gives parents time to establish close attachment with their child and gives them a brief but important respite from the need to balance the demands of work and the demands of child rearing. As with other benefit provision, some countries make generous provision, others have very limited protected leave with limited financial entitlement (Moss 2002). Swedish parents (both mother and father) have protected leave on 90% of pay for over a year (Ruhm 2000). Maternity and parental leave have recently been improved in the UK (Maternity Alliance 2003) but levels remain less generous than in many other European countries. Ruhm (2000) has shown a correlation between levels of parental leave in 17 rich nations and post-neonatal mortality rates from which he postulates that parental leave acts as a protective factor for early childhood well-being.

Early childhood daycare and education

Demographic and economic changes have resulted in an increase in lone parent families and in families in which the mother is the main breadwinner (Howard *et al.* 2001). In households with pre-school children, affordable daycare provision becomes a crucial requirement to maintain the economic stability of the family unit and protect the well-being of the children. This is even more important in countries such as the UK where many parents work long hours. Forty-five per cent of UK women work over 40 hours per week and 30% of men over 50 hours; 61% of working families have parents who work shifts or work during the evenings, nights or weekends (Daycare Trust 2002). In addition, there is good evidence, particularly from US studies (Schweinhart, Barnes and Weikart 1993), that high quality early daycare has positive effects on child well-being and development especially among low income children. High quality, affordable daycare is universally available for infants beyond the age of three years in many European countries and beyond the age of one year in Sweden (Moss 2002). As with other services designed to assist families in the difficult task of child rearing, daycare provision in the UK has been allowed to lag behind comparable European countries and provision is now mainly dependent on the private sector. The Daycare Trust estimate average costs for a nursery place for a child under two years at around £6650/year. Not only does this put daycare for children out of the reach of many families but it also directly excludes the poorest families. In 2002, there was only one subsidized child care place for every 14 children under three living in poverty.

Education as a protective factor

The educational level of a society, especially female education, is likely to be a further mechanism for protecting children and ensuring their needs are met and their rights promoted. Educational failure within rich consumer societies is associated with lower earnings, increased chance of unemployment and social exclusion (OECD and Statistics Canada 2000). Rich nations vary considerably in the investment they make in education and the extent of educational disadvantage (UNICEF 2002). For example, the International Adult Literacy Study of adults aged 15–64 in 22 Organization of Economic Co-operation and Development (OECD) countries (OECD and Statistics Canada 2000) reported that Sweden has more than 70% of its population with document and prose literacy at the higher levels and only a very small percentage at the lowest level, in contrast with the UK and the USA with 50% at the higher levels and 20% at the lowest level. However, among 15-year-olds studied in 2000, the UK had relatively low levels of educational disadvantage (9.4% of pupils scoring below an international benchmark for literacy, maths and science) compared with the USA (16.2%) and Germany and Denmark (both 17.0%) (UNICEF 2000). This variable picture suggests that educational progress has been made in the UK although many adults continue to suffer the detrimental effects of poor functional literacy, with current adverse consequences for the well-being of their children.

Societal influences on parenting

Parenting is the final common factor through which the pathways from society to child neglect exert their effect. We have discussed the social, economic and political context of parenting elsewhere (Taylor *et al.* 2000), reviewing studies showing the impact of economic hardship and low income on parenting and parenting styles and the association of poor social circumstances and problems in childhood. Here we briefly summarize the relationship between factors at the societal level and parenting. Sacker *et al.* (2002) show that parental involvement and interest in their child's education is socially patterned, with both lower social class and higher levels of material deprivation associated with lower levels of parental interest/involvement. Hobcraft (1998), based on the same 1958 British birth cohort (National Child Development Study) but using slightly different measures of socioeconomic status, also reports a close association of poverty with low parental interest, which in turn is associated with high levels of aggression and other mental health problems at ages 7, 11 and 16. These childhood outcomes tend to be transmitted into adult life influencing psychological and physical health as well as health-related behaviours (Hobcraft 2003). Debt and disadvantage in adult life have been shown to increase the risk of maternal depression (Reading and Reynolds 2001). Poor psychological health of the parent is influenced by social risk exposures in childhood and is known to be associated with higher rates of behavioural problems among children. Thus, there is compelling evidence to support the contention that poverty and low income increase the pressures on parents, make the job of parenting more difficult, and increase risks of neglect and other harmful behaviours.

The extent to which economic policies such as family taxation and benefits, employment opportunities and practices such as parental leave, length of working day and unsocial hours support or impede mothers and fathers in their caring, educational and socializing roles, affects the general context and quality of child rearing.

Cultural expectations

Gender roles, cultural attitudes to mothers' and fathers' responsibilities for caring, are further influences on parenting. Assumptions that mothers will instinctively know how to look after children and will be able to provide adequate care in severely limited material and social circumstances, places great burdens on mothers. Lone mothers may have the added burden of being expected to provide competent care even when responsible on their own 24 hours a day. Equally, views that fathers only have a limited caring and socializing role limits their opportunities and relationships.

The cost of stereotypical attitudes to gender can be high. Smyth (1998), working with young people exposed to the troubles in Northern Ireland, gives stark examples of these problems:

> The longstanding 'uncoolness' of articulation of emotional vulnerability or any emotional expression for males (except perhaps anger), is particularly marked in a militarized culture and in situations where violence and danger to life are commonplace. (p.76)

She draws attention to the different routes to satisfaction taken by young women, in a society with increasing numbers of births to mothers between 14 and 16, through personal relationships and child care, and the limitations which these traditional roles impose:

> A number of young women and girls left with the burden of childcare at increasingly younger ages, and young men isolated outside the structure of family and personal life, consigned to the world of unemployment and depersonalized violence. (p.77)

These issues are common to many societies (Garbarino 1995; Wolfe, Wekerle and Scott 1997) forming part of the backcloth to our understanding of contexts of neglect and maltreatment.

Violence, often associated with alcohol abuse, is a major source of stress for parents raising children in disadvantaged areas. Domestic violence is commonly associated with breakdown of family relationships and child maltreatment, yet is surprisingly tolerated (Mullender *et al.* 2000; Scottish Women's Aid 1999; Zero Tolerance Charitable Trust 1998).

Attitudes to physical punishment of children may connect with these values and practices. Among Northern European countries, Britain is in a minority in not having laws which protect children from physical punishment by parents and carers. A vigorous debate continues in the media and in Parliament, but cultural attitudes favouring physical punishment remain strong. The essential principle of the UN Convention on the Rights of the Child, that children have rights as individuals and are not the property of their parents, appears to remain contentious in a number of countries. The convention has been ratified by Britain, but Britain has been criticized by the UN for its record on physical punishment. The Convention has not been ratified by the USA.

The ecological model provides a framework for understanding the wide range of societal influences on parenting and on child well-being, operating at different levels, and the interactions between material, political, social and interpersonal factors.

Local supports for effective parenting

Environmental factors and social support at neighbourhood level have been shown to affect the health and functioning of families, with access to informal support networking helping to lessen some of the adverse consequences of stress and disadvantage (Garbarino and Kostelny 1994; Garbarino and Sherman 1980). The well-being of children within a community has been related to factors such as neighbourhood support available to the family and social support available to the mother (Runyan *et al.* 1998). The concept of social capital has been developed to characterize the extent of perceived support available to families and individuals within a community, although its exact components may not be agreed by researchers (Cooper *et al.* 1999). However, some of the variables used as measures of social capital are strongly socially patterned: size of social networks, degree of network participation and levels of perceived social support increase with socioeconomic status (Cooper *et al.* 1999) suggesting that social capital may be, in part, a reflection of family and neighbourhood economic capital. Cattell (2001), based on a qualitative study of two disadvantaged neighbourhoods, argues that, although social capital may be a helpful construct for identifying conditions which contribute to quality of life, it cannot adequately deal with the extent and range of deleterious effects on health and well-being of poverty and disadvantage. Using a range of country-level measures of economic inequality, social capital and political capital, Muntaner *et al.* (2002) report very weak association of social capital variables with child health status indicators (low birth weight; infant mortality; unintentional injury at less than 1 year) but strong association with economic inequality. They question the extent to which social capital influences health and well-being and argue that economic and political factors at country level are likely to be more powerful determinants.

Too narrow a focus on localities risks placing the burden of change on the most vulnerable, emphasizing the moral and social responsibilities of parents and demonizing young people, without taking full account of wider influences. Regeneration and community development initiatives can only play a part in building safe, healthy and supportive communities alongside far-reaching economic, educational and employment policies. Attempts to increase social capital need to take full and realistic account of these structural factors *alongside* far-reaching economic, educational and employment policies.

The non-random distribution of child neglect has prompted major policy and practice debates related to the optimal approach to preventing child neglect and promoting child well-being. A dominant paradigm in policy and practice is based on the 'risk' approach, in which families at risk (usually multiply disadvantaged families) are targeted for special interventions and enhanced services. This paradigm has informed the development of risk scoring and attempts to improve individualized prevention of child abuse and neglect (Browne and Saqui 2002; Hamilton and Browne 2002). However, there are good theoretical grounds for challenging both the efficacy and the ethics of these approaches as the starting point, or main plank in a strategy to reduce neglect and harm. Rose (1992) argues that risk strategies for the prevention of disease or harmful conditions such as child neglect, which are non-randomly distributed across the population, are flawed. Applied to the prevention of child abuse and neglect, Rose's critique raises the following concerns:

- High risk strategies are limited by a poor ability to predict child abuse and neglect positively.

- High risk programmes professionalize prevention and label and stigmatize parents.

- High risk strategies do nothing to alter the underlying risk exposures and little to achieve overall reductions in child abuse and neglect within a population.

- The expectations for behavioural change associated with high risk strategies are often unrealistic.

Rose argues for an alternative approach, to attempt to change the underlying risk across the whole population. Put simply, this would mean that a strategy to reduce neglect would be based on policies to ensure that all families have access to the resources necessary for safe and healthy child rearing. This is a straightforward public health approach, aiming to eliminate or substantially reduce the conditions in which disease and harm flourish.

Another example which illustrates this approach is the current attempt to change legislation relating to physical punishment of children. Popular acceptance of physical punishment of children is likely to increase the chance of some children experiencing extreme violence and of themselves seeing violence as an acceptable response to others. Changes in general attitudes and behaviour are likely to lead to an increased level of protection for all children. Sweden, a country with well-developed child and family support policies, was the first country to enact legislation (1979) to ban the physical punishment of children. They have seen a decrease of 26% in prosecutions for violence against children since 1982, and child deaths have reduced by 90%. Nine other European countries have now followed this policy. Germany adopted a ban on smacking in 2000, after research established a clear link between childhood experiences of physical punishment and the likelihood of later anti-social behaviour and violence (Children are Unbeatable 2002).

Messages for practice

We have argued that effective responses to problems of child neglect – as to other experiences of harm – must be based on theoretical understanding of the context in which they arise. To change this context demands substantial changes in economic and social policies, with an emphasis on the benefits to society of adequate family income and other child and family supportive policies. It would be unrealistic, however, and unethical, to argue only for structural change, ignoring the possibilities of helping improve the circumstances of children where neglect is already a reality, or whose families are in a downward spiral which increases risk. Current priorities must also include prevention – primary, secondary and tertiary – and treatment, involving equal attention to the minutiae of social and interpersonal circumstances at the level of the individual child and family.

An adequate strategic response will involve collaborative responses from politicians, academics, service managers, professionals and service users. It will be necessary to confront some of the tensions and contradictions of current policies for children and young people, drawing on what is known from research in an integrated way. For example, account needs to be taken of the substantial evidence showing that those being targeted for strong measures of control and punishment through youth offending and anti-social behaviour measures, come from the same vulnerable and disadvantaged groups as those whom government measures are seeking to protect and support through non-stigmatizing, early years provision (Lord Laming 2003; Scottish Children's Reporter Administration 2003; Scottish Executive 2001, 2002a).

Individual practitioners will not on their own be able to achieve the universal provision, free from contradictions and stigma, which we argue for. Nor will teams of workers in health and welfare, however skilled in analysis and planning and creative in practice. However, there are strategic planning mechanisms in place to move towards a more holistic approach (Children's Services Plans; Child Health Strategies, etc.) and others being proposed (e.g. Children's Trusts). Through these mechanisms individual practitioners, with planners and managers and their teams, can help to move the balance from highly individualized, crisis-oriented services, towards a range of interlinked services which aim to prevent harm and promote the well-being of all children.

The approach we argue for – based on current evidence – is expressed diagrammatically in Figure 2.2.

SUPPORTS

Urban and rural initatives –
health, education and social work:
BRIDGES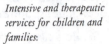

Universal services to respond to the changing needs of children and families:

- *living in disadvantage*
- *vulnerable*
- *in need*

- Early years, school, neighbourhood and family supports
- Range of childcare
- Safe, supervised play and activities
- Community safety and health initiatives
- Employment and educational opportunities
- Advocacy, income maximization

Easy access, non-stigmatizing, supportive, preventive, inclusive

Intensive and therapeutic services for children and families:

- *with complex and multiple needs*
- *needing a range of intensive focused provision*
- *where neglect and risk of harm*

Figure 2.2 A model of family, school and neighbourhood support, based on individualized and population-wide profiling, assessment and planning

Evaluations of responses to child care problems (with a high proportion of neglect cases) from social work, education and health, in a number of authorities across Scotland, show what many previous studies have shown – that responses are often incident driven rather than holistically child focused (Baldwin 2001, 2002; Daniel 2002; Department of Health 1995; Ogden and Baldwin 2001). Little detailed attention is given to the wider problems of income and debt, housing, social networks, health needs. Even where many services have been offered over long periods, these have often been fragmented, poorly co-ordinated, sometimes overlapping or continuing to focus on one aspect of the presenting problem even where there is little change. Comprehensive assessment and long-term, planned collaboration to achieve specific outcomes are only clearly achieved in a minority of cases. Yet the Scottish Executive Audit and Review of Child Protection (Scottish Executive 2002a) showed that where a single worker was able to give these aspects priority, effective work could be achieved.

These are areas where an individual professional can make a major difference, achieving changes for a child, whether through their direct practice, through supervising others or making a contribution in a team. The chapters which follow will provide detailed examples of effective ways of working, from a number of different perspectives. Here we would like to draw out some of the principles which we think will help guide workers in taking a more holistic approach, recognizing that our current systems may not be as child oriented as we would wish, but do allow reasonable scope for working for the benefit of an individual child at the same time as trying to improve conditions for all.

- Assessment of need and risk needs to be comprehensive and continuous, both population wide and individual.

- Services need to be planned on a continuum, with the ability to respond at the earliest identified point of risk or need.

- Where intensive intervention is required, it needs to take account of the range of needs and risks over time, and plan and evaluate specific objectives and changes needed.

- Specialist, intensive services need to be seen in relation to and connected with universal and mainstream support services.

- Co-ordination at all levels of service delivery and intervention needs to be systematic and supported within and across all agencies, with clear lines of accountability and responsibility for resources and tasks.

- Partnership and collaboration across professions and teams, with children and their parents, is a necessary starting point for holistic, child-centred approaches.

- Evaluation of outcomes – for individual children and for populations of children – is an essential component of case and service planning.

We believe that these points can be taken account of in every situation where a professional from health, education, social work or other related services, is concerned about the risk of neglect or other potential harm to children. They are reminders of the importance of working at all levels – looking for opportunities to improve individual practice and organizational systems, at the same time as seeking economic, social and cultural changes to benefit children.

Chapter Three

Research for Practice in Child Neglect

David Gough

Introduction

The potential benefits of research in child neglect are obvious. It can provide evidence about the nature of phenomena, their extent, their cause, and the impact of strategies to change the nature or extent. Policy makers, practitioners, users of services and other individuals and groups, can add evidence to other factors to inform decision-making.

There are also many potential negative aspects of research. Research costs money, it can be mistaken in its conclusions and thus misinform decision-making; it can be used instrumentally to justify actions being taken for other maybe hidden reasons. Research can give the impression that progress is being made, that something is being done, while avoiding difficult questions and decisions. It can make people believe that there is knowledge where there is none. It can undermine professional workers who believe that there is a research evidence base that they could and should know if only they had the time and expertise to understand and utilize it. Investment in research can add to moral panics that define certain groups of people and/or behaviours as something odd and different and thus assist the social construction of social problem making in society. There is nearly always an ethical as well as financial cost of undertaking research and these costs may be higher than the final products of the research.

There is often an assumption that research is intrinsically good, but unless we are clear about the purposes that research serves, for whom or what, as well as its potential negative effects then we cannot properly assess its role and usefulness. Users of research such as practitioners and policy makers are meant to make use of research to inform their policy and practice, but is this a realistic aim? The first section of this chapter examines the nature of academic research and the many challenges for non-academics in accessing and assessing that research and argues for systematic research synthesis to address practitioner, policy maker and service use focused reviews of evidence. The second main section of the chapter then examines whether there are other barriers to use of research. It proposes not a 'research active practitioner' model but a 'practitioner as research driver' model of practitioner engagement with research.

Theoretical and evidential issues

Concepts and definitions

Definitions are important and neglect is a particularly complex concept to define. Research needs to be understood within the conceptual framework within which it was undertaken. These often implicit assumptions determine how a question is framed, the nature of the data collected, the analysis applied and the conclusion drawn.

All definitions of child abuse and neglect are based on concepts of harm to a child and responsibility for that harm (Gough 1996). Neglect is special because it depends on acts of presumed omission rather than commission. Rather than stating that certain acts (for example, physical or sexual acts) towards children are unacceptable it is defining what children need to have. In a sense a definition of neglect is a statement of what a child should be provided with by a society.

HARM

Definitions of neglect often only give examples rather than all-embracing lists of all the different types of harm that might be considered. The harm can be the failure to receive socially acceptable standards of care as a 'normative criterion' or the negative consequences of such care as the 'harm criterion' (Straus and Kantor 2003). For some definitions, abuse or neglect only occurs where certain criteria for responsibility are met. In other cases, the starting point is any harm to the child. So a child suffering from physical conditions such as burns or malnutrition or failing to develop properly (to thrive) without other adequate explanations must be a victim of abuse or neglect.

RESPONSIBILITY

Responsibility for harm can be divided into nature of the responsibility and the scope of who or what can be considered responsible (Gough 1996). The whole concept of neglect implies a failure to undertake responsibilities of care. Not surprisingly, there are differences of opinion about how that responsibility is attributed because it involves moral judgements about children and their care in our societies. Should definitions of neglect:

- only apply to direct intentional lack of care or also apply to lack of care due to parental poverty, physical illness or mental illness?

- apply to harm caused by observance of religious or other beliefs where the parents are concerned that health care (such as blood transfusion) or lack of certain ritualistic acts (such as circumcision) may cause greater harm to the child?

- apply equally to lack of care caused by circumstances within or not within the carers' control? If so, then to what extent are carers responsible for lack of care due to substance abuse, or relationship conflict and separation?

In terms of scope of responsibility, the English guidance refers to parents and carers as responsible agents, so the focus on mothers as carers of children is even more pronounced than in other forms of child protection. Those deemed as having the responsibility of care who do not fulfil that responsibility in the absence of any morally allowed exceptions (maybe, for example, poverty or illness) are deemed to have committed neglect. In contrast, sexual abuse is frequently used to describe acts by non-family members (though interestingly physical abuse is usually limited to carers). It is possible to apply the concept of neglect more widely. In France, it is an offence for anyone including strangers not to come to the aid of others in certain crises and with explicit needs for help. Similar responsibilities could be placed on individuals or organizations to respond when they know or suspect that a child's needs are not being met for any reason.

In addition, society can be considered neglectful by allowing children to be at risk of harm or infringement of their rights. This could include risks of disease or of accidents or of other forms of abuse such as violence. Intra-familial violence can be seen as 'an inevitable by-product of selfish, competitive and inegalitarian values and of dehumanizing, authoritarian and exploitative social structures and dynamics which permeate many contemporary societies' (Gil 1979, p.1). Physical abuse and sexual abuse can be seen as due to societal neglect of unequal power relations between adults and children and between males and females (Dominelli 1986; Ennew 1986).

All of these, often implicit, issues within definitions of neglect will affect the population of situations and scenarios that will be considered neglect in defining research samples. This will vary, not just on value judgements about caring responsibilities, but also on the purpose of the research. Definitions determining whether child protection responses are necessary are likely to be different from those constructed to examine the differential cause and effect of different child care situations or the prevalence of neglect in the population. Definitions created for different purposes will vary in the relative extent that they have been constructed on *a priori* ideological and theoretical reasons or built up from empirical data on cases (and the extent that these have been qualified by data on cases falling outside of the definition). Until all these issues are made explicit in reporting of research and the presentation of cases and case typologies, conceptual clarity and practical use of research findings are likely to be limited. Not only should practitioners and policy makers be cautious about making use of research evidence that does not provide these details, but also the lack of accountability of much research evidence seriously hampers the potential for the accumulation of evidence over time.

Research evidence from primary studies

Although there may seem to be a large amount of primary research on social and psychological issues such as neglect, there are relatively few studies considering the enormous numbers of research questions that could be asked within all the different definitional positions available. The amount of information provided by these studies is further limited by:

- the quality of the studies and study reporting

- limits to generalizability and sampling error

- accessibility of these primary studies.

QUALITY OF THE STUDIES AND STUDY REPORTING

Many research studies, including many of those referred to in other chapters of this volume, are well executed but many are not. A first problem commonly found in studies is a lack of clarity and thus conceptual confusion and inconsistency about the topic under study, for example, lack of consideration of the definition of the topic and thus of the recruitment of participants or other sources of data for the study.

A second problem is the lack of an appropriate research design to address the research question being asked. This may occur for practical reasons. A study may want to assess the impact of an intervention to reduce the likelihood of neglect within families, but this may not be possible because the research was not built into the development of the intervention, there were not sufficient resources to support such a study or there are ideological objections to the use of experimental designs (Oakley 2000).

A common problem is the use of descriptive studies to draw conclusions about the effects of a service initiative. A funder, such as a government agency, may commission research to study the impact of an intervention but require or only provide sufficient funds for a research design that is based on monitoring the implementation with some outcome data. Such descriptive studies are limited in what they can conclude about the efficacy of service. Without some form of experimental or internal control it is not possible to determine whether other uncontrolled variables (from selection bias and the effects of other variables over the time period of undertaking the study) are influencing the reported results.

These implementation studies may include data on participants' views of the service. Such data can provide needs assessment and information about the acceptability of a service, ensure users' views are represented, and identify possible adverse or positive effects of the intervention for further study. Participants' views about the efficacy and appropriateness of a service are essential but there is a need for further data in terms of evidence of the effects of interventions. Users are unlikely to be able to control and thus fully know the effects of all the variables that might be affecting their experiences. For example, many users of hormone replacement therapy believed it to be an effective therapy but it is now known to have many adverse effects. Similarly, the views of parents in families with children considered to be neglected should inform service delivery but parents may not know for sure which services do, or do not, change the level of care for their children.

Lack of fitness can also occur where a study failed in its original aims. Studies may have been set up to assess the impact of a service but for many reasons be unable to execute a fully fit-for-purpose design and collect good quality and relevant data. Such studies may make most use of their descriptive data to give insight into the process of intervention. The results may be of some use but such studies would probably have been more useful if they had been originally set up with an appropriate qualitative design to assess process.

Even where a study is conceptually sound and uses an appropriate research design the design may not be implemented well. Technical limitations may include non-systematic sampling, inappropriate or wrongly applied measures, analysis, or interpretation. In addition, studies are often reported without giving full details about the methods employed, so even if one has the relevant technical skills and background knowledge it may not be possible to assess the extent to which the findings are reliable (would be found again if the study was replicated) or valid in terms of measuring what they purport to represent.

LIMITS TO GENERALIZABILITY AND SAMPLING ERROR

Studies not only differ in their purpose, conceptual frameworks and definitions of neglect, they also vary in many other aspects of the context in which they occurred. In general a study on a small number of cases will provide rich detail on those cases, which may be highly informative for developing conceptual insights and hypothesis generation, but provide less clarity about how representative these findings are for different contexts. Large-scale studies may cover more contexts but are less likely to have the richness of detail of the small-sample studies.

In statistics the extent that a sample is representing a population is often built into the logic of the analysis. In an experimental study, those receiving the experimental and control interventions are samples from a hypothetical population of all those who could receive the intervention. The statistical analysis attempts to identify if there is a difference in outcome between the intervention and control groups; in other words, to try to determine if they came from the same or different (hypothetical) populations. The problem is that any differences between the samples in outcome measures might be due to chance variation in sampling (sampling error). This can be illustrated by an example where we know that there are differences suggesting two 'populations'. For example, we know that eight-year-olds are on average taller than six-year-olds, but if you tried to test this by using only small samples of six and eight-year-olds – relatively tall six-year-olds and relatively short eight-year-olds – you could wrongly come to the conclusion that children of different ages are the same height and that it is no problem that a child has not grown over two years! Significant tests reporting in terms of percentage chance of significant levels are merely stating the chance that any difference in outcome measures found could have been due to chance from sampling error. Even studies reporting that an intervention has a significant effect (difference in outcome measures) at the 0.05 level have a 5% chance of drawing a wrong conclusion (that there is a real difference and therefore that there is an effect when there is not one) due to sampling error.

How are these issues related to the study of child neglect? Many research studies on child neglect are based on small samples of cases known to health and welfare agencies. First, these cases are not likely to be representative of all the instances of neglect occurring in the community. The factors that lead to their identification by agencies may be as significant as any features of the neglect. Second, the cases may be described without reference to how they differ from other children and families. Some studies try to overcome this by comparing children experiencing neglect with children and families that are similar on a range of variables such as age, family history and structure, and socioeconomic status. The problem is that controls identified by this matching process may not be representative of 'normal' families. The tighter the matching the less representative the controls are likely to be and may even include hidden cases of neglect within the sample. Third, the samples may be small, which is useful in case studies where you are trying to obtain detailed data to develop insights into the processes by which neglect occurs or how children and families react to services provided to help. The limitation is the extent that you can be sure that the results generalize as the small sample may not be representative and any comparisons with control groups may identify differences which are just due to chance (sampling error).

This is not to argue that we should not try to understand the phenomenon of neglect by describing its features and its processes. For example, Gaudin and colleagues (Gaudin et al. 1996) classified neglectful families as chaotic/leaderless or dominant/autocratic and suggested that they need different sorts of preventive intervention. Such classification to enable understanding seems to be an ingrained and effective human strategy for understanding the world around us, for everything from typologies of abuse (including child neglect) to syndromes to explain sudden infant death. These strategies are powerful for developing working hypotheses to help us deal with pressing practical issues but the limits to the explanatory power of these models do require testing.

ACCESSIBILITY OF PRIMARY STUDIES

A further issue is the accessibility of studies to different users of research. Research on neglect is reported in a diverse range of academic journals, books, and unpublished research reports. The factors influencing academics' decisions about where to publish do not necessarily encourage reporting in similar journals or in places which are accessible to other users of research. Reports of research reported in the publications aimed at practitioners, policy makers and the general media for the public may not be from the best studies nor provide the best evidence about services. Special initiatives that seem plausible, exciting, and fitting with current fashions but have little research evidence to support (or undermine) them are frequently reported in such publications. For example, home visiting services are often enthusiastically championed in the public and professional media. These are caring and plausible strategies for helping parents who are finding it difficult to cope with the care of their children, but what evidence is there that they make any difference in practice? There is much evidence from the USA of the positive effects of directive nurse visitation (Olds, Henderson and Eckenrode 2002) but there is less evidence to date for the effects of the more empathic model of nurse and volunteer home visitation support in the UK (Wiggins *et al.* 2003). There is not only the possibility that these services may have no effect but they might even do more harm than good. There is evidence, for example, that mothers' support groups can negatively impact upon the parents' existing social networks (Stevenson and Bailey 1998). A more dramatic example related to concerns that infant deaths could be related to neglect or active abuse is the change of advice to parents on the sleeping position of infants. For years, professional knowledge stated that putting babies on their backs to sleep risked them choking on their vomit and that head turning could result in flattening of one side of their heads. Since the knowledge changed to a belief that it is safer for infants to sleep on their backs, the incidence of sudden infant deaths in the UK has dropped by two thirds (Chalmers 2003).

The problem for busy social care and health practitioners, policy makers, users of services and members of the public is that the popular public and professional media is a major source of information on research evidence. This may not give a full overview of what is known about a topic and may give greater prominence to some new initiative, idea, or research report. Individual studies may be misleading because of the quality of execution of the study or simply because of the sampling error involved in research. In medicine these problems are well known. The 'Hitting the Headlines' project at the Centre for Reviews and Dissemination, University of York, reviews research reports in the national media and examines the broader research evidence and places this on a website for doctors and others to check. General practitioners who are then contacted by patients interested in receiving the new treatment can access the National Electronic Library for Health website to clarify the wider picture and knowledge about the condition and its treatment. Maybe we should have a similar service for busy social work managers and practitioners.

Synthesis and quality assessment

These problems of quality of research, study reporting, generalizability and sampling error make any individual study on child neglect vulnerable to giving misleading conclusions. In addition, the diversity of places where research reports are found makes access to such evidence for social care practitioners and other non-academic users of research problematic.

EVIDENCE REVIEW AND SYNTHESIS

All of this suggests the need for some form of synthesis of the research evidence for practitioners and other users of research. This is the function of reviews of research to identify, quality assess and summarize what is known about any particular topic. Literature reviews should enable us to be better informed about what is known, what further needs to be known, the extent to which decision-making can be evidence informed and the extent to which any new study may add to what we already know. Until recently such reviews did not have any clear methodology. How to undertake reviews was not taught in methodology courses and when people were expected to undertake a review they just had to attempt a logical approach to this task.

There are many types of literature review. Some are undertaken to take forward an area of research and so are focused on those research needs. Straus and Kantor (2003), for example, wished to develop knowledge on the prevalence of child neglect. A brief review of the major prevalence studies showed an over 50-fold variation in prevalence rates from less than half a per cent to 27%. Straus argued that, in addition to the real variation in the populations studied, the variation in results was also likely to be due to methodological differences in sources of data of neglect (such as child, parent, professional or agency report), the criterion of neglect, the reference time period, and the dimensions of neglect mentioned. This focused literature review led him to develop a new measure of neglect and undertake a large cross-national study of over 5000 students in 14 nations. The study found that even with methodological consistency there was huge variation in reporting between the research sites. The number of respondents who reported childhood experience of one form of neglect varied from 20% to 95%, those reporting three or more forms of neglect varied from 3% to 36% (Straus and Kantor 2003).

Other reviews are undertaken to argue a case and use research literature to support their argument. These can be powerful resources to inform policy and practice but they need either to be exhaustive and systematic in terms of the studies they include and the way these are assessed or the review needs to be contested by other academics to check that other evidence could not support different arguments.

Many reviews are less argument focused in attempting to review all that is known about a certain area or research question. These can provide a full account of what is known about the review question, but traditional literature reviews have not been explicit about their methods of review. It is therefore difficult to assess whether the review has been undertaken in a systematic way. Just as with primary research, secondary research that is reviewing primary research needs to specify its methods for the results to be checked and potentially replicated by others and thus be accountable and believable.

The same analysis can be applied to academic expert opinion. How do you distinguish trustworthy from not trustworthy experts or, maybe even more difficult, two trustworthy experts who differ in unknown ways in the range of their knowledge and the assumptions that underlie their assessments of the quality and relevance of the research that they are summarizing? Some experts may seemingly provide a full account of knowledge in an area, but it is difficult to assess the extent to which this has been achieved. The process of knowledge production is not explicit and the believability of the experts' view may thus depend upon the acceptability to the listener of the conclusions or the status of the expert. An expert with high status may have that status for good reason but it can be difficult to assess when an expert goes beyond their area of expertise. This can also be a problem in courts where expert witnesses with high status for practice or clinical skills provide expert views on research data.

SYSTEMATIC RESEARCH SYNTHESIS

The need for explicit systematic methods has led to the setting up of the Cochrane and Campbell Collaborations to co-ordinate the systematic review of research literature on 'what works' questions in health and social science respectively. The Campbell Collaboration has three main topic areas of social welfare, education, and crime and justice. The focus of both collaborations on questions of efficacy means that the reviews are principally statistical meta analyses of quantitative data from experimental studies. This has led some to believe that systematic reviews are only concerned with such research designs and data. This is a misunderstanding as the logic of being systematic and explicit about research synthesis applies to all research questions and thus all review questions (Gough and Elbourne 2002). It is a misunderstanding that stems partly from the unfortunate polarization of research into quantitative and qualitative communities rather than seeing research methods as fit for purpose (Oakley 2000).

Some argue that systematic research synthesis is a mechanistic process but this is again a misunderstanding. All research requires some form of process; the intellectual work and judgement comes in the framing of the question, the conceptual assumptions within the questions, and operationalizing those ideas in every stage of undertaking the review.

Different review questions will need to consider different types of research design so systematic reviews may have to consider all types of research data including qualitative data to answer process issues and concepts for conceptual synthesis in areas such as meta ethnography. For example, the types of study, and thus evidence, used in a systematic review of the efficacy of interventions for families with non-organic failure to thrive is likely to differ from a review of the evidence of the processes by which such interventions have their effects. Some studies may inform both outcome and process questions as with, for example, Iwaniec and colleagues' twenty-year follow-up of non- organic failure to thrive families (Iwaniec 1995). Outcome and process evidence reviews also differ from a synthesis of the concepts professionals and researchers use to understand and describe neglect and failure of children to develop in the ways expected of them.

There are many different approaches to undertaking systematic reviews ranging from statistical meta analysis, to systematic narrative reviews, to conceptual reviews including meta ethnography. The basic main stages of undertaking a review are relatively similar but differ in detail and in terms of the content and processes involved at each stage (Gough 2004; Gough and Elbourne 2002).

Improving quality and relevance

If the context of research is increasingly the role it plays in accumulative synthesis with each new primary study being evaluated on its contribution to previous known knowledge then this should also lead to a much greater focus on relevance and quality than reporting of individual studies on their own as interesting in their own right. It should also lead to greater clarity about what research method will be appropriate for addressing different aspects in the gaps in research. All of this should increase the bringing together of quality assessed research evidence, thus increasing the cumulative nature of research enquiry and making this more accessible to the range of people who have questions that can be answered by such research findings. This approach is currently being taken forward by a number of organizations including the Centre for Evidence-Based Social Care, Barnardos What Works publications, the Social Care Institute of Excellence (SCIE), Research into Practice, and the

EPPI-Centre (see lists of evidence-based initiatives on the Electronic Library for Social Care at: www.elsc.org.uk/index.htm).

A fundamental aspect of this approach is the nature of the research questions being asked and examined through systematic research synthesis. There is not just one form of knowledge. There are many different conceptual and ideological differences which result in different research review questions, consider different evidence and come to different conclusions. For example, six systematic reviews of accident prevention included altogether sixty-four different primary research studies but because of different review questions and inclusion criteria only one study was common to all six reviews (Oliver 1999b). If different types of studies are included in reviews then one would expect the conclusions also to be different.

Currently it is primarily academics who make these sorts of decisions. As academics are major users of research they should be involved in the research agenda but so should other users of research. In many areas of social research there are a large number of research studies representing a substantial investment of research, but this does not necessarily mean that the questions relevant to users of research have been addressed.

Messages from research

- Research on child neglect can have negative as well as positive effects. To justify research the benefits need to be greater than the ethical and resource costs involved.

- Providers of services also need to ensure that they do not do more harm than good, and that the services they provide do not have unknown negative attributes.

- The concept of neglect is problematic and any research, policy or practice on neglect needs to be understood within its (often implicit) definition of harm (including current and developmental status, risk, normative expectations and infringement of rights), scope of responsibility (duty of care) and interpretation of responsibility (such as intention including culture and religion, within actor's control, moral assessment of actor).

- Much research in the social sciences does not provide much benefit because of weaknesses in the choice of design, execution or reporting of studies, generalizability, sampling error, reliability and validity, accessibility of studies, and lack of cumulative focus of research.

- Non-academics are major users of research. These include social care practitioners, policy makers, and users of services. These non-academic users of research cannot be expected in these circumstances to develop a detailed knowledge of individual studies and the relevance of their findings.

- Literature reviews and academic expert opinion can provide summaries of findings in a research area. Unless there is explicit information that systematic methods were used then it is not possible to know whether the results are trustworthy. Similar arguments can be applied to the lack of transparency and accountability of expert knowledge.

- Systematic research synthesis (SRS) uses explicit systematic methods for identifying, assessing and synthesizing research findings related to specific research questions. SRS can synthesize research evidence on any research questions involving all primary research designs including statistical, qualitative and conceptual data.

- SRS brings together what is known in an explicit quality assured process, enables the accumulation of knowledge and increases accessibility for all users of research.

- The findings of any research study are dependent on the research question asked. Issues of relevance to non-academic users of research should be important drivers of the primary and secondary research agenda. An increasing number of resources and initiatives to enable practitioner involvement in research are being developed.

Implications for health and social care practice

The discussion so far has suggested that research should be used in a rational way to inform decision-making. The reality, though, is that it can instead be used instrumentally to support decisions made for other reasons or simply to distract attention or to initiate time-taking responses that avoid decision-making (Weiss 1979).

Even if research is used rationally it is just one influence on policy and practice. During the development of the movement for the use of systematic research synthesis the term 'evidence-based medicine' was frequently used which gave the unfortunate impression that medical care was to be determined only by research evidence. This did not take into account all the other factors that need to be involved in any decision-making including ethics and human rights, resources, user needs, professional skills and knowledge, and other political issues. In order to avoid such confusion terms such as 'evidence informed' or 'enabled' are used to emphasize that decisions should be informed but not determined by research. Other influences on decision-making are as legitimate as research, but making the research component more explicit and rational should also enable the other influences on decision-making to be more transparent.

The evidence from research on the use of research is that there are many barriers to its use in social care. How many readers of this book have the time and other resources to have an up-to-date understanding of all the research evidence relevant to their work on child neglect? Sheldon and Chivers (2000) have reported on the very limited knowledge of social workers of research studies. In education and social care, initial training and ongoing professional development focuses on practice rather than declarative research knowledge (Hargreaves 1996). In medicine and other disciplines there is a more even balance between these different types of knowledge.

If practitioners' knowledge of research is limited then it is unlikely that research evidence is having much impact on practice. Even if the research was well known there would be other barriers to its use in practice. To address these issues SCIE has commissioned the Research Utilization Research Unit (RURU) at the University of St Andrews to review the use of social care research. Previous work by RURU has shown that common barriers to research utilization are lack of resources for engaging in research, organizational resistance to use of research evidence, poor communication of research, and lack of relevance of research (Walter, Nutley and Davies 2003). To enable implementation research needs to be translated into local contexts and research needs to be integrated within organizational activities and systems.

How might this be achieved? Non-academic users of research cannot spend all their time being researchers. They can take leave from their normal work to be involved in a particular research project or be involved in research, including action research, undertaken within their workplace. This may provide insight into the research process and the particular research issues within the study in question. What is more difficult is for practitioners and policy makers to have an ongoing role as active participants in the research process.

Secondary research through systematic research synthesis provides an additional model. Involvement in primary research studies provides direct experience of doing research and the methods and practice of this direct form of knowledge production. Involvement in secondary research provides a different type of experience. It is less direct but provides a broader overview of how different research has, or has not, and can, or cannot, answer different questions. It provides a more strategic view of what we know, how we know it, what we do not know and what research, by what methods, would be best placed to help answer these unanswered questions. Users of research such as practitioners, policy makers and users of services are in a sense researchers/experimenters as they adopt different strategies and respond to the feedback that they receive. It is just non-systematic investigation. A more strategic view of research from involvement in secondary research can assist such users of research to adopt research thinking into their daily practice and thus make better use of their experimentation.

As argued earlier, research questions and research review questions need to be driven by the users of that research. This leads to agenda setting of what research questions need to be answered. In this way, practitioners and other non-academic users of research become in a sense managers of the research process and become more sophisticated about the research that will be of use to them without needing to spend time undertaking the time-consuming and technical issues of the primary research or of the systematic synthesis. Systematic research synthesis is sometimes criticized for being controlling of what research is undertaken for what purpose. On the contrary, it provides a means for all users of research to begin to control the research process. Not only does this enable practice-driven research, it also enables more democratic participation in what we study and how we study it by all users of research including users of services. Research is too important to be left only to researchers.

Messages for practice

- Research evidence is only one driver of decision-making.

- Making the rational role of research more explicit could make the ideological and resource issues more transparent.

- Research evidence is only one type of knowledge and we need greater clarity about how research and practice knowledge can be combined to different effect.

- We need greater clarity about how research is utilized in practice and how this could change.

- Practitioners, policy makers and other users of research can benefit from involvement in primary research; involvement in secondary research allows a more strategic view of research, its methods and its potential impact on policy and practice.

- Involvement in systematic research synthesis can also lead to a much more powerful role in setting the research agenda. Research is too important to be left to researchers alone.

Chapter Four

The Nature of Emotional Child Neglect and Abuse

Brian Minty

Introduction

The aim of this chapter is to try to clarify the nature and definition of child neglect, emotional neglect and emotional abuse and to demonstrate their inter-relationships. It is hoped that it will help practitioners better recognize emotional neglect and abuse, and respond with sensitivity. In particular, the significance of emotional neglect is emphasized, without downgrading the importance of physical neglect. The basic argument is that physical abuse and neglect have a character and impact that are as much emotional and psychological in nature as physical, but that there are also other forms of abuse and neglect that are not expressed physically (or sexually) at all, and these are best categorized as emotional neglect and abuse. The impact and harm of these other forms of maltreatment have not always received the attention due to them. Also, emotional abuse and neglect can be used as residual terms. Types of abuse that are not physical or sexual should be categorized as emotional (or psychological) abuse. Types of neglect that are not physical should be categorized as emotional (or psychological) neglect.

The justification for undertaking this task is two-fold:

1. Experts in this field (Clausen and Crittenden 1991, p.6) suggest that the difficulties of defining terms and assessing aspects of child maltreatment have been a major obstacle in writing about child abuse and neglect.

2. Unless the full nature and diversity of child maltreatment is recognized, there is a danger that professional intervention may sometimes fail to grasp the reality of the harm done to children, and the nature of the help children and families require.

The category of child neglect seems to have been somewhat under-used (relative to abuse) because some professional workers have held inadequate assumptions about it:

- that neglect is simply dirty children in dirty homes

- that, on the whole, neglect is a lesser form of maltreatment than abuse

- that neglect is simply a consequence of material poverty.

Our previous article about neglect (Minty and Pattinson 1994) arose as a response to social work colleagues who held such views. All three beliefs are far from the whole truth. Many of the most appalling cases of fatal child maltreatment have involved both severe neglect as well as abuse; for example, Maria Colwell (Department of Health and Social Security 1974), Jasmine Beckford (London Borough of Brent 1985) and Victoria Climbié (Lord Laming 2003). However, these are extreme cases, and may be misleading. They might, in fact, lead social workers and health visitors to assume that neglect is relatively uncommon, whereas, at least in its emotional form, it is very common, and has the potential to seriously impair children psychologically and socially. It also seems near the heart of child maltreatment, as has been confirmed by Bifulco, Brown and Harris (1994), who found over several studies that of all the types of child maltreatment, neglect was the most closely correlated with the other types.

In relation to the belief that neglect is simply an effect of material poverty, two things seem clear. The first is that poverty and (physical) neglect are often found together, although the nature of the relationship is not agreed. In a study for the National Society for the Prevention of Cruelty to Children, Creighton (1992) found that parents who had a child registered for neglect were significantly more likely to live in families where nobody was in full-time employment than was the case in the total population. However, unemployment has a wider significance for families than that of reduced income by itself – serious though that may be. Families with children where nobody ever goes out to work or school may sometimes, in effect, be participating in their own social exclusion, with repercussions over more than one generation. At about the same time as the publication of Creighton's British study, Pelton (1992), on the basis of a nationwide survey in the USA, advised the US Advisory Board on Abuse and Neglect that there was a close association between poverty and neglect.

The second point that must be made is that there are good reasons for believing that child neglect is not simply caused by poverty. The vast majority of families who live in (material) poverty have not had their children registered for child neglect; and, in fact, when children in the Third World are dying from hunger, due to poverty, we would in no way accuse their parents of neglecting them. Something different is needed for society to decide there is neglect. Of course, it could well be that chronic poverty plays a part in many instances of physical child neglect, possibly by reducing morale, or by increasing a sense of general hopelessness and passivity (see also Chapter Two). It is also clear that there are stressors which could be related to neglect both directly and indirectly such as alcohol and drug abuse, and that some forms of mental illness might cause neglect directly, or cause it indirectly by dragging families into poverty.

The language of child maltreatment

Physical abuse (Non-accidental injury: NAI), sexual abuse, emotional abuse and neglect are all official categories for registering children as maltreated, or at risk of maltreatment. Emotional neglect by itself is not recognized as such, nor is it often discussed apart from neglect in general. An exception is Iwaniec's book (1995). Before going further it is necessary to try to analyse the language of child maltreatment. This chapter attempts to describe the terms 'neglect', 'physical neglect', 'emotional neglect' and 'emotional abuse', and to examine the extent to which it is possible to disentangle aspects of emotional neglect from the physical neglect and emotional abuse of which it is often a part, and sometimes an accompaniment. In practice, of course, some children have to suffer several types of maltreatment and neglect, either together, or at different times – parents can be both abusive and neglectful. Emotional abuse often goes with emotional neglect, but there are aspects of parental behaviour (such as the prolonged ignoring of children) which could be described as either emotional abuse or neglect, depending on the nature of the parental behaviour and the 'intention' of the carer. The 'intention' behind neglect seems to be indifference, rather than a wish to hurt or a lack of control.

Definition of neglect

Stevenson (1998a, p.4) quotes the definition of neglect used in the Nottingham Area Child Protection Committee (ACPC) Procedures for 1997: a 'severe and persistent lack of attention to a child's basic needs, resulting in a significant harmful impairment of health or development, or the avoidable exposure of a child to serious danger, including cold or starvation'. This seems a good definition, but a lot depends on how we define 'basic needs'. A certain amount of disagreement among professionals caring for children arises out of different assumptions about their basic needs, and the relative importance of each of them. Emotional neglect needs to be distinguished from both abuse and physical neglect. Neglect in general is distinguished from abuse by the fact that abuse consists of acts of commission, and neglect of 'acts' of omission, although this is strictly a contradiction in terms. It follows from this that in distinguishing neglect from abuse, the question of intent is very relevant. On the whole we are reluctant to use the word 'abuse' where the failure to meet basic needs is unintentional or arises out of indifference. We could say that physical neglect is distinguished from emotional neglect by the presence of clear physical signs, such as untreated medical conditions, lack of adequate clothing, food or shelter, and failure to supervise young children properly.

However, it would be unhelpful to think of neglect as consisting of two sharply distinct types: physical and emotional. At the heart of both types is the serious failure to meet children's basic needs, physical and/or emotional. Box 4.1 describes a study whose findings suggest that where there is physical neglect there is also likely to be emotional neglect, and that if children are to have their needs attended to, their emotional and cognitive needs must also be recognized, and addressed. On the other hand, it is my experience that CAMHS (Child and Adolescent Mental Health Services) Teams rarely see cases of routine physical neglect, but not infrequently see cases where severe emotional neglect and abuse are crucial. It follows that the relationship between physical and emotional neglect appears to be asymmetrical. Physical neglect often includes emotional neglect, but the reverse seems often not to be the case. On the whole it would seem that parents who fall seriously short of meeting children's physical needs also fall short of meeting their emotional needs, but (as we have already seen) many parents and carers fall seriously short of meeting children's emotional needs, but do manage to meet their physical needs. To talk of physical neglect is usually shorthand for talking of *both* physical and emotional neglect. In fact it could be said that the physical neglect of children is a very cognitive and emotional matter, and children who experience it are almost always impoverished both cognitively and emotionally.

Box 4.1 Correlations between physical and emotional neglect

Minty and Pattinson (1994) found, in one NSPCC team in the North of England, correlations between indices of traditional (physical) child neglect and what could be called emotional neglect. Physical neglect was measured by social workers rating the absence of adequate:

- food and nutrition

- health and hygiene

- warmth and clothing

- safety.

Emotional neglect was established by ratings regarding:

- the absence of a responsiveness to children's emotional needs

- a lack of any guidance over television watching

- a marked incapacity to control even young children
- frequent marital rows in front of the children
- suicidal gestures or threats in front of the children.

Ratings were made by child protection workers on a four-point scale. On Spearman's rho tests (a test of correlation through ranking), we found correlations between the aggregate score for 'emotional' neglect and aggregate scores for aspects of 'physical' neglect that ranged from 0.68 for food and nurture to 0.84 for safety; with warmth/clothing scoring 0.68, and health/hygiene 0.7 ($n = 41$). It is not clear to what extent the sample studied was typical of clients referred to community NSPCC teams, but there was no reason to assume that it was very different from the families referred to other NSPCC community teams.

Emotional neglect and abuse can also be distinguished from physical and sexual abuse, in that the former are rarely single events or even a series of events. Emotional neglect is similar to emotional abuse in that they both constitute the air some children have to breathe, and the climate they have to live in, rather than isolated events or a series of events. Emotional child neglect and abuse often appear to constitute a persistent 'background' which does not become noticeable until a striking event in the foreground alerts us to their importance. This event may be physical or sexual abuse, or a particularly gross expression of emotional abuse. Examples of this happening are shown in the case example in Box 4.2. In terms of the child's welfare, attending to the 'background' may be more important and more challenging than attending to the abusive incident.

Box 4.2 Case example: John

John (eight years of age) was the younger son of a working-class couple, and was referred by education social workers for chronic school non-attendance. At first sight this seemed to be a fairly typical case of school refusal, with John and his mother over-anxiously attached to one another, until John alleged his father had tried to strangle him. A case conference was called, but the claim could not be substantiated. However, further investigation revealed that the parents had a chronically unhappy marriage, and that the older son and the father were involved almost daily in physical fights. In addition, his teacher had stated at the case conference that John regularly came to school with his bottom plastered with layers of faeces and paper, and his trouser turn-ups full of fragments of faeces. It also emerged that his mother refused to let him have birthday parties, and had prevented him from having contact with other children in the area. Social services applied for care proceedings, and a Care Order was eventually granted – the judge being impressed by the level of emotional, as well as of physical, neglect. He also criticized social and educational services for delay in bringing the case to court.

Definition of Emotional Abuse

It has now become widely accepted that there is a need for a specific category of emotional abuse, separate from physical or sexual abuse and neglect, for children who have been the victims of rejection, humiliation, isolation, ignoring, tormenting, terrorizing, corruption, constant criticism and marked discrimination in comparison with siblings (the Cinderella syndrome). The categories were recognized by Hart and Brossard (1991) and Garbarino and colleagues (Garbarino, Gutteman and Seeley 1986), and have received further attention from Bifulco *et al.* (1994), who propose that the term 'psychological abuse' be reserved to refer to sadistic abuse, leaving the rest of emotional abuse to be covered by the term 'parental antipathy'. The term 'parental indifference' is used by Bifulco and colleagues to refer to the absence of warmth, and the lack of comforting or support, described in this chapter as aspects of emotional *neglect*. Some of these distinctions are (rather crudely) set out in Table 4.1.

Table 4.1 Distinctions between different forms of abuse and neglect

Maltreatment	Acts of commission	Intentionality	Harm to child	Physical signs
NAI	yes	yes	yes	yes
Emotional abuse	yes	yes	yes	no
Physical neglect	no	no	yes	yes
Emotional neglect	no	no	yes	no

There are analogies between the way in which the terms 'emotional abuse' and 'emotional neglect' are used. Just as with physical neglect, so also with physical abuse, it is impossible not to acknowledge that virtually all physical (and sexual) abuse involves emotional distress and cognitive effects. As with emotional neglect, emotional abuse can also be used as a residual category for all types of abuse that are not physical or sexual. Practitioners have, on the whole, refused to make official such terms as 'cognitive abuse' or 'psychological abuse', preferring the one residual category: 'emotional abuse'. This does not prevent researchers subdividing existing categories in order to try to discover the consequences for children suffering very specific forms of abuse. As already indicated, Bifulco and colleagues (Bifulco *et al.* 2002) reserve the category 'psychological abuse' for particularly sadistic and malevolent forms of abuse, such as are perpetrated by sociopathic parents, and use the milder term 'parental antipathy' for expressions (verbal or practical) of parental dislike (which are none the less extremely hurtful), or constant criticism. Whether or not area child protection committees and child protection workers make official use of the idea of 'sadistic' abuse (in addition to the currently used category of psychological or emotional abuse), it is important that they recognize sadistic abuse and are very wary of failing to protect children from it when it exists. The case in Box 4.3 shows parental behaviour verging on the sadistic.

Box 4.3 Case example: Peter

Peter is aged 10. Peter's father had been imprisoned for causing severe bodily harm to his mother. He also had other convictions for violence. His relationship with his son varied. At times he was generous, and at other times downright selfish; for example, on one occasion, finding himself short of cash, he sold Peter's bicycle. The night before he was discharged from prison, he phoned Peter, and told him to let his mother know he was to be discharged the following day, and that his first priority would be to come and 'sort his mother out'.

This is a case of emotional abuse, with the abuse verging on the sadistic.

Forms of emotional neglect

Examples of specifically emotional neglect could include failure to show any warmth or stimulation to children, or appreciation of their efforts and achievements. Neglectful parents rarely attend school open days, show their children positive attention, play with them or take them on outings. In extreme forms neglect could involve completely ignoring a child, or hardly acknowledging he or she existed. It could include failure to send children to school at all, or to take them to a doctor when they are sick. At a hardly less significant level, neglectful parents offer little comfort or reassurance when a child is ill or upset.

Such failures to respond to children's emotional needs often seem to indicate a marked lack of empathy, or an inability or unwillingness to act on it, rather than a deliberate intent to make the child suffer, even though they can involve gross indifference to a child's welfare or feelings.

Department of Health publications

There has recently been considerable interest shown in the concept of emotional neglect, although under the aegis of response to children in need, and parental capacity to meet children's needs, in two Department of Health publications.

The Department of Health's guidance (2000) entitled *Framework for the Assessment of Children in Need and their Families* states children's 'basic needs' to be for 'health, education, emotional and behavioural development, identity, social relationships, social presentation and self care skills'. Serious failure to pay attention to these needs would be regarded as forms of emotional neglect.

Although few would want to deny the importance of the developmental needs enumerated in the guidance, it seems initially surprising that so little reference is made to basic 'physical' needs such as those for safety, protection, hygiene and warmth, but it needs to be borne in mind that the Department of Health requirements were originally drawn up in relation to the needs of 'looked after children' (Ward 1995). The authors of the guidance may assume that we no longer need to be concerned about physical neglect in foster and residential care, but that we do need still to show considerable vigilance in relation to possible emotional neglect. The emphasis on emotional neglect seems admirable, but clinical experience suggests that there is still need for vigilance in response to physical neglect in the community, especially because of the seriously harmful situations in which some children have to live, which are described at the end of this chapter. Some almost inevitably lead to child neglect. Moreover, the title of the first Department of Health publication refers to 'children in need', not 'looked after children'. However, the main point is that almost all the needs just referred to in the Department of Health document are emotional (including cognitive and psychosocial) rather than being at least partly physical in nature. The only exception is health, which clearly has both physical and psychological aspects.

Many purely emotional needs are biological in origin and their fulfilment is essential for mental health. The Human Givens Approach (Griffin and Tyrrell 2002) claims that all human beings, including children, have biologically based psychological needs which have to be met to enable individuals to achieve and maintain psychological health. These are only slightly less essential than the needs for food, protection, safety, supervision and medical help. The Human Givens Approach suggests that the basic emotional needs of virtually all human beings are for:

- security and safety

- attention

- connection with others

- a sense of belonging and status

- being psychologically stretched

- a balance between autonomy and control

- a sense of purpose and meaning – for many people to be found in relationships.

It is not possible in the space of this chapter to comment on the nature of all these needs. The most we can do is to select two for further analysis and discussion. The first of these needs (for security and safety) has both objective and subjective aspects, with the objective aspects referred to by the word 'safety' and the subjective by the word 'security'. Some parents unwittingly increase their children's anxiety by failing to protect them from marital rows, and threats of suicide. The need for security, and the consequences of having to adjust to less than ideal attachment figures is elaborated in attachment theory. Disorders of attachment can be caused by neglect and abuse and set children on risky pathways. Gross inability to provide safety and security – except in times of war or severe parental illness – indicates serious neglect, both physical and emotional.

Attention is the second need chosen for further discussion. It has both emotional and physical aspects. We all need, in some measure, to be noticed. Attention has also a protective, or physical aspect. Parents who have no idea where their children are, who do not prevent young children walking unsupervised along the verges of busy main roads, or check where their children are, clearly expose them to serious risks. Parents who can only give their children negative attention, and who do not give children a sense of positive status in the family, are grossly neglecting them in an emotional sense. We would all accept that professionals working in the field of child care and protection should be aware that children have needs for positive attention, affection and support, and that difficult behaviour in children can arise out of a lack of positive attention. In fact, when toddlers are placed in day nurseries or family centres for observation with a view towards court proceedings, emotional neglect and insensitivity seem often to be as much the focus of scrutiny as 'physical' care.

Establishing that the levels of physical and emotional care are inadequate

Bifulco and colleagues point out (Bifulco *et al.* 2002) that in assessing child maltreatment it is important to have a standard by which it can be established that what has occurred is abusive or neglectful. The definition for establishing neglect given in the Children Act 1989 puts the onus on local authorities to establish that 'the child's health or development has been significantly impaired', and that this is 'attributable to the absence of a reasonable standard of parental care'. However, this is difficult to establish in relation to particular children. Garbarino and colleagues (Garbarino *et al.* 1986) argue that all instances of child maltreatment go beyond what is acceptable to society, and are defined by this, rather than by their consequences to individual children. However, evidence, in general, of the long-term consequences for children who are involved in abuse and neglect informs professional and public opinion, and in this way affects what we regard as the threshold of unacceptability. At present in England and Wales, we seem possibly to be at a point of change. Some judges appear to need specific evidence that particular children have suffered significant harm in the form of impairment of health and development, in order to make Care Orders when the maltreatment alleged is emotional abuse or neglect, and this may be difficult to establish. Others seem to be satisfied with a careful history of persistent neglect or emotional abuse. The case in Box 4.2 (earlier in this chapter) is an example of a judge not insisting that the local authority prove that John had been impaired in his health and development. His concern was that John should suffer no further neglect. It could be argued that there is an analogy with sexual abuse, where it is not necessary to establish that the abuse has harmed the child. Once it is accepted that serious sexual abuse has occurred, that in itself is sufficient to establish significant harm.

Situations conducive to emotional neglect, or a mixture of emotional abuse and neglect

Not infrequently neglect is a by-product of some parental state of ill health, disability or other preoccupation, such as the effects of alcohol or drug abuse. There seem to be at least four common situations in which we can speak of children frequently being at risk of emotional neglect. In many instances the harm appears to be inflicted unintentionally and indirectly. In any case it frequently emerges that certain children suffer from both *emotional abuse and neglect*, as when it is claimed that the emotional climate in which physically and/or sexually abused children are raised is frequently one of high criticism and low warmth. Parental rejection of children can involve all kinds of maltreatment, but particularly emotional abuse and neglect.

Three of the common situations in which children are exposed to emotional neglect have recently been the focus of considerable study by the Department of Health (Cleaver, Unell and Aldgate 1999). They are domestic violence, parental mental illness, and parental abuse of alcohol and drugs. Children growing up in these situations are more likely than others to be at risk from child maltreatment, including physical and emotional neglect. However, child maltreatment is by no means inevitable in these situations, and they are not the only situations in which children are likely to be subjected to emotional neglect. Cleaver *et al.* entitle their study: *Children's Needs – Parenting Capacity.* The terms 'seriously inadequate parenting' and 'emotional neglect' often refer to the same parental deficits as each other. The Department of Health study has a wider remit than this chapter. It is concerned with all forms of child maltreatment in the three situations described. This chapter confines itself to emotional neglect and abuse, but examines four areas: the three areas already mentioned, and one further area: the aftermath of marital separation and divorce.

Whether or not children caught up in the predicaments of parental struggles and violence, parental drug and alcohol abuse or mental illness suffer from emotional neglect and abuse depends on the nature of their maltreatment, its chronicity, intensity and periodicity, and whether stressors come singly or in combination. Whether children suffer from child psychiatric disturbance as a result of the emotional neglect they have endured seems to depend on the outcome that emerges from the interplay between stressors and protective factors in the child and the situation. The main protective factors seem to be at least one loving parent to whom the child is securely attached, and whether the child has other supports such as good friends or concerned adults. The child's temperament, intelligence and problem-solving skills can also be protective factors.

Exposure to marital violence and rows

The first of the three situations selected by the Department of Health in which children were deemed to be particularly vulnerable to emotional child neglect and abuse was witnessing marital rows, when parents fail to protect their children from their own hurtful arguments and fights. It is difficult to be precise about the prevalence of domestic violence but, however it is defined, its prevalence seems to be high, with just over half the families where a child protection conference is held, admitting to parental domestic violence (Thoburn 1996). Nor is it safe to assume that the instigator is always the male. Moffitt and Caspi (1998) in a review of this field found that whoever instigates the episodes, women and children seem to be the main victims. It is tempting to suppose that the parents often have no intention to hurt the child, but cannot contain their own anger or keep their arguments from the children. However, children are also often physically attacked, sometimes for trying to intervene. Child physical abuse was found by Moffit and Caspi (1998) to be between three and nine times more prevalent in families where parents hit each other. Emotional abuse of a particularly distressing type occurs when a parent, almost always the father, insists on having the children present when he batters or humiliates his wife. This situation would seem another instance of the sadistic form of emotional abuse. Bifulco *et al.* (2002) found that such abuse is relatively rare, but that there was a strong association for women between having experienced situations of sadistic abuse as a child and suffering depression as adults. There is evidence that children can be as upset and emotionally disturbed by watching parents hitting each other, as by being physically abused themselves (Jaffe, Wolfe and Wilson 1990); and emotional neglect is likely to be increased when the mother falls into depression or avoids social contact because of her shame.

Children of separated and divorced parents

When unhappy partners separate, in theory this should help the children involved, by removing them from distressing parental rows, but in some cases the bitterness only continues or even increases; and the child's need to see an absent parent regularly is sometimes resisted, as part of the persisting resentment over past hurts. This itself could often be described as a serious form of emotional neglect. However, the level of emotional abuse and/or neglect may intensify when children are used as messengers between divorced parents who find it difficult to communicate directly themselves. One of the commonest occasions for misuse occurs when parents leave the arrangements for contact to the children. However, what has been agreed with one parent frequently does not fit in well with what the other parent wishes, and the child is left carrying the responsibility for the disagreement. Another common situation when children are left to carry messages is when the parent with residence tells the child to inform the other parent that it is time he/she pays for shoes, clothing or school trips – expenses that had not been previously agreed between the parties. There seems to be a scale of misuse of children as message carriers stretching from on one hand parental fear of the ex-spouse, and, at the other extreme, the deliberate use of the child as a guided missile.

Another unpleasant form of emotional child abuse occurs when one parent will make giving the child a treat dependent on the 'reasonable' behaviour of the ex-partner, for example 'if your Dad won't agree to this, you won't be having a birthday party'. This is doubly destructive, since it is meant to hurt both the father and the child.

Parents abusing alcohol or drugs

A further set of situations in which parental neglect can impact on children involves parents who are dependent on alcohol or drugs. As Cleaver *et al.*

(1999) point out, not all parental alcohol or drug abuse seriously harms children, but children can be grossly distressed and/or neglected by parents who are unable to play with them, protect or feed them because they are drunk or semi-conscious, and who may spend most of the family income on alcohol or drugs. Alcohol and drug abuse may lead to unemployment, debts, evictions, and crime to sustain a drug habit, with increasing isolation for the family. In addition, alcohol abuse is often a factor in physical and sexual abuse, and also of acute embarrassment to children, as when birthdays and Christmas celebrations are ruined by a parent's alcohol abuse. The partner of a drug or alcohol abuser may be so worried and upset in relation to coping with the abuser and the situation that they have little time for the children, who consequently get emotionally neglected by both parents.

The children of mentally ill parents

Third, there are situations where mental illness in one or both parents leads to a deterioration in parenting capacity, and failures to meet children's needs, both physical and emotional. The subject is vast, and can only be briefly dealt with here. Depression is by far the commonest form of severe mental illness affecting mothers. The effects on the children are mediated considerably by severity, frequency and the presence or absence of an intimate spouse or partner who can offer support and mitigate the effects of the mother's depression on the children. Depression could be described as a state of misery and hopelessness, often leading to irritability with others, agitation or retardation, marked changes in eating patterns and in difficulties either in getting off to sleep, or in early morning waking. It is often accompanied by anxiety and deficiencies in self-presentation and the care of children. Depression occurring in the post-partum period may have serious and lasting consequences for the child's cognitive development (Murray et al. 1996), and affect security of attachment formation (Sroufe 1983). Depressed mothers and their children will be likely to get out of step in their relationship, and such important aspects of parenting as praising, supporting, planning ahead, playing games and sharing homework will either not occur, or will be conducted less appropriately than when the parent was not depressed. Caring and patient fathers may be a lifeline to children and to the mothers, but some fathers find the situation more than they can cope with, and stay away from the home more than they need, or even find other partners. Social workers need to know that depression lifts, and also to be familiar with support groups like Newpin (Jenkins 1996) for depressed and isolated mothers. In my experience many depressed mothers have a resistance to taking anti-depressants. It could be said that the ultimate form of parental emotional neglect and abuse is suicide, and this is strongly associated with being depressed. Social workers and health visitors should acquire the skills to be able to ask gently but firmly about suicidal ideation and plans, and what action to take to help the seriously suicidal (see Box 4.4 for a case example).

Box 4.4 Case example: Sean

Sean (four years old) seemed to be the butt of his mother's frustration and depression. His father had recently obtained a job as a newspaper distributor after many months of unemployment, during which time the family had got seriously into debt. His present job involved working long hours, but was well paid. The mother was left to cope with Sean and Lindsay (two years old). Sean appeared to spend much more time in his bedroom than with his mother and Lindsay, having been sent there by an angry mother, who had been obliged to do all the child and household care, and also work two half days a week in a fish and chip shop. She had very little support from her husband, who dealt with her emotional outbursts by laughing at her, or leaving the house. As a psychiatric social worker working with Sean and his mother, I was phoned at 4.30 pm one evening by a debt collector from the housing department, to say she had called, and the mother, Debbie, had just slapped Sean hard across the face for no good reason. Debbie was extremely angry with me when I called. Her husband was present and sat silently and was apparently amused, until the 'storm' blew over. He neither supported his wife, nor attacked me. The father and mother agreed to attend a planning meeting, and the whole incident seemed to jolt Debbie and her husband into a realization that she really was depressed and needed help for herself and in relation to Sean, and that her husband had to assist. The father pledged himself to be more supportive, and he kept his word. The mother began to attend a parenting workshop, and improved greatly in herself.

SCHIZOPHRENIA

Schizophrenia is a serious mental illness usually striking in the late teens or early twenties, which causes sufferers to experience particular kinds of auditory hallucinations and delusions, usually involving grandeur or threat. There are also what are called 'negative symptoms', including apathy and withdrawal. It is difficult to see how parenting in severe cases could not at times be neglectful both physically and emotionally. However, there is a huge range of severity of symptoms, and new atypical anti-psychotics seem capable of reducing the symptoms very considerably – provided, of course, they are taken regularly.

Children are particularly at risk if they become involved in the patient's delusions.

PERSONALITY DISORDER

Individuals with a severe personality disorder tend to suffer from a chronic lack of empathy, and awareness of other people's rights and feelings. They tend to abuse illicit drugs and alcohol in order to numb the pain of their existence. They have usually experienced abusive and/or neglectful parenting, and may have a considerable criminal record. Some are prone to making threats of injury to others and self-harm, sometimes in the presence of partners and children. Some may enjoy hurting other people.

Issues of whether and when it is safe to allow children, especially young children, to live with birth parents with a personality disorder or schizophrenia, severe depression or bipolar disorder need to be dealt with by multi-disciplinary discussion, involving psychiatrists, social workers, GPs and relatives, and not simply by social workers or psychiatrists.

These situations are not the only ones in which children get neglected. The children of parents with moderate or severe learning difficulties may lack adequate care and control unless there are other supports in the community; and the same could be said of a number of parents who suffer from chronic and severe physical illnesses and disabilities.

Conclusion

Neglect can seriously damage children's health, their physical and psychological development, their education and well-being. Social workers' recognition of, and response to, neglect would be more appropriate if they accepted the validity of the term 'emotional neglect', as meaning a gross and persistent inability to meet children's emotional needs, and if they were regularly on the look-out for it, and knew what to expect.

Practitioners need a repertoire of appropriate questions such as:

- 'What are her teachers at school saying about her?'
- 'What are David's good points?'
- 'What does Joan do when she gets upset?'

Positive answers to these questions suggest that parents can be helped to be less emotionally neglectful or abusive to their children. Complete failure to answer them can be very telling. Emotional neglect frequently accompanies emotional abuse and neglect in general, and in fact all other types of child maltreatment. It is not the purpose of this chapter to argue strongly for another distinct official category of child maltreatment: emotional child neglect, but practitioners must

recognize it as a reality, and realize that the greater part of child neglect is emotional. We need to react in ways that help parents become better parents (where
that is possible) and create opportunities for neglected children to catch up, as
far as is feasible, on the severe deficits and distortions in their lives and development. However, there will be cases where parents cannot or will not change,
and the only means of protecting a child from further deficits in parenting is his
or her long-term removal.

Messages for practice

- Neglect is a serious form of child maltreatment.

- Child neglect (both physical and emotional) is often found with
  other forms of maltreatment.

- Emotional child neglect can be defined as a persistent failure to
  attend to children's basic emotional needs, although physical
  neglect, by itself, always involves emotional neglect.

- Emotional neglect arises out of failures of omission rather than
  commission.

- Emotional neglect frequently only comes to light when other forms
  of child maltreatment are being investigated.

- Emotional neglect implies indifference to the child's basic emotional
  needs – to his or her distress and achievements and need for control,
  guidance, security, protection, praise and affection.

- Emotional neglect seems to occur particularly in situations where the
  parents are preoccupied with other concerns, for example, in
  situations of marital violence, and where marriages end in increased
  bitterness. It is also frequently found in situations where parents are
  dependent on alcohol or drugs, or suffer from mental illness or
  disorder.

- On the whole, emotional neglect is not usually a specific event, or
  series of events, but the daily atmosphere in which neglected
  children have to live.

- Certain negative parental styles, for example, a rejecting style, are
  often associated with emotional abuse and neglect.

- Recognition of emotional neglect often depends on careful
  observation and listening. Practitioners need to have a repertoire of
  questions which elucidate the extent to which parents appear to be
  adequately and sensitively involved in caring for and controlling
  their children.

Chapter Five

Is This Child Neglect?

The Influence of Differences in Perceptions of Child Neglect on Social Work Practice

Jan Horwath

Introduction

A social worker participating in a research study of child neglect asked the following question:

> How do I know what I consider to be neglect is the same as everyone else working with the child?

At one level the answer appears obvious; there are both working definitions of neglect and lists of signs and indicators. However, the definitions and the lists are open to individual interpretation and this is where the differences described by the respondent can occur. Lally (1984) notes that different perceptions of child neglect are determined by cultural agreement and belief systems, social systems and the personal views held by individuals. Sullivan (2000) summarizes ways in which these views influence both professional and media attitudes towards neglect. In an overview of the literature she found the following beliefs exist about child neglect:

- child neglect does not have serious consequences
- it is inappropriate to judge parents involved in poverty-related neglect
- child neglect is an insurmountable problem
- other forms of child maltreatment are more compelling
- ambiguity and vagueness make it difficult to define neglect

- child neglect provokes negative feelings and is therefore
marginalized.

It is against this backcloth that social workers, together with other professionals, have to struggle as they make assessments and plan interventions in cases of
child neglect. Social workers have a key role to play in assessing cases of child
neglect. If the family, members of the community or other professionals are
concerned that the needs of a child are not being met as a consequence of
neglect then the child should be referred to the social services department for
an assessment of the needs of the child and the parents' ability to meet these
needs. The social worker is usually responsible for co-ordinating this assessment through working together with the child, the family and other professionals. The early 2000s have been a period when significant attention has
been given to standardizing assessment practice in Great Britain; this is exem-
plified by the introduction of the *Framework for the Assessment of Children in Need
and their Families* (Department of Health 2000) in England and Wales. The
Framework emphasizes that standardized practice is most likely to occur if the
use of professional judgement is informed by an evidence-based approach
towards a case. However, if social workers are to achieve better outcomes for
children and families, it is necessary to reflect on the factors that can influence
the way in which they make judgements. Using the findings of an Irish study of
social workers' practice in cases of child neglect together with other reported
studies in this field the chapter begins with an analysis of the factors that can
influence social workers' assessments and interventions in cases of child
neglect. The chapter concludes with a practical exploration of the lessons learnt
from the studies together with a framework for assessment to assist social work
practitioners in identifying ways in which their beliefs influence their practice.

Child maltreatment services in Ireland are managed on a regional basis by
ten local authorities known as health boards. Each region divides into community care areas with social work teams working in child care. The team is made
up of three different types of workers: social workers who take the lead responsibility for investigating cases of child maltreatment, family support workers
who work in the home with carers to develop their parenting skills, and community child care workers who work primarily with vulnerable children. The
study details are included in Box 5.1.

Four themes were identified as a result of the analysis which give some
insight into the ways in which differences in perception of child neglect influence the way social work departments define and work with cases of child
neglect. These are:

- the effect of individual beliefs

- the influence of the team in establishing working definitions of child
neglect

- the assessment process: differences between theory and practice
- the use of language.

Box 5.1 The study

Aims

The study sought to:

- identify front-line workers' understanding of child neglect
- increase understanding of the factors which inform decision-making when assessing cases of child neglect
- explore professionals' perceptions of their professional and organizational needs
- make recommendations to the senior management team regarding ways of standardizing agency responses to the assessment of child neglect.

Methodology

- An audit of case files was completed. The aim was to identify ways in which front-line child care workers actually worked with child neglect. The advantage of an audit is that it provides recorded information about the child and family, details of their involvement with the health board and an outline of the services provided.
- An anonymous postal questionnaire was designed to collect quantitative and qualitative information regarding ways in which staff believe they work with child neglect. The questions were designed:
  - to elicit detail regarding themes that emerged from the case audit
  - to begin to explore the attitudes of respondents towards child neglect
  - to identify the professional and organizational factors they believe influence practice.
- Peer-based focus groups provided opportunities for staff to explore the themes that emerged from both the case audit and questionnaire and to consider ways in which both themselves and the managers within the health board could develop practice in cases of child neglect.

THE SAMPLE AND DATA COLLECTION

A randomly selected sample of 57 cases from the different social work teams designated as cases of child neglect were read and qualitatively analysed by the researcher using a standardized content analysis framework. The framework was developed based on knowledge of file content obtained from reading a randomly selected sample of child care files prior to the case audit.

All front-line child care staff, practitioners and managers, were sent the questionnaire. There are potentially 75 front-line staff employed in child care teams. However, long-term sickness and staff vacancies meant the potential sample size was reduced. Information was not available regarding the actual level of absenteeism and unfilled posts at the time the questionnaire was sent out. Based on a sample size of 75 a response rate of 40 meant a 53% response rate. However, it would seem the actual response rate was higher than this bearing in mind the number of available staff.

Four focus groups were held. All staff working in child care fieldwork teams at the front line were invited to attend the focus groups. Three child care teams operate within the health board. Each team had its own focus group. This provided opportunities for data to be obtained to compare and contrast the views held by members of the different teams. Managers were invited to a separate group to avoid practitioners being placed in a position of being intimidated in expressing their views because of the presence of their manager. Nine managers attended this focus group.

Analysis

- The researcher collated the data regarding the case audit using the standardized content analysis framework. An analysis of themes and sub-themes of the framework content was completed.

- The quantitative data in the questionnaire was analysed using SPSS and content analysis was used to identify themes from the qualitative data.

- Content analysis was also used for the focus group data.

Limitations

The study is small-scale and based on the views of social work practitioners and managers working in a region of the Republic of Ireland. One cannot make national or international generalizations about social work practice in cases of child neglect based on the findings from this study.

The effect of individual beliefs

Respondents to the study questionnaire were asked to comment on statements regarding parenting, decision-making and damaging environments for children using a Likert scale (a scale offering five options from 'strongly agree' to 'strongly disagree'). The statements were adapted from the work of Daniel (2000). The responses indicated a diverse range of individual assumptions and perceptions of parenting and the needs of the children that are likely to influence attitudes towards neglect. As emotional neglect is perhaps the most significant and damaging component of neglect (Iwaniec 1995) the most concerning opinions were those held by respondents regarding the link between neglect and emotional abuse. Although 53% ($n = 21$) of respondents considered that the most damaging environment for children was one of high criticism and low warmth, 28% ($n = 11$) were not sure and 20% ($n = 8$) disagreed. Second, 33% ($n = 13$) considered the essential aspect of parenting to be providing for a child's physical needs and safety. In response to the statement '*a child who is physically neglected is likely to be experiencing emotional neglect as well*' 75% ($n = 30$) of practitioners and managers agreed. These responses would seem to indicate that a minority of respondents do not fully understand the nature of emotional neglect. This lack of attention to the emotional aspects of neglect was also striking in its absence from case files. These findings contrast to those of Daniel who found not only a high level of consensus amongst qualified social workers in Scotland regarding the importance of emotional factors in the parenting environment but also workers being highly sensitive to the emotional needs of children (Daniel 1999, 2000).

Social work practitioners did however share similar views regarding a child's home environment. The questionnaire respondents were asked to give examples of what they considered to be unacceptable in a house where a three-year-old was living with regard to the soiling of the kitchen floor; general decorative order; uncared-for child's clothing and so on. There was a high level of consensus. For example, the most frequently cited factor regarding soiled kitchen floor was the presence of human or animal faeces or urine cited by 53% ($n = 21$). Regarding children's clothing 38% ($n = 15$) of respondents declared that not washing children's clothing regularly was unacceptable. 30% ($n = 12$) objected to clothes that were inadequate or unsuitable for the weather, and 25% ($n = 10$) to ill-fitting clothes or shoes. Respondents commented that there was a degree of personal judgement involved in making assessments of unacceptable levels of dirt. Recognizing variations in the application of standards was a striking theme of the study.

These double standards operated amongst the social work professionals in the study. Only 13% ($n = 5$) of respondents to the questionnaire stated that they use the same criteria for assessing the parental behaviour of clients that they would use for themselves or their friends. Differences in standards between social workers and other professionals were noted by 50% ($n = 20$) of question-naire respondents. They believed that staff in social work departments accept lower standards of parenting than other professionals in contact with children.

In response to the statement '*I have a baseline of what is good enough for children that I will not step over*' 45% ($n = 18$) agreed while 35% ($n = 14$) disagreed and 8% ($n = 3$) were unsure. What is not clear from these responses is how this baseline is determined and the factors that influence those practitioners who would step over the baseline. Social workers do not make decisions about what is good enough for children in isolation. Their own beliefs and values and those of society, as with any other professional, will determine their decision. The degree to which this influences decision-making is open to debate. Ringwalt and Caye (1989) note that people's perceptions of child neglect are affected by sex, race and education. The researchers found black ethnic minority groups were marginally more likely to rate the vignettes as severe than white respon-dents. Females were more likely than males to rate them severely while severity ratings varied negatively with education. Hong and Hong (1991) found that the Chinese in the USA were more tolerant of parental conduct than the His-panics and whites. Portwood (1998) found that parental experience and personal experience of maltreatment had only a minimal effect on assessments. However, professional experience of working with maltreatment predisposed individuals to view ambiguous acts as less likely to constitute abuse.

What is child neglect? The influence of the team in establishing working definitions

Scourfield (2000) notes that two influential and contrasting professional dis-courses operate within teams working with child neglect. He argues that practice will be determined by the discourse that dominates team practice. The first discourse is that taken by the Bridge Childcare Consultancy, an independ-ent organization who have prepared a number of case reviews following deaths of children from neglect (Bridge Childcare Consultancy 1995). Scourfield argues the emphasis is on the physical care of the child 'servicing the child's body', recognizing that dirty, smelly children may be suffering maltreatment. The other discourse is that emphasized through the Department of Health's publication (1995) with a focus not on the physical care provided by the parent but on the emotional impact of parenting on the child. Scourfield, in his ethnographic study of a social work team, found that social workers con-structed child neglect by concentrating on the 'children's bodies and parental body maintenance for children'. He noted that social workers made judge-ments about the emotional climate within the home but that if this was positive but the standards of physical care were unacceptable then the family was still seen as a cause of concern. However, Stone (1998) interviewed social workers in a metropolitan borough in England about their work with neglected children on the child protection register. He found that these practitioners considered relationship issues and family dysfunction to be central to their understanding of how children become neglected. This could be seen to support Scourfield's argument that the organization and team play a crucial role in shaping practitioners' perception of neglect.

Turning to the Irish study, there was general agreement amongst those that attended the focus groups that perceptions of child neglect vary from worker to worker and the responses to the questionnaire would seem to bear this out. However the review of the case files completed as part of the study indicated that the perceptions of child neglect varied depending partly on the location of the worker. That is, workers in the different comunity care areas tended to assess child neglect in different ways. This was influenced by the context in which the teams operated. For example, the systems, resources available and workloads. As a result of this, in one area with clear established systems for processing cases of child maltreatment the focus when defining neglect tended to be on the incident that could pose an immediate risk of harm to a child. The cases were thoroughly investigated with this focus. For example, if a child was left home alone, the assessment focused on the act of leaving a young child at home alone. In a second community care area the focus of both assessments and interventions were more varied. Some cases records indicated the focus was on keeping children safe and meeting their needs, whilst other records showed workers attempting to do this as well as improving parenting capacity. However, the records on the files indicated that pressure of work resulted in short term interventions Finally, in the third area that had services available to families that were not available in the other areas the workers were able to focus not only on the impact of maltreatment on the child, they were also addressing issues related to parenting capacity and the parenting environment. In addition, the threshold for intervention was lower in this area than in the other two areas.

The way in which the social work professionals define child neglect has a direct influence on the assessment process. In the case audit included in the Irish study, 48 out of the 82 reasons for referral (referrers often cited more than one cause of concern) focused on a specific incident such as children being left alone or the parents being seen drunk whilst caring for the children (Table 5.1).

When completing assessments in response to these referrals notable differences were recorded on case files based on team response. In 20 cases predominantly from one community care area, social workers dealing with the referrals appeared to focus on the *incidents* of possible neglect rather than considering the *impact* of neglect on the child. In a further 18 cases, mainly from a second team, there was a generalized assessment of the children's needs. This included eight cases where information was obtained from other professionals with no discussion with families recorded and ten cases where the information was based on contact with the family and professionals. The records included

Table 5.1 Reasons for referral

Nature of referrers' concerns	Frequency and percentage
Alcohol use by carer	8 (9.8%) single source of referral 11 (13.4%) combination
Children left unattended	7 (8.5%) single source of referral 6 (7.3%) combination
Home conditions	2 (2.4%) single source of referral 3 (3.7%) combination
Drug use	3 (3.7%) single source of referral 2 (2.4%) combination
Suspected child sexual abuse	1 (1.2%) single source of referral 3 (3.7%) combination
Children hungry	4 (4.9%) combination
Lack of supervision	4 (4.9%) single source of referral
Inappropriate carers	3 (3.7%) single source of referral
Children witnessing domestic violence	3 (3.7%) combination
Carer's ability to care	2 (2.4%) single source of referral 2 (2.4%) combination
Non-attendance at clinics	2 (2.4%) single source of referral 1 (1.2%) combination
Non-school attendance	1 (1.2%) single source of referral 2 (2.4%) combination
Carer's mental health	1 (1.2%) single source of referral 1 (1.2%) combination
Child begging	1 (1.2%) combination
Carer gambling	1 (1.2%) combination
Carer's company	1 (1.2%) combination
Homelessness	1 (1.2%) combination
Lack of stimulation	1 (1.2%) single source of referral
Carer's aggression	1 (1.2%) combination
Vulnerable adolescent	1 (1.2%) single source of referral
Carer's lifestyle	1 (1.2%) single source of referral
Physical abuse	2 (2.4%) combination

generalized descriptions, for example 'the child is well though her weight remains a problem'. In these cases, it was difficult to establish what was the cause of concern. For example, was the weight a problem because the child was under or over weight? In 18 cases largely from a third team, the initial assessments explored the specific needs of the child and the carer's ability to meet these needs. The analysis of case files would seem to indicate that workers and managers take one of three different perspectives towards the assessment process:

- to confirm whether child neglect has occurred

- to assess whether the child has suffered or is likely to suffer harm as a result of the perceived neglect

- to assess both for harm and the impact of the harm caused by neglect on the well-being of the child.

Rose (2001) notes that any assessment of a child that aims to understand what is happening to the child has to take account of a child's developmental needs, the parenting capacity to meet these needs and the wider community in which he/she lives. Yet, the review of the case files highlighted that in many cases these factors were not considered in detail.

The review of case material indicated that the interventions planned for the children in many ways mirrored the assessment, that is, perceptions of neglect and its impact on the child influences the approach to interventions. Interventions could be seen to operate at three levels each having a different purpose: protecting the child from the presenting concern; protecting the child and promoting the child's welfare; or safeguarding and promoting the welfare of the child and working to improve parenting capacity. The suggested interventions in response to a questionnaire scenario about a family where increasing concerns about neglect were described. Some respondents focused on the abuse the children were suffering and considered care proceedings as a means of keeping the children safe. Others focused on ways in which the children could be protected and have their needs met. Suggestions included regular medical checks, respite care, daycare and monitoring. Other respondents considered ways of influencing parenting capacity through parenting courses, alcohol counselling and treatment for the mother's depression. It appears that different services are offered depending on the attitude towards not only the assessment but also the perceived purpose of intervention.

If teams are incident focused and view child neglect as failure to service children's bodies then, as Minty and Pattinson (1994) comment, social workers can under-estimate the seriousness of child neglect believing it is either a consequence of maternal poverty or a matter of 'dirty children in dirty homes'. That is, social workers can be 'under-whelmed' to the point where practitioners normalize the neglect (Graham 1998, cited in Buckley 2002). However in teams that take a broader holistic approach towards child neglect and consider relationship issues and family dysfunction in addition to poverty and physical neglect workers may feel 'over-whelmed' by the complexity of the case.

The role of the supervisor

If, as would seem to be the case in the Irish study, teams respond differently to cases of child neglect then this raises questions about the role of the team manager. Practitioners and managers in the study were asked to respond to the statement '*the criteria for triggering child protection procedures can vary depending on which manager is involved*'. Seven of the nine managers agreed with this; however, only 53% of practitioners agreed. If team managers recognize different approaches while a large number of practitioners do not it would appear that many practitioners are unaware of the differences in practice between the community care areas accepting their team approach as 'normal'. It may be that some team members are unaware of the influence of the manager in setting thresholds and the focus for assessments and interventions. In addition, the respondents in the focus groups believed that team members played a significant role in supporting fellow team members and acting as a sounding board when exploring concerns about children and families. It would seem the team members play a part in reinforcing the standards set by the manager.

The assessment process: differences between theory and practice

A number of factors influence the way in which social work practitioners define and assess cases of child neglect. Differences were also found between what workers believed they did and what happened in actual practice.

Listening to children

The questionnaire highlighted discrepancies amongst respondents regarding their approach to working with children. Respondents were asked whether decisions about a child should be made on the basis of what the young person wants (provided they have the ability to understand and make informed choices). Thirty-five per cent ($n = 14$) believed this should be the case most of the time, 48% ($n = 19$) some of the time and 15% ($n = 6$) occasionally. A further question required respondents to consider the extent to which communications with the child influenced their decision-making. Forty-nine per cent ($n = 19$) stated that it influenced their decision-making all the time, 30% ($n = 12$) some of the time and 5% ($n = 2$) claimed never to be influenced by this factor. The

Bridge Childcare Consultancy (1995) state that they 'cannot stress too highly' the importance of communicating with children in cases of neglect.

Yet, the review of case material indicated a lack of meaningful communication with children about their lives. In only five cases was there clear evidence on the files of workers ascertaining the wishes and feeling of children regarding their experiences. Not only were children not listened to, but in 15 of 21 home visits made following a referral there was no evidence on the file of the children actually being seen. As neglect centres on the impact of parenting behaviour on the child (Dubowitz 1999), it is difficult to see how workers can assess neglect without at the very least seeing the child.

Working with parents: aggression, resistance, collusion and stereotyping

Seventy-five per cent ($n = 30$) of respondents to the questionnaire had a strong view that decisions about the child in cases of child neglect should be based on workers and the family exploring all possible outcomes and weighing up the costs and benefits of each. Sisty per cent ($n = 24$) of respondents went on to indicate that decisions were made according to information from the family most of the time while 33% ($n = 13$) said they do this all of the time. Although there was evidence on the files that working together with parents did take place, on many occasions it was not always the case. In some cases, the views of both parents were not obtained. For example, there were alleged concerns about both carers in ten cases however only the mother or the father were seen. In five of these cases, the father came to the office and the mother was never seen. In four cases the social worker only met with the mother even though the concerns centred on the behaviour of the father. In two additional cases, although the referral related to the impact of marital conflict on the children, the focus for assessment and intervention was the mother rather than both parents. All these cases were closed without evidence on the file of discussion of the causes of concern with both carers. Swift (1994) notes that early definitions of neglect were personalized and gendered, 'seen as failure of individual mothers to carry out their mothering responsibilities' (p.72). Scourfield (2000) has argued that in the recent 'rediscovery of neglect' the dominant construction of neglect among the social work practitioners in his study was 'maternal failure to service children's bodies' (p.365). Neglect is usually constructed as an omission in care, and the gendered nature of care means that neglect is associated with deficiencies in mothering (Turney 2000) (see also Chapter Fourteen). This was borne out in the case scenario. Only three respondents saw the lack of support the mother received from the father as a cause for concern and only five respondents identified the father's perceived lack of interest in the parenting role as an issue. What emerges is a picture in some cases of the mother being perceived by workers as totally responsible for the care of the children.

A number of respondents acknowledged, when asked to state factors that *did* contribute to decision-making, that aggression was influential. The review of the case files would also seem to indicate that in practice not only physical and verbal aggression but also passive resistance can influence the decision-making process. There were ten cases where carers avoided meaningful contact with the social worker. For example, carers cancelled or did not attend home or office visits. In some cases the carers did allow social workers to visit; however, they managed to avoid meaningful contact. For example, one social worker noted 'Mother is seen but when one gets in a conversation it is difficult to conduct because of constant interruptions'. All these cases resulted in closure without any meaningful discussion with the family about the concerns of child neglect.

The use of language commonalities and differences

The Irish study highlighted some interesting findings regarding the use of terminology amongst social work professionals and differences between the social workers and other professionals. In some cases perceptions regarding the meaning of terms were similar, in other cases there were considerable differences. These findings regarding different use of language are explored through the use of the term 'good enough parenting'.

GOOD ENOUGH PARENTING

Throughout the records on the files references were made to 'good enough parenting', for example 'parenting is good enough case closed'. Case records also indicated that social workers ask other professionals the question 'Is parenting good enough?' In order to elicit whether social work practitioners were consistent in the use of this term respondents were asked to define the term 'good enough parenting'. The responses were coded into seven common themes (see Table 5.2). The most common answer, given by 17 respondents (42.5%), referred to parenting which meets the child's physical needs, that is those for food, shelter, warmth, clothing etc. However even this was open to dispute as two practitioners specified that 'good enough parenting' did not meet the needs of the child, saying 'it is at times very difficult to define the term, but good enough parenting will not meet the needs of the child' and 'the standard of parenting is such that the child's health, welfare or development is, has or will be seriously affected'.

Table 5.2 Definitions of good enough parenting

Valid	Frequency *	Percentage of respondents*
Meeting child's (physical) needs	17	42.5
Parents provide love/nurture/attachment/emotional warmth	11	27.5
Child is safe/not at immediate risk	8	20.0
Promoting child's development/stimulating child	6	15.0
Parent does best/puts child first	5	12.5
Parenting is (just) adequate/acceptable	5	12.5
Not meeting child's needs	2	5.0

* Some respondents gave multiple answers

The second most common answer (27.5%, $n = 11$) was that parents provide children with love, nurture, emotional warmth, etc. while the third was that the child was safe or not at (immediate) risk (20.0%, $n = 8$). Six respondents (15%) felt that 'good enough parenting' promoted the child's development, or provided stimulation for the child, but again one specifically mentioned that 'good enough parenting' did *not* promote child development or stimulate the child. This respondent wrote: 'Parent meets child's basic material and emotional needs but has limited insight into child's developmental needs.'

Five (12.5%) believed 'good enough parenting' means the parent(s) do(es) their best, or 'putting the child first' and the same number (12.5%, $n = 5$) felt that 'good enough parenting' was just adequate/acceptable (and no more).

Only a minority of respondents provided a holistic definition that his/her needs for food, warmth, education, stimulation, emotional growth, development etc. are met and 'good enough parenting promotes the child's development'.

The term was originally used by Winnicott (1964) to describe a facilitating parenting environment that enables the child's needs to be met. However what is apparent from the responses is that respondents confuse the term and some practitioners use 'good enough parenting' to describe what Cooper refers to as 'border-line' and 'bad-enough parenting' (Cooper 1983). In addition, as Pugh, De'Ath and Smith (1994) comment, what is good enough parenting for one child may be inadequate for another child. This was not noted explicitly by the respondents in the Irish study.

Messages from research

- The assessment framework emphasizes that standardized practice is most likely to occur if the use of professional judgement is informed by an evidence-based approach to care.

- Social workers display a diverse range of individual assumptions of parenting and the needs of the children that are likely to influence attitudes towards neglect.

- Personal judgement and double standards operated among the social work professionals in this study.

- In the Irish study there were regional variations regarding defining neglect which in turn influenced the assessment process.

- There were differences between what workers believed they did and what happened in actual practice.

- There was a lack of meaningful communication with children about their lives.

- The focus for assessment and intervention tended to be on the mother.

- Social workers differed in their understanding of 'good enough parenting'.

- If practitioners are to be more open-minded when assessing cases of child neglect they need an *aide memoire*.

Lessons learnt and the implications for social work practitioners and managers

Munro (2002) argues that child protection workers tend to act like barristers defending one particular viewpoint. She believes that workers would be more effective if they acted like detectives searching for the truth, keeping an open mind and testing the conclusions they reach. The Irish study would seem to support this argument. Findings indicate that social work professionals take a particular perspective towards child neglect that is influenced by their personal beliefs, the team and team manager. Once a case is categorized in a particular way then interventions reflect the categorization. The issue for practitioners and managers is how to make the shift from barrister to detective bearing in mind some of the other findings from the study. That is, social work professionals have standards and beliefs, which influence their perceptions of what constitutes child neglect and good enough parenting. And there is a difference between what practitioners believe they should be doing when working together with children and families and what actually occurs. Members of the focus groups had a number of ideas about developing practice in light of these findings, which have been developed by the author and are outlined below.

From Rumpole of the Bailey to Sherlock Holmes: assessing the needs of children and families

If practitioners are to be more open-minded when assessing cases of child neglect then they need an *aide memoire* (Macdonald 2001) or prompts reminding them what they should be considering when assessing cases of children in need. Assessment frameworks such as the *Framework for the Assessment of Children in Need and their Families* (Department of Health 2000) can be seen to provide an *aide memoire*. However, the Irish respondents who attended the focus group believed that they would work more effectively with children and families if they had a detailed assessment framework that gave them specific prompts to remind them what to consider when assessing cases of child neglect. Using data obtained from the study the author developed an assessment framework, which has been successfully piloted amongst social work personnel; this framework is shown in Table 5.3. Members of the focus groups believed the following principles should underpin the framework:

- Assessments and interventions should be child focused.

- Effective management of child neglect requires an ecological approach.

- Child neglect impacts on the developmental needs of the child.

- Working with both children and families is crucial to assessing and addressing issues of neglect.

- Effective assessment and intervention in cases of child neglect requires an ongoing multidisciplinary approach recognizing the contribution of professionals working with carers' issues.

- Professional knowledge, values and skills should inform assessment, planning, intervention and evaluation of neglect cases.

The framework builds on the definition of child neglect used by the Department of Health and Children (Ireland) (1999) in *Children First: National Guidelines for the Protection and Welfare of Children*. Child neglect is:

> an *omission*, where the child suffers significant harm or impairment of development by being deprived of food, clothing, warmth, hygiene, intellectual stimulation, supervision and safety, attachment to and affection from adults, medical care. (p.31)

Table 5.3 Horwath framework for assessing child neglect

Area of Concern	The child	The parent/carer	The outside world
Intellectual stimulation	Consider:	Consider:	Consider:
	Level of school/playschool attendance	Importance attached to educational activities and social opportunities	Engagement in learning at school/pre-school
	Freedom to play with toys Time for play	Provision of toys and books and opportunities to use them	Access to activities outside home
	Interaction with adults and other children	Interaction and stimulation from carer Ability to listen and communicate with child	Relationships with peers
	Type of activities undertaken, for example, watch TV all day	Encouragement for intellectual development	Opportunities for extra-curricular school and social activities
	Particular educational needs of child	Recognition and ability to meet special needs	Provision of service to meet special needs
Basic care – food, clothing, warmth and hygiene	Appearance and quality of clothing, seasonal, fit and level of cleanliness and repair	Provision of clean fitting clothes appropriate for season Ability to recognize when child needs help with basic care, for example dressing	Attitude of school and peers to the appearance of the child
	Physical presentation including level of cleanliness, condition of hair, body odour, skin infections, dental and optical care	Encouragement to or commitment to wash/bath child regularly Attitude to changing nappies regularly Treatment of infections	Condition of home, for example, human/animal excrement, soiled bathrroom, broken toilet, old/decaying food on floor, evidence of infestation
	Child's development using centile charts	Attendance at clinics, dentists, opticians etc.	Child's development and ability to meet basic care needs in relation to peers

Continued on next page

Table 5.3 continued

Area of concern	The child	The parent/ carer	The outside world
Basic care – food, clothing, warmth and hygiene (cont.)	Child's attitude to food	Attitude and ability to provide regular and balanced meals	Provision of food for school Attitude to food outside the home
	Whether child is warm/cool as appropriate	Ability to keep child warm/cool according to season	Warmth of house, fo example, damp, source of heating, broken windows, bedding, financial ability to provide heating
Medical care	Child immunized if appropriate	Parents' attitude to immunization	Ability to keep appointments through lack of transport, finance, child care commitments
	Receiving necessary medical checks	Response to medical, dental and optical appointments, use of medication, treatments and therapies	
	Child receiving any medical care as considered necessary by health professionals	Commitment to meeting child's specific medical requirements	
Supervision and safety	Child given appropriate amount of freedom dependent on age and ability, for example, left at home alone, playing in streets unsupervised, time of day when out playing	Carer's ability to meet the child'a needs for dependence/ independence and establish appropriate boundaries Carer's level of awareness of child's whereabouts	Norm in the area for playing out, being left unattended etc.
	Child's physical safety in the home	Ability to recognize and provide protection against hazards in the home	Home environment, for example dangerous electric sockets, broken windows, no fireguard, hazards in garden, medication and alcohol kept out of reach of children
	Child protected from inappropriate behaviours, for example, domestic violence	Ability Ability and commitment of parents to demonstrate and model appropriate behaviours	Support network for child outside home in situations of domestic violence etc.

Continued on next page

Table 5.3 continued

Area of concern	The child	The parent/carer	The outside world
Supervision and safety (cont.)	Child able to demonstrate appropriate behaviours according to age and ability, for example, anger management	Ability to protect children from harm and danger Recognition and commitment to protecting child from unsafe adults/children including siblings	
Attachment and affection	Child's feelings about themselves, for example, self-esteem, self-worth	Attitude of parents to child	Child's positive relationships outside home Attitude of teachers to the child
	Sense of own identity taking into account culture and disability	Value placed on the child	Attitude of significant others to child's identity
	Attitude to parents/carers and significant others Response to others	Parents' ability to consistently demonstrate warmth, love and affection verbally, cognitively and physically Parents' emotional availability	Significant people in the child's life
	Sense of belonging to family and other relevant groups	Appropriate physical contact, ability to make child feel important member of the family	Identity in out-of-home settings
	Feelings of security	Ability to feed back on negative behaviour in a manner that encourages growth Ability to praise and reward	Activities that increase child's sense of self-worth

This framework can be used alongside the Department of Health framework (2000) as the prompts link into the three domains that are central to the English and Welsh framework: child's developmental needs, parenting capacity and family and environmental factors.

The framework should encourage practitioners to act as detectives rather than barristers when assessing child neglect as the prompts remind workers of the variety of direct and indirect causes and consequences of neglect on a child.

The effective use of the framework will be determined by managers using the framework with team members to create a culture that encourages practitioners to act as detectives rather than barristers.

The study highlighted that different perceptions of child neglect were influenced not only by the gathering of information but also by the assessment process and planning interventions. Munro (2002) notes that assessment is not only about being more open-minded when gathering information, it is also about explicit and clearer use of reasoning processes. As she notes this increases the empowerment of children and parents as issues can be explained to them and their role in the assessment process becomes clear. The assessment process has several phases, which overlap and lead into planning, interventions and evaluation of those interventions (Adcock 2001). The prompts shown in Box 5.2 are designed to assist practitioners together with team managers to work their way through this process. Moreover, the questions act as reminders to practitioners of the importance of working in partnership with children and families in order both to gain information and to make sense of that information. The section on making judgements offers practitioners prompts to enable them to draw conclusions about the parents' or carers' ability to be the good enough parents that provide the 'facilitating environment' a child requires as described by Winnicott (1964).

Box 5.2 Prompts to use when carrying out assessments

(Adapted from unpublished work undertaken by Buckley, Horwath and Whelan).

Who should I contact when gathering information?

- Using the appropriate prompts included in the assessment framework what are the views of the child regarding their situation?

- What are the views of each significant carer?

- Are family members in agreement with information being obtained from professionals?

- Which professionals should be included in the assessment?

- Are there any blocks and barriers that are influencing information-gathering?

What does this information mean?

Consider current and pre-existing factors that could jeopardize the child's well-being including:

- vulnerability of child to abuse or neglect (current, further and/or future)
- needs of the child not being met.

Consider new and ongoing strengths of child and family that could promote the child's well-being including:

- protective factors provided by adults
- child's resilience and ability to protect themselves.

How can I use this information to make a judgement?

- What are the pre-existing and current factors that indicate that the welfare of the child is not being promoted and/or that they are likely to suffer significant harm?
- What are the pre-existing and current strengths that protect the child and promote their welfare?
- What is there about the current situation that increases or decreases risk of significant harm and meeting the developmental needs of the child?
- How does the current situation fit with past patterns of carer's behaviour?
- What are the child's views? What do they want to change?
- What insight does the carer/s have in relation to the treatment of the child?
- What are the indicators that carers have both the capacity and motivation to make changes required to promote the welfare of the child?

Reaching a decision

Consider whether:

- the needs of the child are being met
- the needs of the child are being met currently but the child is in a vulnerable position and there is potential that needs will not be met

- the needs of the child are unlikely to be met without the provision of services

- the needs of the child are not being met and their health and development are being impaired.

What services are required?

What interventions are needed to:

- protect the child from immediate harm?

- meet the needs of the child?

- effect change amongst carers in order to protect and promote the welfare of the child?

Effective use of the team and team manager

One of the most striking findings from this study has been the importance of the team in terms of setting the standards for thresholds, content and process of assessment and interventions. Based on the findings of this study insufficient data has been obtained to establish the extent to which it is the team manager, team members or a combination of both that influences the team approach towards working with cases of child neglect. Irrespective of who has the most influence in the Irish study there are lessons that can be learnt by drawing on theory related to group process. Brown (1996) analysed the social influences that operate within groups. He found that individuals tend to conform to the attitudes and behaviours of the majority. This can occur to the degree that individuals are willing to deny the evidence of their own senses to conform to the group perspective. Brown identified three reasons why this occurs:

- the need to depend on others for information about the world and to test the validity of our own opinions

- pressure from within and outside team to achieve group goals

- the need for approval arising out of not wishing to seem different.

This has a number of implications for social work teams. First, practitioners may adjust their own standards to meet those of the team. This could be either advantageous or disadvantageous depending on the individual standards and those of the team. Second, Daley (1999) in a study of decision-making amongst newly qualified nurses found that there was a reluctance to learn from experience. Instead the nurses tended to focus on using memory, accumulating information and waiting for others to tell them what to learn. This could apply equally to newly qualified social workers who would look to the team members and manager for guidance as to what is important in cases of child neglect. Third, in a performance-driven culture, which is dominant in the statutory social services, group goals are becoming explicit. These goals in England are linked to targets used to determine quality and funding. A culture can develop in teams where the priority is meeting the targets irrespective of their impact on outcomes for children and families. Finally, front-line social work teams are working under intense pressure (Jones 2001a). In these circumstances the implicit team goal may be survival: the price paid is to be a barrister rather than a detective because of the consequences on workload of taking an open approach towards cases of child neglect.

Brown (1996) makes reference to the work of Janis (1972) who explored the notion of 'groupthink' or group standards. He believes groups that are most vulnerable to groupthink are those which are very cohesive; are insulated from information outside the group; rarely search systematically through alternative options; are often under stress and are dominated by a directive group leader. If teams are to avoid distorting assessments of child neglect then antidotes to groupthink are required. These can include:

- using professional advisors outside the team

- ensuring the team devotes time to keeping abreast of practice developments

- holding regular meetings between team managers to compare and contrast team approaches

- managers taking a more facilitative approach towards team decision-making.

Messages for practice

As can be seen, social work practice in cases of child neglect is influenced by a number of factors. If practice is to be developed in ways which promote better outcomes for children and families then work needs to be done with teams, and by team managers and practitioners. The following questions are designed to assist teams of social work professionals, team managers and practitioners in this task.

The team

As a team, select a number of cases of child neglect and audit the cases with the following questions in mind. Alternatively devise a number of case scenarios for team members to consider individually in terms of ways they would assess and intervene in each case:

- Do we as a team tend to focus on the incident of neglect, safety issues or the developmental needs of the child?

- Do we always make a point of engaging the children and all key carers in the assessment process?

- How do we make judgements in this team? For example, through team discussion with colleagues or through discussion with manager 'on the hoof' through regular case supervision?

- What organizational pressures influence our approach towards our work? How do they influence our work?

- How can we address issues of groupthink?

Team manager

As a group of managers, audit a number of cases of child neglect from each team. Alternatively devise case scenarios for team managers to consider individually in terms of ways their teams would assess and intervene in each case:

- What are the differences between the teams?

- What accounts for these differences? Consider organizational, professional and personal factors.

- How can we develop a standardized approach towards child neglect?

- How can we obtain professional support to encourage an objective approach towards assessment and intervention in cases of child neglect?

The practitioner

- What are my personal values and beliefs about child neglect?

- What are my expectations of parents' ability to meet the needs of their children?

- Under what circumstances do I tend to reduce/raise my standards? For example, poverty, young lone mother, aggressive carers.

- What systems can I put in place to ensure I keep an open mind when assessing cases of child neglect?

Summary

This chapter has highlighted some of the differences that exist amongst social workers in terms of assessing and intervening in cases of child neglect. Social work personnel need to find ways of standardizing practice in a way that safeguards and promotes the welfare of children. The exercises above and the lessons learnt from the Irish and other studies described in this chapter are designed to assist this process. Social workers need to standardize practice in ways that are child centred by focusing on the impact of neglect on the child for two reasons. First, to ensure that the assessment offered to children is of the highest quality irrespective of which social worker assesses the needs of the child. Second, social workers need to give consistent messages to other professionals, family members and the public at large about the cases that will receive an assessment and services.

Chapter Six

Working Together in Cases of Neglect
Key Issues

Olive Stevenson

Introduction

It is beyond dispute that working together across disciplines and agencies is a prerequisite for effective assessment and intervention in cases of serious neglect (see Chapter Nine). It is also clear that many serious case reviews, including those in which neglect was a factor, have revealed major flaws in communication and co-ordination. However, we must beware of extrapolating from these tragic examples and assuming that they represent a general failure in 'working together'. Despite certain negative findings, the major research reports by Birchall and Hallett (1995) and Hallett (1995) on this topic do not suggest widespread failures. Admittedly, this work is now nearly a decade old, but there is no reason to suppose that there has been a general decline in the UK, even though, in certain localities, pervasive staff shortages have created major problems. Gross deficits in practice revealed in the Laming report (Lord Laming 2003) should not be taken as typical of the UK as a whole.

However, there had been sufficient evidence of failures in interagency working in certain high-profile cases to have made it more or less inevitable that there would be political pressure for change when the harrowing Victoria Climbié case became the focus for media attention. Indeed, the breakdown of communication between agencies was a key criticism of the report. It seems likely that most of the recommendations for structural change in the Green Paper *Every Child Matters* (Chief Secretary to the Treasury 2003) will be generally welcomed. These likely changes in England have a bearing on some of the issues raised in this chapter, and will be discussed later.

Despite legitimate criticism of poor 'working together' in certain particularly difficult cases, my own experience as Chair of five area child protection committees (ACPCs) over seven years does not suggest that there was a pervasive failure by individual professionals to co-operate, nor that ACPCs neglected to offer guidance and training in such matters (Stevenson 1998b).

This chapter, then, and its evidence base, is in part derived from direct experience, as well as from available research evidence and the reports of the Social Services Inspectorate in the English Department of Health. Data from the different sources is confirmatory and in a sense can be used to triangulate evidence. It draws only on the situation in the UK in contrast to Chapter Seven by Buckley in this volume. Buckley points out that neglect as an aspect of child abuse received less attention than other aspects. However, in recent years, in the UK, it has been given much more prominence.

This chapter is focused on serious neglect. Jeyarajah Dent and Cocker (Chapter Nine) point out that in England 'neglect constitutes the largest category for registration and has increased every year over the last five years'. Registration alone is not 'a true measure of the incidence of neglect', which is likely to be considerably higher. Daniel (in press) refers to the finding of the Scottish Multidisciplinary Child Protection Review (Scottish Executive 2002a) that, of the children surveyed, at least 45% were experiencing some form of neglect. The developmental harm which may be done to children who are neglected is not in dispute; of particular interest in recent years is the evidence of the effects of under-stimulation and weak bonding on the development of the infant brain.

There is, then, considerable consensus amongst professionals in the UK, that serious neglect is seriously harmful and that, to intervene effectively, inter-agency and interdisciplinary co-operation is essential. Professional concern is evidenced by the increased use of this registration category. However, it is also apparent that to live up to the standards set by English and Welsh government documents (for example *Working Together to Safeguard Children* Department of Health, Home Office and Department for Education and Employment 2000), and by numerous procedural documents at local level, is exceedingly difficult. This chapter is an attempt to pinpoint some of the issues which appear to be crucial if we are to diminish the gap between the ideal and the reality of working together.

The way forward for interdisciplinary assessment

Buckley (in Chapter Seven) points out that there is some ambiguity and confusion as to the nature of interdisciplinary assessment. This chapter explores certain aspects of this process in the context of the current system in England and Wales. The English *Framework for the Assessment of Children in Need and their Families* (Department of Health 2000) marked an important stage in the development of policy in an area of work in which all are agreed that interdisciplinary co-operation is a prerequisite for effective practice. There have been some contentious aspects of its implementation and the materials designed to support it. (The issues are not explored here.) Nonetheless, the basic building blocks of the assessment process, epitomized in the familiar 'triangle' (Figure 6.1), is a sound working tool to ensure all relevant considerations are taken into account. It is of particular value in cases where neglect is a major feature since, almost by definition, such families exhibit a range of difficulties across many dimensions of family life.

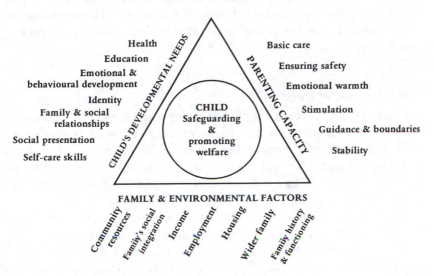

Figure 6.1 *The Department of Health (2000) assessment triangle*

The 'framework' document stresses that:

> effective collaborative work between staff and different disciplines and agencies assessing children in need and their families requires a common language to understand the needs of children, shared values about what is in a child's best interests and a joint commitment to improving the outcome for children. (Preface p.x)

However, Chapter Five, entitled 'Roles and Responsibilities in *Inter-agency* Assessment of Children in Need' (my italics) refers only to agencies, not to the different disciplines (as in the preface). The chapter emphasizes the responsibility of various professionals in the assessment process but says virtually nothing about the distinctive nature of the contributions which the different professionals are expected to make. So far as I am aware, there has not been significant research into the content of assessment records and the contribution of different disciplines to it. It remains to be seen, therefore, if the speculation which follows is borne out by empirical work.

The English Green Paper *Every Child Matters* (Chief Secretary to the Treasury 2003) has proposed changes to ensure that, at least at a basic level, there is a common assessment framework for professionals to use based on a common data base. 'The aim is for core information to follow the child between services to reduce duplication' (p.51). This assessment is to be designed as a relatively simple tool, suitable for use by a wide range of workers. This marks a first step towards more effective communication but in cases of serious neglect, on which this chapter is focused, the complex issues raised by the Assessment Framework as a multidisciplinary tool will necessitate more radical and more sophisticated consideration.

The role of social workers

The official guidance is unambiguous in giving social services the lead responsibility for the completion of assessment for children in need. In practice, this means responsibility for the co-ordination of information provided by others as well as by themselves. The guidance does not, however, identify the distinctive professional contribution which such social workers can make, in addition to the co-ordination of other people's work.

Implicit in much of what is written about social services is that a designated social worker will carry out the direct assessment of parenting capacity and of 'family or environmental factors', even if others are involved. Similarly, the guidance in 'communicating with children' seems to assume that the social worker will have a duty to 'see, observe, talk to, and engage in activities' with children (Department of Health 2000).

Although these responsibilities apply generally, they have particular significance in cases of neglect. Yet there are unresolved doubts and ambiguities in the social work role. First of all, constant references to the gathering of 'information' on many dimensions does not ensure that workers will be able to integrate it into a coherent theoretical framework, thus making sense of the data. Second, there are two elements in the process which may need specific attention. These are, first, the factors outside the immediate family and, second, direct communication with children.

Since the Assessment Framework was published in 2000, it seems that the bottom line of the assessment 'triangle', 'family and environmental factors' may have received less attention. This may have been partly a simple visual problem – the subcategories on the bottom line are more difficult to read! But it may also reflect the ebb and flow of professional interest in aspects of users' lives.

The first five subheadings are:

- Community resources
- Family's social integration
- Income
- Employment
- Housing.

It is hard to imagine issues more important in the assessment of neglectful families than these five. For example, their 'social pariah' status in some neighbourhoods ('the neighbours from hell') is an extremely destructive element in some situations; aggressive interactions breed paranoia. They also make allegations of child maltreatment from neighbours more likely. These are very difficult for professionals to assess. Are they malicious or well founded? Similarly, the material problems arising from debt, unemployment and poor housing are all too familiar.

It seems clear that social workers are likely to be best placed to consider these issues. It is also clear that, if such matters are not considered in depth, a crucial dimension of holistic assessment is weakened. As was pointed out in my earlier work (Stevenson 1998a, pp.20–27), it is not enough to note that such parents may be at, or below, the poverty line. The question is why this is so, and what impact it is having on family life. For example, the existence of unpayable debts may so reduce weekly income that there cannot be adequate nutrition for the children.

The last two subcategories of the 'bottom line' of the triangle are 'wider family' and 'family history and functioning'. Indeed, these two are indivisible. History may be alive in the present, perhaps members of the extended family living just down the road, for better or for worse, so far as the family is concerned! Again, the social worker in the assessment team is the most likely to have access to this part of the family story, which may be critical in understanding the dynamics and evolving possible strategies for intervention. It seems, therefore, that social workers, whatever else they do, should ensure that, in all cases of neglect, these dimensions are thoroughly probed.

The second important role for the social worker to consider in the assessment process concerns the children within the neglectful family. There will be other expert contributions, of course, such as those from paediatricians, health visitors and teachers. There may be professionals called in specifically, perhaps in the context of the courts, such as psychologists or child psychiatrists. However, social workers who visit such families, often over a substantial period of time, are in an important, perhaps unique, position to observe ordinary interactions between adults and children and between children. These may be different from encounters with other professionals and cast fresh light on aspects of the dynamics. Social workers may be able, in a less formal, more everyday, environment, to notice individual children and to talk, perhaps through play, to them. They are sometimes overlooked in the chaotic interactions so characteristic in such families. There is something in the way that neglectful families often present themselves, in crisis and in turbulence, that may make it particularly difficult to follow through the assessment of each child.

More generally, it is apparent that there is a lack of professional confidence in assessment skills, combined with resentment at being perceived as 'second-class citizens' by some other disciplines, especially in the eyes of the courts. There is justified anger at the way Guardians *ad litum* are accorded status denied to the local authority social worker (who may be, after all, the same person a few years later). If the role in assessment is seen as *only* drawing together other people's words of wisdom, this may perpetuate feelings of inadequacy.

Health care professionals

Thus far, we have concentrated upon the aspects of the 'lead role' of the social worker in the assessment process. There is also, however, a complex and problematic issue in relation to the role of health care professionals in cases of serious neglect. There is ample evidence from serious case reviews, of which 'Paul' (Bridge Childcare Consultancy 1995) is perhaps best known, that neglectful families have often subverted the best efforts of health professionals to provide care. In the case of Paul, no fewer than thirteen health professionals and agencies were involved. More recently, my own experience, in relation to a review involving children with learning disabilities, has brought home to me the complex physical health needs many such children have. Similar problems in Scotland in co-ordinating health information are noted by Daniel (in press).

The underlying reasons for the difficulties experienced in seeking to provide for the health needs of neglected children are not difficult to find. Yet, overcoming them has so far proved intractable. Neglectful parents, especially those with a number of children near in age, often have difficulty meeting the diverse health needs of their children. Characteristically, they do not keep appointments. It is common for the children to have a range of health-related problems, some of which may in themselves have been caused or exacerbated by parental mismanagement. Thus, there may be a downward spiral, in which children become more ill, 'poorly' and difficult to manage, and parents more desperate to avoid blame.

The families tend to be involved with a number of health professionals situated in various agencies: different hospitals, different outpatient departments; primary health care teams; a range of community health services, including those for schools, and so on. There can be a large number of individual practitioners with some direct responsibility. Some children have relatively minor problems, such as squints or (in Down's Syndrome) weak ankles; others have more serious and potentially grave problems, such as speech delay, which can adversely affect the child's future career at school. Health professionals have distinct identities and very different roles, and often have little or no contact with each other. Furthermore, they may not have shared governance.

The present system is meant to ensure that the general practitioner will receive notification of hospital outpatients' appointments, including 'did not attend' notes (DNAs). But there is little to suggest that such information is followed up or collected in any systematic way. Sadly these 'DNAs' often only rise to the surface when a serious case review is undertaken. In any case, contact with health professionals is not restricted to such formalized appointments.

It would seem imperative to devise a method within the framework of health agencies by which such information could be systematically brought together and its cumulative significance assessed. Even the bare facts of attendance and non-attendance at health appointments over (say) the course of a year would be invaluable. Leaving aside the obvious value of the health information *per se*, it would give important indications of the parents' capacity to handle the problems. The neglect of children's health needs can be a key factor in overall assessment. (See also Chapter Thirteen for a discussion of the health needs of disabled children.)

Every Child Matters (Chief Secretary to the Treasury 2003) proposes an ambitious programme to improve information collection and sharing (p.52). A 'local information hub' is suggested which would ensure that every authority has a comprehensive list of basic details about all children in their area. The aim would be to ensure that concerns about their well-being and safety would be flagged up. Whilst this should prevent the grosser failures of communication, it does not address the difficulties of sharing information about neglected children and their health needs which require more detailed attention. (The 'information hub' (p.54) presented in diagrammatic form does not even list hospitals as a relevant agency!)

There are, however, other recommendations which could have a bearing in the better co-ordination of information. One proposes the creation of Children's Trusts (p.72), the second identification of lead professionals, where children are known to more than one specialist agency (p.51), and the third integration of professionals through multidisciplinary teams (p.51). The implications are far reaching and cannot be explained here except in relation to sustained intervention which is discussed later.

The discussion above has been selective; it refers only to a few dimensions of the vital process of interdisciplinary assessment. There is a case for exploring each element in turn. The role of schools more generally in the assessment of neglected children is of particular importance. *Every Child Matters*, in the proposals for bringing together educational and social services for children, opens up the possibility of very significant improvements in the crucial relationship between the school and social services in care for seriously neglected children.

Questions for practice

- What 'content analysis' of completed assessments has there been? If none, why not? Such an analysis could provide evidence as to whether the three sides of the 'triangle' are each being tackled in the appropriate depth and whether these different dimensions were adequately integrated. Such practice research could form part of regular audit and would have many uses in training.

- Content analysis might also be used to assess the relative weight given to the contribution of different disciplines and to consider whether that seems appropriate. It could lead to a helpful debate between the disciplines and to greater awareness of the usefulness of particular inputs to the whole.

- What steps can and should be taken by senior managers to increase appropriate confidence in the value of the part played by social workers? This is likely to be a two-way process; there is a need to enhance their skills but also to emphasize to other disciplines, perhaps particularly the lawyers and the judiciary, the distinctive, perhaps unique, value of their contribution.

- How can health professionals begin to collect systematically the health information available to them in their own systems, specifically the practical details of attendance or non-attendance at appointments, clinics, etc? In the event of this revealing serious concerns about the children's well-being, how should this be used to feed into the overall family assessment? Is this best done in the context of the primary health care team? How can evolving technology help?

- For children from the age of four or five, the schools can play a critical part in ensuring that health needs are noted and that the links between schools and health services are close. For children with special needs who attend special schools, such links are often well managed. It is less clear whether children from neglectful families who are not at special schools, but who nonetheless may have diverse unmet needs, are generally well served. Anecdotal evidence suggests it is patchy.

The organization of work to fit long-term cases of neglect

Despite the increased awareness of the significance of neglect in the abuse of children and of the substantial increase in registered cases of neglect, there has been little informed debate within the UK of the possible implications for the way services are organized. Here, we consider two aspects of the issue: first, the organization of work within social services and, second, the arrangements made to foster interdisciplinary working.

The role of social services is of central and critical importance in such cases. Within our present system they are pivotal in co-ordinating a range of other agencies. Therefore, unless their responses to such cases are satisfactory, effective interdisciplinary work is impossible. The ways in which social services can best deploy their staff and the degree and type of specialization which they use is a complex matter. It has never been satisfactorily analysed or addressed since the major (now fast fading) Seebohm Report (1968) which recommended far-reaching changes in the organization of social services and embedded the generic ideal for the practice of social work in the new structure. Whilst this is of fundamental importance, the architects of the 1970s reorganization failed to recognize the need for specialization which can be built on the common foundation (Stevenson 1981). There are two distinctive elements in the idea of specialization: one is about the particular knowledge and level of skill required to operate effectively; the second is about the way the work itself is organized to achieve maximum efficiency. Both are important in relation to working together with neglectful families and the children. These two elements are not necessarily incompatible although tensions arise when (as in social services) there are many different types of work to be performed as in services for children and families. Of course, how 'maximum efficiency' is defined in this context is of central importance.

In the years since the 'Seebohm reorganization', a number of related trends led to greater emphasis on the importance of more purposeful intervention with clearer goals than heretofore. There was also stress on the value of time-limited 'task centred' encounters with clients, sometimes underpinned by so-called 'contracts' (Reid and Epstein 1972; Reid and Shyne 1969). These professional developments fitted quite comfortably with the increasing pressure from the 1980s towards more effective use of scarce resources and the general trend towards tighter managerial control, with specification of outcome measures. Most recently, in the last three years, we have seen in English and Welsh services a dominant preoccupation with government targets, many of which are designed to avoid 'drift' in a range of service activities for children and families.

Whatever the merits of such professional and managerial pressures (and there are many), it is very clear that in certain vital ways, families who seriously neglect their children 'buck the trend'. This is not to suggest that the avoidance of 'drift' is irrelevant. On the contrary, it is often tragically apparent that children have been left sinking (not swimming) whilst courts and professionals dither. But it *is* to suggest that if a well-considered decision is taken to leave certain children at home, it is highly likely that continuing support will be needed over a long period – sometimes the lifetime of the family cycle. Tanner and Turney (2003) have helpfully explored these matters. They point out that, in cases of chronic neglect, as distinct from 'reactive' neglect, the evidence (which they cite) clearly shows that long-term intensive support may be necessary. 'In the absence of sustained, targeted work, a revolving door syndrome develops, in which families repeatedly return to agencies with the same unresolved difficulties' (p.31).

Tanner and Turney stress that such sustained work is to be based on 'clear assessment, objectives re change, strategies for achieving change and way of evaluating whether change has taken place' (p.32). They suggest that the consequences of such an emphasis will be a 'rethinking of the concept of dependency'. They recognize that 'current social work thinking has tended to regard dependency as a bad thing' (p.32). The authors use the phrase 'managed dependency' to describe a relationship in which the worker 'can offer the parent an alternative model of attachment and way of relating, and perhaps allow them to recognize previous damaging internal working models, which will, in turn, affect their parenting capacity' (p.32).

In short, the authors propose a model for working in serious and chronic cases which is founded on the familiar theory (at present somewhat out of favour) of the inherent value of long-term relationships in such cases but in which they have tightened the prerequisites for such an approach. These are the careful assessment of a case as 'chronic', the use of 'managed dependency' as a key element in long-term work, and, finally, the need for a continuing focus on the children which has been discussed earlier in this chapter.

If the general thrust of this argument is accepted, what are the implications for the organization of work? Current arrangements do little to facilitate such an approach and at times positively hinder it. Behind practical arrangements may lie managerial disapproval of long-term dependency and of a perceived insatiable demand for services.

There has, therefore, to be a shift in thinking so that this 'managed dependency' is made more possible by the way social services staff are deployed in relation to such cases. This means affording opportunities for consistent and longer-term working with a relatively small group of families. There remains the question of whether such specialized work would be attractive to social workers. The strains and problems are well understood. Certainly job satisfaction from this type of work is partly a matter of temperament and professional inclination. But it is possible that some workers would be receptive to the idea of a steadier, more concentrated specialized focus over a longer period in working with such families.

The suggestion of the crucial importance of a key relationship with the family, which is acknowledged on both sides, does not imply that it should be exclusive. The key worker, in addition to working with other disciplines, is certain to utilize the services of others who can support the family in other ways. But crucial to the plan is that one social worker is recognized as having a special, if not unique, role in the life of a family, some at least of whose members are likely to be very needy.

Some compromise is inevitable; whatever families may need, the practicalities of staff shortages and mobility and the intense demands of such work means that it is not often feasible to offer such families the security of very long-term relationships. However, a 'neglect sub-team' with a small group of social workers would offer a real opportunity for more consistent, focused and planned intervention than is usually the case. It would also offer a much sounder basis for interdisciplinary co-operation, which is discussed later.

There may seem to be a tension between such initiatives and the present emphasis, given strong impetus by the Lord Laming recommendations (2003), on a continuum of support for neglectful families. Services are not to be sharply distinguished at the point when the children are seen to be 'in need of protection' rather than simply 'in need'. This report is not alone in suggesting that the consequences of moving children on to child protection registers has been to unlock resources which would not otherwise be available and which might at an earlier stage have prevented deterioration. This is clearly perverse and it is essential that bureaucratic categories should not dominate practice. However, acknowledgement of the value of a seamless service to families where there are problems of neglect is not inconsistent with a decision to provide particularly intensive services over substantial periods of time at certain stages in a family's life cycle. Certain families who had been extremely dependent, but who were improving, should and could remain on the case load of the sub-team for significant periods of time, whilst they are helped to utilize wider sources of support of different kinds.

An additional complication in realizing this proposal is that the services involved in supporting neglectful families are by no means themselves seamless. Recent years have seen a proliferation of services, located within different agencies, of which 'Sure Start', programmes designed to intervene at early stages of neglect, is the best known example. There are also long-standing arrangements with the large voluntary children's organizations for intensive work to be undertaken with certain families. These involve partnerships with local authorities. Indeed, some may wish to argue that such work is best done in such settings. At the level of social policy, careful consideration needs to be given to the effects of such diversification. There would seem to be a real danger that the local authority social worker may be left in the unenviable position of having neither the satisfaction of early preventative work nor of focused specialized intervention. That would seem a recipe for disaster.

Questions for practice

The preceding section has addressed the organization of work within the context of social services. However, the 'questions for practice' which follow have implications for those health professionals, notably health visitors, whose contribution to these services is so vital.

If managers and practitioners accept the need for some alteration in the pattern of work, they will need to explore the best ways of achieving this within their own particular organizational context, which varies considerably across authorities and agencies. (Voluntary agencies and family centres are examples.) The geographical or agency location must be determined at local level. It is suggested that the following issues are explored:

- In a given locality, how many families would be judged to be in need of intensive long-term help at a particular time? (This may well lead to reassessment, which is in itself valuable at certain stages.)

- Are there workers who would be prepared to take on work with such families for a significant period of time? (Perhaps two years?) Would the following influence their decision?

- Initial agreement as to 'manageable' case loads and regular review: this needs sophisticated discussion. It is not simply a matter of numbers but of ebb and flow and of the nature of intervention.

- The certainty of *some* reflective consultation/supervision outside the formal line management process: the aim of this is to encourage flexible modes of intervention and to help workers with the anxieties and despondency such cases generate.

- The certainty of easily accessed information/research on neglect in line with 'evidence based practice'; such material can be used as part of the consultative arrangements.

- The possibility of instituting other forms of reflective learning: for example, planned peer group consultation between social workers or between disciplines.

Interdisciplinary work

Thus far, the argument has concentrated on the possibility of special work arrangements within social services. However, it can justifiably be argued that whatever is done to improve the position of social workers in undertaking such work is of little avail without improving the ways in which interdisciplinary co-operation can be facilitated. It is frequently asserted that physical proximity is the best aid to effective co-operation.

The Green Paper (Chief Secretary to the Treasury 2003) has made important proposals for the creation of a wide range of multidisciplinary teams across the whole field of 'safeguarding services' (p.60). It suggests 'co-location' 'in and around the places where children spend much of their time, such as schools, Sure Start Children's Centres and primary care centres' (p.62). None of these is currently part of social services provision. The debate and controversy which the implications of such proposals, rather than the essential idea, are likely to raise may push into the background the specific needs of seriously neglected children and their families. The key factor in providing better service lies in the model of consistency and in medium to long-term intervention.

It is possible to envisage social workers and health visitors as full-time members of such a team, the latter being seconded for an agreed period. Other professionals, such as community paediatricians and special needs teachers, might be involved on a sessional basis. This would provide structured opportunities for planning of intervention, for review of progress and for sharing of anxieties. Such a grouping would be particularly valuable in ensuring that the focus is kept on the well-being of individual children. It should point to the need for the involvement of other disciplines whose contribution is less extensive, but very important for certain individuals at certain points in time. In fact, one might see such working groups at the core of interdisciplinary activities, drawing in as necessary a range of others.

Questions for practice

The suggestions above are relatively modest once the principle of dedicated workers (such as social workers and health visitors) is agreed, with sessional input from others. Some of this work already occurs but it would give formal acknowledgement to the importance of tackling neglect in a systematic way which recognizes the interdependence of the disciplines for effective work.

Area child protection committees (or their successors in England to be styled 'Local Children's Safeguarding Boards') can initiate discussion with agencies concerning innovatory projects designed to improve the quality of interdisciplinary work with seriously neglectful families. The essential elements of such innovations is to provide opportunities for more co-ordinated, concentrated and long-term work. This can be done in the context of the work suggested in the 'questions for practice' sections in the first two parts of this chapter.

Working together: getting below the surface

It is time to find new approaches in the key task – on which we are all agreed – of working together more effectively. Exhortation and prescription are not enough. Sincere attempts are being made to formulate the standards which should underpin multidisciplinary work, illustrated in the recent second phase consultation paper, issued by the Department of Health (2003). Whilst it may be important to itemize these standards (though it has to be said that the risk of platitude is high), we are whistling in the wind if we believe that such measures will have a positive impact on practice unless we are prepared to examine the reasons for the difficulties in achieving improvement.

Reder and Duncan (2003) have recently pointed out: 'A major concern is that precisely the same failures are occurring now as in the past… How can this be explained?' (pp.83–84). The focus of their argument is upon the complexities of communication. They assert that issues are 'far more complex than has ever been envisaged by panels/case reviews and that their more practical recommendations only address a small part of this complexity' (p.84). Their article is valuable. It unpacks some of the factors involved in the process of communication.

The discussion here is not intended to diminish the importance of understanding other aspects of interdisciplinary work, such as those explored in earlier work (Stevenson 1998b). Rather it seeks to raise awareness of the feelings and perceptions which are likely to be aroused in cases of serious neglect and the ways in which they impinge and affect the process of communication. What may be behind the message? These are not only questions to be asked of the other party. They must form part of the dynamics of reflective interaction. 'What is going on between us?'

Evidence from research (Glennie, Cruden and Thorn 1988; Tresider, Jones and Glennie 2003) supports the view that certain powerful feelings are commonly present in at least some of the professionals involved in serious cases of neglect (as well as others). These include: diffuse anxiety; confusion; hopelessness, even despair; denial and over-optimism, linked to powerful identification with adults in the family. These feelings arise from the very nature of the cases. Quite often, for long periods of time, there is concern and anxiety about many different aspects of the family's functioning but none so sharply focused and grave that the course of action which must be followed is clear. Characteristically, such families seem to exist in considerable confusion, bordering on the chaotic; frequent crises demand attention and divert workers from planned intervention. The very size of the files, and the knowledge that much previous work seems to have effected little change, can breed a sense of hopelessness, which is contagious. The sheer effort of 'fire fighting' may consume energy which might otherwise have been available for sustained consistent work. When the situation is grave and there is recourse to the courts, it is not uncommon for goals to be set by which parental effort and capacity may be judged. (Parents with learning disabilities often feature in such cases.) The involvement of certain workers in such court requirements places on them a heavy responsibility, knowing that the future of the children may depend on the outcome. This may lead to a wholly understandable but risky identification with the parent (usually the mother) and a reluctance to acknowledge that parental effort may, sadly, not be adequate to ensure the well-being of the children.

We owe it to the professionals to acknowledge that they are engaged in an extremely difficult area of work. Such emotions as are described above are natural reactions to highly stressful work, the more so when, as is usual, there is a strong commitment to bettering the lives of such families. These feelings cannot be avoided; nor is it 'professional' to ignore them. Rather, they have to be worked with. They will sometimes be at their most powerful when the issue of 'thresholds' is underlying interprofessional discussion. That is to say, when the functioning of the family and, in particular, the capacity of parents to offer 'good enough care' is becoming an urgent focus for debate.

There is a pressing need to provide forums for professionals to discuss the difficult issues underlying work with cases of serious neglect, so that differences of perception may be aired and, if possible, consensus reached. Of particular importance is shared understanding of the various dimensions of neglect and exploration of their effects on children's development. This is the basis on which effective working relationships can be constructed; if this is sound there is less potential for misunderstanding and conflict.

However, even if groundwork is done on the core topic of neglect, there remains in the hurly burly of daily work, a constant stream of 'messages' which professionals must exchange; somehow, there has to be increased sensitivity to the ambiguity which some of these messages carry, especially when the 'feeling context' is high. As Reder and Duncan (2003) put it:

> Communication involves information processing in order that it acquires meaning; it is a function of interpersonal reality; and it is a manifestation of interagency relating... Both parties need to be aware of these influences and must monitor them. (p.94)

When considering the feelings aroused by serious neglect, it is worth asking such questions as: 'Why am I giving or receiving this message? Is it to offload anxiety? Is it to offload despair? Is it to cover myself? (If so, is this necessary and justifiable?) What do I, or they, expect to happen as a result?'

In short, there needs to be much greater sophistication about the process. The roles of supervision, staff development and training are critical in this. Neither organizational change nor technological improvements, important though they may be, will reduce the need for improved interpersonal awareness. This work is about professional people working together; agencies lie behind this. They affect but do not determine the process.

Questions for practice

It is hard to over-emphasize the importance of incorporating this dimension of professional people giving and receiving messages, into strategies for the improvement of working together. This is not simply a matter to be hived off to multi-agency trainers, although training has a critical part to play. It is obvious that these initiatives cannot be sensibly restricted to the issue of neglect. However, different aspects of child abuse and child protection give rise to particular areas of tension in interdisciplinary working. Neglect is one. These particular tensions need to be identified so that the unpacking of 'the messages' relates more precisely to the nature of the case. It seems, therefore, that area child protection committees, or their successors, have a vital role to play in:

- Developing audit processes to include analysis of the quality of 'the messages' and an understanding of the distortions of the content which may arise and why.

- Influencing agencies to work towards a cultural change in which all levels of professional staff are aware of the need for, and difficulties in, achieving unambiguous communication. What are the best means of achieving this?

- Developing the content and delivery of single and multi-agency training programmes to ensure appropriate focus on issues concerning communication.

Conclusion

This chapter has selected three key issues for those who work with seriously neglectful families. They focus on particular aspects of assessment, of the organization of work and of interdisciplinary work. There are many other strands in this complex area of work but from the current evidence on policy and practice, it seems that improvement in these areas is critical if progress is to be made.

Chapter Seven

Neglect

No Monopoly on Expertise

Helen Buckley

Multidisciplinary involvement in child neglect, in fact in all protection and welfare work, is a notion that has been long debated and promoted. As a desirable way of working, it is cited regularly in reviews of child abuse cases and child protection systems and its absence is constantly identified as an underlying cause of poor outcomes and outputs. However, it is also a concept that is heavily laced with assumptions and implications and open to many different interpretations. Inevitably, any social assessment or intervention will be multidisciplinary in the sense that the different domains and dimensions of a person's environment will be considered and will undoubtedly compel some level of communication with, or participation of, a variety of staff whose views or input will be sought. The defining element of multidisciplinary work is essentially the process that is operated, which can vary considerably from case to case and terms such as 'pooling' skills and perspectives can be so loose as to be meaningless. The term 'multidisciplinary assessment', for example, can be interpreted to mean one person carrying out an assessment in the course of which he or she will seek the views of other relevant professionals specializing in different areas. Alternatively, it could be understood as a one-person co-ordinated assessment, where different elements are carried out by a selected group of professionals within their own frameworks for practice but remain the responsibility of the co-ordinator who will draw conclusions from it. Or, it could mean a multidisciplinary group carrying out a joint assessment of one situation using different pieces of an agreed approach and jointly deciding on outcomes and recommendations. The same rationalizing can be applied to interventions into child protection and welfare cases, where, essentially, the crucial questions are how aware each professional is of the involvement of other practitioners, how far the work of each individual dovetails with the inputs of others and ultimately, who has overall responsibility.

Multidisciplinary work in practice

The ambiguity applicable to the term 'multidisciplinary' as it refers to child protection and welfare work mirrors, I would suggest, the hit-and-miss situation that exists in the daily work-world. The abundance of research on impediments to working together, as well as the dearth of material offering examples of positive and workable practice, illustrate that the notion of a seamless multidisciplinary approach to work with child abuse or child welfare cases is somewhat abstract. Instead, child protection guidelines and frameworks for assessment of children in need are generally social work driven (Department of Health 2000; Department of Health and Children (Ireland) 1999; Department of Health, Home Office and Department for Education and Employment 2000), and built on the presumption that social workers can elicit the required amount of co-operation from relevant disciplines to deliver a comprehensive service. Administrative arrangements may assist this process, and there is generally a stricture laid down about joint responsibility and shared duties. However, experience shows us that the expectation of unproblematic communication and co-operation is, to say the least, idealistic (Buckley 2003a; Hallett 1995; Hallett and Birchall 1992; Lupton, North and Khan 2001; Reder, Duncan and Gray 1993). Research has also shown that the chances of success are greatest when personal relationships between professionals are strong, a foundation which is generally not particularly enduring in a climate of rapid staff turnover (Buckley, Skehill and O'Sullivan 1997; Hallett 1995). Otherwise, naturally occurring tensions concerning claims to expertise, differing professional perspectives and statuses and a host of other interactional dynamics tend to determine the nature of inter agency and interprofessional relationships, are difficult to shift and need to be constantly grappled with. This applies particularly to the field of child neglect, fraught as it is with definitional differences and associated as it is with complex and unquantifiable social problems.

Feasibility of a social work led child protection response to child neglect

This chapter will focus, not on the actual nature of multidisciplinary work with child neglect, but on the complexity of current organizational arrangements and professional norms and practices which limit access between families and child welfare and family support services. While it will not confuse multidisciplinary work with interprofessional/inter-agency co-operation, it will inevitably link these two concepts. Principally, it will challenge the orthodox approach of the social work led child protection system by making visible its inherent weaknesses, specifically in relation to child neglect, and will question both the feasibility and the advisability of giving social workers prime responsibility for assessing and intervening in these types of cases. On this basis, it will make a case for promoting interventions into child neglect by agencies and professionals who are working within a framework that is not necessarily statutory itself but is accountable to a statutory authority.

Potential for tense relationships between statutory child protection social workers and other professionals is particularly endemic, and strongly linked with issues such as power and obligation between on the one hand, the statutory social workers' responsibility and on the other, their lack of influence over those professionals on whose co-operation they depend. Research has shown that certain professionals, such as teachers and social care workers, associate social workers' responsibilities with power and can feel marginalized and excluded by the control that they seem to exert over the child protection process (Berry 2003; Buckley *et al.* 1997). In practice, however, as Lupton *et al.* (2001) point out, social workers have had difficulty attaining full professional status and find it problematic to control their spheres of work, possibly because of its association with altruism rather than science. Research carried out on child protection practice in a statutory setting in Ireland has demonstrated the perception held by statutory social workers that they tended to be left with the difficult, confrontational elements of the work, and that other agencies wanted to do 'therapy in isolation', avoiding the 'unpleasant, action taking bits'. The statutory social workers in this study resented the implication that 'co-ordination' meant them taking on the 'nasty' bits to facilitate the treatment agencies doing the 'nice' work (Buckley 2003a). It is clear that social workers as case managers do not hold sufficient authority to compel a satisfactory level of co-operation and sharing of responsibility from other professionals, particularly those outside the statutory system. Normally, inter agency arrangements have to be negotiated by them within organisational contexts and cultures. Yet, despite their sense of powerlessness in the inter agency sphere, social workers in statutory settings do have a strong gate-keeping role that in many cases effectively determines children and families' access to a range of services. Where referrals are placed on waiting lists for assessment or fail to qualify for a service (a trend frequently associated with child neglect) this can impede or seriously delay their access to support or treatment. This could be seen as a negative use of power or control by statutory social workers.

One of the principal weaknesses of the type of statutory child protection system commonly operated in Ireland, the UK and elsewhere is the fact that child neglect has traditionally been accorded low priority in the continuum of child abuse. Despite what we know about the detrimental and long-term effects on children of failure to meet their basic needs for nutrition, supervision, emotional attachment and stability, research in England, Ireland, the USA and Australia has substantially demonstrated that proportionately, the majority of referrals of suspected child abuse to statutory agencies concern neglect and that the majority of these are filtered out, often without a service, at an early stage (Berry 2003; Berry, Charlston and Dawson 2003; Buckley 2003a; Gibbons, Conroy and Bell 1995; Horwath and Bishop 2001; Sedlack and Broadhurst 1996). As Stevenson (1998a) has observed, 'the nettle has not been grasped' despite the acknowledged concern of professionals about the unsatisfactory response being made to reported child neglect. Its relegation to a lower priority is commonly explained as a consequence of the crisis-driven nature of child protection social work, and the inevitable development of defensive practice despite the acknowledgement in child law and policy of the importance of early intervention and family support. Spratt (2001) argues that while statutory social workers express an attitudinal desire to adopt a welfare orientation, they experience constraint at an organizational level and still tend to prioritize the management of risk. As he points out, this trend has been underpinned by a realistically based fear that too wide a swing from child protection to child welfare may leave them open to criticism if child protection issues are seen to have been inadequately addressed. The refocusing debate in England was based on the notion that a less forensic approach to the problem of child neglect would yield more effective outcomes, but as others have argued (Parton 1996; Parton, Thorpe and Wattam 1997) it would require more than a different mindset to achieve universal acceptance of a change of approach within a system that demands a high level of certainty and an elimination of risk.

The tendency of the child protection system to downgrade child neglect is also explained by Graham (1998) who suggests that the structures within which statutory social workers operate lack clear procedures and systems for dealing with neglect, unlike cases of physical and sexual abuse where causes and effects are easier to identify. Child sexual and physical abuses are crimes, thus, because of the structures set up to facilitate co-operation between the police and social workers, clearer channels exist for processing reported cases. Clinical examinations and forensic interviewing may also provide corroborative evidence of harm or injury and such procedures form a normal part of assessment. Interprofessional and inter agency work is easier to achieve in such circumstances, and multidisciplinary involvement is automatic.

However, under Irish child protection guidelines (Department of Health and Children (Ireland) 1999) child neglect (unless deemed 'wilful') is not reportable to the police as it does not involve law enforcement if it is deemed 'unintentional'. As a type of child abuse, it is less likely than others to threaten a child's immediate safety or cause a direct injury, and is therefore considered less dramatic and less urgent. Research has also shown that the low priority assigned to child neglect by statutory social workers is strongly linked to its complex nature and a combination of pessimism on the part of practitioners about the value of intervention together with ambivalence about the boundaries between poor quality and unacceptable care in a context of general adversity where an accusation of child abuse would further undermine the carers' already stretched parenting capacities (Buckley 2003a; Stevenson 1998a; Thorpe 1994). A much earlier study in the UK demonstrated that it was only when the boundary of 'parental incorrigibility' had been breached by some spectacularly and visibly harmful caregiver behaviour that the child protection system would assert itself in cases where parents were seen to be entrapped by social inequality and struggling against the odds (Dingwall, Eekelaar and Murray 1983, 1995).

Research on statutory child protection social work in Ireland, the UK and Australia has also demonstrated that, once thresholds for intervention have been breached, there can be a tendency for assessment of neglect to employ a kind of 'sense-making' which is based more on pragmatic rationalization than on any theoretical reasoning and focused more or less exclusively on caregiver performance and the extent to which they acknowledged culpability, in other words, their moral behaviour and attitude. There is less concentration on the physical, psychological or emotional needs of children, or evidence of knowledge about the specific impact of various factors such as parental alcohol problems or poverty on their development (Parton et al. 1997; Thorpe 1994). Social workers can be somewhat shy about drawing explicitly on theory (Buckley 2003a; Howe 1996a; Stevenson 1989), unlike their counterparts in child health, psychology, clinical speech and language therapy and nursing who operate a more empiricist style of assessment by drawing on quantifiable evidence of delayed development or impaired well-being. Moves towards more needs-based assessments (Department of Health 2000) and the type of evidence-based practice advocated by Macdonald (2001 and Chapter Sixteen in this volume) and others should rationalize professional approaches to child neglect and by demonstrating convincing and systematically gathered data, validate its detrimental effect on children's welfare and development. However, in the meantime, neglect suffers within the orthodox child protection system, which continues to give a higher profile and more urgent response to cases with more dramatic manifestations. The case example in Box 7.1, taken from a study of child protection practice in a statutory agency in Ireland in the mid 1990s (Buckley 2003a), demonstrates an approach adopted by statutory social workers that essentially ignored the contextual issues compounding the reported neglect.

The limited response to child neglect within the statutory social work system, and the potential for multidisciplinary involvement in treating it, are further undermined by a lack of confidence on the part of potential key referrers. Research carried out recently in Ireland and Australia has demonstrated the reluctance of community-based nurses to refer neglect cases to social work because of anticipated lack of response or feedback (Buckley 2002; Graham 1998; Horwath and Sanders 2003). Hanafin's (1998) analysis of a high-profile

Box 7.1 Case example of the response of a statutory social work service to reported child neglect

This case was referred to the statutory child protection social work team by a member of the public who had been out canvassing for a forthcoming local election and had come across four children under ten in a house on their own at ten o'clock at night. This person had waited with the children for three hours until their parents' return at which point she informed them that she would be reporting them to social services for child neglect. The parents (here called John and Mary) apparently displayed distress at this and said it had never happened before.

However, the referrer, who was very concerned, had already spoken to neighbours who said that the children were frequently left alone at night and for periods during the day. The matter was reported to the duty social worker by telephone. When it was discussed at the weekly intake meeting with the social work team, it was decided to write to the parents and ask them to come to the office and discuss the complaint. One week later Mary came to see the duty social worker, partially in response to the letter, but principally looking for help. Mary explained that she and her husband were both problem drug users and had run up serious debts, they were on a waiting list for methadone treatment, they had been seeing people in different agencies in their (unsuccessful) efforts to get help. They were about to be evicted from their rented accommodation and had lost their welfare allowances due to previous fraudulent claims. Neither parent had contact with their extended families and because of their tendency to move frequently and the isolation linked with their drug problem, they had virtually no connections with the local community.

Mary told the social worker that her objective in coming to social services was to find someone who would see the family's difficulties as a 'package', not just separate bits, and who would give her some advice and advocate on her behalf. She expressed concern about the effect on the children of recent instability, poor diet, frequent moves, arguments between herself and her husband as well as both parents' substance abuse. The social worker brought up the matter of the children being left alone, and Mary explained it by saying that she worked late at night in a pub, and her husband got part-time work in the same place on occasions. She had claimed that the children were quite safe in bed at that time, but acknowledged, after talking to the social worker, that it was unacceptable to leave them alone.

The social worker made two telephone calls on her behalf, neither of which were successful, first to the welfare officer about a rent allowance and second to a charity dealing with housing problems. No further action was taken in relation to the reported neglect as the mother appeared to show insight into her difficulties and had expressed what was considered to be appropriate contrition for leaving the children unsupervised. The children were not seen, and the case was closed with no further action recommended.

child abuse case in Ireland where a child had died of wilful neglect (Western Health Board 1996) and Nadya's (2002) Australian study of community nurses' reporting behaviours when they encounter child abuse both illustrate that nurses experience a sense that their opinions are neither valued nor taken seriously, and in the latter study, this acted to deter them from activating the child protection system. Faughey (1997) makes an argument based on her Irish study that although public health nurses share corporate responsibility under child care legislation, the high threshold of entry into the child protection system means that not only do families not get a service, but also public health nurses lose credibility in their eyes when their assessment of need does not result in an intervention. In areas where child protection social workers are the gate-keepers of family support services, this can be a crucial issue. Research in Ireland and the UK has also shown that the ambivalence felt by teachers in relation to the reporting of suspected child neglect is influenced by their sense that no response or feedback will be forthcoming, based on past experience (Baginsky 2000; Briggs 1997; Kelly 1997). A group of school principals interviewed by Berry (2003) were extremely vociferous in their expression of frustration at the poor communication from statutory child protection social work services in relation to children they had referred. In an earlier study on the role of secondary schools in supporting pupils who had been victims of child sexual abuse, Bradshaw (2000) points out that 'teachers feel insignificant and undervalued by health board professionals' (p.94), a factor that undermines their willingness to collaborate in child protection work.

Effective interventions with children and families where neglect is a problem

It can be reasonably inferred, therefore, that despite the lead role assigned to it in child protection procedures and guidelines, the response of the statutory, social work led, child protection system to concerns about child neglect is often inadequate for a variety of reasons. It could further be suggested that child protection social workers are not always best placed to deal with concerns of this nature due to the constraints imposed by their agency function. At the same time, there are many examples of programmes conducted within communities by non-statutory social workers, community-based nurses, schools programmes and family support services that have been highly effective with cases of neglect, once families have been linked with them. Community-based nurses who have access to universal populations of children and families are ideally placed to intervene with vulnerable children and families. One of the best-known programmes in Ireland is the Community Mothers' Programme, managed by public health nurses in Dublin, which has been evaluated and found to achieve significant improvements in children's health and diet, and mothers' parenting skills and self-esteem following their involvement in the programme (Johnson 1999; Johnson et al. 2000; Molloy 2002). Programmes based in early years settings, schools, family support projects and community-based youth projects have been evaluated and found to produce evidence of considerable progress with families where neglect has been a problem (Buckley 2002; Holt, Manners and Gilligan 2002; McKeown 2000). Berry et al. (2003) cite many examples of positively evaluated home-based programmes delivered in the USA by nurses and other multidisciplinary service providers, aimed at enhancing child health and safety as well as interpersonal relationships in neglectful families.

Further afield, a very effective and carefully evaluated programme in New Zealand, called Social Workers in Schools, capitalizes on the opportunities provided by schools to intervene with vulnerable children over a period and offers a good example of the usefulness of early intervention before problems become complex (Department of Child Youth and Family 2002). The important role played by teachers in both observing potential or actual abuse and at the same time developing resilience and improving the quality of life for many children has been highlighted by Gilligan (1998). A review of Irish research on child protection and welfare practice demonstrates the skill and commitment of a range of practitioners including public health nurses, early years workers, family support workers, youth workers and community-based child care workers in responding to and intervening with actual and potential child neglect (Buckley 2002). Box 7.2 gives a case example of intervention in a case of 'failure to thrive' (Faughey 1996, cited in Buckley 2000) which demonstrates task-focused intervention by a public health nurse in which effectiveness is easily measurable because of the clear links between aims, process and outcomes. This case had been initially referred by the public health nursing service to the statutory child protection team because of serious concern over the child's delayed development and high number of hospitalizations, but no action was taken in response to the referral.

Interestingly, while the public health nurse in this example emphasized that progress was achieved not simply through her own interventions but in combination with the work conducted within the multidisciplinary network, she had encountered considerable difficulty in communicating with the other professionals involved in the case, either through their unavailability or apparent lack of interest. However, on the positive side, she suggested that similar interventions could provide exciting opportunities for public health nurses to engage in direct work with multiproblem families and avoid the proliferation of specialist referrals that often have a disempowering and marginalizing effect on families.

Box 7.2 Case example: failure to thrive

In this case example, a public health nurse designed, carried out and evaluated a specific intervention in a case of non-organic failure to thrive, a condition where a young child's physical development is observably delayed with no obvious organic cause. In this case, there was a suspicion that the failure to thrive was linked with neglect. The child, here called Joanne, was eleven months old and well below her expected rate of development. Joanne lived with her mother who had suffered from depression, had been a problem drug user, was taking care of five children with little support from her partner and was socially isolated from her family.

The public health nurse assessed Joanne's family composition, their financial position, background, the health of Joanne's mother, the family's social support, the child's own history and development, her relationship with her mother and her feeding habits and patterns. On the basis of her assessment, the public health nurse designed a programme to be carried out over ten weeks, involving the family, herself and a community child care worker. The intervention was aimed at:

- increasing Joanne's weight above the third centile

- improving the parent–child interaction during feeding

- correcting the delay in Joanne's gross motor, fine motor and language development

- empowering the mother and raising her self-esteem.

The nurse, as key worker, outlined individual action plans designed to address target behaviours and problems and achieve desired results, identifying specific goals and proposed actions to be taken in relation to each of the difficulties identified. For example, she linked Joanne's lack of interest in food and poor appetite to a combination of factors, including her mother's depression and apathy, the fact that she was not sitting where she could see her mother and the way that she was not included in family mealtimes. Other areas targeted were the lack of routine and stimulation, Joanne's insecure attachment to her mother, the mother's sense of being overwhelmed by caregiving and the relationship problems between the mother and her (non-resident) partner. Many of the ameliorative strategies involved other personnel, including the community welfare officer, the community care child care worker, general practitioner, addiction counsellor, staff in the day nursery and the paediatrician.

The public health nurse's own contribution to the multidisciplinary plan of intervention was to visit weekly with the aims of tackling feeding in a constructive way, providing information, listening to the mother's concerns and positively reinforcing any changes that were observable. She also kept a diary in which she recorded events that affected the family, any changes, the content of each visit and observations of the mother–child interaction.

Although the mother and her partner were initially reluctant to participate, the nurse managed to engage them in the process. Using a standardized measure, she was able to demonstrate that the previously identified goals were being achieved in relation to Joanne's gross and fine motor development, and the mother–child relationship. Ultimately, Joanne became far less insecure and her interaction with her mother became more positive and began to include smiles and laughter. Joanne displayed a new capacity to explore independently and seek comfort from her mother when she was upset, all illustrating a healthier attachment. Noticeable improvements were observable in relation to the mother's mental health and her interest in the programme. Goals in relation to Joanne's language, weight and feeding and the parents' relationship had been partially reached, which is understandable within the

One of the key elements identified in the success of some of these projects described above is the relationship that is developed between the workers and families (Buckley 2002; Department of Child Youth and Family 2002; McKeown 2000). An important aspect of this is that practitioners in these services are seen as 'friendly' by families to whom the 'heavy' image of statutory social workers is a source of threat. However regrettable the latter, it now appears to be a fact of life that continues to pervade child protection and welfare work. There also appears to be a significant difficulty in merging different interventions satisfactorily with the child protection social work service, and in receiving feedback, support and acknowledgement. Yet, as we now know, child neglect can be as dangerous and critical as any other form of abuse in terms of risk to children's immediate safety and long-term well-being and must be taken seriously (Bonner, Crow and Logue 1999; Bridge Childcare Consultancy 1995; Fitzgerald 1998). If the statutory system is not the most appropriate channel for bringing direct assistance to families, it cannot abrogate its responsibility; it must still ensure that child neglect is addressed, albeit by services outside the statutory system, and assume accountability over the process by developing clear contracting arrangements with whatever agency is carrying out the task.

Many metaphors are used to describe the formal process of child protection. It has been described as a fishing net, where only certain-sized fish survive. Another striking illustration has been offered by Thorpe (1997) and adapted by Ferguson and O'Reilly (2001) in the shape of a funnel, demonstrating the filtering process that is normally applied to child protection cases, and showing how a number of families are moved out of the system by the time a decision for intervention or allocation is made. I would propose a further extension of that illustration, turning the funnel into an eggtimer shape, the lower half illustrating the range of services which are available to families and are known to be effective where child neglect is a problem, but which are accessible only by service users who have qualified for them by squeezing through the narrow middle part, which could be said to represent the gate-keeping function of the child protection system.

The challenge is clearly to find a way of eliminating the isthmus that divides the two phases of the process described above and broadening out the filtering process thereby responding to families where neglect is a problem, whilst making sure that services are neither fragmented nor duplicated, but joined up by their accountability to an over-arching authority.

What we now know from research and evaluations of existing policies and practices clearly demonstrates that the statutory child protection social workers system has difficulty in addressing the problem of child neglect. This is attributable in part to the sort of screening and gate-keeping practices operated by them which tend to prioritize incidents of child abuse that have a more

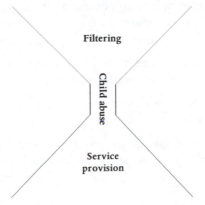

Figure 7.1 The 'eggtimer' model of filtering

dramatic and urgent manifestation. It also appears that the 'heavy' image of statutory social workers does not lend itself to the approach required by families where neglect is a problem. It is clear, as this chapter has already demonstrated, that many significant interventions are already being made into families where neglect is a problem, by a range of multidisciplinary services. While the independence and non-threatening nature of these services undoubtedly facilitates their capacity to engage with families, it is important that they see themselves as part of a network interlinked in various ways, accountable to and supported by the statutory system responsible for overseeing a comprehensive response to vulnerable children and families. The next section will offer some pointers towards the accomplishment of this goal.

Messages from research

- Multidisciplinary involvement in child neglect is a concept laced with assumptions and is open to many interpretations.

- Unproblematic co-operation and communication is idealistic.

- Child protection guidelines and frameworks for assessment tend to be social work driven and are built on the presumption that social workers can elicit the required amount of co-operation from relevant disciplines.

- The majority of referrals of suspected child abuse to statutory agencies concern neglect, and the majority of these are filtered out at an early stage.

- Child neglect is traditionally accorded low priority in the continuum of child abuse – many reasons are given to explain this phenomenon, mainly attributing the trend to a combination of the complexity of neglect and pessimism of practitioners.

- Social workers can be 'shy' about drawing explicitly on theory, whereas their counterparts in other professions operate a more empiricist style of assessment drawing on quantifiable evidence.

- Nurses and teachers can be reluctant to refer cases of neglect to social work because of anticipated lack of response.

- Community-based nurses are ideally placed to intervene with vulnerable children and families.

- Home and community-based programmes have produced evidence of considerable progress with families where neglect has been a problem.

Implications for practice

One of the principal advantages of multidisciplinary work is that it takes into account the interplay of various factors in a child's life. It also provides families with options, which increases the likelihood of their identifying an acceptable intervention. Reinforcement of the same messages by different agencies gives confidence to service users and improves working relationships between services and service users. Crucially, however, interventions into cases of child neglect must be co-ordinated at an authoritative level. The objective is to provide a range of multidisciplinary interventions that are appropriate, effective and non-threatening, but which are at the same time, accountable to and supported by the system that is statutorily obliged to ensure that concerns about children's safety and welfare are satisfactorily addressed. In order to achieve this, a number of messages for practice suggest themselves, at management and front-line levels.

Implementation of an assessment framework that is multidisciplinary in nature

The most logical place to situate the basis for multidisciplinary work is at assessment. Though each profession working with children tends to operate a framework for assessment that elicits information appropriate to each professional perspective, the concept of multidisciplinary assessment of child neglect is strongly associated with a statutory social work led process. However, speech and language therapists, teachers, health visitors, community-based nurses, early years workers and a host of other professional service providers are probably more likely to witness first-hand evidence of child neglect, and for the many reasons cited above, may find it unsatisfactory to refer their concerns to the child protection social work service. There is a need for an assessment framework that is formally established within a local team or sector and that permits assessments to be carried out by a range of professionals but, importantly, ensures that they are co-ordinated and recognized at a level which has the mandate to allocate resources and which will 'log' the concern in a system where it immediately becomes accountable and auditable. Consultation and support as well as regular communication will have to flow between disciplines in order for this process to work effectively, and it will not be sufficient to assume that each service can manage child neglect on its own. This will require a significant change of approach for many agencies and organizations and is not something that can be undertaken without considerable self-challenging by individual professions and service managers. While the substantial content of a framework for assessment is important, the process by which it is implemented and operated will determine its capacity to reach its full potential.

Management

The Climbié report (Lord Laming 2003) has been very strong in its insistence that managers assume more accountability for the range of interventions being carried out at front-line level, and must actually acquaint themselves with the detail of routine work by consulting files and holding regular reviews. Effective multidisciplinary work will be achieved when this accountability, with concurrent levels of support, is extended to all agencies and professionals in regular contact with vulnerable children. Lord Laming made a biting criticism of the gap that he perceived to exist between front-line services and management in the Victoria Climbié case, and called for the establishment of 'a clear line of responsibility, from top to bottom, without doubt or ambiguity about who is responsible at every level for the wellbeing of vulnerable children' (p. 6). The Climbié inquiry suggested a four-tier structure emanating from a Children and Families Board at central government level in England. It may be possible to situate at some point in this configuration a means of co-ordinating services to neglected children in some way that makes them visible and accountable.

Training

Much has been written about the benefits of inter agency and interprofessional training as a means of promoting multidisciplinary work (Buckley 2003b; Charles and Hendry 2001; Horwath and Morrison 1999). While there is certainly evidence to indicate that it is one of the most effective ways of breaching barriers and promoting understanding, particularly of each other's professional roles, as Horwath and Morrison (1999) point out, caution must be exercised about over-optimistic expectations of the potential for training to sustain interagency and interprofessional relationships.

Interprofessional training on child neglect needs to cover substantive issues, such as causative factors, short and long-term effects of neglect and evidence about effective interventions. It must inform participants about each other's roles but, importantly, it must focus on the dynamics of inter agency relationships and actively promote team working or one of the main benefits will be lost. One of the most useful inter agency models is where the training is delivered by a multidisciplinary peer group of trained trainers, who are likely to have more credibility with colleagues than an external consortium (Buckley 2003b).

Information management

One of the most commonly recognized impediments to multidisciplinary working is failure of communication. In the absence of a good data management system, practitioners can find themselves in the dangerous position of acting in ignorance of vital information about a child or family, particularly concerning the patterns or trends that are so significant in child neglect. Duplication of information can exist, for example, in the records of public health nurses, psychologists, public health doctors, speech and language therapists and family support workers and yet be inaccessible to the different members of the professional network who are engaged in work with the same children and families. This type of practice is not only time-wasting and inefficient, but increases the sense of hopelessness and confusion that already exists in neglectful families. Parents in need of help and support are far less likely to have confidence in professionals who mirror their own chaos and disorganization. Password or otherwise protected access to data by appropriate professionals and managers is fundamental to good multidisciplinary practice, and should be a universal commodity.

Commitment to promoting multidisciplinary work by focusing on the process and developing links

There must be a strong commitment from senior management in all organizations providing services to vulnerable children to promote collaborative work. If this is absent, staff in less senior posts will be unable to either represent their organizations or carry any mandate for co-operation. Organizations could usefully appoint a link person to promote inter agency co-operation, or develop some strategy to maintain partnerships/links between agencies or disciplines in an overall sense. Whatever process is implemented, it is vital to understand and acknowledge that co-operative multidisciplinary working relationships will not develop without active facilitation. Consistent and regular efforts should be made to maintain partnerships with agencies that have been contracted to do work so that roles and mutual expectations are negotiated, agreed and reviewed. Contracting obligations need to be absolutely clear so that 'cherry picking' by non-statutory agencies, a practice that was noted in Irish research (Buckley 2003a), is not an option.

Good practice

In front-line work, consistent adherence to basic norms of good practice could make a significant difference to the quality of working relationships. An example is the matter of feedback; as this chapter has demonstrated, the experience of lack of response and feedback from statutory agencies to referrers acts as a deterrent to collaboration. Mundane as it sounds, staff should always respond to phone calls and other forms of contact as soon as possible and give feedback to other relevant professionals about the nature of their work with a given family, particularly any changes in the circumstances or work plan.

Proactive communication is relatively easily achieved by regular exchanges of information regarding, for example, changes of staff, locations and new policies, and can pave the way for more complicated negotiations by establishing positive relationships on a consistent basis.

Overcoming obstacles in contact and communication

Certain staff may have heavy workloads or inflexible working arrangements that limit their availability for meetings or discussions, teachers and police being two examples. This can be addressed by identifying one point of contact for referral and receipt of information in order to ensure that it is managed carefully and efficiently. Nominating specific personnel between whom information can be shared, and agreeing the most appropriate contact times and means of communication can overcome potential frustration and slippage. It is important to have arrangements that will endure beyond staff changes, therefore this practice should become firmly enshrined in local strategies.

Norms about the exchange of information

Despite assumptions to the contrary, it cannot be assumed that all organizations providing services to children and families have a shared understanding about confidentiality. Therefore protocols must be agreed regarding the nature and extent of information to be shared in different circumstances, together with the necessary consents to be obtained. While the requirement to share information if child abuse is suspected is generally understood, the question of sharing information about the type of need or vulnerability often associated with child neglect is more sensitive and requires careful consideration. Child-centeredness, clarity about the rationale for communicating information and assurances about the uses to which information will be put should help to determine the necessary protocols.

Promoting multidisciplinary work at the front line

Most of the literature on promoting inter agency and multidisciplinary work focuses rather broadly on actions to be taken by management, but individual practitioners also carry a level of responsibility. For example, they should familiarize themselves with the roles of other professionals within and outside their own organizations so that they are aware of the optional services available to families. They should also ensure that they understand the responsibilities, policies and procedures of their own and others' professions and organizations, and should make it their business to be aware of the nature of any agreements between their profession, department and organization and any others.

Providing a needs-based service

Finally, the most effective way of responding to vulnerable and neglected children is to ensure that assessment and intervention are focused on the needs of children and their caregivers. Front-line workers who are in regular contact with families and children are in a good position to identify and draw attention to gaps and overlaps in multidisciplinary service delivery and present consistent evidence of their observations to management.

Messages for practice

- Interventions into cases of child neglect must be co-ordinated at an authoritative level.

- Assessment frameworks need to be multidisciplinary in nature.

- Accountability, with concurrent levels of support, is integral to the management of effective multidisciplinary work.

- One of the most useful inter agency models is where training is delivered by a multidisciplinary peer group of trained trainers.

- Protected access to data by appropriate professionals and managers should be a universal commodity.

- There must be a strong commitment from senior management in all organizations providing services to vulnerable children to promote collaborative work.

- Consistent adherence to the norms of good practice could make a significant difference to the quality of working relationships, including jointly written protocols.

- There should be one point of contact for referral and receipt of information.

- There should be a familiarity with the roles and responsibilities of other professionals.

- Assessment and intervention should be focused on the needs of children and their caregivers.

Conclusion

The complexity of child neglect, its pervasive nature and the number of challenges involved in addressing it make it a particularly difficult problem to assess and tackle. Its multifarious nature means that no one profession or service can deal with it in isolation and it demands a certain type of synchronized response if change is to be achieved. We are now aware of positive interventions carried out with children and families by a range of disciplines that can successfully reduce the risk of child neglect. We also have evidence to demonstrate that the statutory social work led child protection system has not been effective in leading a co-ordinated response and that it frequently acts to ration rather than expand the range of services available to vulnerable families. The challenge is to create a system that can co-ordinate the programmes and services that have a proven positive record in order to assess comprehensively and intervene effectively in an integrated fashion, so that neither replication nor fragmentation of interventions occurs. Multidisciplinary work involves consistent effort to overcome the inevitable difficulties caused by differences in professional approach, structure and perspective, but essentially, it is the managed combination of diverse skills, resources and expertise that offers the best possibilities for children whose needs are not otherwise being met.

Chapter Eight

Common Operational Approach Using the 'Graded Care Profile' in Cases of Neglect

O. Prakash Srivastava, Janice Stewart,
Richard Fountain and Patrick Ayre

Introduction

Neglect has serious consequences for children in terms of health, growth and development. The protection of children from neglect is therefore of paramount importance but it can be difficult to achieve because of the problems of identification which it poses. Subjective judgements often come into play because this form of abuse is relatively nebulous, yet the harm it causes can be nonetheless devastating. Without timely intervention, the point may be reached where the effects are irreversible. The English and Welsh Children Act (1989) requires local authorities, working in collaboration with other agencies, to safeguard children from all forms of abuse including neglect. However, the wide variation in practice in dealing with neglect is evident from the variation in the number of children on child protection registers under this category across authorities. It is particularly difficult to recognize it in its milder forms and it has seemed that severe damage must often occur before the child protection system becomes meaningfully engaged (Ayre 1998).

Another group of children who may suffer in similar ways are those who are not neglected but are exposed to other adversities outside their carer's control which do not allow their needs to be met. Such children need support in addition to that which their carers can provide in order to help them to maintain or achieve their potential. These are collectively called 'children in need' (Children Act (1989), Section 17) and local authorities are expected to identify and assist them, in collaboration with other agencies. There appears to be even more variation in the ways in which their needs are addressed.

One of the main reasons for the variability of response to neglect is a lack of clarity on its operational definition. While *Working Together to Safeguard Children* (Department of Health, Home Office and Department for Education and Employment 2000) clarifies the role of professionals in different agencies and provides guidance on structure and processes, it does not provide clinical guidance. It was not until the advent of the *Framework for the Assessment of Children in Need and their Families* (Department of Health 2000) that the understanding of this concept began to develop, and work in this area began to improve and take shape. Local authorities have developed their own multi-agency procedures under this guidance to identify, assess and support such children and their families. This is a welcome development.

The boundary between the families unable to provide optimal care because of circumstances beyond their control, such as poverty, and those inhibited by factors within their control, such as lack of commitment to care, is very thin, but in each case there are adverse consequences for the child. In some cases, both these factors may co-exist, exposing the child to double jeopardy. Therefore, both these strands must be identified and dealt with individually. It is well recognized that increased social adversity may erode the capacity to care which may precipitate overt neglect in incipient cases. Helping such families in time serves not only to minimize the negative impact on the child but also to prevent neglect by enhancing the caring capacity. However, the level of adversity that may precipitate neglect will vary from family to family, depending on their own initial caring strength. In any given set of adverse circumstances, some carers will go on making sacrifices to optimize care for children, while others will not.

Families that need support must be supported, but those that lack commitment to care must be recognized and tracked as in such circumstances the level of care may not improve even when support is forthcoming. In some cases, practical support provided to families for the benefit of their children may even be exploited by carers to further their own individual interests. In two well-documented cases, the material assistance provided to the carers did not improve the lot of the children because the furnishings and equipment which were purchased were subsequently sold to raise cash for the parents. In each of these cases, a child subsequently died through severe neglect (Bridge Childcare Consultancy 1995; Lynch and Stevenson 1990). The level of commitment to care needs to be kept sharply in focus or there is a danger that disproportionate sympathy for the carer, because of the adversities which they face, may result in tragedy for the child.

The process of caring

What seems to be required is a linear measure of care which could be used both by referring agencies and by social services. Such a measure could help with the task of maintaining a focus on the process of caring. It could also be used in tracking progress in the early stages of concern, before referral to social services, and also in the context of formal assessment undertaken under the *Framework for the Assessment of Children in Need and their Families* (Department of Health 2000).

It is impossible, within the confines of this chapter, to undertake a comprehensive review of the literature relating to parenting and the process of caring. However, it may be helpful to draw attention to some key sources. Bentovim (Bentovim and Bingley 1985) proposed three areas for the assessment of parenting in the context of neglect:

- the 'level of living' provided for the child
- present family functioning
- the significance of family history.

For the first area he advocated use of the 'Childhood Level of Living Scale' developed by Polansky *et al.* (1981). This contains a list of 99 items in nine clusters, each cluster having a variable number of items. Clusters include:

- general positive child care
- state of repair of house
- negligence
- quality of household maintenance
- quality of health care and grooming
- encouraging competence
- inconsistency of discipline and coldness
- encouraging superego development
- material giving.

There is one point for each item with a maximum score of 99. Higher scores denote better care and a score below a preset threshold is categorized as neglect. However, individual scores are not weighted. If a mother does not use a thermometer (Item 15), allows (reason not specified) a five-year-old to sleep with parents (Item 27), allows at least one of the children (age not specified) to sleep with parents (Item 28), if the family does not own a camera (Item 62), if the child does not say prayers at bed time (Item 63) and if the child has not been taken to the fire station (Item 66) or fishing (Item 67), the mother will lose a point for each of these items. On the other hand, if she is given credit for being tuned into the child's indirect emotional signals (Item 56), this is deemed to be worth only one point as well. Furthermore, it may be argued that though family functioning may influence care, they are not the same thing.

Reder and Lucey (1995) have suggested five thematic headings for the assessment of parenting:

- the parent's relationship to the role of parenting
- the parent's relationship to the child
- family influences
- the parent's interaction with the external world
- the potential for change.

Here, the first two themes directly represent parenting or the care process while the others seem to represent indirect influence.

After an extensive review of literature, Mrazeck (1995) proposed five key dimensions of parenting which form the basis of the Parenting Risk Scale. Those five dimensions are:

- emotional availability – degree of emotional warmth
- control – degree of flexibility and permission
- psychiatric disturbance – presence, type and severity of overt disorder
- knowledge base – understanding of emotional and physical development as well as of basic child care principles
- commitment – adequate prioritization of child care responsibilities.

This type of assessment is highly specialized and requires psychiatric training in relation to the third dimension, 'psychiatric disturbance'. The fourth dimension, 'knowledge base', is very fluid, changing with new developments, as we have seen in relation to cot death (until the early 1980s, parents were advised to lay the baby prone before the advice was changed in favour of a supine position after new evidence). With respect to the second dimension, a high level of control does not equate with neglect in the normal sense and in fact may be negatively correlated with it. The fifth dimension 'commitment' appears to mirror caring instinct more closely. This scheme may be more suitable for assessing children in child psychiatric settings.

In child welfare and child protection practice the starting point may be recognition of parenting deficit by front-line staff and 'level of commitment to care' may be seen as a good proxy for this. These first-line professionals, such as midwives, health visitors, general practitioners, nursery nurses, teachers and education welfare officers, play a pivotal role in the identification of caring deficit and the success of the whole support system may depend upon their readiness and ability to pick up cases early enough. A tool that can be used across all these agencies would provide a very useful support to them in this difficult task. It would help first-line professionals to identify cases early and to provide promptly the support which falls within their own remit. In cases in which this proved insufficient, use by all agencies of a common tool would allow seamless referral to social services when a predetermined level of concern had been reached. A common tool would promote a shared understanding of different levels of care deficit and help to build a common language. It could also inform the decision about which route to take: 'child in need' or 'child protection' and could help to reduce interprofessional tension emanating from mismatched expectations. A more detailed specialist assessment of parenting could be commissioned at any stage of the process if indicated.

The authors of this chapter have nearly four years of experience in using such a tool, the 'Graded Care Profile (GCP)' scale, which centres on commitment to care and is described below.

The 'Graded Care Profile (GCP)' scale

To understand the GCP it is important to be aware of the theoretical basis upon which it was founded. It is based on the notion of a continuum which starts with the acknowledgement that parents are biologically attuned to care for their children. Donald Winnicott (1957) called it 'a thing called love' and John Bowlby (1988) referred to an innate biological ability to parent. This 'caring instinct' is distinct from other attributes that a carer might have like temperament, disability, habits and behaviour and different individuals will have it in different measure. It may be eroded or enhanced (or fully expressed), depending on the presence or absence of socio-environmental support systems, the nature of other personal attributes and the relative demand of caring. In any given case, if these secondary influences are positive, care may get better (and may be fully expressed), if negative, it may get worse. This is the basis for thinking of care as being on a continuum.

Belsky (1984) proposed eight grades of care based on different combinations of these factors which in practice were difficult to delineate. In fact, what is seen in practice as the net care delivered, is the final product of strength of caring instinct expressed after its interaction with these factors. In a prospective cohort study of outcomes in children care was assessed in three grades: satisfactory, unsatisfactory, and variable, measured in terms of what the carer actually did by way of caring (Miller, Court and Knox 1960, 1974). Unsatisfactory and variable care correlated with poor outcomes for children. For the GCP, it was decided to adopt five grades of care. These five grades are on a bipolar continuum: grade one being the best and five the worst. The whole scale is made up of a number of areas and sub-areas and is thus capable of capturing different ratings of performance, both positive and negative, with respect to a large number of distinct aspects of care. The general qualitative basis on which the grading is based is illustrated in Table 8.1.

Table 8.1 The Categorization of different grades of care

Parameters	Grade 1	Grade 2	Grade 3	Grade 4	Grade 5
1	All child's needs met	Essential needs fully met	Some essential needs unmet	Most essential needs unmet	Essential needs entirely unmet/ hostile
2	Child first	Child priority	Child/carer at par	Child second	Child not considered
3	Best	Adequate	Equivocal	Poor	Worse

The next task in constructing the scale was to isolate the areas of care to which these grades should be applied. For this purpose, four main areas were adopted from Maslow's hierarchy of human needs (1954) chosen for its universality, comprehensiveness and exclusivity. These areas are:

- physical care
- safety
- love and esteem.

The self-actualization element of the hierarchy was not deemed appropriate for this purpose. These main areas were each divided into sub-areas and some sub-areas into smaller units referred to as items, based on established psycho-logical and developmental principles. The actual care observed can then be scored by matching it with descriptors set out in the manual. These describe five grades of care for each sub-area or item. The descriptors are based on developmental outcomes rather than a professional group opinion. From the scores obtained for the items or sub-areas, the overall score for their constituent area can be calculated according to a standard procedure. An example illustrat-ing the sub-area of Disapproval within the area of Esteem is shown in Figure 8.1.

In order to make it easy to collate scores, a specialist record sheet was devised. All the scores for individual elements of assessment are transferred to the reverse of the record sheet. The aggregated score for the main 'areas' and 'sub-areas' could then be calculated and recorded on the front side of the record. It is possible to denote any individual element of assessment by using a simple notation consisting of three characters – a capital letter for an 'area', a number for a 'sub-area', and a lower case letter for an 'item'. Items or sub-areas scoring particularly poorly may be highlighted for follow-up re-scoring after a period of intervention by entering the identifying characters in a box provided on the form for this purpose.

Sub-areas:

1. **Stimulation**
2. **Approval**
3. **Disapproval** *(to disapprove undesirable behaviour)*
4. **Acceptance**

(constructs for different grades)

1	2	3	4	5
Mild verbal, consistent	Mild to terse verbal, mild sanctions, consistent	Terse/ shouts, inconsistent	Harsh/ shouts, severe sanctions, inconsistent	Terrorised, ridiculed, cruel

Figure 8.1 A schematic representation of one of the sub-areas in the 'Graded Care Profile':
D – Self Esteem: Disapproval

The Graded Care Profile approach thus has two key components. The first is a manual which contains the full scale, including the descriptors for each grade of care in each unit of observations, and instructions for its use. The second is the record sheet which allows the scores to be noted and aggregated. These materials have been described in more detail elsewhere (Srivastava *et al.* 2003) and are published by the Luton Social Services Department (Richard Fountain, Social Services, Unity House, 111 Stuart Street, Luton LU1 5NP).

The scale has been tested for inter-rater agreement amongst health visitors, nursery nurses and social workers on two samples of children – one from community nurseries and another from those on the child protection register for neglect. An almost perfect level of agreement was achieved in 'Physical' (k = 0.899; CI 0.885–0.948), 'Safety' (k = 0.894; CI 0.854–0.933), and 'Esteem' (k = 0.877; CI 0.80 –0.946) areas, and a substantial level in the area of 'Love' (k = 0.785; CI 0.720–0.849). The mean time taken for scoring was 20 minutes and those who used it more often took considerably less time (Srivastava and Polnay 1997).

In summary the GCP is a linear scale which gives a qualitative measure of care on a bipolar scale, yielding a profile of care across a range of developmentally sensitive areas. Because it identifies difficulties in specific aspects of care, it also provides a means to target intervention. It can also be used to monitor progress over time objectively. It lends itself to the development of a multi-agency protocol for the assessment of parenting, since it is a tool which can be used by practitioners in health, social care and education.

Developing existing provision

Health services are usually the first point of contact with families, starting in most cases antenatally. Therefore, from the point of view of prevention, health service provision for children and their families seems a sensible place to start the process of identification, intervention and tracking. Within health, there is a well-established programme of child health surveillance and health promotion aimed at preventing or minimizing disability arising from impairment of health, growth and development. This programme ante-dates the *Framework for the Assessment of Children in Need and their Families* and within it, all children are tested, assessed, observed or screened for various problems at different ages in the hope of early identification of problems.

In the second chapter of their influential book of guidance on child health promotion Hall and Elliman (2003) place considerable emphasis on addressing parenting concerns in order to prevent adverse effects on the developmental and emotional well-being of a child. One of the recommendations which they make after reviewing the evidence is that parenting problems need to be addressed individually, as well as on a group or locality basis, an approach which links neatly with that enshrined in the 'Framework for Assessment'. Whilst these linkages need further development at the national level, they can be pursued locally. Protocols for the identification of 'children in need' or 'vulnerable children' and within that group those cases where there is also a parenting deficit highlighted by using the GCP, can be developed as part of that linkage.

Other factors such as parental mental health problem, drug and alcohol problem, domestic violence and overt neglect and emotional abuse would need to be considered in their own right. Using the GCP alongside other forms of assessment in such cases will further stratify the case allowing finer analysis. For example the GCP can differentiate between alcoholic carers who are actually providing poor care (GCP 3, 4, 5 in some or all areas) and those who are not currently doing so but about whom there are anxieties. Using this approach, the existing child health surveillance and health promotion programme within health could be made to blend in seamlessly with the assessment framework for children in need obviating the need for developing an add-on service. A suggested pathway is outlined in Figure 8.2.

It is logical to replicate this approach with respect to other services interfacing with social services. In the field of education, nursery nurses (pre-school staff), Sure Start staff, teachers and education welfare officers could initiate the process in the same way as health staff. Considerable interest has been expressed in the possibility of expanding the use of the GCP to this field but further development work is required.

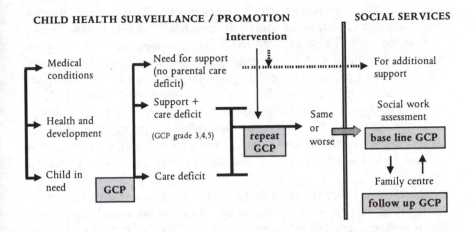

Figure 8.2 Suggested pathway between child health and social services

Strategy for assessment

The assessment of early care deficit or neglect is not a straightforward exercise in terms of its links with adverse outcome for children. There could be a number of other factors operating simultaneously, which could also exert an important influence. Further, a problem may even be encountered in separating the process of caring from the outcome. Professionals often fail to distinguish between the two in making a case for neglect (see Box 8.1 for case example).

Box 8.1 Case example

A head teacher was quite concerned about a six-year-old Asian boy who was said to eat a lot at lunchtime (free school meal) and who was also quite thin. He was being weighed weekly by the school nurse because of a strong suspicion of neglect. He was expected to climb up the weight centiles, but did not. This led to referral to social services for neglect. After an assessment of the home situation, it became apparent that his parents were cooking enough food for the whole family in traditional style and that the child was given adequate love and affection. On paediatric assessment it was found that he had a very sensitive tongue, which caused soreness with spicy food. Once this problem was eliminated, he began to eat well at home but still his weight did not climb up the centiles. It was concluded finally that this was his normal constitution.

Other factors that might affect outcomes for the child include genetic influences, the child's temperament, and any undiagnosed developmental disorder and it is important that these be addressed when neglect is being considered. A two-year-old child with poor weight and developmental delay along with poor hygiene and clothing was on the child protection register for neglect. Her mother was a lone parent with a learning disability and lived in very inadequate accommodation. In this case, all these factors were used cumulatively as evidence for neglect. It later transpired that the child had a medical condition, which was responsible for short stature and thinness, and the developmental delay was genetic rather than due to lack of stimulation. This mother, in spite of her limitations, was fully committed and the child was quite securely attached to her.

Therefore, the 'care process' must be analysed in its own right to assess the severity of any deficit, while taking account of other influential factors. The GCP is uniquely suited to this purpose and will identify strengths as well as weaknesses across a wide range of aspects of care. This will help to pinpoint the factors which are contributing to the adverse outcome for a child and the extent of the contribution of each. It is worth noting that though some children may not present with adverse outcome despite neglectful care, this does not invalidate the identification of neglect. The relatively positive outcomes may be explained by resilience on the child's part, the degree of severity and duration of the neglect, or the presence of nurturing elements within the wider care milieu.

Bentovim and Bingley (1985) have confirmed that observation of the child and observation of parenting and family functioning need to be looked at separately. This is to avoid unsubstantiated assumptions and connections being made on the basis of the 'common knowledge' that parenting affects children's development. Neglect can be both physical and emotional, and can involve rejection including deliberate withholding of affection; abandonment; and inability to provide continuity of care. In such cases there needs to be an assessment of the child, the parents, family interaction, the environment, and the impact of external forces as each can affect the capacity to care (Adcock 1985). However, the final common pathway through which these are expressed would be what the carer actually does by way of caring. The GCP grades the care that is actually delivered directly rather than extrapolating it from other factors.

Messages from research

- Neglect has serious consequences for children in terms of health, growth and development.
- Families that need support must be supported, but those that lack commitment to care must be recognized and tracked.

- A linear measure of care that can be used by referring agencies and by social services could help maintain focus on the process of caring.

- 'Level of commitment to care' may serve as a proxy for recognition of parenting deficit.

- The 'Graded Care Profile' is based on the notion of a continuum which starts with the premise that parents are biologically attuned to care for their children.

- Five grades of care on a bipolar continuum are applied to four main areas adopted from Maslow's hierarchy of human needs; descriptors are based on developmental outcomes rather than on professional opinion.

- It can be used to target intervention, monitor progress over time, and be used reliably by practitioners in health and social care and in education.

- Assessment of early care neglect is a complex exercise and the care process must therefore be analysed in its own right to assess the severity of any deficit.

Developing an operational protocol

The next question is how to put the GCP into use to improve early recognition, institute appropriate intervention and monitor progress in cases of neglect. This can best be elucidated by describing how it was done in one local authority. The GCP was introduced at a point when working with neglect had already been identified as posing a problem. Having been accepted by the local area child protection committee, the GCP was initially piloted by the health visitors in 1999. They found it to be a useful professional tool which helped them to quantify care objectively in cases of neglect, something which they had been unable to achieve previously. Following this successful trial, it began to be used by social workers. It was introduced to staff in both sectors by providing them with three hours training and was characterized as a useful practical tool rather than as a management-led burden being imposed from above. Since its introduction, the expansion in its use has been driven largely by grass-roots enthusiasm, with management support, rather than being compelled by management.

A multi-agency protocol was developed whereby health visitors were encouraged to use this scale whenever they had substantial concerns about parenting. If the grade of care was three, four or five in any area, this would be picked up, worked on, and tracked. If the score did not improve or got worse, a referral to the social services was indicated. After receiving the referral, social workers were expected to incorporate the use of the GCP in their initial assessment. The scores obtained would be analysed alongside other findings and would help to inform decisions. If the case was allocated to a family centre for parenting work, a baseline score was obtained and areas and levels of care deficit were identified, helping to target intervention where it was most needed. Figure 8.3 shows the record sheet on which the score is recorded.

In September 2003, an evaluation of the current use of the GCP was undertaken by convening a conference of those professionals who had been trained in its use and were employing it in day-to-day practice. Feedback was gathered through workshops and a structured questionnaire. This is being analysed in detail but the initial findings are outlined below. At the present time health visitors are the most frequent users within the health sector. They employ the GCP in making referrals to social services in accordance with the agreed local protocol. Social workers are then undertaking a baseline scoring for planning further intervention. Some cases are passed on to family centre workers for work on areas of deficit.

Family centre workers are the most frequent users in the field of social care and are finding the GCP very helpful in identifying parenting needs, targeting intervention and monitoring progress. They select those areas from the GCP where grades of care are poor (three, four or five), and institute matching intervention, setting a pathway towards the goal of achieving the next better grade and making sure it has been achieved before moving further. It is found easy to explain the process to carers, who usually share the same goal. Progress is scored periodically and even small improvements or deteriorations of a single grade are measurable. If the care does not improve or actually deteriorates, appropriate feedback is sent to the relevant social worker who connects the case with the child protection process for further deliberation.

It was noted that in the past, in the absence of the GCP, empathy and compassion for carers which had developed over time could sometimes interfere with effective assessment and intervention. This was felt to be no longer the case as GCP scores are relatively unaffected by one's feelings and depend upon observation undertaken according to externally established guidelines. However, it was noted that where grades of care remained poor, some workers felt the need to provide justifications for the lack of progress. They were advised to enter their comments in the box provided on the forms without letting this affect the scores themselves. At times, this approach could appear to workers to be harsh towards the carers but it was explained that the scoring was designed to safeguard the interests of the children rather than those of the carers. Some carers who took part in the scoring had commented on the negative wording in some of the grade descriptors, particularly those leading to a score of five. However, this could not readily be changed without losing the grade separation, since a score of five in principle represents the most negative end of the continuum. The GCP is scored individually for a particular child with a particular carer which usefully highlights differential care within the same family where it exists.

GRADED CARE PROFILE (GCP) SCALE

Name (Child) ....   Main Carer/s ....

Date of Birth ....   Rater's Name ....

Unit Number ....   Rater's Signature ....

Date of Scoring ....

Other Identification Date ....

AREA	Sub-area	SCORES					AREA Score	Comments
(A) PHYSICAL	1. NUTRITION	1	2	3	4	5		
	2. HOUSING	1	2	3	4	5		
	3. CLOTHING	1	2	3	4	5		
	4. HYGIENE	1	2	3	4	5		
	5. HEALTH	1	2	3	4	5		
(B) SAFETY	1. IN CARER'S PRESENCE	1	2	3	4	5		
	2. IN CARER'S ABSENCE	1	2	3	4	5		
(C) LOVE	1. CARER	1	2	3	4	5		
	2. MUTUAL ENGAGEMENT	1	2	3	4	5		
(D) ESTEEM	1. STIMULATION	1	2	3	4	5		
	2. APPROVAL	1	2	3	4	5		
	3. DISAPPROVAL	1	2	3	4	5		
	4. ACCEPTANCE	1	2	3	4	5		

TARGETING PARTICULAR ITEM OF CARE

Any item with disproportionately high score can be identified by reference to the manual as: capital leters for an 'area', numericals for a 'sub-area', and small letter for an 'item'. (A/1/b = physical – nutrition – *quantity*)

	Targeted items	Current Score	Period	Target Score	Actual Score
1.					
2.					
3.					
4.					
5.					

Figure 8.3 The record sheet on which the final GCP score is recorded

From the children's social services perspective, it was originally intended that the GCP be used as a 'snapshot' assessment, visibly displaying the care profile at a particular point in time. It was later discovered to be effective in many other ways including:

- contributing to the usefulness of pre-referral assessments by health staff wishing to refer a family to social services

- as a contributory assessment tool for initial assessments

- as a means of assessing parenting capacity during the completion of core assessments

- providing a baseline and allowing ongoing monitoring of progress.

Although some of the professionals who had been trained had not used the GCP for a variety of reasons, there was a consensus that it was a useful tool in its own right. It also complemented conventional assessment methods in providing an objective sense of direction, particularly in chronic cases and in between detailed assessment points. It had been used in a wide variety of ways. Some professionals had used it in conjunction with the carers, some in conjunction with other professionals and some in conjunction with older children to get an insight into their perspectives on their own care. It was generally felt to be working as intended but needed a rolling programme of interactive refresher sessions to monitor the quality of its use and to address such difficulties as arose from time to time. It was hoped that it would gradually become embedded as one of the armoury of tools habitually deployed in the field of family assessment.

Since the inception of the use of the GCP locally, there had been a significantly enhanced focus on identifying issues of neglect both at early stages and within the child protection arena. In consequence, work with families where neglect is a primary concern had increased markedly. It might be speculated that, in the absence of the GCP, some of these additional cases might not have been identified until the consequences for the children involved became grave and unmistakable in their impact.

Messages for practice

- Health visitors have found the objective measure of care a useful professional tool.

- Family centre workers too have found the GCP helpful in identifying parenting needs.

- In the absence of the GCP empathy and compassion for carers could interfere with effective assessment and intervention.

Summary

The assessment of neglect should be a continuous process which aims to identify problems early enough to allow the adverse consequences on health and development to be reversed or minimized. It is an intricate and time consuming undertaking but the Graded Care Profile has a useful part to play within it by providing a visible, objective measure of parental care at a particular point in time. It can be used by all professionals and even carers and older children (under supervision) and can promote the provision of a seamless service. It also helps workers to identify strengths and weaknesses, to choose suitable interventions, to set targets (by grades), and to monitor progress. It provides a sense of direction in long-standing cases where it complements other detailed assessments. There seems no reason why it cannot be extended to the education–social services interface and it is proposed that exploration of this possibility will form the next stage in its development.

Learning points

- In order to prevent or reverse the adverse effect of neglect on children early intervention is necessary.

- A 'Children in need' framework is an ideal starting point.

- In addition to assessment for need of support, this should also focus on identifying and monitoring early signs of parenting deficit.

- This should be a 'caring process' based approach rather than outcomes based because children may still suffer without manifesting readily observable signs.

- This needs to be a seamless process involving a systematic approach adopted by the referring agencies (pre-referral) such as health and education.

- An existing programme of child health surveillance could be adapted to include this activity where parenting deficit may be tracked alongside medical, developmental and health problems.

- A single tool that can quantify parenting deficit and can be used by all professionals including social workers would provide a common reference and would promote seamlessness.

- The 'Graded Care Profile' scale is one such tool which quantifies 'commitment to care' on a bipolar continuum in different areas of care.

- Thus it quantifies both positive and negative aspects of care and has been used on a multi-agency basis for nearly four years.

- While areas of deficit provide targets for intervention and tracking, areas of positive care provide means for engaging with carers and have been shared with carers and some older children.

Acknowledgements:

We would like to thank all the health, social services and family centre staff who volunteered to adopt this new way of working using the Graded Care Profile and provided essential insight into its usefulness and its limitations. We would also like to thank Luton Borough Council for printing the manual which can be obtained from Richard Fountain, Social Services, Unity House, 111 Stuart Street, Luton LU1 5NP.

Chapter Nine

Serious Case Reviews: Lessons for Practice in Cases of Child Neglect

Renuka Jeyarajah Dent and Christine Cocker

Introduction

The death of a child under any circumstances is tragic. When that death has been deliberately caused by the very adults who were expected to cherish their child, a sense of disbelief permeates not only those individuals directly involved with the child and family but also the wider community. In the face of such difficult circumstances, often our society needs a focus for blame, whether that be a particular individual, or an organization charged with the responsibility of protecting children from abuse and maltreatment.

In England and Wales it is estimated that between one and three children die of abuse or neglect each week whilst in the care of their parents (NSPCC 2001). The majority of these children are very young. An NSPCC working party has shown that in a three-year period, each week up to three children under the age of ten were killed or suffered serious injury, and 83% of these youngsters were under two years old (*The Guardian* 2003). The Department of Health indicate that approximately 90 child deaths each year are the subject of a formal case review and there is concern that there are still more cases each year which should have been reviewed (Sinclair and Bullock 2002). In the USA patterns are similar. In 1998, 77% of the children who died as a result of mal-treatment were between the ages of zero and three (US Department of Health and Human Services 1999). Neglect is more likely to result in fatality than any other form of child maltreatment (Petit and Curtis 1997; US Department of Health and Human Services 1999) and causes the highest rate of fatality due to maltreatment in children between the ages of zero and five (Gustavsson and Segal 1994; Petit and Curtis 1997; US Department of Health and Human Services 1999). In the UK it is noted that although most child deaths are caused by a physical injury, child neglect is often identified as a factor within the child's circumstance (Reder and Duncan 1999; Sinclair and Bullock 2002). According to Reder and Duncan (1999) in cases of neglect the final episode resulting in injury or death to the child is either an avoidable illness or an avoidable medical accident superimposed over a profile of often long-standing concerns about parental neglect of the everyday needs of a child.

Child neglect: definitions

There is broad consensus that neglect is a very complex and multifaceted concept and this is reflected in the process of constructing a definition of what constitutes neglect (Stone 1998). Contemporary definitions of neglect incorporate both the physical and emotional elements where the result is significant harmful impairment of health and development, or the avoidable exposure of the child to serious danger, including cold and starvation (Department of Health, Home Office and Department for Education and Employment 2000).

Neglect is viewed from both the perspective of parental behaviour and from that of impact on the child. Although there is no prescriptive baseline standard for what constitutes adequate care, and 'no universal agreement about what is "normal" or "desirable" child-rearing practice' (Stone 1998), there is substantial agreement and general understanding cross-culturally of what constitutes the adequate care and protection of children (Dubowitz *et al.* 1993). The notion of adequate care is strongly associated with the healthy development of children in which 'children's physical, social, intellectual and emotional needs have to be met' (Stevenson 1998c).

Additionally, neglect and emotional abuse are based on relational factors as opposed to specific incidents of abuse (Glaser 2002; Reder and Duncan 1999). This distinction of parental behaviour is based on characteristics such as 'hostile' or 'indifferent'; 'omission' or 'commission' is crucial in understanding the pervasiveness of neglect on the developing child. Golden, Samuels and Southall (2003) argue that 'neglect has its roots in ignorance of a child's needs and competing priorities... The carer is without motive and unaware of the damage being caused' (p.105). However, a persistent lack of response or inaction from a parent can be just as damaging for a child as an over-reaction or an inappropriate reaction from a parent to the signals from a child. Child neglect is concerned with the persistent failure of a parent to respond adequately to the emotional and/or physical needs of their child, whether this is via omission or commission. The lack of insight and understanding shown by the parent into the consequences of the neglect for the child is indicative of the complexity of the situation for the social worker or health worker in assessing parental capacity for change. Iverson and Segal (1990) report that neglect is thought to be the most damaging type of abuse with regard to the long-term consequences for the child.

A number of studies have indicated that child neglect features very prominently in child abuse referrals in the UK, either by itself or where associated with other forms of maltreatment, notably physical abuse (Stevenson 1998a;

Wilding and Thoburn 1997). In England at 31 March 2002 the numbers of children on the child protection registers for neglect was 10,100 of a total of 25,700, that is 39% (Department of Health 2002). It is recognized that neglect constitutes the largest category of registration and has increased every year over the last five years. In the USA in 1998, more than half the children who were maltreated experienced neglect (US Department of Health and Human Services 1999) and again this number is growing. Child protection registers are not a measure of the true incidence of neglect but they do give some measure of the scale of the problem. If anything these figures represent an under-estimate of the problem (Cawson *et al.* 2000; Thoburn *et al.* 2000). Baladerian (1991) suggests that ten times as many children survive severe abuse and neglect as die from it, and that a staggering 9.5 to 28% of all disabled persons in the USA may have been rendered thus by child abuse and neglect. Paul and Cawson (2002) report that there is very little UK data on disabled children that is comparable to the US data. The recent national prevalence survey of child maltreatment gives the most comprehensive data on child maltreatment in the UK (Cawson *et al.* 2000 cited in Paul and Cawson 2002) and this found higher levels of maltreatment for disabled children than for those children without disabilities.

Factors associated with neglect

There is evidence of a strong association between poverty and neglect (Bifulco and Moran 1998; Stevenson 1998a). However it is unlikely that income or lack of material goods is the primary impediment to child rearing (Crittenden 1999). Indeed the findings of several serious case reviews indicate that the provision of material resources to the family did not reduce the risks faced by the child (Bridge Childcare Consultancy 1995; Bridge Childcare Development Service 1999; Lord Laming 2003; Newham Area Child Protection Committee 2002; Scottish Executive 2002a).

Jowitt (2003) and Berry *et al.* (2003) have summarized some of the characteristics of families who neglect. These include:

- Severe difficulties in sustaining interpersonal relationships. Parents who neglect their children generally lack an understanding of the complexity of social relationships, particularly meeting the needs of another. Domestic violence is likely to be a feature within the adult relationships.

- Significant deficits in both physical and psychological attachments between parent and child, which can lead to serious impairments in the psychosocial and emotional development of the child. In addition it is likely that these parents have themselves grown up in unstable, over-critical, non-nurturing homes.

- Stress associated with low self-esteem and isolation. In minority ethnic groups, additional issues of discrimination and racism from the wider community may intensify experiences of socioeconomic disadvantage, social isolation and low self-esteem.

- Physical, intellectual and mental health problems including alcohol and drug misuse and associated financial and partnership problems.

There is broad consensus that child neglect occurs as a result of a complex inter-action between a range of psychosocial and environmental factors that are known to significantly impair parent–child relationships and child-rearing practices.

Findings from serious case reviews

The Department of Health in England and the National Assembly for Wales require all area child protection committees (ACPCs) to undertake serious case reviews whenever a child has died or been seriously injured as a direct result of actual or suspected child abuse or neglect (Department of Health, Home Office and Department for Education and Employment 2000).

Key themes from these reviews have been collected in a handful of studies, most notably Falkov 1996; Hill 1990; James 1994; Munro 1996; Reder and Duncan 1999; Reder *et al.* 1993). Sinclair and Bullock (2002) have completed the most recent review for the Department of Health in England. The common themes identified in Sinclair and Bullock's study are:

- limited interagency co-operation both at a strategic and operational level

- poor communication between and within agencies

- inadequate links between social services and mental health services

- poor recording

- inappropriate response to referrals – for example practitioners not being aware of risk factors

- inadequate supervision

- failure to utilize cumulative information to assess risk factors

- lack of shared understanding of individual agency thresholds

- inadequate comprehensive family assessments

- absence of shared decision-making

- failure to plan a co-ordinated response

- lack of practical tools especially for key decisions.

Although hindsight brings with it distinct advantages, these themes have featured repeatedly in previous studies reviewing the findings from serious case reviews, and emerge again in the Scottish Executive's (2002a) audit and review of child protection. More than one third of children who die of abuse and neglect are not known to social services but are known to primary health services (Reder and Duncan 1999; Sinclair and Bullock 2002).

Occasionally a fatal case of child abuse will become the subject of a public inquiry. The most recent tragic and high-profile case, which resulted in a public inquiry in the UK, was the death of Victoria Climbié in 2000 at the hands of her great aunt and her great aunt's boyfriend. The eight-year-old had lived in the UK (London) for only ten months when she died but in that time was 'known' to a number of professionals across four local authorities within the statutory services of health, social services, police and housing. A relative (anonymously on two occasions) and an unregistered child-minder were concerned enough to alert social services and health respectively to Victoria's abuse but despite this, Victoria died a long, lonely death, neglected, beaten and starved. Toward the end of her life she was incarcerated in an unheated bathroom, lying in a bath inside a plastic bin-liner containing her excrement (Lord Laming 2003).

Professionals involved would need enough information to suspend the assumption that no human being would deliberately allow a child to suffer to this extent. This is one of the major challenges for professionals in undertaking child protection work – considering the unthinkable. In Victoria's case a public inquiry chaired by Lord Laming (2003) found that a catalogue of errors occurred due to a number of basic tasks not being carried out to a satisfactory standard by a number of different professionals. Examples of these include:

- Arrangements for discharging Victoria from hospital that had allowed Victoria to be returned to her great aunt on two separate occasions despite suspicions amongst medical staff that some of Victoria's physical injuries might be non-accidental and that further assessments were necessary.

- Social workers had spent no longer than 30 minutes speaking to Victoria and that had been without the necessary interpreter.

- Social services responded to the information they had by treating the family as requiring assistance with housing and needing financial support.

- Victoria did not benefit from her right to an education. A referral was not made to education welfare services by any of the involved agencies to enable them to check why it was that Victoria was not attending school.

- For those agencies that were involved, interagency communication had been poor with conclusions drawn from minimal evidence without the presence of a comprehensive assessment.

- Whilst in the UK Victoria attended three different Pentecostal churches on an occasional basis with her great aunt. Her great aunt reported to two of the churches that Victoria was enuretic and the pastors separately formed the view that Victoria was possessed by an evil spirit. Both pastors advised that the problem could be solved by prayer, until Victoria's last visit to church just before her death when the second pastor finally recognized Victoria's need for medical care. It was a mini-cab driver who in the end took Victoria and her great aunt to an ambulance bay in North London as he was so concerned at Victoria's appearance.

Although Victoria's case is particularly horrific, themes within it are true of many other tragedies where children have died through abuse and neglect. Lord Laming (2003) found that the 1989 Children Act legislation informing child protection in England and Wales was sound. He made recommendations and emphasized that it is doing the basic things well that can save children's lives.

Relevance of findings from serious case reviews in relation to neglect

Not all child deaths or injuries through abuse and neglect are predictable and preventable (Sinclair and Bullock 2002) but in cases where they are, competent and timely professional involvement can make the necessary difference. Whilst neglect demands efficient multiprofessional work, the evidence from practice and serious case reviews indicates that many professionals find it a difficult issue to address effectively (Bridge Childcare Consultancy 1995; Bridge Childcare Development Service 1999, 2001; Macdonald 2001; Munro 1996; Reder and Duncan 1999; Reder *et al.* 1993).

Multidisciplinary work and communication

The vast majority of case reviews (in the UK and beyond) point to a lack of multiprofessional dialogue that is crucial in the complex area of child protection. This can be caused by:

- failure to recognize and thus share important information (Sanders, Colton and Roberts 1999)

- tension or conflict in the communication (Reder and Duncan 1999; Sanders *et al.* 1999)

- fear of breaking rules of confidentiality.

In cases of child neglect where the sharing of information is crucial at a relatively low threshold, maximizing dialogue is important. Clear communication can avoid misunderstandings arising between professionals. This is an issue that was widespread in the Climbié case and Lord Laming commented extensively on the need for improvements to the exchange of information. Two quotes used in the report that evidence this point are:

> I cannot account for the way other people interpreted what I said. It was not the way I would have liked it to be interpreted. (Dr Ruby Schwartz)

> I do not think it was until I had read and re-read this letter that I appreciated quite the depth of misunderstanding. (Dr Mary Rossiter)

Children suffering from chronic neglect and emotional abuse come from families with complex needs. It is entirely unrealistic to believe that social workers alone can assess and intervene successfully with these families on an ongoing basis. For example, in some cases, particularly those involving mental health, the lack of shared expertise between adult and child care professionals has seriously inhibited the assessment of risk. A review of child death inquiries, concerning parental psychiatric illness and fatal child abuse, by Falkov (1996) highlighted this.

Decision-making

Decision-making in child protection is a very complex process and has significant impact on the lives of children and families. Practitioners bring their knowledge, practice wisdom and professional judgement to assessments of risk and subsequent decision-making. This is influenced by the legal and policy frameworks/guidelines and the resources available. The impediments to decision-making identified in the literature are:

- *Knowledge*: Serious case reviews have repeatedly highlighted alerting evidence not being recognized as such (Bridge Childcare Development Service 2001; Newham Area Child Protection Committee 2002). This is proportional to the level of skill, experience and training that staff have, or have access to in order to undertake their duties competently.

- *Personal beliefs and values*: Personal beliefs and values strongly influence professional judgement and reasoning in child protection work (Jones 1993; Macdonald 2001). In the case of Victoria Climbié there is evidence that her regimented behaviour in front of her great aunt was interpreted as being 'cultural' as she was from the Ivory Coast rather than due to her being deeply frightened. In a serious case review of a little girl with moderate to severe learning difficulties, her neglect was thought to be because of the stress caused by her complex needs rather than the possibility of the reverse being considered (Bridge Childcare Development Service 1999). See Box 9.1 for a case example. Racism and prejudice are also powerful inhibitors to good practice.

In neglect and emotional abuse in particular, where risk may be less extreme or immediate, personal values, beliefs and intuition play a much greater part and can lead to bias and errors in decision-making.

Box 9.1 Case study

Girl Two and her twin were the youngest of six children who were living with their mother, father and/or stepfather at the point when Girl Two was removed from home in August 1997. The family had been known to several agencies for a very long time.

Her removal followed a visit by a social worker two days earlier. The Serious Case Review report comments (Bridge Childcare Development Service 1999, p.2), 'In her case recording, the social worker reports that mother was cleaning the house, while Girl Two's twin brother was playing outside with no shoes on; Girl Two was in her bedroom asking for milk and trying to get out; the doorway into Girl Two's bedroom was obstructed by three boards nailed across it, to a height of approximately four feet six inches, and there was also a board nailed across the window; there was no bed, the mattress being on the floor, and no carpet; the room smelled of urine...the bedroom was a downstairs lobby area. There was no light bulb... There was no carpet on the floor; it was covered by lino tiles and appeared very dirty...there appeared to be nothing else in the room. Photographs taken by Gwent police on 14 August show that parts of the house were reasonably well maintained and furnished' (p.2).

All of the children in this family at various stages in their lives were assessed as having developmental delay (some global), learning difficulties and serious speech difficulties. In Girl Two's case health services had gone to considerable lengths to try to establish the cause of her developmental delay and learning difficulties.

Each of the three main agencies (health, social services and education) held a great deal of information about the past history of the family (and the extended family) that was not brought together either within each agency or across organizations until 1997. This meant that no one professional had oversight of this case and each professional was dealing with a very small percentage of the information available on the family. There were over 173 different professionals involved with Girl Two's

> family, and this was considered an under-estimate as many of the teachers could not be identified. These features are not limited to this case (Bridge Childcare Development Service 1999).

Bias and errors in decision-making

Human psychological processes affect decision-making in child protection. We tend to form judgements in line with evidence that is readily available (Macdonald 2001; Reder and Duncan 1999) and approach problems of categorization on the basis of simple resemblance between different cases with similar features. These particular factors, particularly when combined with selective perception and emotional commitment, can distort professional judgement and contrive to persuade practitioners that child abuse exists when it does not, or the other way round (Macdonald 2001; Sheldon 1987).

There is strong evidence from serious case reviews that once practitioners have formulated a hypothesis they are reluctant to change their mind in spite of information to the contrary being available (Bridge Childcare Consultancy 1995; Munro 1996, 1999). This is not surprising since the psychological literature confirms that we tend to pay more attention to evidence that supports our beliefs rather than challenges them (Kahneman, Slovic and Tversky 1990). Reviewing decisions and in fact changing one's mind is a sign of good not bad practice (Munro 1996, 2002). Mistakes which were at first 'unavoidable' because of lack of information become 'avoidable' as more information joins the system.

Repeatedly, serious case reviews emphasize the importance of a good assessment that includes historical information and frequent multiprofessional reviews to stop 'drift'. Yet Macdonald (2001) indicates that a completed assessment is still likely to be an exception rather than the norm in case files. Similarly Sanders et al. (1999) found in their review of 21 serious case reviews undertaken in Wales between 1991 and 1996, that assessments were either not undertaken or were insufficiently structured to be useful as a basis for planning.

Child protection conferences have been seen as one way to hypothesize and take decisions relating to risk in a multiprofessional forum. However, Kelly and Milner (1996, 2000) in a rigorous analysis of case conference minutes extracted from child death inquiry reports found strong indications that the original perceptions of a family constructed by the individual decision-maker and the subsequent management of the case are likely to be supported, maintained and endorsed in 'group decisions' within the conference forum and this persists even in the face of contrary evidence. This is supported by Munro (2002). Group pressure for conformity ensures that the initial dominant position in the group will emerge as the group choice. The child protection conference is not then necessarily a forum where previous decisions are challenged or reviewed and in chronic cases of emotional abuse and neglect there is often no one serious event that may act as a trigger to re-evaluate the original hypothesis. This lack of very immediate danger also raises the probability of 'drift' as cases may not hit agency thresholds, thus professionals mentally categorize the case as relatively 'safe' in relation to others where issues of risk are defined in more tangible terms.

Case complexity

As the introductory section highlights, neglectful families have a multiplicity and complexity of needs. Reder and Duncan (1999) describe a process of 'assessment paralysis' in which the focus of professional attention on a parent or carer's mental health diagnosis takes over the whole case, rather than looking at the effects of the parent's behaviour on the child. Although Reder and Duncan use this term specifically when referring to parents with mental health problems, this could apply to other areas of assessment. The important factor is that there is a danger in the needs of the parent becoming the point of focus, and this then becoming the context for all decisions relating to intervention, with other relevant factors relating to the child not given sufficient attention. 'Paralysis' can also result because of poor training, lack of confidence, lack of credibility and an over-reliance on the opinion of other professionals (Skinner 2002). Professionals can experience an overwhelming sense of need within the family. Invariably the practical needs are the easiest to identify and the danger is that the case goes down a path of intervention that does not tackle the fundamental reasons for the problems.

Keeping the child central

Many serious case reviews have indicated that cases were being dealt with as 'in need of practical resources' like housing or finance when in fact the situation for the children required a far more intrusive intervention (Bridge Childcare Consultancy 1995; Bridge Childcare Development Service 1999, 2001; Newham Area Child Protection Committee 2002).

Resources have to be monitored in order to consider how to *recognize the success or failure of the intervention* in relation to the child or whether the child or other children in the family would suffer in the time it took the intervention to work.

In order to assess risk there must be sound evidence of:

- The severity of risk: based on evidence which includes *observation and dialogue with the child* and analysed against the backdrop of a *sound knowledge of child development.* Almost all serious case reviews have inadequate information directly from the child.

- The capacity of the parents to change: based on their insight and the resources available.

Several serious case reviews (Bridge Childcare Consultancy 1995; Lord Laming 2003) have pointed to the 'rule of optimism' at play, where despite evidence that contra-indicates treatability (Fitzpatrick 1995) more resources are used to try to enable change. According to Hill (1990), the term 'rule of optimism' was first used by Dingwall *et al.* (1983) but was taken up by Blom-Cooper (1985) to describe how 'social workers were too ready to believe the best of parents or even over-identify with their perspective, so that lies were not seen through and evasive action not circumvented' (DHSS 1981, cited in Hill 1990). Alternatively a lack of engagement is seen as a reason to close the case. If the severity of risk to a child is high and the parent cannot change to alter this then removal must be considered.

Resources

Evidence from case reviews (Lord Laming 2003), audits of practice (Chief Secretary to the Treasury 2003; Department of Health 2002) and anecdotal reports point to an acute shortage of qualified and experienced staff within the health and social care sector, especially in the inner-city areas of the UK. A lack of continuity of staff adds to the risk contained in a case.

These documents also point to difficulties and pressures with financial resources available for work with children and families in need. Whilst managers and those that take decisions on financial and other resources have a responsibility to ensure that their decisions do not impact adversely on children and their families (Lord Laming 2003), the Safeguarding Review (Department of Health 2002) highlighted some of the complexities in achieving this in reality. Most notably the review commented on the different priority given to the safeguarding agenda by relevant statutory agencies as not all these agencies have this as a national priority for funding and resources. This will have a direct implication for resources available to those members of staff working directly with service users in the area of child protection. In addition the Laming report commented on elected councillors choosing how to allocate resources to children's services, which left one inner-city borough (Brent) being allocated just over half the government recommended amount under the Standard Spending Assessment. This political decision would have had an enormous impact on child protection services in the borough concerned.

Finance for families is important. However, Rosenberg and Cantwell (1993) comment, 'the distinction must be made between the neglect caused by financial poverty, which can be alleviated by financial help and that caused by emotional poverty. These may co-exist, but relief of the former condition does not relieve the latter'. For some families the parents' own emotional impoverishment is so great that they do not know how to parent, do not understand the needs of their children and despite massive intervention are unable to meet the needs of their children. Where money and other supports result in no change then a hypothesis of maltreatment through the parents' own emotional impoverishment must be considered (Fitzgerald 1998).

Case recording

Examining historical or background information held by a variety of agencies is critical in cases of neglect and emotional abuse as there is often no one event that generates a crisis. Responding to the case on an event-by-event basis will not enable the crossing of a threshold between need and risk. At the very least a *chronology* of important events, of agencies involved and the dialogue between them is essential. In many serious case reviews the risk contained within the information on file has never been grasped simply because no one person had read the file.

Lord Laming emphasized the value of basic good practice in relation to recording. Fact, opinion and hypothesis testing should be easily recognizable on file, especially in the context of frequently changing personnel.

Issues of race and culture emerging from serious case reviews

Sinclair and Bullock (2002) noted in their report that the ethnicity of the children subject to serious case reviews was not routinely recorded or discussed within the reports they reviewed making it impossible to discuss the possible impact of racism.

There have been a significant number of well-publicized inquiries into the deaths of black children through abuse and neglect in the UK (London Borough of Brent 1985; Lord Laming 2003; Newham Area Child Protection Committee 2002). Occasional comments have been made by the public inquiry reports or serious case reviews about the impact of a child's ethnicity on decisions made by professionals. For example, the inquiry held after the death of Tyra Henry concluded that the white social workers from Lambeth council tended to be too trusting of the family, and made assumptions about extended family, because they were black. On other occasions, such as in the serious case review report into the death of Ainlee Labonte, the child's ethnicity was not acknowledged or commented on (Newham Area Child Protection Committee 2002; Sinclair and Bullock 2002).

Lord Laming acknowledged in his report into the death of Victoria Climbié (2003) that:

> Victoria was a black child murdered by her two black carers. Many of the pro-
> fessionals with whom she came into contact during her life in this country
> were black. Therefore it is tempting to conclude that racism can have had no
> part to play in her case. But such a conclusion fails to recognise that racism
> finds expression in many other ways other than in direct application of preju-
> dice. (p.345)

However, in the report of more than 400 pages written by Lord Laming, just under three pages of the report deal directly with issues of diversity. He made no recommendation relating directly to issues of diversity.

In fact there is very little research regarding cultural competence in child protection practice generally (Walker 2002), although there is acknowledge-ment of inequitable, oppressive and poor quality services to black and other ethnic minority adults, especially in relation to mental health (Bhui and Olajide 1999; Cole, Leavey and King 1995). Walker (2002) reminds professionals that, although it instinctively feels right, there is no substantive evidence to support the view that cultural or ethnic congruence between clients and staff is a good strategy to improve acceptability and accessibility. Although it is important, simply employing more minority ethnic staff cannot be assumed necessarily to improve services. Evaluations of what works and for whom are important. Without this there could be an over-reliance on ethnic minority staff to provide 'cultural and related expertise' in what is sometimes a rapidly changing context. Britain is a multicultural society, particularly in urban areas where the minority ethnic population can be as high as 20%–30%. There is evidence that child neglect is more likely to occur in families experiencing multi-deprivation factors and there is a disproportionate presence of minority ethnic communities in areas of high social need. Some of these families will have suffered before their arrival and as asylum seekers will suffer the stigma associated with this. Accessing services and being honest about problems is inevitably difficult in a place in which you do not feel at home. For other individuals, where they live is indeed where they feel is home, but problems which make people feel different are emphasized by the real or perceived impact of racism even with the advan-tage of adequate finances and a good education. Working with diversity brings added complexity to the already complex work in child protection. However, it seems to us that the following is important in working with minority ethnic neglecting families:

- Make sure you have available to you the language that will enable the family to communicate their needs and views.

- Child development and the factors associated with fuelling distress in children are very similar across all races/cultures. Begin with a thorough initial assessment.

- Formulate a hypothesis but discuss it with others who have experience of the context in which the family live or from which they might have originated. Do this especially if your hypothesis is similar to a commonly held stereotype about that minority ethnic group. For example, 'she's running away because her father will not let her socialize with friends' about a Muslim girl who might, in fact, be running away because of direct abuse.

- Make sure the interventions make sense to the children and families. Sometimes particular families will give more status to religion, spirituality and perhaps fate than others might.

- Recheck your hypothesis frequently.

We acknowledge that none of this should be different for any client. However, we believe that reminding ourselves of basic good practice in relation to all children whilst acknowledging the increased complexity of working with diversity is important. Managing across race/culture can also be more difficult. Supervisors have to challenge and be challenged and if evidence is based on 'cultural knowledge' held by either one then challenging is more difficult. We believe that a multicultural society is certainly an advantage but we also believe that working with diversity brings with it added complexity (real or perceived) which we have a duty to discuss and be honest about.

Messages for practice

Serious case reviews tend to deal with extreme cases where a number of factors are in operation (Reder and Duncan 1999). This means that it is not easy to predict exactly which cases will result in serious injury and/or death (Sinclair and Bullock 2002) or to isolate specific lessons for cases of neglect. However the following lessons are pertinent:

- Chronic neglect can and does kill. In the USA neglect is more likely to result in fatality than any other form of maltreatment, most commonly through physical injury due to lack of care.

- Neglect is viewed as the most damaging type of abuse over the long term. Neglected children face a multitude of risk factors known to impair development. Neglected children's resilience is constantly under attack and they are at high risk of social exclusion.

- Poverty is unlikely to be the primary cause of chronic neglect. However, poverty is a risk factor and thus increases the probability of child abuse and particularly neglect occurring. The impact of this for social welfare and social policy considerations is important.

- Whereas physical and sexual abuse are in the main specific *events* that children are subject to, neglect and emotional abuse characterize the *relationship* between the parents and the child (Glaser and Prior 1997).

- Professionals have to share information and work together if risk is to be recognized and addressed. Communication between professionals has repeatedly been found to be poor in serious case reviews both in relation to relational dynamics and recording/sharing of information. Recording is generally poor across all professionals in the field of child protection.

- Remember that neglect requires a multi-agency response. It is impossible to conduct good assessments of neglecting families without the co-operation of other agencies. As well as co-operation it also needs a practitioner to take control and to co-ordinate activities.

- A multi-agency integrated chronology of events should be compiled, including background material, which enables all agencies to see a history of the family. This is a necessary tool for ensuring that agencies can then agree when the threshold for concern has been reached. Often one agency can have information that another agency is not aware of. Pulling together pieces of the multi-agency 'jigsaw' can change professional perceptions, dependent on the information available.

- Make sure that you have recorded evidence directly from the child and marry your information with measures of usual child development. Use this in order to set realistic targets and as a constant check on harm to the child and constantly predict forward to assess if harm will become significant.

- Remember that the first few years of a child's life are crucial in terms of cognitive and other areas of development. Neglect is characterized by an absence of parental care and attention. Make sure you compensate by arranging a child-minder or nursery. Children do not have the time it might take for an intervention to work. Make sure other protective factors are in place such as a good enough school. Neglected children may not be the highest on each agency's priority list but their needs merged together mean that they will find it hard to benefit from interventions if they are not tackled quickly.

- Consider using a risk assessment tool – especially if you have been involved with the family for some time and have completed a comprehensive assessment. It is not easy in cases of chronic neglect to pull out from the mass of information those points that are alerting of danger. Practice wisdom is always important but standardized tools can enable workers to obtain a more objective view of difficulties within a particular family (Bridge Childcare Development Service 1999; Macdonald 2001); see also the tools in the Assessment Framework Pack (Department of Health 2000))

- Remember to use a theoretical model that fits current theories on neglect (see Box 9.2).

Box 9.2 Theoretical models: the work of Peter Reder and Sylvia Duncan

During the last decade Reder and Duncan (Reder and Duncan 1999; Reder, Duncan and Gray 1993) have published extensively on child deaths and serious case reviews. Over 90% of abusing parents are neither psychotic nor criminal personalities but tend to be lonely, unhappy angry people under heavy stress. They bring with them their own experiences, especially of being parented, and their own resolved and unresolved conflicts from these experiences. Their children have their own characteristics and psychological meaning for their parents that might or might not fit harmoniously with their parents' expectations. Other significant factors are the context in which the family live which can exaggerate the situation, as can the level of insight (or lack of it) that the parent shows regarding the effects of their parenting on their children, or particular demands on the relationship at any one time. In order to understand the meaning of the neglecting behaviour for the child, the context in which the behaviour occurs must be examined.

Reder and Duncan have used this theory to form the basis of reviewing child deaths through abuse and neglect in order to understand what may have gone wrong. We believe that in cases of chronic neglect, this model will guide professionals to look at the various dynamics in the situation, understanding the impact of lots of factors rather than over-emphasising particular factors and dealing with them one by one.

- The Assessment Framework (Department of Health 2000) does seek information relating to the parent, the child and the context in which they live. However we believe that useful though this information is, it will need to be seen in the context of fuelling factors in order to be a dynamic rather than a mechanical tool. The interactional model described by Reder and Duncan (1999) is a means of doing this.

- Attachment is a fundamental aspect of child development and understanding the parent–child relationship in the context of attachment theory and disorders is important (Ainsworth *et al.* 1978; Bowlby 1969; Howe *et al.* 1999).

- Remember that in order to use theoretical models properly you need to know who is in the family and obtain information about significant others. Draw a family tree and make a chronology. Look at risk factors in the adults and the children. Think about the whole family. Do not forget, as often happens, the men involved.

- Remember the difference between material neglect and emotional neglect. The provision of finance and services will improve the situation of children in need but will not improve the situation of those children maltreated through neglect.

- Remember that most children who die of abuse and neglect die when they are young. Look for risk factors even in the ante-natal period.

- Acknowledge that there is a shortage of experts in the field of child protection. Arrange for observations from different sources to be brought to a forum with a consultant/s from another discipline/s. Observations can also lead to hypothesizing about the quality of attachment. Intervention may need to address this as simply working on a practical level may not improve the quality of attachment for the child with her/his parents.

- Remember to consider the hypothesis that developmental delay may be the result of maltreatment through neglect.

- If a case is frequently opened but equally frequently closed because it does not meet the threshold for risk (often referred to as the 'revolving door family') then do something different, for example seek consultation, read the file(s), use a risk assessment tool.

- Remember that although some children die of neglect, many survive but live dreadful lives. Remember the poor outcomes for children with chronic neglect. Put protective factors in place but recognize that leaving the child in chronic neglect for too long will have effects that are not easy to reverse.

- Provide adequate social welfare in order that this can be a backdrop to the assessments in general.

- In considering resources required for practice and intervention, recognize that in many circumstances there is a rapid turnover of staff and that families move. Neglect and its consequences require relatively long-term intervention and so excellent recording is required if risk is to be assessed properly. Make interventions time-limited, clearly stating intended outcome, how you will recognize it and the hypothesis driving the intention. Make sure other professionals know and agree and that your actions are based on evidence-based practice. Make sure you put resources into the initial assessment as often the initial hypothesis sticks. Make sure you regularly review cases.

- Remember to consider auditing neglect cases within your organization. We know that neglect cases are frequently on the child protection register for the longest period. An audit of cases may raise issues that you can then follow up at a local level.

Conclusion

Serious case reviews can tell us a great deal about where practice can be improved in relation to neglecting families. Although the majority of child abuse deaths were probably not predictable, the literature suggests that repeatedly the same mistakes are made. These relate to multiprofessional communication, issues of confidentiality, lack of staff expertise and continuity and resources generally.

We contend that if children are to be better protected then there are some fundamental changes required both from individuals and from the agencies in which they work.

Social workers need to take personal responsibility for their work but they cannot by themselves perform all the tasks required. Believing that adults can do the unbelievable to those children that are desperate for their love needs a wider skills base than any one professional can bring.

Neglected children are amongst the least resilient. Advocating for them is important. In too many cases the large and busy nature of the school system mitigates against a nurturing approach that is so important to vulnerable children and the process of entry into secondary school still means that the most vulnerable children continue to have least choice. This ultimately affects the self-esteem and self-efficacy of the child concerned, potentially leading to social exclusion.

Neglect is often, though not always, associated with those that are poor and deprived. This means that there needs to be the political will to help people overcome their problems, in order that they can care for their children safely, if this is possible. This in turn means respecting those that are brave enough to try work with them to stop child abuse and neglect. In the current climate social workers in particular are criticized for not intervening enough or intervening too much. Child neglect is complex. When the outcome of neglect can be as terrifying as death, society needs to appreciate the complexity of the issues raised and consequently the complexity of the solutions. Time and time again reviews completed after child deaths appear to point to simple solutions. However the solutions are in reality not that simple.

Acknowledgements

The authors would like to express their thanks to Peter Reder for commenting on an earlier draft of this chapter.

Chapter Ten

What is Weight Faltering (Failure to Thrive) and When Does it Become a Child Protection Issue?

Charlotte M. Wright

Introduction

Failure to thrive (FTT) is strongly associated with child neglect in professional understanding. This is so much the case that failure to thrive was until recently listed as a category of abuse under child protection guidelines (and still is in Scotland). When I first encountered this condition in the 1980s, I was working in a deprived inner-city area with an active interest in child protection. At that time it was assumed that most children with failure to thrive were living in conditions of extreme poverty and neglect and the only recognized intervention was removal into care. This stimulated us to start a programme of research into community-based treatment approaches in partnership with the NSPCC. However within a few years it was obvious that in fact most children with failure to thrive were neither neglected nor ill and that this was primarily a dietary or behavioural problem. Much of our energy since then has been directed to reframing practitioners' ideas about this condition so that it can be managed more successfully and with less stigma. However, although only a minority of all cases, neglected and abused children are still more likely to fail to thrive than other children and tend to be the most challenging of such cases to manage.

This chapter will first outline the history of research into this subject and the evidence that has led to this shift in our understanding of the causes and consequences of failure to thrive. It will then outline the process of routine weight monitoring, how growth charts may be used to identify children whose weight gain is a cause for concern and how they should ideally be managed in primary and secondary health care. Then it will discuss how we may identify and manage the few but highly challenging children where poor weight gain is a reflection of parental neglect and abuse.

The history of failure to thrive as a condition

In 1915 Chapin (1915) described a syndrome of delayed growth, development and emotional changes resulting from institutional care which he termed 'hospitalism'. From the 1930s onwards evidence accumulated (Bakwin 1949; Spitz 1945) of the disastrous effects of being raised in institutions, and the striking recovery seen when children were transferred into nurturing environments (Skeels 1966). In the post-war period Bowlby first described the effects of 'maternal deprivation' (Bowlby 1973) which was to have a profound effect on child rearing attitudes. In the same year, Widdowson (1951) published a study of German orphanages in which the effect of supplemented diet on growth appeared to be over-ridden by emotional influences. She concluded with a since often quoted verse from the Book of Proverbs: 'Better a dinner of herbs where love is than a stalled ox and hatred therewith'.

These studies were important in reforming the care of children in institutions and also stimulated interest in apparently similar children seen outside institutional care. However they also established the idea that this stunting occurred despite adequate dietary intake. In 1957 two cases of 'hospitalism' were described in children living in their own families (Coleman and Provence 1957) and by the 1960s the term 'failure to thrive' had come into regular use to describe such children, used interchangeably with the term 'the maternal deprivation syndrome'. Early studies of this 'syndrome' (Barbero and Shaheen 1967; Bullard *et al.* 1967; Elmer 1960; Leonard, Rhymes and Solnit 1966) described the families and emotional circumstances in great detail, but referred only fleetingly to nutritional intake, which was thought to be unimportant (Patton and Gardner 1962; Powell, Brasel and Blizzard 1967). Others though showed that under-nutrition was actually the common underlying mechanism (Talbot *et al.* 1947; Whitten, Pettit and Fischhoff 1969). By the end of the 1960s, 'failure to thrive' was widely used to describe a syndrome of growth failure associated with neglecting or disrupted homes and adverse developmental outcome.

However, a problem with all these studies was that they relied for their clinical material on children referred to specialists and diagnosed by them as having failure to thrive. At that time there was no accepted objective growth-based definition of failure to thrive (Wilcox, Nieburg and Miller 1989) and no characteristic emotional or developmental features had been found (Drotar 1985). In these circumstances only children meeting the perceived profile of failure to thrive would be identified, while those who did not remained undiagnosed. This has been well illustrated by a study (Batchelor and Kerslake 1990) which found that children with the same growth pattern were identified as failure to thrive if living in deprived circumstances, but labelled constitutionally small if not.

In the 1980s it was recognized that what was needed were community-based studies, where all cases in the population were identified, using consistent growth-based definitions so that their true characteristics could be established without bias or subjectivity. A number of such studies were conducted from the late 1980s onwards and it is these that have persuaded us to radically alter our view of the condition. However the earliest research with its paradigm of failure to thrive as a syndrome of emotional deprivation, where children can somehow eat and eat and not grow, remains firmly embedded in the collective subconscious and is hard to shift. The following sections will outline what research tells us about the true correlates of weight faltering and failure to thrive as well as un-picking why our clinical experience may give us a different impression.

Why do children fail to thrive?

Organic disease

The majority of children with slow weight gain will have no underlying organic disease (Drewett, Corbett and Wright 1999; Skuse, Wolke and Reilly 1992; Wright *et al*. 1998). Children with serious medical conditions appear actively ill and are normally referred straight to hospital, so detailed medical tests in apparently well children rarely yield positive results (Berwick, Levy and Kleinerman 1982; Sills 1978). Despite this, much emphasis is placed on the possibility of organic disease, particularly by doctors, but also often by parents and social workers. This is probably because, without an understanding of the nutritional and behavioural features described below, it is not clear why they are not gaining weight and alternative medical explanations are sought.

Poverty

Poverty is probably the most important risk factor for poor weight gain world-wide, but in the UK there is actually little evidence that it has an important influence in young children (Skuse *et al*. 1992; Wright, Loughridge and Moore 2000; Wright, Waterston and Aynsley-Green 1994a). The reason for this lack of association is probably the major food safety net provided by the UK welfare foods scheme which provides free formula milk for children under one, the age when they are most at risk (Department of Health Committee on Medical Aspects of Food Policy 2002). It is of interest that there is evidence of poorer growth in older children living in poverty in the UK, when children are no longer eligible for the welfare foods scheme (Wright and Parker 2004).

What this means is that in whole-population surveys most cases of failure to thrive are found in 'average' homes. This will not accord with practical experience, but this is because the selection process described above ensures that 'typical' cases in vulnerable families are referred while cases in more affluent families either go unrecognized or are labelled as something else (Wright et al. 2000).

Neglect and abuse

Early descriptions of groups of cases of failure to thrive included accounts of subsequent serious physical injury (Evans, Reinhart and Succop 1972; Koel 1969)and even deaths (Hufton and Oates 1977). However, again, these were all children referred to hospital and were thus highly selected. In contrast in population studies, evidence of abuse or neglect has been found in only a minority of cases of failure to thrive. One early US study (Sherrod et al. 1985) found no overlap between failure to thrive and abused children. Skuse et al. (1995) found 6 of 47 cases (13%) were subject to either child protection case conferences or registration while our own study found only 5 out of 97 (5%) cases (Wright et al. 1998). Two other studies have failed to find psychological similarities between abusing and parents of children who fail to thrive, with the latter nearer to normal controls (Dubowitz et al. 1989; Oates 1984). Thus the majority of children meeting the case definition for failure to thrive do not show evidence of neglect and abuse.

However, children with failure to thrive *are* at increased risk of abuse and neglect. The rates of child protection issues found by Skuse and ourselves were four to five times the expected rate in the general population (Sidebotham et al. 2001). This apparent discrepancy is because weight faltering is much more common than abuse and neglect (see Figure 10.1). Five per cent of all children will show weight faltering, while even in high-risk groups only 1–2% will suffer abuse or neglect (Sherrod et al. 1985; Skuse et al. 1995). This suggests that around a quarter of abused or neglected infants will also have failure to thrive. It is thus important always to consider whether an abused or neglected child is achieving their growth potential. One study found that over half of a group of children removed from their families following abuse showed marked catch-up growth in foster care (King and Taitz 1985), which strongly suggests that they had been chronically under-nourished previously.

Under-nutrition

What has been consistently found in population-based studies of failure to thrive is evidence of under-nutrition. Most studies have reported that failure to thrive children are thin (Black et al. 1995; Skuse et al. 1992; Wright et al. 2000). Our study found that the great majority subsequently showed at least some catch-up growth and that in two thirds there was some evidence of dietary insufficiency (Wright *et al.* 2000). Other studies have shown that failure to thrive children eat less than normally growing children (Heptinstall *et al.* 1987; Pollitt and Leibel 1980).

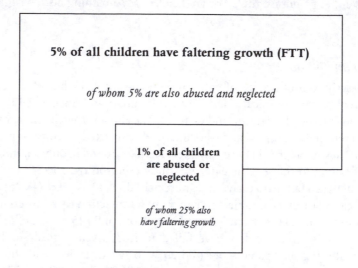

5% of all children have faltering growth (FTT)

of whom 5% are also abused and neglected

1% of all children are abused or neglected

of whom 25% also have faltering growth

Figure 10.1 The relationship between faltering growth and abuse and neglect

What is initially puzzling is how children can become under-nourished if well and living in normal loving homes. Things become clearer when you appreciate that all young children are naturally at high risk of under-nutrition. Young babies and toddlers have very high energy requirements which they need both for maintenance of their relatively inefficient body systems and to fuel extremely fast growth. Newborn infants will double their weight by the age of four months and treble it by a year and to do this must consume 15% of their weight in milk daily (Department of Health Committee on the Medical Aspects of Food Policy 1991). Toddlers have equally high energy needs partly because they are extremely physically active. At the same time they have small stomachs and limited feeding skills and are often embarking on the battle of wills that characterize the toddler years. This means that all young children need to consume high-energy foods or drinks frequently and regularly.

Because pre-verbal children rely entirely on their parents to recognize and meet their feeding needs, quite a small problem with feeding can thus lead to weight faltering. A mother need only be otherwise preoccupied by family stresses or offering a well-meaning but inappropriate diet such as the high-fibre low-fat diet recommended for adults, for a child to fail to quite meet their energy requirements and for their weight to begin to falter. Our own research has shown that children with slow weight gain have poorer reported appetites and like all foods rather less (Wright *et al.* 2000). They eat a narrower range of foods (Wright *et al.* 2000) and have subtly different patterns of satiation (Kasese-Hara, Wright and Drewett 2002). We have also found that quite modest dietary changes can produce much improved weight gain (Wright *et al.* 1998). Thus we have come to understand that in general weight faltering due to under-nutrition is a common natural hazard of early childhood, rather than a shocking rarity necessarily caused by overt neglect.

The consequences of weight faltering

The consequences of weight faltering vary depending on the severity of the weight faltering, but in general recent research has demonstrated that they are not as serious as was initially thought. Mild weight faltering may have no lasting effects at all, with a natural tendency for weight gain to improve over the pre-school years (Kristiansson and Fallstrom 1987), although children with weight faltering in infancy are generally shorter and thinner (Drewett *et al.* 1999). At the other end of the spectrum severe under-nutrition is associated with a significant risk of mortality, usually from overwhelming infection.

Many studies have found significant developmental delay in children with weight faltering (Kerr and Black 2000; Skuse *et al.* 1992; Wilensky *et al.* 1996). But, reassuringly, this seems to lessen with age, though it appears to be associated with a deficit of up to five IQ points in childhood (Drewett *et al.* 1999).

An important question is whether these effects are reversible. Few studies have formally examined the effect of intervention. Most that have lacked untreated controls, were often very small and tended to find no difference in outcome between children receiving one treatment or another (Black *et al.* 1995; Drotar and Sturm 1988; Raynor *et al.* 1999). At the other extreme, case studies have shown dramatic improvements in both growth (King and Taitz 1985) and cognition in children removed from their families because of neglect or abuse (Money, Anecillo and Kelley 1983), but made no comparison with controls remaining in the family home. Our own trial, comparing community-based care with no treatment found that both groups improved, but that those receiving the intervention were significantly heavier and taller at age four and also had better reported appetite (Wright *et al.* 1998).

How should weight faltering be managed?

In general as our understanding of weight faltering has grown, our concern about its possible correlates and consequences has diminished. It has become clear that the majority of cases are not occurring in the context of abuse or neglect, that the risk of occult (that is unrecognized) organic disease is very slight and that the sorts of factors that seem to be relevant are difficult to assess and manage outside the home setting. This thus makes it a condition ideally managed in the community by the primary care team. In the UK health visitors are the members of that team best qualified for this, because they provide a universal, non-stigmatizing service to all infants and most commonly make the diagnosis in the first place. They already know families, have ready access to the home and are expert in assessing normal diet and feeding in young children. Our trial of community-based treatment successfully used health visitors as key workers (Wright *et al.* 1998) and this approach has now been adopted in a number of districts and the central role of the health visitor in this work endorsed by a number of publications (Hampton *et al.* 2002; Underdown and Birks 1999). Health visitors are also well placed to identify the important minority of these children who are failing to thrive because of abuse or neglect, but in this area of work they ideally need the support of a multidisciplinary team.

The rest of this chapter will discuss the management of weight faltering in more detail and explore in particular when such children should raise concerns about possible neglect and what should be done about them.

Messages from research

- The majority of children with slow weight gain will have no underlying organic disease.

- Most cases of FTT are found in 'average' homes.

- Most children meeting the definition of FTT do not show evidence of abuse and neglect.

- However, children with FTT are at increased risk of abuse and neglect.

- Around a quarter of abused or neglected children will also have failure to thrive.

- In studies of FTT there is evidence of under-nutrition, but this is a common hazard of early childhood rather than a consequence of overt neglect.

- The consequences of weight faltering vary depending on severity, but are generally not as serious as was thought initially.

- Few studies have examined the effects of intervention, although it appears that community based intervention has a significant effect by age four.

- Health visitors are ideally placed for delivery of intervention.

Routine growth monitoring

Faltering growth is usually identified during routine weight monitoring in primary care by the family health visitor. All babies should be weighed regularly so that trends in weight gain can be seen, but not too often, as minor variations in weight can cause unnecessary anxiety (Hall and Elliman 2002). Healthy children should be weighed once every 2–4 weeks in the first few months, every 1–3 months till the age of one, but then only at routine checks or when seeing the doctor for illness. If a child appears to be gaining weight too slowly, they should be weighed more often, but still not usually more than once per month. If weight gain is poor at least one measurement of length or height is also helpful, but two people using special equipment are needed to measure length in young children, so it is not measured routinely before school entry. If both height and weight are available the body mass index (BMI), which is a measure of thinness and fatness, can be calculated.

Growth charts

There are charts for height and weight as well as for head circumference and BMI (Freeman *et al.* 1995). Growth charts are important, as measurements on their own tell us little or nothing about growth over time or how a child compares to others. When measurements are plotted they tell you how big a child is compared to the UK average. For example a child on the 75th centile is a large average child while a child below the second centile is in the smallest 2% of children. New, more accurate weight charts were introduced in the mid 1990s (Freeman *et al.* 1995) and these are the ones that should now be used (Wright *et al.* 2002).

After the age of 6–12 weeks children usually track roughly the same centile line and this reflects how naturally small or large they are. However most children show occasional drops or gains from that line (Wright, Waterston and Aynsley-Green 1994b). As long as it is less than the space between two centile lines on the new UK 1990 charts (one 'centile space') this is entirely normal. Fatness varies a lot during childhood, with toddlers being naturally plump while older children tend to be very thin. It is therefore particularly important always to plot BMI on a centile chart (Cole, Freeman and Preece 1995).

How is failure to thrive/weight faltering diagnosed?

It can sometimes appear as if the definition of failure to thrive was developed by Humpty Dumpty:

> It means just what I choose it to mean, neither more nor less. (Carroll 1872)

Until recently we knew little about what constituted normal weight gain and even with this knowledge, variations in weight relative to height relative to parental heights can still make the definition complex in individual children. However we can now say when a pattern of weight gain is unusual, and just how unusual it is compared to normal children of the same age. Weight gain can be said to be subnormal if there has been a long drop down the weight centile chart. Only 5% of children will show a sustained drop of at least two centile spaces, with only 1% dropping through three, but very large and small babies show different weight gain patterns, making standard charts hard to interpret. This led us to design a special *weight monitoring chart* which has been shown to improve the accuracy of diagnosis of weight faltering over the first year (Wright *et al.* 1998). In primary care a drop through the equivalent of two or more weight centile spaces should usually trigger some sort of assessment by the health visitor. We cannot then say whether any one child showing a fall down a centile chart is definitely under-nourished, but it becomes increasingly likely the longer the fall. If such children are also thin for their age (i.e. having a low BMI), this makes it most likely that this in fact reflects relative under-nutrition. If a child also shows evidence of slower than expected height gain, compared to previous height measurements or parental heights, then this is powerful evidence to suggest that they are chronically under-nourished.

Unfortunately, those children who ultimately turn out to have been failing to thrive because of neglect and abuse do not usually show particularly severe or characteristic growth patterns that allow them to be picked out at an early stage.

The basic assessment of faltering weight gain

This assessment should ideally be done by a health visitor in the UK primary care setting, but could be done by a paediatrician, GP, psychologist or social worker, depending on the child's circumstances. The important principle of the assessment is to look globally at the child and family in relation to feeding and establish the current situation before giving any advice. In general this assessment will be most informative if at least part of it is undertaken in the family home. While home visits can be time consuming, they supply a wealth of information, much of which can never be obtained in the lengthiest of office-based consultation.

The first question to ask in any assessment is what the family perceive the problem to be.

- Are they worried about their child's growth, feeding or both and why are they worried?

- Have they always felt that there was a problem with their child's feeding or growth, or has their anxiety been raised solely as a result of health professionals telling them that their child is not gaining weight?

The next issue to rule out or contextualize is the possible role of medical issues.

- Have there been important health problems in the past such as prematurity or severe chronic illness?
- Are there currently any symptoms suggestive of illness?

If so, a paediatric assessment will be needed at an early stage. However even if medical problems are identified usually the general management approach will be the same, so it is still important to proceed to a broader assessment of the child's feeding. This needs to consider everything about food and eating systematically, rather than merely concentrating on, for example, what was reported as being eaten the day before. The food chain (Figure 10.2) illustrates the general areas needing to be considered.

THE FOOD CHAIN	EXAMPLES OF ISSUES THAT MAY BE UNCOVERED
Money & Knowledge ⇓	Family in the grip of a loan shark
Purchase ⇓	No car, no local supermarket
Preparation ⇓	Living in one room without a cooker
Giving ⇓	Mum depressed and force feeding
Taking ⇓	Eats walking around room
Absorbing ⇓	Coeliac disease
Using	Rapid growth in hospital

Figure 10.2 The food chain

The sorts of questions you might ask would be:

- What are the family circumstances? Do the family know what food they should be giving their child and have they the money to buy it? How do they shop and where, and can they cook?

- What sorts of foods are given? This assessment is easier if the family complete a three-day food diary, which is far more informative than relying on parental recall. The family may have an inappropriately restrictive diet due to religious beliefs or ideas about food intolerance, both of which can lead to a very low-energy diet. Some children are genuinely food intolerant, most commonly of milk, and this may greatly restrict what they can eat. Milk intolerance should never be diagnosed in a child without assessment by a paediatrician, and such children should always be under the supervision of a paediatric dietician.

- How is the food given to the child and where, and how does the child react to it? Are there meals or settings or types of food that the child will eat better? This part of the assessment is made much easier if a meal can actually be witnessed or viewed via a video made by parents.

- Finally, it is important to examine the child's growth pattern over time and link events in their life to periods of poor weight gain or catch-up. If there was a period of particularly poor weight gain, what was happening then? If the child showed a period of rapid recovery, what precipitated this and why did the improvement not continue? Sometimes the information from the growth chart may in effect contradict all the remainder of the assessment. For example a child may be presented as eating very well at home and yet show much more rapid weight gain during a brief admission to hospital. Similarly, a child's poor weight gain may coincide very precisely with major family upsets or changes in the organization of care.

Intervention

Once the whole picture is outlined, obvious areas capable of change may have been identified which clearly explain the poor weight gain. More often things are not that clear, but there are aspects that, if changed, should result in improved intake. Commonly the assessment itself results in improved intake, as the parents spontaneously develop a clearer view of what needs to be changed, though this is not always shared explicitly.

When it comes to offering advice, as in any area of behavioural change, it is important to remember three basic principles.

1. Reinforce and commend whatever is already going well. Families often feel demoralized and may only need help in recognizing where to concentrate their efforts. In other circumstances it may be very difficult to find anything worthy of praise, but without some positive reinforcement it will be difficult to engage families in changing any other behaviours.

2. Discuss possible changes with the family and identify those which are most important and achievable. The family should then implement a limited number, ideally no more than two or three at any one time.

3. If possible put this advice in writing to the family with copies to all others working with the family, to ensure a consistent message to the family.

The sort of advice that might be given depends very much on the individual child. Generally, dietary advice would aim to maximize the energy content of the food given: for example adding butter or cream to foods, using full-fat dairy products, offering a sweet as well as a savoury course at each meal and encouraging solid foods – which have the most energy – over purées or drinks. It may also be important to widen the range of food types given or make them more age appropriate.

Other advice commonly relates to mealtime routine. There should be regular meals and snacks (a toddler must eat five times a day to meet their high dietary requirements), yet constant grazing on snack foods, or drinking large volumes of fluids should be avoided. Suitable seating can make a big difference, as can meals shared with parents or other children. A vital behaviour to advise against is coercion of any kind in relation to food, particularly force-feeding since it can have such an adverse effect on the child's experience of meals. Many parents probably resort to force-feeding at some stage in these circumstances, so it is a sensible precaution to advise explicitly against it in advance.

Advice is most likely to be successfully implemented if it is followed up within 1–2 weeks. At this contact progress can be discussed and the advice restated if necessary. Actual changes in weight gain take longer to identify: at least a month in a child under one year and two to three months in toddlers. It is important to check progress, but not to weigh too often, as over short periods of time random variations can mislead.

Specialist assessment

If there is no sustained improvement after this assessment, more specialist assessment may be needed. In the ideal model these assessments inform and support the health visitor as a key worker rather than subsuming their role (see Figure 10.3). The most helpful first specialist to see the child would usually be a dietician. In some districts referral can be made direct to dieticians, in others a referral to a paediatrician would be necessary first. Where there are concerns about medical issues paediatric assessment will be necessary at an early stage. Otherwise, if there is sustained unexplained weight faltering, even after dietary input, paediatric assessment will be necessary prior to referral on. If the child is described or witnessed as having difficulty chewing or swallowing they may also benefit from speech and language therapy input. If the weight faltering clearly relates to severe feeding behaviour problems, a referral to a clinical psychologist may be appropriate. Finally there will be some children where weight faltering persists for no very clear reason or where there are emerging concerns about their care and it is in these cases that a risk assessment should be undertaken in order to decide whether to involve social services.

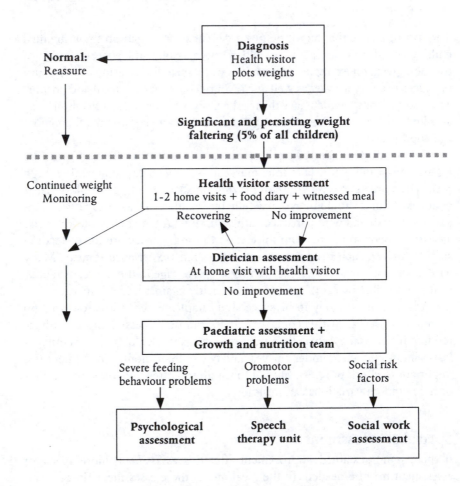

Figure 10.3 The multidisciplinary pathway of care for weight faltering

Dietician assessment

Dietary assessment is excellent for obtaining a detailed picture of the types of food offered and the meal pattern, which can then form the basis of advice. However, it is important to realize that dietary assessment can rarely diagnose under-nutrition and can never exclude it, as food diaries are inaccurate at best and may often be falsified where families perceive themselves to be under investigation. The diagnosis of under-nutrition should be made from measurements of weight-for-height and weight gain; a child with weight faltering who is significantly underweight is under-nourished, whatever the food diary shows.

Dietary assessment is best undertaken at a home visit, after the family have completed a three-day food diary. Hospital or clinic-based assessments, though less time consuming are much less informative. If done jointly with the health visitor no follow-up dietetic input is usually needed.

Paediatric assessment

Paediatricians have three roles in assessing children with weight faltering:

1. *Assessment of growth.* Their help may be needed to arrive at a clear diagnosis of under-nutrition by collecting a reliable measure of height and relating it to their previous growth and parental heights. Some very small children are in fact growing very well and the anxiety about them is unfounded. Where the diagnosis is confirmed the paediatrician can offer the parents a fuller explanation of the basis for concern about the child's weight gain and explain why it is that young children commonly become under-nourished.

2. *Investigation to rule out organic disease.* There may be medical symptoms or signs that need to be explored further, or possible hidden organic disease to be ruled out. These investigations should be completed promptly to avoid inadvertently signalling to parents that there is a medical cause that has simply not yet been identified. Once the tests have been completed, it is important that the doctor reassures parents about the absence of a medical cause while reinforcing the need to improve their dietary intake.

3. *Management of severe cases.* In practice referral to other specialists must usually be made through the paediatrician and it is s/he who should take an overview of the case and decide how such children may be best managed. These decisions are much easier if made collectively with a multidisciplinary team, which might include:

- liaison health visitor
- community-based paediatric dietician

- psychologist
- speech therapist
- social worker.

Social risk assessment: what factors might suggest a need for social work input?

Deciding whether to involve social services can be straightforward, or can be very difficult. If it has become obvious that a child with weight faltering is living in a family with other major social problems, such as domestic violence or drug or alcohol abuse, a referral to social services should be made, as in any case where there is evidence suggesting abuse or neglect. The much more difficult situation is where there are suspicions that the weight faltering may be a result of neglect or emotional factors, but there are no other concerns about the care of the child. In this case a referral would usually only be considered if there was very severe weight faltering which persisted despite appropriate advice and support. It is important to ensure that families have been appropriately advised and have truly *heard* this advice (Wright and Talbot 1996). Sometimes it may need to be repeated by different people or with different degrees of authority before the message finally gets through.

A global picture should be built up and the consideration of possible referral returned to as new information is obtained. The health visitor is usually the most well aware of family circumstances, but may need the prompt of discussion with a multidisciplinary team or from one of the other specialists involved, to arrive at a decision to refer. Most of the factors to be taken into account are themselves part of a spectrum and Table 10.1 summarizes the sorts of issues that should be considered and how they might influence the decision.

How might social services help?

Children can usually be referred as children 'in need' unless there are active concerns about concurrent abuse. A planning meeting or informal case discussion should usually be convened to discuss the range and extent of the family's problems and what would be the best therapeutic options. Possible initial options would include:

- social work assessment
- social work aide input
- family centre input
- specialist nursery placements
- sponsored child-minding.

Table 10.1 Risk Assessment grid: indicators for referral to social services

	Category 1	Category 2	Category 3	Category 4
Growth pattern	Worsening, severe, weight faltering and underweight	Lack of improvement in growth pattern or relapse after initial improvement	Partial improvement only or partial relapse	Steady catch-up or risen to <2 centile spaces below expected weight
Child's feeding behaviour (at a witnessed meal)	Family known to withold food	Child observed to be hungry	Child observe to eat poorly	Child observed to eat well
Development (assuming medical factors excluded)	Worsening developmental delay	Some developmental delay		
Concerns about abuse or neglect	New evidence of physical or sexual abuse	Concerns about global neglect of child or siblings	Some concern about general care or paternal competence	
Growth of siblings		Siblings currently under-nourised	Sibling faltered in the past	Other siblings not affected
Family situation	Major social or financial problems	Multiple social or financial problems	Apparently isolated issues	
Family motivation	Family seeking social services input	Family willing for social service input		

Any item in **Category 1** should usually trigger referral, as should two or more in **Category 2** or four or more in **Category 3**.
Any item in **Category 4** would normally lessen the level of overall concern, but would not over-ride other major concerns.

Box 10.1 Case example: Anne Marie

Anne-Marie had prolonged involvement with health and social services because of early concerns about neglect. Concerted multi-disciplinary work began with the family when she was 12 months old. She was registered at the age of 33 months on the ground of neglect, with her two siblings who also had faltering growth. The family then received intensive daily support, but it became apparent that nearly all food and care was now being offered by social services, nursery staff and extended family members. There were also signs of emotional and physical abuse. When the care package was wound back, family conditions deteriorated rapidly. Finally, after the parents had failed to engage with formal assessment of their parenting, all three siblings were removed into care when Anne-Marie was 4½ years old.

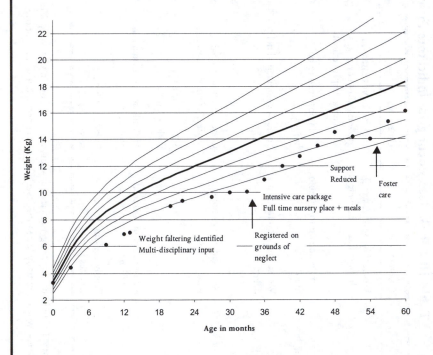

Figure 10.4 Anne-Marie's weight gain pattern over time plotted on a standard UK growth chart

Box 10.2 Case example: Paul

Paul showed early severe weight faltering which was investigated at an early stage and revealed no organic cause. Although there were concerns about possible physical abuse and the mother was known to be depressed, she proved difficult to engage in any way.

After showing rapid catch-up weight gain during a hospital admission aged 19 months, but no further improvement, social services' involvement was sought. They were initially reluctant to play a role but at the age of 27 months a social worker was allocated, a nursery placement was found and his mother accepted counselling.

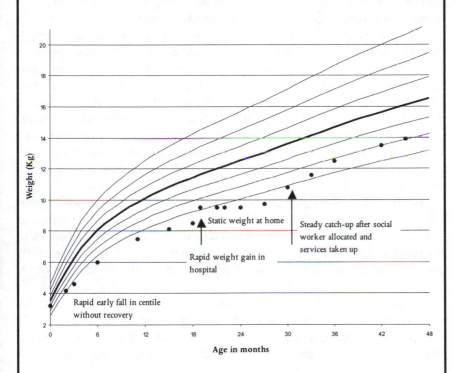

Figure 10.5 Paul's weight gain pattern over time plotted on a standard UK growth chart

Monitoring progress

Clear goals should be set for the family in terms both of engagement with services and of the expectation of sustained weight catch-up. Dramatic improvement can be seen while still at home and alternative care is not usually needed. While parental co-operation is important neither this alone, nor their reports of their child's diet, can be used as a robust measure of progress unless they are reflected in actual changes in growth.

Progress should therefore be assessed using a series of weights plotted on centile charts. Any single weight may not be representative so it is important not to let the last weight measured influence decisions in isolation. Children with continuing failure to thrive usually do gain weight over time, but at too slow a rate, with the result that their weight tracks along the low centile they have fallen to. Catch-up weight gain is occurring when a child gains weight more rapidly, with most plotted weights being at a higher centile position than the last. This means that over time the child's weight moves from their low centile to one more appropriate to their genetic potential.

Catch-up weight gain can begin rapidly after dietary change has occurred, but it is usually two to three months before this can be clearly recognized on a growth chart. Recovery can be said to have occurred when a child's weight and height have caught up to within two centile spaces of their expected centile, taking into account early weight and height gain and parental heights. Where there has been a long fall in weight this will take between one and three years, and may never be complete. However, if there is continued catch-up over 6–12 months, with one to two centile spaces (or their equivalent) crossed upwards, social services input could probably then be safely withdrawn, with monitoring only by health.

Interpretation of progress can be difficult where there is a conflict between the parents' account and the child's objective progress. It is important to remember that all foods eaten must be used by the body in some way except in rare medical conditions that will have been excluded before referral. Therefore, whatever parents report, if there has been no catch-up there has not been an overall increase in intake.

Alternatively, if very extensive support is provided for the family and child, any recovery seen may result solely from external input, rather than family change. If this is thought to be the case, there should be a period of continued monitoring after withdrawal of intensive support before the case is closed.

Conclusions

Weight faltering is a common problem in early childhood and most children experiencing it live in normal unexceptional families and respond well to simple primary care based intervention. Some children with sustained or severe weight faltering need the input of specialists to assess them fully and in a minority of cases faltering growth may be an indicator of global neglect or abuse. These cases require multidisciplinary assessment and management, either as children in need or within the child protection system. Successful management requires an understanding of the underlying growth problem and a healthy scepticism about reported diet, while supporting parents to implement and sustain the necessary dietary and behavioural change.

Messages for practice

- Faltering growth is usually identified through routine weight monitoring by the family health visitor.

- BMI should always be plotted on a centile chart.

- Assessment should be global in relation to feeding. Home visits provide the most complete picture.

- After a medical history, a broad assessment of feeding patterns is necessary.

- Intervention is sometimes obvious after assessment; commonly the assessment itself can result in improved intake.

- Reinforce and commend whatever is already going well.

- Discuss possible changes, and put these in writing.

- Dietary advice and mealtime routine are the most common focus of information giving.

- If there is no sustained improvement more specialist assessment may be needed – from a paediatrician, dietician, clinical psychologist, social worker.

- Careful monitoring of progress is essential.

Chapter 11

The Theoretical and Practical Issues in Attachment and Neglect

The Case of Very Low Birth Weight Infants

Gill Watson and Julie Taylor

Introduction

> I couldn't really see his face because of the eye pads on and erm...his little
> body was covered in all these tubes, so I couldn't really see him very well...
> what a mass of wires, ha, an absolute mass of wires and he was in bubble wrap.
> I was just, erm, just amazement...it was quite dark as well and he looked sore,
> so red and sore, I was scared to touch 'cause he looked so sore.
>
> *(Mother of very low birth weight infant, Scotland, 2003)*

Usually babies are born weighing around 3200g (7lbs). If they arrive earlier
than expected, and/or if there have been ante-natal complications, they may be
born weighing very much less than this, putting them at risk from a whole
gamut of biological, social and developmental challenges. Very low birth
weight (VLBW) infants are those who are born, usually preterm, weighing less
than 1500g – less than half the weight expected. It is this group of infants in
particular whose defencelessness affords a potential for child neglect. Our
argument explores the pluralistic nature of this vulnerability, a kind of 'double
whammy': not only do the circumstances and consequences of being born with
a very low birth weight provide a potential for neglect, but also the antecedents
of VLBW may in and of themselves also have associations with neglect.

Issues of neglect within the very low birth weight population have received
little recent attention. Over the past thirty years changes in medical technology,
combined with clinical developments, have led to the increasing survival of
preterm, very low birth weight infants born at the lower extremes of pre-

maturity. The degree of physiological fragility experienced by this vulnerable population often creates a different set of outcomes compared with those infants born at the end of a full term pregnancy. This is an issue for a range of professionals in health, social care and education across the lifespan of the child. Yet it does not appear to be an area that attracts interprofessional interest (except perhaps from a medical or technologically oriented perspective), nor consideration within any child care and protection assessment framework.

A major outcome considered in this chapter is the overall effect of the circumstances of VLBW that can impinge on the attachment process between compromised infants and their parents. A secure attachment relationship can do much to enhance the overall development of VLBW infants as they progress into childhood. The road can be fraught with challenges for many parents as their infants continue to experience chronic disease and in some cases disabilities. This is a vulnerable infant population, potentially exposed to numerous biopsychosocial challenges. All of these are individually worrying, but a direct consequential factor of VLBW is the unnatural, but at times necessary, physical and psychological separation between the infant and the parents. This separation experience has the ability to affect the attachment process, therefore influencing the security of the infant–parent attachment relationship (Goldberg and Di Vitto 2002). This poses a number of challenges in relation to the global development of the child. For some parents taking their fragile infant home from hospital does not lead to the much longed for security of normality, because more frequent feeding and other specialist requirements have to be considered within the context of other family commitments. This situation can increase tension and conflict relating to roles and expectations of other family members. Within such a context are many factors that may lead to neglectful child care, whether intentional or otherwise.

For committed and sensitive parents with appropriate support networks the challenge of parenting is awesome. For less resilient parents, or for those whose social, psychological or environmental circumstances are compromised, there is the potential for an increased chance that their preterm, VLBW infant's needs will not be safely met. There are those who will argue that there is little point in spending valuable resources on the study of this population because they account only for approximately 2% of national births. While this may be the case, we would argue that although the actual numbers may be low, the antecedent risk factors and resulting consequences in delivery of the preterm, VLBW infant need to be addressed in practice. Many of the risk factors relating to neglect and preterm births are reducible and in some cases avoidable.

The very low birth weight infant

In developed countries infants classified as of either very or extremely low birth weight are also likely to have been born preterm (Wilcox 2001) – that is, before

37 weeks gestation. Figure 11.1 provides a summary of classification adapted from the World Health Organization (2003)

Table 11.1 Definitions of term, preterm and birth weight of newborn infants

Infant	Definition
Term infant	Born **at or after** 37 completed weeks of gestation
Preterm infant	Born **before** 37 completed weeks of gestation
Very preterm infant	Born **before** 32 completed weeks of gestation
Extremely preterm infant	Born **before** 28 completed weeks of gestation
Low birth weight (LBW)	Birth weight **less than** 2500 grams
Very low birth weight (VLBW)	Brith weight **less than** 1500 grams
Extremely low birth weight (ELBW)	Birth weight **less than** 1000 grams

The more preterm the birth and the lower the birth weight, the greater the chance of problems immediately following birth and indeed in the longer term. The general consensus within the literature (Birch and O'Connor 2001; Darlow *et al.* 1997; Foulder-Hughes and Cooke 2003; Horbar *et al.* 2002; Strathearn *et al.* 2001; Valkama 2000; Waugh *et al.* 1996) is that infants born at the earlier extremes of gestational age present with greater risk of:

- experiencing higher rates of mortality
- requiring more medical and nursing interventions
- carrying a greater burden of morbidity.

And whilst the mortality rate for infants weighing less than 1500 grams in industrialized countries has fallen over the last 30 years, from 50% to 15–20% (Valkama 2000), it is still a major challenge. These outcomes are quite different compared with infants born closer to term.

When a VLBW infant is born active resuscitation is likely to be required. The parents in all likelihood are ill-prepared for such events. Instead of a healthy and robust infant comforted by parental warmth, there is a mottled and limp 'rag-doll' that hardly resembles a baby at all. This 'worm-like' creature (parental quote) that would fit in the palm of an adult hand is then quickly removed into the neonatal intensive care unit, placed in an incubator, with tubes and machines and lights and noises and alarms…very frightening, very unexpected, and very very threatening.

Preterm, VLBW infants are not a homogenous group, therefore their needs vary. The earlier the gestational age at birth the more physiological functions are compromised and thus more interventions are required which although life saving, can also be harmful to an infant of such small stature (Fraser Askin 2001). The margin for error therefore remains very narrow (Keeling, Bryan and Fearne 1999). The optimal intrauterine environment ideal for the developing foetus is not readily available for the infant following birth (Goldberg and Di Vitto 2002). Aggressive interventions, longer hospital stays, readmissions to hospital and lingering health problems have an attendant effect on the direct physical interaction and proximity experience between the infant and the parents.

The double whammy

There is now extensive evidence that childhood experiences have a substantial influence on brain development. For all parents this can be challenging, but for those with a preterm, VLBW infant the obstacles facing the immediate and long-term goals of a healthy developing child can be immense. By their very being preterm, we argue that VLBW infants are potentially more vulnerable to neglect (and possibly abuse) when compared with their term counterparts. Meeting their complex and often diverse needs increases opportunities for negligent events. These may be accidental or intended acts of omission or exposure to harm within the environment, from infancy into childhood. Difficulties related to feeding, ongoing disease processes, neurological, behavioural and cognitive disabilities are just some of the components that increase the potential for neglectful events for the VLBW infant.

Contemporary data from the ongoing Avon Longitudinal Study of Parents and Children (ALSPAC) has reported that children born prematurely or with low birth weight are more than twice as likely to be maltreated subsequently than are children of normal birth weight (Sidebotham, Heron and The ALSPAC Study Team 2003). There are numerous postulations threaded throughout the literature for explaining such findings – such infants may be less attractive to their parents; there is disruption to the bonding process; and there is increased health surveillance – all of which probably have some substance. It is important to note that the majority of low birth weight children are not subsequently abused or neglected and thus low birth weight should not be used as a predictive factor (Sidebotham et al. 2003). The ALSPAC Team are finding though that birth weight, health, hospital readmission, development and behaviour are important variables in children who are subsequently placed on the child protection register. Given that the VLBW child is likely to experience all of these factors, it is not too great a leap to suggest that such findings highlight the vulnerable status of the VLBW infant.

The factors that lead to VLBW are also factors that have independently been identified as potentially associated with child neglect thus highlighting the double vulnerability of this population:

1. The characteristics and consequences of VLBW may enhance risk of neglect.

2. The pre-existing parental and environmental circumstances at the time of birth, which may have contributed to prematurity and low weight birth, also present a potential for ongoing neglect.

Characteristics of the VLBW infant

Physiological frailties predispose the vulnerable VLBW infant to increased susceptibility to damage of the vital brain structures resulting in neurosensory disabilities (Valkama 2000). Disabilities of this nature are considered an important measure of long-term outcomes among preterm infants, of which the main examples are:

- cerebral palsy
- visual difficulties and blindness
- hearing loss and deafness
- learning disabilities and developmental delay.

Although mortality rates for VLBW have reduced significantly over the last 30 years, morbidity rates have not fallen at a similar pace, although morbidity is improving. A number of robust studies collated in a meta analysis have demonstrated that in industrialized countries the percentage of surviving VLBW infants experiencing no disability has increased from 25% to 50% (Lee et al. 1995). Other studies support this view, reporting lower rates of disability compared to 20 and 30 years ago (Escobar, Littenberg and Petitti 1991; Hack et al. 2000; Piecuch, Leonard and Cooper 1998). This is all good news. However, it is the ELBW infant that now poses greater concerns and challenges with regards to disabilities (Muraskas et al. 1999; Vohr and Wright 2000). One study followed prospectively for four years 352 extremely low birth weight infants. Fifteen per cent of those children were referred to child protection services. Cognitive development in children referred for neglect was significantly delayed (Strathearn et al. 2001).

Indeed it is the long-term consequences that are worrying. There is growing evidence that very preterm infants, previously considered unscathed in the pre-school period, are now demonstrating greater difficulties when entering formal education (Foulder-Hughes and Cooke 2003; Hogan and Park

2000; Sullivan and McGrath 2003). Recent neuropsychological assessments have identified varying problems relating to language, visual-spatial dysfunction and daily living skills in the pre-school and older child and adolescent (Darlow *et al.* 1997; Minde 2000; Valkama 2000).

Another area of concern relating to preterm birth is that of behavioural outcomes and psychopathology. A number of studies suggest that although many preterm, VLBW infants are of normal intelligence, a higher proportion go on to experience problems associated with eating difficulties, fussiness and over-activity, temper tantrums, attention seeking and poor concentration (Minde 2000; Szatmari *et al.* 1993).

In summary, therefore, preterm, VLBW infants are at increased risk of a range of neurological and cognitive disabilities. Higher levels of behavioural problems are also found within this population. The special needs of these children can increase their potential vulnerability to neglect, whether intentional or otherwise. For some parents this challenge creates extra stress within the family.

Parental and environmental circumstances

Most VLBW infants are born preterm and some 20–30% of these deliveries occur spontaneously and without a recognizable cause following an uncomplicated preterm labour (Mires and Patel 1999). There are a number of risk factors, however, that are recognized as predisposing mothers to early labour (Steer and Flint 1999):

- cervical weakness
- premature rupture of membranes
- infection
- multiple pregnancy
- age of mother (under 15 years and advanced maternal age)
- previous preterm infant
- lower socioeconomic class
- being unmarried or unsupported
- being underweight
- cigarette smoking
- drug use.

There are a number of biological factors influencing the length of the pregnancy, but also a range of socioeconomic and psychosocial factors. Adverse pregnancy outcomes generally rise with increasing socioeconomic disadvantage (Kramer *et al.* 2001; Kramer *et al.* 2000). There is still a lack of clear under-standing of the interplay between those risk factors but it has been suggested that lifestyles and even parenting styles more commonly adopted by families within lower socioeconomic groups can be disadvantageous to the pregnancy (Kramer *et al.* 2000). Smoking, for example, is a more common activity within this group and is a major indicator of low birth weight. We would agree with Spencer and Baldwin (Chapter Two), however, that the chronic stressors related to socioeconomically disadvantaged mothers and their families are embedded within their environment. Indeed, one of the variables frequently used to measure disadvantage is that of low birth weight. Poor living condi-tions related to financial insecurities; poor and overcrowded housing; and unsupportive relationships can all erode personal resilience factors. Kramer *et al.* (2001) suggest that this leads to feelings of helplessness; heightened per-ceived stress; anxiety and depression. Of particular interest is the presence and quality of social support networks. Previous research has identified that quality support from others, especially intimate partners, can buffer the effects of stressful events (Kramer *et al.* 2001).

Regardless of the exact nature of the links between disadvantage and VLBW, the VLBW infant born into a deprived household will be affected by that environment anyway, and, like other children in poor circumstances, may be at increased risk of referral for neglect.

Issues of environment

The unique birth experience, intensive care and medical sequelae for VLBW infants create a particular circumstantial chain whereby vulnerability of the child to neglect may be increased. Although we do not at all suggest neglect as a probable outcome of VLBW, it is a possibility. Practitioners need to be aware that the child's environment, both pre and post-discharge from hospital, affords another potential arena for neglect in the VLBW infant.

The hospital environment

It is a general expectation that patients will be well cared for within an institu-tion, such as a hospital, and will not come to any harm because of being in such a place (Bross 2001). This expectation is of course questionable. Institutional abuse and neglect is defined as:

> …any system, program policy, procedure, or individual interaction with a child in placement that abuses, neglects, or is detrimental to the child's health, safety, or emotional and physical well-being or in any way exploits or violates the child's basic rights. (Gil 1982, p.9)

Neglect could be envisaged when policies and protocols within a hospital and in particular the neonatal and obstetric areas, do not meet the needs of the VLBW infant and the parents. This includes obtaining the resources, staff, equipment and environment to provide an adequate standard of care. For example, the neonatal intensive care area may be closed due to a lack of equipment or trained staff and consequently preterm, VLBW infants need to be transferred to another centre. The cost to the infant in terms of medical risk is great, further complicated by increasing separation from the parents in physical (geographical) terms, but also psychologically. Another factor, not unrelated, is the ratio of staff to infants within the neonatal unit. Iatrogenic complications become more common when staff workloads are higher, leading to a reduction of surveillance and an increased variability in nursing skills. VLBW infants exposed to this environment are at greater risk of mortality and morbidity (Callaghan et al. 2003).

Programme neglect refers to a fall in what have become acceptable standards of care. In accordance with present-day standards neonatal nurses are aware of the need to promote attachment and to incorporate parents in the decision-making process (Lawhorn 2002). Indeed recent debate in the literature has begun to question who in fact owns the child in hospital (Shields et al. 2003), emphasizing the importance of communication between staff and parents.

The home environment

Once VLBW infants have reached a point where their *expected* birth weight is attained and they are physiologically stable, they are discharged home to parental full-time care. Yet these are still very small and very vulnerable infants. The parents suddenly become sole providers for an infant that has experienced profound insult and interruption to normal development. The early disruptions of the biological and social aspects associated with preterm birth reduce the time parents have in their preparation for parenthood, or in making the pragmatic home preparations necessary when having a baby. The degree of perceived stress attributed to the pregnancy and the events of labour and the delivery have been found to influence emotional processing of parents. Those parents found to be preoccupied with past perceived stressful events experience greater difficulties adjusting to parenthood which affects their availability for their infant (Dulude et al. 2002). Increasing anxiety and low confidence levels in parenting ability is, quite predictably, the experience of parents when caring for their VLBW infant in the home environment.

Previous studies have demonstrated that mothers of preterm, VLBW infants experienced episodes of anxiety and depression and are predominantly socioeconomically disadvantaged, having poor quality social support networks, and are often single mothers (Dulude et al. 2002; Kramer et al. 2000;

Mackey, Williams and Tiller 2000; Steer and Flint 1999). Mental health problems experienced by the mother in the antenatal and postnatal period are recognized as having harmful effects on the attachment relationship. This makes commitment to the attachment process far more challenging and increases the risk of parents not being available for their infant (Shandor Miles *et al.* 1999). Indeed preterm, VLBW infants are more vulnerable to relationship disharmony, especially if the parents are experiencing some degree of psychological dysfunction in the form of depression or severe anxiety – which given the circumstances would not be unusual.

The complications of VLBW not only prolong hospitalization following birth, but are instrumental in the development of chronic health problems throughout childhood. The development of chronic lung disease (CLD) and other related conditions can predispose the VLBW infant to ongoing problems. Discharge home with supplementary oxygen therapy is sometimes an outcome. However, infants with lung disease can endure difficulties with feeding, oesophageal reflux, poor weight gain, developmental delay and ongoing chronic lung problems (Avent, Coile and Mathai 2001; McLean *et al.* 2000; Shaw 1999).

Professionals in the field often use weight gain as a marker of health and development. However, there are many intervening variables that influence the process of weight gain. Many VLBW infants are discharged home requiring a very frequent feeding regime throughout a 24-hour period. Bottle-feeding can be a slow process and for others tube-feeding is the only means of providing dietary requirements. Meeting the correct calorific and environmental needs to promote growth, especially when the infant requires supplementary oxygen, can be problematic. Other influences in the weight gain process are the characteristics and skills of the parents. Much depends on their availability, sensitivity, commitment and understanding of the technicalities involved in their infant's care. Caring for a baby with the degree of special needs that are common with VLBW can be physically and emotionally draining. On top of the practical and physical problems are the difficulties relating to infant temperament. More often than not they are fussy infants, taking longer to settle, and they appear to be more emotionally demanding. While these infants do require the necessary stimulation for development they have more limited boundaries for interaction, becoming over-aroused more easily. This picture identifies a number of threads that create an environment leading to a greater vulnerability to neglect.

Attachment

The circumstances relating to conception and the early birth of an infant can also influence the attachment process. In the 1980s parental experiences of attachment with preterm infants were found to be problematic. However, these difficulties were time limited and the majority went on to develop secure relationships (Goldberg 1988; Goldberg *et al.* 1986). This knowledge is comforting. However, the boundaries of viability have moved beyond those perceived appropriate in the early 1980s. Survival of infants born as early as 23 weeks gestation, weighing less than 1000 grams, is more common but they are cared for in a highly technical environment where their physiological condition is monitored continuously. This requires a clinically skilful approach to care with minimal interference. The physiological needs of the infant at this time are paramount, with the psychological needs of the parents falling into second place.

Further, these are parents who are not only unable to fulfil any of the normal parenting roles, they are very often unable to hold or at times even touch their infant. Visual closeness too can be partially obscured by necessary equipment, while at the same time this closeness can be influenced by the infant's appearance, behaviour and disease experiences (Brunssen and Miles 1996). Anxiety relating to the possible loss of their infant is gradually replaced by concerns about the long-term future. Some mothers have reported that feelings of anticipating the loss of their baby has influenced their ability to become psychologically close, therefore placing the attachment process on hold (Feldman *et al.* 1999; McHaffie 1990). This acute stressful experience becomes more chronic as the infant experiences more crisis situations through illness events. The burden for parents can be immense as they attempt to meet other family responsibilities while at the same time visit their hospitalized infant. In some circumstances, visiting patterns change and become more infrequent reducing further physical contact and interaction. These circumstances have been recognized for many years as influencing negatively the attachment relationship between a mother and her infant (Sandford Zeskind and Iacino 1984) and in some cases this has contributed to later abuse and neglect (Fanaroff, Kennell and Klaus 1972).

Messages from research

- Very low birth weight infants born at the early extremes of viability are generally more at risk of death or disability.

- There is an association between neglect and children with disabilities. A substantial number of very low birth weight infants experience some residual disability.

- The extreme and very preterm infant is at increased risk of developing some degree of cognitive developmental delay.

- Very low birth weight infants and their parents more commonly experience greater periods of physical and psychological separation immediately following birth and for some time after.

- Parents take longer to get to know their infants, with a potential impact, therefore, on the attachment process.

- Parents of VLBW infants may find them difficult or unattractive.

- Institutional arrangements can in themselves be considered neglectful, reducing infant and parental proximity and affecting the attachment process.

- Very low birth weight infants require more frequent feeding than term infants when discharged home. They may also have special needs in relation to the process of feeding or oxygen therapy.

- There is an association between cognitive developmental delay and neglect in extremely low birth weight infants whose parents are socioeconomically disadvantaged.

- The vulnerability factors associated with preterm labour are closely matched to the factors associated with children being referred for neglect.

Exploring practice implications: interactive framework to guide practice

We suggest an interactive framework as a model for guiding practice (see Figure 11.1). The framework consists of three separate yet interactive components that are shown as layers. The lower component represents clinical governance that contains the essential elements required to provide the infrastructures for quality care. Clinical governance and all the elements should be visualized as the building blocks to support evidenced-based practice within all service delivery points. Clinical governance is structured within a multidisciplinary context. The second or middle layer in the framework is communication that is composed of a number of elements, or processes, necessary to deliver interventions within the service delivery points. The third and final component within the framework is that of service delivery.

To support practitioners in the development of their practice we aim to use a single case study of a young woman called Marsha and her story is presented in four parts, each representing a service delivery point found within the framework. Marsha is fictitious, but her history demonstrates the diversity and complexity of circumstances often experienced by parents of preterm, VLBW infants.

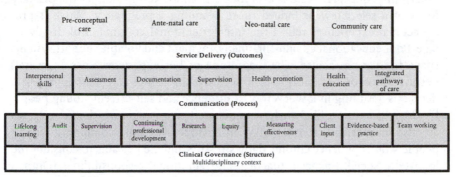

Figure 11.1 Interactive framework to support parents of preterm, very low birth weight infants

Pre-conceptual care

Box 11.1 Case history: Marsha's Story: Pre-conceptual period

Marsha is 17 years of age and lives with her 34-year-old mother and 15-year-old brother in a rundown council estate within the central belt of Scotland. Marsha and her mother have a volatile relationship that often results in Marsha leaving home for short periods. Her brother Tom has attention deficit disorder and has been excluded from school on a number of occasions. Tom has also been in trouble with the police. Marsha left school without gaining any qualifications and has not been able to obtain full-time employment. She has a boyfriend called Jim who is also unemployed and lives with his sister. Marsha and Jim frequently drink alcohol and both are prone to binge drinking at the weekends. Due to their intake of alcohol both Marsha and Jim use their shoplifting skills to supplement their low income. Jim has a previous conviction for stealing cars. Their relationship is also volatile and Jim has physically abused Marsha twice, once causing her to be admitted to hospital for treatment. They have an active sexual relationship without using any form of contraception.

Today, pre-conceptual care is everyone's business and no longer the primary focus of a select few or indeed those planning a pregnancy. Marsha's pre-conceptual experiences reflect the intergenerational continuum of disadvantage. Poor educational attainment, unemployment and volatile support systems shape her very existence. The magnitude of her experiences has an overall negative effect on her ability to form secure relationships and make appropriate decisions, resulting in low levels of confidence and self-esteem. Young people like Marsha are more likely to have unplanned pregnancies which in some cases are also unwanted. Preterm, VLBW infants are also more common in young people who experience chronic daily stressors and are less able to consider the long-term social, financial, practical and emotional responsibilities (Dignan 2000).

The Scottish Executive in Nursing for Health (Elliott *et al.* 2001) has redirected the focus of nursing practice from a medical to a more social and community development model. Health promotion activities require practitioners to work with service users and other disciplines at the community level, while at the same time playing a major part in empowering individuals through appropriate health education.

An example of this multidisciplinary action is highlighted through two recent government initiatives to address the exclusion factors recognized as having a negative effect on the global development of children and families living with some degree of disadvantage. Sure Start initiatives and the New Community Schools project aspired to enhance the development of children by supporting their environment, including families and local communities. The main objectives for both projects are listed in Table 11.2.

Table 11.2 Objectives for Sure Start and the New Community Schools projects

Sure Start Initiatives	New Community Schools
Improve children's social and emotional development	Equip pupils with knowledge and skills to make health-related decisions
Improve children's health	Encouragement of healthy lifestyles
Improve children's ability to learn	Promotion of self-esteem for all pupils and their families
Strengthen families and communities	
	Positive staff–pupils relations
	Good links between the school and home

Evidence from the United States, where similar initiatives have been ongoing for much longer, are positive, recognizing that early interventions and ongoing support throughout childhood has many positive effects (Rivers *et al.* 1999). The overall effect of such interventions is to improve the individual's global development through family and community support. This can reduce vulnerability to unplanned, unwanted pregnancies, preterm labour and childhood neglect. The aspiration would be to reduce the likelihood of other young women finding themselves in the same position as Marsha.

Antenatal Care

Box 11.2 Marsha's story: Antenatal period

Marsha thought that she was pregnant but was very unsure about what to do or who to tell. She eventually went to see her GP. Her pregnancy was confirmed and she was found to be at approximately 22 weeks gestation. She told her boyfriend about the baby. Her mother wanted her to 'get rid of the baby' while Jim was very pleased with the news. Marsha attended the local antenatal clinic but only on the second appointment. Marsha felt very frightened and uncomfortable with the way she was spoken to on that occasion. She avoided telling the doctors and midwives about her alcohol use and the fact that she felt that she did not want the baby. Marsha's mother was not pleased about the pregnancy and threatened to kick Marsha out of the house. When she was 26 weeks pregnant Marsha started to feel unwell but could not say exactly what was wrong. She had pain in her back and her abdomen and she felt that she was dribbling urine constantly. This went on for two days before she went to see her GP. She was admitted to the local labour ward where she was found to be in preterm labour. Marsha delivered a daughter weighing 890 grams (1lb 9oz). The baby was immediately transferred to the neonatal intensive care unit. The baby required support with breathing and was to go on and develop many other problems. Marsha was on her own throughout this experience. She felt very frightened and did not understand what was happening to her. Nobody asked her how she was feeling and she could not stop crying. A doctor, caring for her infant, stated that her infant was very ill and might not live. He left a Polaroid photograph of her baby but Marsha could hardly make out what was actually in the picture. Marsha was now more upset and very concerned about her baby. She felt alone and isolated but did not want to call her mother or her boyfriend who was out drinking with his friends. Marsha felt that the midwives did not understand how she was feeling.

Antenatal care extends from confirmation of pregnancy through to delivery, marking an important step in the transition to parenthood. Marsha's story, a realistic portrayal for some, highlights a number of issues related to the practice of midwifery (see Box 11.2).

Midwives are ideally positioned to identify circumstances such as parental behaviours and ambivalent attitudes that may lead to disruption of the parent–infant attachment relationship (Chapman 2002). Yet styles of communication adopted by nurses and midwives have in the past received some negative attention (Coyle 1999; Johnson and Webb 1995; Kirkham 1989) with the 'inverse care law', first described by Hart (1971), as relating to those in greatest need of health care being associated with the poorest provision. This has been identified as a continuing problem in midwifery practice (Kirkham *et al.* 2002) and questions the transparency of clinical governance within midwifery practice.

Interpersonal communication skills influence the degree and quality of engagement between the midwife and client. Documenting assessment findings, for example, supports planning of care while at the same time enabling a means of measuring effectiveness through audit. There are many positive outcomes that are achievable through the development of sensitive, responsive, trusted and therapeutic engagements with clients, including:

- systematic assessment of needs
- identification of interventions to promote positive parenting
- involvement of other disciplines to meet identified need
- sharing of health education information.

Due to their immediate circumstances greater effort is required to engage in an effective interaction with women experiencing socioeconomic and psychosocial disadvantage as they are the very individuals who perhaps more than others experience difficulties in the transition to parenthood. The barriers that can prevent expectant mothers receiving information can be usefully overcome by enhancing the quality of professional communication, including:

- being aware of the quantity of information given to parents
- being careful of the language and jargon
- taking culture into consideration
- accounting for age, experience, education, motivation and belief systems
- making oneself open and accessible to the parents
- assessing the need for and extent of knowledge
- reducing competing commitments.

Neonatal Care

Box 11.3 Marsha's story: Neonatal and after-care

On her arrival on the neonatal unit a nurse told Marsha to wash her hands before touching anything. When shown her daughter Marsha could not believe that this was her daughter. She had never seen anything like this before. The infant was in an incubator surrounded by lots of tubes and wires. The infant's eyes were covered and her skin looked 'see through' and very red. Her legs were moving in jerky movements. Marsha was terrified to touch her, which was just as well because the nurse caring for the infant told her not to. Marsha felt sick because she was in so much pain, the room was hot and all the noises and lights from the monitors were frightening. The nurse told Marsha very little about her infant and Marsha was scared to ask. She only stayed for a short time and returned to her room where she cried herself to sleep. Marsha did not return to see her infant until Jim appeared on the third day. Marsha and Jim felt they were treated coldly by the staff and were repeatedly informed that their daughter was very sick and might not survive. They named their daughter Tanya. Marsha and Jim visited their daughter daily for the first few weeks but they soon became tired of the same old routine. Tanya experienced a number of serious setbacks, however by the time she was four months old was developing well. Her parents were now attending more frequently and taking greater responsibility for their daughter's care. Marsha lacked confidence in this area and was often criticized by the nursing staff or Jim for not doing things properly. Tanya was slow to feed by bottle and this area of Tanya's care made Marsha feel frustrated, often leaving a nurse to take over and complete the feed. By the time Tanya was ready for discharge at four and a half months old her parents were living together in a third floor, two-bedroomed council flat. Marsha was to 'stay in' the hospital with her daughter for 24 hours to get used to caring for her on a continuous basis. At this time Marsha was feeling very low and considered walking out. The next day she took her daughter home with a list of instructions. Tanya's parents were told that the health visitor would visit in a few days. Marsha was given a follow-up appointment for her daughter in two weeks time.

The neonatal period extends from the time of birth until the twenty-eighth day of life. For the very preterm, VLBW infant the majority of hospitalization days extend beyond these 28, but they remain within the neonatal intensive care unit (see Box 11.3). The process of delivering neonatal intensive care often takes place within a bright but artificially lit, often noisy, hot and highly technical environment. This is necessary to support infants requiring extensive medical and nursing interventions to sustain and maintain life.

Marsha's experiences reflect the strangeness of the parental position in the neonatal environment. Her anxieties and discomfort are compounded by her social isolation. The neonatal staff offered no support to Marsha at a time when she was struggling to come to terms with parenthood. Failing to assess Marsha's needs therefore did not set the scene for future parenting preparation (Bialoskurski, Cox and Wiggins 2002).

With good interpersonal communication skills neonatal nurses can use their knowledge base and technical nursing ability to:

- provide parents with information about their infant therefore empowering their position as parents and addressing the power imbalance often experienced at this time

- draw parents into the cycle of providing and caring for their infant by encouraging breast milk production and active visiting, to 'be with' their infant

- supporting parents to maintain contact with their infant and to gain a balanced and realistic set of expectations of the short and long-term outcomes

- carry out an ongoing assessment of parental needs.

As Riley (2000) suggests in relation to nursing in general, 'despite the complexity of technology and the demands on a nurse's time it is the intimate moments of connection that can make all the difference in the quality of care and meaning for the client and the nurse'.

Riley clearly identifies that even in our technological world the (neonatal) nurse's communication skills remain a major source of comfort (or discomfort) for parents, while at the same time acting as a catalyst for education, enabling parents to learn and develop new skills, attitudes and behaviours.

There is growing evidence to highlight the important role and influence of neonatal nurses in the promotion of the attachment relationship between parents and their very preterm, VLBW infant (Curran, Brighton and Murphy 1997; Franck, Bernal and Gale 2002; Moore 2000). In the early days physical proximity is often not possible, however psychological closeness can be enhanced through day-to-day 'chatting' between the nurse and the parents about daily happenings (Fenwick, Barclay and Schmied 2001). As the infant passes the unstable phase parents will gradually experience more psychologically pleasing and physically interactive experiences with their infant, for example by:

- talking
- touching
- massage
- skin-to-skin contact
- feeding
- moving from incubator to cot
- dressing infant for the first time
- bottle/breast feeding
- playing.

Becoming involved in care enables the parents to develop a sensitive and confident understanding of their infant's developmental needs. Nursing skills are therefore pertinent in teaching and enabling parents to 'read' their infants safely, identifying their needs from a very early age (Gottesman 1999). Many specialized neonatal units have integrated protocols for discharge planning incorporating positive parenting approaches in preparation for going home. The aims of such interventions are to move from the medicalization of care towards parental recognition of infant need. Parents also learn about community resources to support their parenting (Pearson and Anderson 2001).

After-care in the community

Box 11.4 Marsha's story: After-care in the community

Marsha was pleased to be home but was anxious about caring for her baby. Feeding Tanya took a long time and she was often sick. Jim helped to prepare the milk feeds but was reluctant to attend to Tanya's other needs. Marsha was becoming very tired and resentful at always having to drop everything to attend to her daughter. During the night, Tanya was being left to cry for longer periods. Jim would shout at Marsha if Tanya cried. This became an area of friction between Marsha and Jim.

The family health visitor (HV) knew nothing of the family until the day of Tanya's discharge. Tanya had been discharged for five days before the health visitor called unexpectedly. She arrived at 4pm to find Marsha and Tanya at home. She heard Marsha shouting at the infant. Marsha told the HV that she was tired but managing. Marsha looked tired, was still in her night clothes and her breath smelt of alcohol. The living area was cluttered with clothes and used nappies. Tanya continued to cry, look anxious and pale. The HV left after 15 minutes, saying she would return the following week. The HV recorded the visit in the case files. She had a gut feeling that things were not going well, but knew nothing about preterm babies.

Over the next few weeks Marsha's limited ability to care for her infant became more obvious. Jim was rarely at home. During her second out-patient appointment Tanya was noted to be very pale and dehydrated and had lost weight. Marsha stated that she could not look after her daughter. Tanya was taken into care following social work intervention. Following a case conference four weeks later Tanya was returned to her mother's care. One month later, Tanya was noted to have lost weight, was becoming more irritable and was not reaching developmental milestones. She also had a severe skin rash over her buttocks where the skin was exco-riated and bleeding. Marsha admitted that she had been feeding Tanya on cow's milk, as she had run out of baby milk. She also stated that some-times she left Tanya alone in the house while she went to the shop to buy alcohol. She did not always hear Tanya crying through the night there-fore she had missed out on her night feeds. Tanya was admitted to hospital for investigations and treatment. She was found to be dehy-drated, hypothermic and septicaemic.

Moving from secondary to community care can be problematic especially for parents who are taking their infant home for the first time and who experience many challenges to test their confidence (see Box 11.4). The degree of prepara-tion is therefore important. Neonatal units approach this area of planning jointly with many of their community colleagues. For Marsha there was little evidence of preparation for discharge or planning of supports. The health visitor lacked the skills to support a vulnerable family. She obviously worked in an area without the infrastructures needed to support quality care and safe practice. Marsha's experiences reflect institutional neglect.

Standard neonatal practice is now focused on planned neonatal discharge with early follow-up within secondary care within a multidisciplinary context. The aims of such approaches are the early recognition of abnormality in relation to the physical, emotional and social development of the infant and planning of appropriate interventions to support parents in the care of their infant and therefore reduce further possible morbidity.

Integrated pathways of care are designed for specific clinical conditions, identifying the necessary tasks and sequencing of those tasks and indicating which discipline should carry out the task. Documentation is carried out through a single multidisciplinary record. They encourage the tracking of outcomes for individuals and groups to identify variation between expected and actual outcomes (Campbell *et al.* 1998). There is little evidence though that such pathways are in use within antenatal services within the UK. Clearly, there is an advantage to developing such a system for the care of parents and their preterm, VLBW infants in an effort to support their transition to parenthood.

Messages for practice

- Clinical governance infrastructures support the use of evidence-based practices.

- Professionals who care for VLBW infants also have an active role to play in the prevention of childhood neglect and in the management of child protection policies.

- Assessment of individuals or families, by all nursing and midwifery practitioners, requires the use of a framework that enables recognition of child protection issues.

- Interpersonal communication skills are the means by which practitioners develop relationships with clients at the interface of care.

- Practitioners' communication skills are pivotal in the identification of physical, psychological or social factors relating to the parents' ability to care for their VLBW infant safely.

- Equity is a concept that needs to be explored by all in health care to ensure that those in greatest need are in receipt of appropriate care and services.

- Parents of VLBW infants need to be involved in the decision-making process at all levels.

- Multidisciplinary discharge planning for VLBW infants needs to be initiated early to enable the appropriate support necessary for parents.

- Excellent, open and two-way communication is required between secondary and primary care services.

- Audit can be very useful in ensuring effective services for parents and their VLBW infants.

Chapter 12

Parental Substance Misuse and the Implications for Children

Lessons from Research and Practice in one Family Centre

Moira Walker and Mary Glasgow

Introduction

Over the last few years protecting children from harm resulting from their parents' substance misuse has emerged as one of the key challenges facing child welfare services. The number of parents using drugs has increased dramatically, alongside heightened awareness of the potentially damaging effects on children's lives and development. This chapter focuses on what has been learned about how best to support children whose parents are problem drug users. One of the authors is a researcher, the other a practitioner. We start from the premise that research findings and practice experience are complementary sources of knowledge, of equal value and with much to be gained from developing links between the two. In terms of practice we draw primarily on how one family centre goes about safeguarding children and supporting parents affected by drug misuse. We illustrate what the work entails at the micro level, that is engaging, working and talking with parents and children on a day-to-day basis. These accounts are offered in the belief that there is much to be learned from practice, but we make no claim that the ways of working described here are necessarily different or more effective than those adopted in other services or settings. An independent evaluation of the centre has recently been commissioned and will report on the nature and effectiveness of its work in due course.

The terms 'substance' and 'misuse', as used in the chapter, require some comment. 'Misuse' is taken to mean that the level of dependency or consumption of a substance is significant enough to impact on family life and potentially on the care of children. The term 'substance' is used to include drugs, alcohol or other mood-altering chemicals such as solvents. In the experience of staff at the centre, the impact on children can be broadly similar, irrespective of whether parents become dependent on alcohol or drugs. Both can result in serious physical and emotional neglect through insufficient supervision and care, chaotic lifestyles, lack of money and many other associated problems. Alcohol is more often accompanied by violence within the home. However, whereas alcohol is widely used and accepted in our culture, drugs are illegal and feared. This means drug use is more shameful and hidden, while obtaining a regular supply can take over and change a parent's way of life. Involvement in the criminal justice system in not unusual, often for shoplifting or prostitution, and can result in parents going to prison. The consequent disruption to children's lives is obvious.

Because of the distinctive ways in which drugs affect family life and since concern about the effects of parental drug use has captured professional and public attention to a far greater extent than the longer-standing problem of parental alcoholism, the practice described in the chapter is with families where parents' substance use includes, though may not be restricted to, illegal drugs.

The social and professional context

Any professional working with families will be well aware that risk to children from parental drug misuse is currently a major concern, not only for child welfare services, but also for the public at large. During the last five years the growth of interest in this topic has been quite dramatic. As recently as 1999, in an article which argued for more attention to the effects of drug misuse on parenting, Barnard implied that it might be considered offensive to question the parenting capacity of a whole group of parents but that the issue is 'serious in its import' (Barnard 1999).

Since the late 1990s the case has been well made for proactive consideration of children's welfare when parents are known to use drugs (Kroll 2003; Kroll and Taylor 2000). Interest has been fuelled by awareness of an increasing number of children affected by parental drug use and recognition among professionals of some of the potentially harmful consequences (Harbin 2000; Kroll and Taylor 2000). In addition, media coverage of a number of situations where children of drug-using parents were seriously harmed brought the matter to the attention of the wider public (Hannah 2000). As a result it is no longer considered offensive to question the parental capacity of drug-using parents. Rather it is widely accepted that all professionals who come into contact with adults using drugs should take steps to understand how this affects any children for whom they are responsible.

Numbers of children affected

Information on the number of children affected by parental drug misuse can only be approximate. A recent review carried out by the Advisory Council on the Misuse of Drugs estimated that, in Scotland, there are between 41,000 and 59,000 children whose mother or father is a problem drug user (Home Office 2003). This represents 4–6% of all children under 16. The estimated number for England and Wales was between 200,000 and 300,000, this being 2–3% of all children under 16.

The same review requested information from maternity and social work services across the UK. Responses from maternity units indicated that approximately 1% of babies were born to problem drug users, and a similar proportion to problem drinkers. Social work services estimated that parental problem drug or alcohol use featured in a quarter of cases where children's names were placed on the child protection register. In over 80% of authorities, staff routinely asked about drug and alcohol problems in the family, but only 43% provided specific services for drug-using parents and their dependent children.

The social context

In a society characterized by its pervasive preoccupation with risk (Beck 1992; Giddens 1994), drug use and the safety of children are key concerns. Both issues attract intense media and political attention, often being portrayed as indications of social malaise or even the disintegration of society. It has been argued that illicit drug use is particularly abhorred in mothers because they are seen as rejecting the traditional role of motherhood and thus threatening the stability of the family (Taylor 1993).

There is considerable evidence that moral considerations and wider social attitudes strongly influence social workers' assessments of parental capacity and children's well-being (Parton *et al.* 1997). Thus social workers have been found to view heroin use as inherently more problematic than alcohol misuse, even though the effects on children may be similar (Forrester 2000). This means that when assessing the risks parental substance misuse pose in a particular family, additional rigour is needed to ensure decisions are based on accurate evidence rather than poorly informed and biased judgements.

Professional responses

Within the professional context, attention to the needs of children affected by parental drug misuse is consistent with increasing awareness of the potentially harmful ways in which inconsistent parenting, lack of care and chaotic family lifestyles can impact on the developing child (Stevenson 1996). Social workers are no longer to confine their concerns to risk of physical abuse in the present.

Rather, when assessing children's best interests, they are to take into account the effects of negative experiences over time.

Assessment has become a central and complex task for the social worker in child welfare. Assessing risks to children from parental drug use is evidently a very complex task. It is always incomplete, since workers can never know exactly what happens within a family. However the more parents and children trust the worker and are willing to discuss problems openly, the more reliable the assessment can be. Thus to work effectively in this field, workers requires considerable knowledge and skill in engaging with parents and children.

Staff also need to be well supported, with opportunities to review their practice critically. As Tanner and Turney (2003) remind us, over time workers can adjust their expectations downwards and stop seeing when levels of care have become unacceptable. In a similar vein, Stanley and Goddard argue that constant exposure to highly stressful situations can result in social workers unconsciously responding in ways which will protect themselves (Stanley and Goddard 2002). This might mean colluding with parents to overlook poor care, or precipitately removing children from situations where the workers feel threatened. Work with families affected by parental drug misuse is very demanding, so it will be more effective in situations where social workers are appropriately informed, skilled and supported.

What can we learn from research?

Links between parental substance misuse and child welfare

It is generally accepted that parental drug misuse does not necessarily result in children being harmed but that the effects on parenting cause sufficient concern to merit close examination (Barnard 1999; Cleaver *et al.* 1999; Kroll and Taylor 2000). Based on an extensive review of the literature, Cleaver and colleagues reported that there has been no systematic research into the association between problem drug misuse and child maltreatment.

A number of American studies have reported high levels of child maltreatment among substance misusers (Black and Mayer 1980; Jaudes, Ekwo and VanVoorhis 1995) and high levels of drug and alcohol misuse among children who have been abused or admitted to care (Famularo, Kinscherff and Fenton 1992). However these essentially confirm that maltreatment and substance misuse are often present as part of a cluster of characteristics associated with poverty and stress, rather than demonstrating any causal link.

A study by Luthar and colleagues set out to assess the impact of maternal drug use on children as opposed to other psychological disturbances such as depression (Luthar, D'Avanzo and Hites 2003). The findings indicated that maternal depression and anxiety affected children more adversely than drug use. This was consistent with other research evidence that children of drug users showed comparable or better adjustment than those whose mothers were depressed or anxious (Wakschlag and Hans 1999).

In the absence of a body of systematic research, the effects of drug use on child welfare can be inferred from five main sources:

- the effects of maternal drug misuse on babies and their subsequent care
- knowledge of how drug misuse affects parents
- perspectives of young people affected by parental drug misuse
- perspectives of mothers who misuse drugs
- research on the impact of parental alcohol abuse.

The effects of maternal drug use on babies and their subsequent care

There is an extensive medical literature on the effects of maternal drug use on the unborn child and infant. Kelley (1992) summarizes a range of symptoms which include stiffness, irritability, tremors, abnormal sleep patterns, feeding difficulties and over-reaction to sensory stimulation. In addition to the resultant distress to the babies, these symptoms make them difficult to care for and so increase their vulnerability to abuse. At the same time mothers who have continued to use drugs during pregnancy typically feel guilty, lack confidence and may be depressed. Kelley thus attributes the high rate of admission to foster care to difficulties in the interaction between child and mother.

Two British studies which followed the progress of babies born to drug dependent mothers also reported a high rate of social work intervention and admission to care, especially if the mother continued to use drugs (Alison 2000; Alison and Wyatt 1999; Fraser and Cavanagh 1991).

How drug misuse can affect parents and parenting

Acknowledging a dearth of specific research on this topic, Cleaver and colleagues drew on evidence from a range of sources to identify some ways in which drug misuse can adversely affect parents (Cleaver et al. 1999). They describe the impact of drug misuse on psychological state, family relationships and contacts with wider social networks.

In terms of the psychological state, drug-using parents may be subject to depression or mood swings or be emotionally unavailable for children because they are preoccupied with ensuring they have a regular supply of drugs. Each of these would be expected to interfere with the formation of secure attachment, while also potentially resulting in reduced attention to children's physical or emotional care. In practical terms, attendance at school and for medical appointments may be affected, while poor supervision can expose children to accidents or abuse by other people visiting the home. Parents' physical health may also be affected, resulting in hospitalization and periods of separation from the child. Of course many other lifestyle choices also result in mothers being separated from their child and/or preoccupied with matters outside the home.

Within the family, Cleaver and colleagues suggest that parental drug use can result in increased tension or exacerbate other problems. If drug-related tensions result in violence between parents, the experience is particularly harmful for children (Brandon and Lewis 1996; Morley and Mullender 1994). In addition the stigma and association with criminal activity can alienate extended family members, in which case children may become particularly isolated. Isolation can be exacerbated in school or the community, as children may be taunted because their parents are known drug users. In addition lack of money may deprive children of opportunities to attend clubs or take part in social activities.

This would suggest that children are harmed by the social consequences of parental drug use rather than the drug misuse itself, a point also highlighted by Bates and colleagues. In addition the social workers, drug workers and health visitors they interviewed made an important distinction between stable and chaotic drug use, believing that the former need not adversely affect children's welfare (Bates *et al.* 1999).

Nevertheless, it is evident that the social effects of parental drug use can potentially undermine the factors associated with resilience. Correspondingly, Cleaver and colleagues (1999) concluded that, while the impact varies according to age, it is likely to be less adverse when the child:

- has somewhere to go when the family home becomes unsafe
- regularly attends school or pre-school provision
- regularly attends school medicals
- has support from other adults, for example, teachers and other family members
- has a good friend or supportive older sibling
- belongs to clubs outside the home
- has acquired a range of coping strategies and is confident enough to know what to do when the parent(s) are incapacitated
- is in a family which has sufficient income and there are good physical standards in the home.

It follows that where services can boost protective aspects of children's environment, this will help minimize potentially negative effects.

The perspectives of children

Research on children's perspectives on parental drug or alcohol misuse is relatively rare, partly because the associated stigma makes it difficult to find
children who are willing to talk about it. Those who do have generally confirmed that they feel ashamed about their parents' behaviour and are often
reluctant to confide in friends or invite them to their home (Laybourn, Brown
and Hill 1997). Secrecy was even maintained within the home. The children
who spoke with Barnard and Barlow talked of knowing something unacceptable was going on and about their shock when they realized that their parents
were using drugs. Not all the children had told their parents that they now
knew about the drugs, so the secrecy was two-way. This level of secrecy and
denial means nothing is as it seems, so children do not learn to trust their own
perceptions or feelings (Barnard and Barlow 2003). Hoggan also highlighted
that the secrecy of drug use increases the burden on children, since their fears
and distress cannot be shared (Hoggan 2003). Correspondingly children interviewed by Harbin (2000) had observed more of their parents' drug-related
behaviour than parents thought.

Older children of parents who use alcohol have talked about being influenced to copy or model their parents behaviour, viewing drug or alcohol use as
a normal part of life. Some identified benefits, for example that their parents
were in a better mood when drunk. However many felt invisible, aware that
drugs were their parents' priority, and unable to talk to parents or anyone
outside the home about what was going on in their life (Laybourn *et al.* 1997).

The perspectives of mothers who use drugs

Reflecting that women are held responsible for most child care, studies of
parenting and drug use have focused primarily on the role of mothers (Turney
2000). Based on an ethnographic study of the lives of drug-using women in
Glasgow, Taylor reported a high level of concern for their children's welfare.
From pregnancy on women worried about the effects of their drug use on their
child and took what steps they could to minimize the harm. In spite of their
preoccupation with obtaining and administering drugs, Taylor reported that
most of their children were clean and well fed. The women interviewed were
critical of drug users who neglected their children and said that, in situations
where they felt their own capacity was in doubt, they would ask a relative to
care for their child (Taylor 1993).

Mothers interviewed by Elliot and Watson (2000) also reported that they
used a range of strategies to protect their children from the effects of their drug
use. These included only administering drugs when children were not present,
arranging for other family members to care for children at times of stress and
keeping them away from places where drug users congregated. Similar strate-

gies were reported by the parents interviewed by Hoggan (2003), but, under pressure, parents were not always able to protect children as much as they hoped to. Forty per cent reported that their children had seen them using drugs, with a third of parents acknowledging that their children had been present when they injected heroin. As noted above, because parents try to conceal their drug use, it is not spoken about, which means children have to cope with their fear and anxiety alone. Thus the stigma attached to drug use in itself creates stress.

In all of the studies referred to so far, parents have acknowledged that their drug dependence made life worse for their children, partly because associated financial hardship can result in children missing out, for example on school trips, clothes or even at times, food. Parents interviewed by Barnard (2003) reported that they sometimes relied on their own family and friends to make sure children were adequately provided for. In some situations grandparents took over the full-time care of children. Though many parents were relieved that their children were being looked after, there was often tension among family members. Some parents resented that they were not able to care for their own children or felt that their own parents undermined them, despite being grateful when they baled them out. In these situations it could be difficult for all concerned when a drug-using mother wanted her children to return to her care.

Among women interviewed by Taylor (1993), professionals such as social workers and health visitors were seen as keen to remove children from drug users, and were therefore not trusted. As a result women would not ask for help or would try to conceal their drug use. The women's experience indicated that social workers tended to base all hope of them being able to provide for their children on ending the drug use. In contrast the women themselves were realistic about how difficult it would be to stop and looked for support to cope and reduce the harm to themselves and their children.

Research on parental alcohol use

While little is known about children's experiences of parental drug misuse, a number of studies have explored children's accounts of life with an alcoholic parent (Laybourn et al. 1997; Velleman 1993). In addition Velleman assessed the impact of having had a parent as a problem drinker on the lives of young adults (Velleman and Orford 1999). Each study reported that children's experiences vary widely. Common difficulties include increased tension or violence within the home, embarrassment among friends and being required to take on responsibility for others at an early age. However Velleman reported that long-term negative effects only applied when drinking was accompanied by sustained disharmony at home, concluding that the risks of parental alcohol misuse had been exaggerated and children's resilience under-estimated.

Responding in practice

The nature of the service

Research-based knowledge can guide practice by providing useful indications of how children might be affected by parental problematic drug use. However its effective use depends on practitioners' skill to engage with families, make well-informed assessments and provide effective support. Our discussion of practice is based on the experience of a family centre in the outskirts of Glasgow. One of the distinctive features of the project it that it offers open access to any parent of young children living in the catchment area, whilst also working with families referred by social workers and health visitors because of concerns about their safety or well-being. In addition the project has a strong commitment to engaging with both fathers and mothers, and has a city-wide remit to support young parents who have spent much of their life in residential or foster care. Around 100 families are in contact with the centre, of whom just over half receive intensive individual support from a project worker.

The centre works with a diverse group of families, offering a wide range of services which include:

- Practical support: for example, assistance to establish routines, make and keep appointments with support services, get children to nursery/school; respite; advocacy to access benefits and deal with other agencies.

- Individual support to parents: consistent contact with one worker, providing an opportunity for the parent to explore the pressures and personal issues affecting him or her. The main aim is often to raise confidence and self-esteem. In some instances parents may be helped to manage key relationships better.

- Individual work with children: consistent contact with a supportive adult who can be confided in and can support their understanding of their situation, opportunities for positive social experiences and respite from pressures at home.

- Parenting sessions: structured, regular sessions which address identified gaps in parenting knowledge, skill and experience.

- Parenting courses or groups: allowing groups of parents to explore the needs of children in depth.

- Informal groups for women and men: to reduce isolation and offer ordinary, everyday support. Parents are encouraged to participate in other community activities and supported to develop their own potential, for example through learning opportunities at college.

This range of services means that parents and children can be offered a level and type of support which suits their individual needs. Parents who use drugs and their children access services alongside others with different kinds of problems.

Despite the complexity of the issues, there is broad consensus about what constitute key issues and challenges in work with families affected by parental substance misuse. These are:

- being accessible and gaining parents' trust

- assessment: developing realistic understanding of the impact of parental drug misuse on the child and what is required to safeguard the child's welfare

- working towards change: challenging mothers and fathers, increasing their awareness of what their children need from them and helping them provide this.

Effective interagency working and a willingness to take assertive action on behalf of children is crucial throughout each stage of the work.

In highlighting practice issues we focus on the everyday practicalities of service delivery. This is consistent with our view that it is through the minutiae of day-to-day interactions that workers can best:

- gain the trust of parents

- understand the risks to children

- support families in ways which enable them to safeguard their children and promote their welfare.

All parents and children referred to in case examples have given permission for details of their experiences to be included and have read and agreed the relevant sections of the chapter. Names and other details have been changed to avoid identification.

Being accessible and gaining trust

Starting from the premise that parents will feel ashamed and mistrustful when approaching services, it is evident that any agency hoping to engage with parents needs to anticipate any potential barriers to contact from well before the first contact. Location and layout of premises, arrangements for making appointments, approaches to routine aspects of the service and staff attitudes all make it more or less likely that parents will make contact in the first place and, having done so, will feel safe enough to acknowledge and try to reduce any difficulties.

There are three main ways of accessing this family centre. The first is through services open to all parents in the community, for example, the nursery or activity groups for women. Some parents restrict their use of the centre to these open activities, but for others they provide a route to more intensive and formal support (see Box 12.1).

Box 12.1 Case example: Susan

Susan, 19, called into the centre to ask for a nursery place for her six-month-old son. After about six or seven months the nursery worker noticed the child was attending less often, was less well kempt and was increasingly aggressive. The nursery worker raised her concerns with Susan who agreed to meet with one of the project workers.

Susan confided that her new boyfriend was violent to her and had introduced her to drugs. She was struggling to cope but anxious and afraid to ask for help in case her son would be accommodated. Susan met regularly with a project social worker and addressed a number of difficulties at an early stage, before her son came to any serious harm.

A second group of parents are referred directly from social workers or health visitors because of concerns about the children's well-being and/or safety (see Box 12.2). Referral to the centre is typically a means of avoiding the children being accommodated. This can encourage parents to engage, but also adds to fears about being judged and deemed unfit to care for their children.

Box 12.2 Case example: Alison, Matt and Amy

Alison and Matt were referred by their addiction worker. Both were on methadone and their relationship was volatile. Their six-year-old daughter, Amy, was on the child protection register under the category of physical neglect. Their home was in a very poor condition and Amy had no toys and very few opportunities to play or socialize with other children. Amy was refusing to go to school, soiling, bed wetting and displaying aggressive, anxious behaviour. Both parents were reluctant to engage with social workers and were described as hostile and threatening at times.

The priority was to improve conditions for the child from the start, while also overcoming the parents' hostility. The project worker met with the family in their home and arranged to provide a number of practical supports, including money to improve conditions in the home and buy clothes and toys for Amy. For a few weeks the worker called at the family home every morning to re-establish a routine of early rising, encourage Amy to attend school and support the parents in dealing with the tantrums she had been displaying. In time the parents were able to manage this themselves.

The third group of parents simply turn up at the centre and ask for help (see Box 12.3). They can arrive at any time of the day or evening. Among this group are people most desperate for help, but often very wary of getting involved and so easy to 'lose'.

Box 12.3 Case example: Kelly

Kelly came to the project one evening. She was 21 years old, eight months pregnant and heavily under the influence of drugs. She said she felt ill-prepared both practically and emotionally for motherhood and had a great fear of losing her baby to the care system. A worker spent an hour listening to Kelly, then arranged to see her the next day. When she did not turn up staff got in touch with her at home, where she confirmed that she still wanted help.

Kelly had been in foster and residential care from age 12. She left care from secure accommodation at 16, refusing any help because she was 'sick of social workers running her life'. She had begun using alcohol and drugs while in care and her drug use increased when she left. By the time she was 18 she was using heroin and had become involved in the criminal justice system. During her pregnancy Kelly had been attending antenatal services where she presented as coping well on methadone, so had not been identified as particularly vulnerable.

During any first meeting, workers acknowledge with parents that it is difficult to talk to professionals about their most personal problems, and would initially raise concerns about the child and their drug use in a general way. The worker would try to find out what support the parent felt they needed and would usually prioritize one or two of these, for example, housing or financial issues. The parent(s) are given information about the centre, including the policy on confidentiality, child protection and our joint working with other agencies. It is made clear that, though drug use in itself will not be reported to social work services, a referral will be made whenever centre staff believe a child is being significantly harmed. Parents will be informed when a referral is being made and will continue to be offered a supportive service in collaboration with statutory colleagues.

Based on feedback from parents attending the centre, it seems that staff attitudes are crucial to the engagement process. They talk of feeling treated 'with respect' and 'as normal people' and often contrast this with their experiences within other services. In addition they appreciate that the centre is open all day, so there can be more fluid arrangements for keeping in touch with workers, rather than having to attend appointments at a set time. Providing very practical and immediate support in the beginning of the relationship can help gain the trust of parents and build a solid foundation from which to address more challenging issues. It also means workers can be making a difference to the quality of children's lives from the start.

Assessment

For families receiving individual support, there is a distinct phase; however, work with families is cyclical rather than linear, involving ongoing attention of what is happening/changing in the family and how each member is faring. It is crucial to be constantly checking whether the care of the children is still good enough and whether more needs to be done to protect them from potentially harmful aspects of their parents' behaviour.

WHAT ARE ASSESSMENTS FOR?

Assessments of families affected by substance misuse serve four crucial functions.

First they provide some understanding of how the parents' substance use impacts on the child: what the child's life is like and whether the child is being harmed. The second function is to get to know parents, become aware of their strengths and weaknesses and gauge their motivation and potential for change. Having developed understanding of the child and parents, assessments should also indicate what kinds of service are appropriate for a particular family to safeguard the child and improve the family's quality of life. Finally, assessment is crucial to deciding whether a child can safely remain with his or her parents.

HOW DO CENTRE STAFF GO ABOUT ASSESSING FAMILIES?

We can never know exactly what happens in a family's home or what children experience. There are three main ways in which staff in the centre try to form as accurate and realistic a picture as possible of how the family is operating:

- talking with parents and children

- observing parents' care of their children, how they interact with them and how children respond

- taking account of other professionals' assessments and observations, including statutory social workers, health visitors and drug support workers.

What parents and children tell us about their lives will be more realistic and honest if workers are able to build a degree of trust and have the skill to communicate openly on sensitive issues. In the centre a wide range of simple exercises and worksheets have been developed to facilitate this (see Appendix Two). For example, in one exercise parents are asked how they would like their children to describe them, once they are grown up. This gives a good insight into parents' awareness of their children's needs and perspectives.

During 'Family Fun Days', workers can observe how parents put into practice what they might have learned in more formal sessions about warmth, positive reinforcement, distracting or ignoring challenging behaviour. Staff might also note whether improvement has been made in practical ways, for example, whether they come prepared with extra clothes, nappies and so on, indicating whether they are beginning to prioritize children's needs. Are they presenting as under the influence of substances, but nevertheless capable of providing 'good enough' care? On the basis of careful observation, staff can point out to parents the respects in which their child care still needs to be improved or, more positively, is becoming more child-focused and responsive. Direct interaction with older children, either on an individual basis or in the children's groups, is also crucial to checking out what life is like for them and whether they can count on 'good enough' attention to their welfare and care.

Collaborating with other professionals is central to putting together as accurate as possible a picture of how children are faring. Health visitors can readily note whether babies and young children are reaching expected milestones, while teachers, through their daily contact with older children, are well placed to spot changing standards of care, school attendance and behaviour.

It is very clear that how the assessment is carried out to some extent shapes the conclusions reached. The centre's approach is to continually offer parents help to improve their parenting and to assess their capacity to respond. This, and the opportunities staff have to meet with parents in a range of settings, means they are often aware of positives which are not apparent to statutory social workers whose contact with parents is more narrowly problem-focused. In situations where professionals are concerned that children may be harmed, it can be a struggle to ensure these positives are given due weight.

Kelly's experience after the birth of her baby provides useful illustration of several of these points (see Box 12.4).

> **Box 12.4 Case example: Kelly**
>
> Kelly's baby was accommodated at birth after she used heroin on the ward. Centre staff facilitated contact between Kelly and her baby and began to work with her on promoting attachment and basic parenting skills. To centre workers she seemed very much in tune with her baby's needs and readily responded to advice or support. However these positives were less evident when she met with the baby in other settings. She continued to struggle with being 'observed' when statutory social workers were present and there had been less opportunity to establish trust.
>
> In time social work staff were convinced by Kelly's growing capacity to prioritize and cater for her child's needs and the baby was returned to her care. The situation was certainly not risk free. Kelly was at times 'drowsy' and at times 'topped up' the methadone with other substances. However her daily attendance at the centre and her willingness to openly discuss concerns raised by staff (albeit grudgingly at times) resulted in professionals across agencies feeling confident that any deterioration would be picked up before the child came to any harm.

Kelly's situation demonstrates that the context in which parents meet with professionals influences perceptions of risk. Statutory social work services carry responsibility for final decisions about whether the care offered is 'good enough' and would shoulder blame if a child were to be harmed. Yet if the benefits of more proactive work undertaken by voluntary agencies are to be realized, social work staff need to trust their colleagues' capacity to assess and manage risk.

WHAT MATTERS ARE CONSIDERED IN ASSESSMENT?

The central issue to be assessed is *the impact on the child* and whether the care parents can offer is adequate. With babies and children physical health and development can be routinely monitored, while emotional well-being can be assessed through observing responses to adults. If a baby is thriving and able to make attachments, if a parent keeps appointments, and comes prepared with nappies and bottles it tells you that the parents' drug use is not chaotic and that the child's basic needs are being catered for.

With older children it can be more difficult, as they become adept at caring for themselves and do not easily confide in adults. Deterioration in appearance, behaviour, learning and attendance at school would cause concern. Some children will have had very frightening experiences, signs of which can be apparent in their conversation, play or drawings. It is equally important to identify the ways in which children adapt to the drug use and/or support their parents. For example, some take on responsibilities for looking after their parents and siblings, while others withdraw from school or social activities because of the stigma associated with their parents' drug use.

When it comes to assessing *parents' strengths and weaknesses*, typically a number of long-standing difficulties emerge. Most parents have very little confidence, while many have suffered abuse, trauma or neglect themselves. Many mothers have physical and/or mental health problems, many of which have not been addressed. All of these can affect parenting capacity, while also having a bearing on what drug use means to an individual parent. Luthar and colleagues emphasized the importance of addressing mothers' depression and anxiety, since these seriously undermine parenting capacity (Luthar *et al.* 2003). On the positive side, the birth of a baby and/or the wish to be a good parent can provide a major motivation for drug users to address their problematic drug use and some of the issues which underpin it. Their response when help is offered is in itself a strong indication of whether they will be able to provide good enough care.

The *relationship between the parent and child* is perhaps the most important element of any assessment, because this provides insight into the potential for harm and change. Children who have experienced chaotic care as young children often reflect this in their out-of-control behaviour and difficulties in relating to other people. Where parents respond by blaming and/or rejecting the child, there is a risk of emotional or physical harm. Work towards change would involve helping parents develop understanding of children's emotional needs, while also offering practical support to establish routine and order in family life.

In other equally worrying situations, children make themselves almost invisible or take on a supportive role with their parents. Again the priority is to increase parental awareness of their own responsibilities for their children's welfare, while also encouraging the children to recognize and give expression to their own needs.

As Barnard comments (2003), the availability of support from the wider family can be crucial in determining whether a child can remain safely with parents. Yet if parents' drug use is or has been chaotic, there are usually also tensions in relationships with relatives, who typically feel angry and let down by the parent's behaviour. A considerable number of the children the centre works with are being cared for by relatives who have assumed care informally and then been left to rear children without support. As parents stabilize, some want to resume the care of their children, but relatives are often reluctant to expose children to a chaotic life again. Mediation with parents and family members can help them take into account the child's experience and perspec-

tive, while also helping establish patterns of sharing the care which are acceptable to all concerned.

How do we know when parenting is good enough?

Working out what is good enough is an ongoing process which involves bal-
ancing risks and protective factors and realistically gauging the extent to which
support services can make a difference. As is evident from the research, the
quality of emotional care is crucial to children's well-being, so if parents show
warmth and care for their children, it will usually be in the children's interests
to try to sustain the situation, providing additional support to help make the situation 'good enough'. In some situations, for example where children are very
young or the level of physical care is very poor, it is not possible to create a situation in which the care is 'good enough' and it is better for children to be cared
for outside the family home.

It can be very uncomfortable for workers to admit this, especially when the
parent has tried to improve the situation but not managed to sustain any
progress. It can be difficult to get an appropriate balance between giving
parents long enough to make their care good enough, and not leaving children
in situations where their emotional and physical needs are neglected during
crucial periods in their development. Correspondingly it is easy for staff to be
'drawn in' to families, wanting them to succeed, and so failing to see the
negative side of life for the children. It is therefore important that we constantly
check out the reality of the day-to-day experiences children have in living
within a household where drugs are around. This brings us back to the need for
constant vigilance, openness to the communications and assessments of others,
including the children, and frequent opportunities to review the situation in
staff supervision and case reviews.

Working towards change

In a sense working towards change starts from the minute a worker engages
with a parent or child. Engaging their trust, assessing the nature of the difficulties and agreeing how these should be tackled are all potentially part of the
change process. Work at the centre is guided by a plan of work which is shared
with parents and older children and can be reviewed and reshaped as needs and
circumstances change. The availability of a range of flexible services is crucial if
supports are to correspond to what an individual family needs.

Years of drug use and other difficulties cannot be resolved quickly; they
need medium to long-term solutions. An ability to increase support as things
dip or get worse is important and can be helpful in building trust with parents
who see that they will not be abandoned when things get difficult, even if their
drug use increases.

By the end of the centre's involvement staff would expect that parents' drug use is stable and that relationships within the family are supportive enough to ensure children can be adequately cared for. In terms of personal development, some parents make much more progress than would have been expected when they first came to the centre. For example several have gone into further education, training or employment. Yet we would caution against expecting dramatic change, since progress is typically slow, hard won and interspersed with periods when difficulties increase. Work with families affected by substance misuse is usually a process of managing and reducing risk, not creating situations which are risk and anxiety free.

See Box 12.5 for an example of the value of sticking with families through the hard times.

Box 12.5 Case example: Matt, Alison and Amy

Matt was introduced to the dads' group where he could socialize with other men and access information. He felt more able to attend because his male worker co-ran the group.

A female worker helped Alison explore personal issues, including earlier experiences of abuse. Alison later said that she had been able to work well with the worker because 'she talked about me and what happened to me, not just all the things I have done wrong'. This acceptance helped improve her self-esteem and reduce her feeling of shame about her problems.

Joint sessions considered Amy's needs, the reasons for her behaviour and strategies to reassert their position as parents in a positive way.

Amy attended a social skills group with other children to get used to playing and being a child again with clear boundaries and adults in control.

Then all three came together to consider family rules and relationships and to enjoy some shared activities. Amy was encouraged to describe her worries and feelings, helping her parents better understand how she was affected by their behaviour and boosting their motivation to change.

Although these parents responded well and Amy's name was eventually removed from the register there has been ongoing support which has been increased when the situation has deteriorated. The strong relationships between workers and parents have meant that difficulties are identified more quickly.

Direct work with children

The children of drug-using parents have their own needs, deriving from their experience and from the secrecy and stigma which surrounds drug use. Centre staff also work directly with children and an example of this work is reported in Box 12.6.

Box 12.6 Case example: Karen

Karen (six years old) was referred by her social worker because of concerns about her behaviour in school and at home. Karen's parents were both long-term heroin users and her mother was being treated for clinical depression. Karen and her younger sibling's names were on the child protection register and an older sibling had been accommodated. The initial referral noted concerns about poor material standards, lack of routines in the home and her mother's aggression toward social workers. Karen was described as 'a very angry child' who at school was 'violent to other children in the playground and insolent to staff'.

After some introductory visits at home, Karen began to see her project worker at the centre twice a week. At first Karen's mother was reluctant to speak to the worker and was often not at home when Karen was dropped off. This gradually improved as the worker offered informal listening support and some practical assistance to gain financial aid.

Initially sessions centred on activities and outings to develop the relationship with the worker and build Karen's self-esteem and confidence. In time, as Karen's trust developed, one session each week was used to put together a folder which told 'Karen's story'. Karen's mother was also asked to complete sheets about Karen's birth, what kind of baby she had been and so on, which she really enjoyed. The relationship between Karen and her mother improved and joint sessions were held. Worksheets were used to identify things that worried or upset Karen and she began to talk about her embarrassment, shame and anger toward her parents.

Improvement was noted in Karen's behaviour at school and at home, she became much more open about her worries and her confidence grew.

Key issues identified in the work included:

- Karen was angry with her parents but very loyal, and she worried about being 'taken away'.

- Karen's family experience was of chaos and inconsistency, but the worker encouraged them to remember that the early years were positive; there was evidence of warm attachment between them and their current relationship became warmer.

- Karen knew that her parents were 'not well' but no one spoke directly to her about it. She identified in one worksheet that her biggest worry was her 'mum dying because of drugs'. This was used to open up discussion with Karen's mother. This development took place more than a year after work had started, indicating the need for sustained, long-term support to help parents and children acknowledge such painful secrets.

As Barnard and Barlow (2003) acknowledge, the secrecy which surrounds parental drug use makes it very difficult for researchers to learn directly from children what living with a drug-using parent entails and how this affects them. Practitioners who gain children's trust over time are much more able to gain an in-depth understanding. Providing this level of support is time consuming and requires skilled and well-supported staff. However it is potentially a more benign and cost-effective way of keeping children safe than removing them into care, so there is a case for arguing that building this type of capacity within social work services should be a priority.

Concluding remarks

Research to date has been helpful in highlighting the potential effects of drug misuse on children and demonstrating that these will vary depending on the nature of the family's interpersonal relationships and access to material and social support. The practice described in this chapter shows that sustained and thoughtful social work support can make a positive impact on each of these, thus making a real difference to children's quality of life, including whether or not they can remain in their parents' care. Engaging with parents is the first and crucial step, but it is well documented that many parents who use drugs prefer to keep social welfare agencies at bay. This means workers need to develop a range of strategies to reach out to parents, make sure services are accessible and honestly discuss risks to children. Employing agencies need to ensure staff are supported enough to develop appropriate skills and cope with demands of engaging with parents, while constantly being vigilant in considering whether their children are safe and well enough cared for at home.

We have focused on enabling parents to continue to care for their children, but we acknowledge that it is not always in children's interests to remain with parents who use drugs and that some will move to live elsewhere. In these circumstances children will still need sustained, personal support to understand what has happened to them and work through the fear, worries and guilt which are otherwise likely to cloud their life.

Making strenuous efforts to support drug-using parents can be misunderstood by the wider public as encouraging them to renege on their parental responsibilities. Correspondingly it is sometimes suggested that a strong belief in supporting parents implies a reduced commitment to children. Neither of these views is supported by evidence from research or practice, both of which indicate that children do better when they and their parents are offered help. Drug-using parents are an easy target for the media and a society trying to come to terms with a host of new threats, but, where possible, this should not deter professionals from seeking out and developing the strengths of parents and children alike.

Messages for practice

Assessments

- Develop relationships over time using a range of techniques.
- Acknowledge fear, shame and stigma issues and establish groundrules and values for the work.
- Focus on strengths as well as difficulties and convey these clearly to the family.
- Look at all the issues affecting the family, not just the substance misuse.
- Identify and try to evidence the ways in which each member of the family is affected by the drug misuse including parents and children. Share these with the family and other professionals involved.
- Use a range of recording methods and share these with families. Use graphics to visually record feelings, concerns, hopes and fears.
- Convey concerns openly and honestly to parents and help them identify their own concerns about being honest about their difficulties. Make sure that these are reassessed throughout contact and that parents understand the explicit concerns about the impact of their substance misuse on their children.

Working with parents

- Communicate clearly and honestly and with respect and empathy.
- Try to hear and understand 'their story'.
- Establish a positive working and learning environment.

- Use tools which help them identify their own attitudes, concerns and skills as parents.

- Offer support to address practical difficulties while the work is going on.

- Try to create 'opportunities' to observe and engage which can informally build a picture of how the family operates. Use other significant professionals to gain information appropriately.

- Try to encourage opportunities for parents to really hear what life is like for their children.

- Give feedback regularly on progress and strengths as well as concerns.

Working with children (aged 6–12years)

- Make sure that parents give their permission for the child to talk.

- Be clear and explicit with the child and the parents about the purpose of the work, for example, to find out about worries, to raise confidence or to give them a chance to talk.

- Make sure you give enough time to the relationship-building phase.

- Trust and consistency are crucial.

- Work in a warm child-friendly venue and provide transport if necessary.

- Keep regular appointments at the same time each week and be prepared for a long process.

- Plan the work in advance and with the child as much as possible so they know what to expect.

- Be honest with the child about who you might talk to about your work and when.

- Check out your communication style early on with the child, check they understand your questions, practise with them until they do.

- Make it fun and also give feedback to the child and, when appropriate, to the parents.

Chapter 13

Neglect of Disabled Children

Margaret Kennedy and Jane Wonnacott

Introduction

It is paradoxical that we write a chapter on neglect of disabled children which might be perceived as what happens *within families* when, in fact, the whole area of the protection of disabled children within the abuse arena has been almost totally ignored – neglected. For this reason, when we write about the neglect of disabled children, we also need to address this systemic 'invisibleness' of disabled children within society, research, service provision and child protection.

It is estimated that around 400,000 disabled children are currently being brought up in the UK, with over 100,000 being described as being severely disabled (Department of Health 2001). Of these, around 17,000 families are thought to include more than one disabled child, with some 7500 families having two or more severely disabled children (Tozer 1999). Most of these children live at home with their families the majority of the time (Fazil *et al.* 2002).

Almost all research in the UK on abuse of children fails to address the experience of *disabled* children. What has tended to happen is that government departments assume that the research done on non-disabled children will be representative of all children, including disabled children. We argue that this is a 'false assumption', which ignores the impact of impairment, discrimination and prejudice on the protection of disabled children. Anne Wilson Schaef (1992) shows how this did not work for black people during the lengthy debates on equality and racism, nor does it work for women during the debates on sexism. She says:

> When we are deprived of the freedom of exploring what it means to grow up female in a White Male System (read 'disabled in a non-disabled world') *we are robbed of our experiences and our souls.* Our differences give us our identity. (p.77, emphasis added)

Schaef's argument helps us see that it is the non-disabled 'system', profession-als, policymakers and even families, who want to argue that 'we're all the same' and that this ignores disabled people's experience of oppression, discrimina-tion, prejudice and abuse; ignores the 'differences'; and this 'ignoring' allows child protection researchers and academics to leave out disabled children from their samples of study.

It also ignores the various situations in which disabled children are more likely to find themselves, such as short breaks and shared care (respite care), and residential school. Utting *et al.* (1997) highlighted how vulnerable children are in these settings (see also Box 13.1).

Box 13.1 Abuse of disabled children

One noticeable piece of research is the Pam Cooke study, funded by the 'Children in Need Appeal'. This did specifically, rather than incidentally, look at the abuse of disabled children. This was a small study of children conferenced under child protection procedures, and showed that neglect was the registration category used the least often for disabled children. Neglect was the reason for registration in 20% of the sample compared with physical abuse (34%) and sexual abuse (43%).

This contrasts with Department of Health statistics, which show that neglect is the largest category of all registrations, constituting 48% of all children regis-tered in 2001 (Department of Health 2001). This might suggest that for disabled children in the UK neglect is not recognized or acted upon.

We do have some non-UK research which gives us a glimpse of what the situation might be for disabled children in relation to neglect. Gonzalvo (2002), in a Spanish study of 62 disabled children, found that the most frequent type of maltreatment was physical neglect. This category was found to be the type of abuse experienced in 82.2% of the cases.

Sullivan and Knutson's (1998) study looks at children with a range of dif-ferent impairments. Using a hospital-based sample, they found that disabled children were 3.8 times more likely to be neglected than their non-disabled peers. In a later school-based study of 50,278 children, the same researchers found that neglect was the most prevalent form of maltreatment for both disabled and non-disabled children, and that disabled children were 3.79 times more likely to be neglected than non-disabled children.

This study also found that disabled children tended to be maltreated at earlier ages, and that pre-school disabled children suffered more abuse, includ-ing neglect, than the elementary, middle school and high school age groups. It is therefore important to be *alert* to the possibility of neglect early in a disabled child's life.

A model towards understanding

We see the neglect of disabled children as resulting from an interaction between disabling barriers and the capacity of the child's parents to parent (see Figure 13.1).

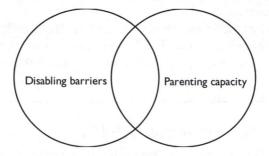

Figure 13.1 Political and personal interaction

When we are considering the neglect of disabled children, we have no reason to believe that the impact of neglect is any different from the impact of neglect on non-disabled children. They are just as likely to experience the same impairment of their physical, emotional and social well-being as their non-disabled peers. The difficulty for disabled children is that we may be less likely to notice the impact, and confuse the signs and indicators of neglect with factors associated with their condition. For example, low self-esteem is a well-documented result of neglectful parenting, yet we assume that the low self-esteem displayed by many disabled children is a *natural* consequence of being disabled.

By focusing on the interaction of disabling barriers and parenting capacity, we aim to acknowledge the similarity of the impact of neglect, yet explore the dynamics which might contribute to the increased vulnerability of disabled children to this form of abuse and our own inability to respond appropriately.

An additional reason for excluding a specific focus on the child and their impairment is that this has, to date, resulted in a child-blaming model which refers to the abuse-provoking characteristics of disabled children. This is offensive to disabled people, and not sufficiently backed up by research.

Disabling barriers

The idea that our society puts up 'disabling barriers' to inclusion was first mooted by Oliver (1999a), and refers to the ways in which disabled people are hampered by prejudice and discrimination with the result that they are disabled. The most crucial point here is that to be 'disabled' is not about the child's impairment *per se*, but about these societal prejudices and discriminatory practices. Therefore when we speak of 'disabled children' we are referring *not* to the impairment but to how these children have had their lives affected by attitudes and stereotypical views about them. They are disabled by society, not their impairments (see Table 13.1).

Table 13.1 Disabling barriers

Disabling barriers create barriers…	…to a fulfilling and positive life
Euthanasia/termination of pregnancy	Life itself
Denial of sufficient resources leading to poverty/hardship	Health and development
Discriminatory and prejudicial practice leading to oppression	Self-esteem, confidence, emotional and psychological well-being
Degrading and humiliating treatment	Human rights
Lack of research on disabled children's experiences of abuse	Safety and protection
Language of 'care' gives image of 'burden'	Empowerment/independence

We are referring here to a discussion about the differences between the 'Social Model' and 'Individual (Medical) Model', which separates impairment from prejudice. This is a crucial distinction, which has been explored by a number of authors (Morris 1991; Oliver 1999; Shakespeare 2000).

If we take one area that is highlighted in Table 13.1, poverty: research has consistently shown that families of disabled children are more likely to experience poverty than families with non-disabled children, and that current levels of service provision do not adequately meet the needs of disabled children and their parents (Beresford 1995). Extra money is needed for things like heating, laundry, clothing, special diets, travel, prescriptions and equipment, and if this is not available the quality of the child's life may well suffer. The Disabled Living Allowance (DLA) is supposed to help. Often parents are turned down and must appeal.

A Scottish survey ('The struggle for Disability Allowance' – pdf available at www.samh.org.uk/news_dla.html) found that 97.3% found the DLA forms difficult to complete; 80% had to get help to complete the form. One mother said:

> My daughter had been diagnosed with a disabling terminal illness and the form had been so heartbreaking to complete that I was almost too upset to appeal.

Problems did not stop there. The family were later served an eviction notice when there was a delay in a DLA decision that in turn led to a suspension of other benefits.

In 1997, 65% of ethnic minority couples with a disabled child surveyed had incomes of less than £200 per week (Chamba *et al.* 1999), although the 'modest but adequate' budget for a family with two children and a car, calculated by the Family Budget Unit, was around £450 per week (Goodinge 1999). Income is lower, despite the fact that it is known that disabled children accrue increased costs for the family. However, the difficulties arise from service provision (Social Model), not from having a disabled child (Individual/Medical Model). Where we attribute the problems is crucial.

The literature on neglect does note that children are often being neglected by official agencies rather than their own parents (Parton 1995), and this may be particularly true for disabled children. Jenny Morris (1998b) found, for example, that disabled children were being denied appropriate communication systems, and argued that this neglect of their communication needs was a form of maltreatment (Morris 1998a). Disabled children, without adequate systems to communicate, will suffer impairment of their development as well as possibly experiencing loneliness and depression as a result of having no means to relate to peers and family. Another example given to us by a participant on a training course was a child being excluded from PE because the school were not able to provide a person to dress them in their PE outfit. Again, this could have a detrimental impact on the child's health and development, as well as isolating them from their peers and increasing the likelihood of bullying.

Whilst poverty and neglect ought not to be assumed to be synonymous, there is a strong association between neglect (especially low-level neglect) and socioeconomic deprivation (Stone 2003). However, what can happen is that workers try to address the poverty by putting in practical solutions, and fail to notice the 'breakdown or absence of a relationship of care' (Turney and Tanner 2001). We know that this can have disastrous consequences for children and cause lasting damage or even death (Bridge Childcare Consultancy 1995). This is perhaps even more likely to happen where the family has a disabled child. Practical solutions *are* necessary but may distract workers from focusing on the relationships within the family. Laura Middleton (1998) found that parents of disabled children felt that social workers concentrated more on physical, as opposed to emotional, issues and that material help was easier to obtain than support or advice. Such an emphasis may leave disabled children vulnerable to neglect and in receipt of services which only partially meet their needs.

Therefore, anyone working with disabled children needs to address 'disabling barriers' and constantly ask themselves:

- What is it about this disabled child's *environment* that is leading to neglect?
- What is it about our service provision (or lack of it) that is contributing to neglect?

- What is it about the family's circumstances (e.g. financial situation) that is contributing to neglect?

- What is it about society's perception of disabled children that causes their neglect?

Can professionals who are 'agents of the State' help both parents and disabled children see their position as one of oppression? Will they be willing to put their heads on the block to challenge policy and financial discrimination? The politics of oppression have to be an integral part of working with families who have disabled children.

Parenting capacity

The idea of 'parenting' and what this means is particularly value laden. Indeed, rather than perceiving that this particular child may need a skilled parent, we often allow parenting that is less than 'good enough'. We base this on a presumption that the child will not experience 'poor parenting' as 'poor parenting' as they may not have the cognitive ability to understand or 'feel' deprivation! There is almost a view that abuse for these children is experienced in a different way, and is, therefore, usually less damaging. This is quite a paradox, since before we argued that the 'difference' of being disabled was ignored (all children are supposed to be the same); yet here we are saying the 'sameness' of being a *child* is ignored (disabled children actually do not feel abuse in the same way as other non-disabled children)!

What is regarded as 'good enough parenting' is, however, fraught with difficulties. This is well illustrated by Hackett (2003). He argues that the concept of 'parenting capacity' is a more helpful one than 'good enough parenting'. He says practitioners are:

> encouraged to move away from assessing whether someone's assessed level of parenting is 'good enough'...to a broader and more dynamic view of their capacity to meet their children's needs within their familial, social and environmental contexts. (p.156)

We agree that assessing parenting capacity does have to include the familial, social and environmental contexts, as this is how the social model and an ecological model works. Looking at the child's developmental outcomes alone, however, may not be a yardstick of 'good enough parenting'. What are the particular complexities of assessing parenting capacity where the child is disabled?

Commentators on assessment practice (Hackett 2003) have pointed out that the level of parenting skills needed for children in different circumstances will vary. However, caution needs to be exercised in using these arguments with disabled children. We could fall into the trap of assuming that different expectations of parenting are acceptable, as are different/negative outcomes for the child. This is a dangerous assumption; this is where a disabled child's developmental delay is perceived as *part of their impairment* when in fact it may be due to neglect and poor parenting. This is exactly why, as we have argued above, the disabled child's needs have been overlooked.

What we are especially concerned about is the tendency to allow a standard of care that would not be acceptable for a non-disabled child. Practitioners who assess 'parenting capacity' allow themselves to be diverted from the 'relationship of care' by the child's impairment and perceptions of 'stress'.

A diversion from neglect and the 'relationship of care' can happen in the stereotypical perception that disabled children cause 'stress' for their 'carers'. Within this perception, called the 'dependency-stress' model of abuse, abuse is thought to happen following the child's dependency on the carer, which causes stress; this stress then causes the abuse. Figures 13.2 and 13.3 show two possible cause of stress, neither of which are due to the child's impairment.

There are very grave dangers with this thinking, and several authors address this dynamic. The first aspect is this notion of 'Carer', rather than 'Parent'. It is now very common to refer to disabled children's parents as their 'carers', rather than parents. Morbey (2002) prefers the term 'caregiving' rather than 'carer' for she says that 'this allows us to recognise that in "caregiving" *caring for* should not be assumed'. This is an important consideration, as there may well be a rejection of the disabled child even though 'caregiving' may be adequate. The term 'carer' also distracts us from the parental role, which is unique and separate from the caring task. Disabled children may well be asked, 'who is your carer?' rather than 'who is your parent?' and may feel that they have lost this special relationship. Another danger may be that the 'canonization' of carers (Morbey 2002) may inhibit the 'caree' (the disabled child) from complaining and expressing how stressful their own situation is. It seems as though only the 'carer' may talk about 'stress'. Forbat (2002) also notes that 'stress and care are seen as integrally linked, and the anger or difficulties that occur are to be expected and tolerated'.

This is well illustrated in Cooke's study of a social worker's views regarding *why* there had been neglect of an eight-year-old girl with severe/profound learning disabilities. She had been found to be severely neglected with bedsores, loss of weight, poor hair and ear care and lacking in stimulation. She was admitted to hospital where 'she ate voraciously' (Cooke 2000). The social worker did not believe the neglect was deliberate, rather that the mother had carried a *heavy burden* with three other very small children, one a new baby, and that she had also lacked some skills relating to safe care. The social worker had articulated the problems as 'stress' related, and therefore almost understandable. McCreadie's (1996) *précis* of research on elder abuse states, 'There is no convincing evidence that the stress of caring on its own is the principal reason for abuse'.

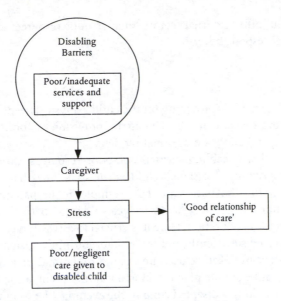

Figure 13.2 Poor child care as a result of inadequate service provision

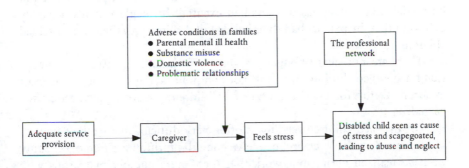

Figure 13.3 Abuse and neglect as a result of adverse family conditions despite adequate services

Sobsey (1994) reviews the research evidence relating to the 'dependency-stress' model of abuse and finds that:

> Dependency related stress in the families of children with disabilities, however, must be considered to be an unsupported and largely disproved model for understanding the abuse of people with disabilities. As such, it has little potential value for guiding prevention efforts. (p.150)

Clearly it is useful if parents can talk about 'stress' but it becomes dangerous when the disabled child is blamed for that stress, rather than the *difficulties in the relationship* and other external factors, such as poor resources, or if it detracts from personal responsibility.

Basic care

This dimension involves providing for the child's physical needs, and appropriate medical and dental care. It includes the provision of food, water, shelter, clean clothing and adequate personal hygiene.

It is here that 'disabling barriers' of poor resources, little support and negative stereotyping of disabled children *do* sometimes have an impact on parents' ability to offer basic care. For example, if the parents have to wait months for a hoist to lift a very heavy 14-year-old into a bath, then bathing may be eliminated for the duration. Here it is crucial to assess *why* care tasks are not done or addressed sufficiently, but the worker must be constantly alert not to collude with 'excuses', for excuses are easy to find…and believe.

In a poignant example given to us at a training event, a social worker told us the story of visiting a disabled child in the evening. She went up to his room to find him sitting in his buggy (wheelchair) facing the wall. He said to her, 'I'm waiting to be seen to'. He had been in this position since coming home from school. This was not the first time this had happened, and the practice had not been challenged. Previous workers had excused this neglect of his needs by believing that the parents had their hands full dealing with their non-disabled children.

There are a number of issues that may arise under the 'basic care' dimension for disabled children. It almost goes without saying that one of the most important factors for any child is *to be fed*. Children who are neglected are often *not* fed.

For disabled children feeding is often very difficult due to their impairment. How these children are to receive enough nutrition is paramount. Sadly we have realized during our work that there are a number of reasons why disabled children do not get fed, either in a care or home setting. At the start of life, or for very young, seriously impaired babies with conditions such as Down's Syndrome, Spina Bifida or brain damage, who remain in hospital for care, withdrawal of feeding and hydration is sometimes offered as an option. Whether we call this 'euthanasia' is debated. Whether we call it discrimination or service (hospital) neglect is never debated. It would seem anomalous to 'allow' the withdrawing of food/water as 'treatment' in a hospital setting, yet for it to be neglect in a home setting.

So feeding or lack of it can be the result of the following factors:

- Feeding/hydration is seen as a 'treatment/medicine', therefore can be withdrawn to 'allow the child to die' (this followed the Tony

Bland case when feeding/hydration was declared a 'treatment' and could therefore be withdrawn (Keown 2002)).

- We know of several cases where disabled children are not fed *enough* so as to keep them 'light' for carrying purposes, this even to the extent of malnutrition. It is very difficult to assess weight and appropriate weight for some disabled children, however, what tends to happen is that *away from home* these children eat voraciously and gain weight.

- Parents (and carers) may fail to give children enough food because it is difficult, and so they 'give up' half way through meals.

- Parents who will not allow gastrostomy feeding (tube into stomach) as this is 'abnormal' even in the face of failure to thrive and malnutrition. Some social workers try to 'work with' these parents, to persuade them towards surgery rather than take care proceedings; meanwhile the child suffers and continues to lose weight.

- Parents who *insist* on gastrostomy feeding despite the fact it is not medically required. This is usually requested when it is time consuming to feed a child. This is sometimes the case for children who are difficult to feed but, nonetheless, are receiving sufficient nutrition orally. This denies the disabled child the sensory input of taste (chocolate mousse can taste wonderful!). There are occasions when surgeons accede to the demands for such surgery when they perceive that the parent is under stress. This is a parent-focused model, rather than a child-focused one. It would seem easier to do surgery than pay for a helper for the family.

- Food is used as a reward or denied as punishment. This focus on food for behavioural purposes is unethical.

- Some parents 'fabricate' illnesses by the judicious use/non-use of food.

Professionals need to be vigilant regarding the feeding of disabled children. Poor growth, or thinness, is not necessarily a part of the child's impairment or illness (though it can be). Lesley Carroll-Few, from Westminster and Chelsea Hospital's feeding clinic, said at SCOPE and MacKeith Meetings in 2002 that many teenagers and young adults with cerebral palsy were reaching a 'degree of emaciation shocking in the 21st century', with some weighing as little as three or four stone. School lunches were often rushed, food unsuitable and independent feeding encouraged at the expense of eating enough. Dr Martin Bax said at the same conference that too much work was focused on improving motor disorders, whilst issues such as feeding were ignored. 'The idea still pervades that cerebral palsy kids don't grow, but we need to answer why they aren't growing'.

We have discovered that professionals prefer to believe that poor growth and thinness is not neglect but is instead due to the child's condition. This could have disastrous consequences. Indeed, we know of one case where a child died of pneumonia as a result of malnutrition; in this case it was put on the death certificate 'died of natural causes', much to the distress of the child's social workers, who had persistently tried to get the neglect issues addressed.

Another area of concern is around hygiene and toileting. Disabled children may well be incontinent. However, there are disabled children still in incontinence pads (we should not refer to these as 'nappies', which is demeaning and humiliating for older disabled children) far beyond what is necessary, and when they are not, in fact, incontinent in the clinical sense. This is often due to lack of/or unwillingness to persist in toilet training; it is quicker and easier to leave a child in incontinence pads but parents often argue 'It's too difficult for my child'. In some cases it is simply benefit fraud; you can get money for incontinence pads!

Children may be left in pads for long periods in school – 'we don't have a nurse to change them' – or in respite care or home. This is a staffing/resource issue that harms the child. Many disabled children who are able to articulate their needs find their hygiene and toileting needs are humiliating, and failure to meet their needs properly constitutes emotional and psychological neglect. It may also constitute 'degrading and humiliating treatment' under the Universal Declaration of Human Rights, Article 5 (Disability Awareness in Action 2003).

Also common is the changing of pads or dressing/undressing disabled children in public areas such as sitting rooms, classrooms or in full view of passers by. Some children (even aged five, six or seven) are put on potties in classrooms or sitting rooms. This denies privacy and the concept of privacy so needed for safety. If a disabled child learns that they can be undressed publicly, then he or she also learns that their body is an object of others and not their own. This neglect may set them up for sexual abuse.

In relation to clothing, some disabled children are dressed inappropriately, in clothes that either make them look 'frumpy' or 'childlike'. Others have to make do with second-hand clothing, either on the basis that they 'ruin clothes' or 'What's the point in dressing her/him up, after all she/he's *disabled*'. In other words, they are not worth bothering about. We do, however, have to be careful not to judge if this is done due to poverty or low income.

Some of this discussion may sound harsh, but there is anecdotal evidence to suggest that these practices are reasonably common. We would like to see such practices under the remit of the neglect of basic care.

There is research which shows that basic health and dentistry needs of disabled children are neglected (Payne 2000).

Keeping the 'basic care' of disabled children in focus is complex and can be guided by the following:

- *'Care' may not mean 'competent', and 'competent' may not mean 'care'.* Too often meeting 'caring' parents suggests to the worker that what they do is 'competent', and the task of the professional is to analyse what the parents *do* (competency) as well as how the parent responds to the disabled child (care). The reverse can be the case: that parents do well to provide for all the disabled child's needs, are competent, but actually do not care for the child. This we must also try to detect.

- *'Doing your best' is not the same as 'good enough parenting'* (Horwath 2002). Because workers see children with very complex needs, with serious impairments or illnesses, they can fall into a 'feel sorry for parents' mode, which cuts them off from assessing well (Kennedy 1995). It is as if the shutters come down and the worker sees only the fact that *something* is being done, is well intentioned, the parents care...but it simply does not meet the child's needs and is not competent or 'good enough'; this is often difficult for the worker to see if they are enmeshed in the parents' difficulties. These workers may well operate under the 'child-blame' model described above, so that their focus is not 'child-centred' but has shifted to 'parent-centred'. This is more easily done where there is a disabled child.

Ensuring safety

Parents are required to ensure their child's safety. This includes protection from harm or danger, and from contact with unsafe adults/other children and from self-harm. This dimension suggests that what we are doing is protecting children from unnecessary pain and/or suffering. We would also like to address here the protection of the disabled child from excessive surgeries or other 'treatment' modalities.

Parents of disabled children are usually very concerned about safety issues. They fully appreciate that their children are vulnerable, particularly from physical harm. Paradoxically, children learn about safety by taking certain risks, and one of the hardest aspects of 'safety' for disabled children is to take those risks. Riding a bike, crossing the road, going to the shops alone, are all developmental tasks. Learning to do these things in safety is an essential tool for everyday living. For disabled children, over-protection may be the problem. Over-protection, in our view, constitutes neglect, particularly when it involves a child who can do more than is allowed. We know children who are not allowed to go on school trips, go out alone, stay away from home over night: all ostensibly to keep the child safe.

One disabled man said:

Before that most of my life was spent in my parental home. Too much so, for it left me ill-prepared for self-management. Independent living should be inherent for every disabled person's life. Part of their conditioning from birth should be that one day they have to fend for themselves. No matter how difficult it is, putting it off can only make it harder.

This is also one dimension where disabling barriers, lack of services, put a disabled child in danger. Parents, perhaps tired and needing a break, if only to go down to the shops, may invite anyone in to 'baby-sit'. Whilst this is also the case for non-disabled children, parents of disabled children may not see the need for vigilance, as it may be perceived that no one will harm a disabled child (still a very common myth). Some parents may even leave the child alone, as the child may not be mobile and therefore assumed to be safe in a bed, cot or wheelchair. Some are locked into rooms while parents go out.

Practitioners have told us that social services are sometimes leaving disabled children in neglectful and dangerous homes *even though siblings may have been removed* based on the myth that they will not be harmed, or on the belief that abuse will not impact so much on this particular child. Often this happens because there are no appropriate facilities for accommodation. We are quite stunned to hear this time and again on training courses around the UK.

Bullying of disabled children, particularly in mainstream schooling, is very common. Whilst some parents do bring to the attention of schools what is happening to their disabled child, this is often ignored. There is a real problem of how parents protect their disabled child from bullying if the school perceives the problem as the child, not other children or the school environment.

Other parents tell their child 'just ignore it' but this approach is not addressing the core issue of discriminatory and abusive practices by non-disabled children. As workers we may need to work hard with parents to take bullying seriously. Middleton (1999) quotes from Randall's work (1997, p.10):

> As soon as they found out I couldn't see very well, they started taking my things and hiding them. It's been going on for years now. When I start looking they sing things like 'Bottle Bottom's on the trail again' and slap me with rulers. (nine-year-old in independent school)

Another child said:

> My deformed spine makes me all bent over and doubled up. Some of the girls started calling me 'Quasi' after the Hunchback, then they started saying my father buggers me standing up. I complained to the teacher but she thought I was lying. (14-year-old boy in a mixed comprehensive)

Middleton writes that rather than receiving help to understand or address the structural issues around discrimination or bullying, the respondents found themselves pathologized and in need of psychiatric help. Parents were told that disabled children went through 'phases'. There is educational neglect when the disabled child is not kept safe in these environments.

Other controversial areas around pain and suffering are the often extensive surgeries or other 'therapies' that disabled children undergo, sometimes for little benefit, or to make the child appear more 'normal' and therefore more 'acceptable' for their parents and society. For example, is it really acceptable for Down's Syndrome children to have facial reconstructive surgery so that they do not look as if they have Down's Syndrome? Is it acceptable to do repeated lower limb surgeries to help a child walk when, long term, this child will probably use a wheelchair when older and heavier? At what point do we argue that repeated hospitalization to make a child more 'normal' will have a negative impact on education, and therefore constitute neglect of educational needs? At what point will we say that not allowing a profoundly deaf child to learn British Sign Language (now a recognized language in Britain) is an infringement of his or her right to their *own* language and therefore cultural and linguistic neglect or, indeed, a form of racism? Are cochlear implants simply more sophisticated hearing aids billed as 'cure', to make a child more 'normal', or are they a denial of a cultural heritage within a Deaf Signing community? Will exclusion from the deaf community cause additional pain, suffering and unnecessary isolation? Can it constitute neglect?

These latter points about pain and surgery, language and education are based on what non-disabled people perceive as important, and also on assumptions about 'normality'. The end results may be medically fulfilling and satisfactory for doctors, aesthetically pleasing to parents, but at what cost to the disabled child? At what point is the lived experience of disabled adults incorporated into our thinking about child care?

This is a very complex discussion, and it would be simplistic to represent it as a clear-cut, polarized debate between non-disabled people and disabled people. The notion of 'normality' will be perceived differently by different people, but it is influenced by a general cultural belief that impairment is a problem. It will also be influenced by experience.

Another serious area of concern is the increasing medication of disabled children, particularly of children labelled 'challenging' or 'hyperactive'. There is anecdotal evidence to suggest that some professionals and parents are 'over-medicating' disabled children. Two spoons of tranquillizer are cheaper than an additional carer for the parents, or the respite care centre. However, it is stupefying and may lead to a poor quality of life.

These are all issues that need to be addressed, but have not received sufficient attention in the National Assessment Framework (Department of Health 2000). No one suggests the discussion is easy, but a *disabled* child-centred approach is imperative.

Emotional warmth

If chronic neglect includes an 'absence of a relationship of care' (Turney and Tanner 2001), the degree to which the parents of disabled children are able to show genuine emotional warmth and thus facilitate the development of a secure pattern of attachment needs attention.

Unfortunately the focus of work with many disabled children and their parents is on the provision of basic care needs, with the result that consideration of emotional needs of the child and the relationship between child and parents receives scant attention. Research confirms this bias (Middleton 1998), with the parents of disabled children reporting that social workers were interested in physical problems not emotional ones. For Marks (1999) this concentration on the physical aspects of the lives of disabled children starts from birth:

> Medical intervention demonstrates the centrality of the body as a functioning system rather than the newborn as a relating person with emotional needs which are crucial for survival and growth. (p.44)

This lack of understanding of the emotional needs of the child and the importance of developing a relationship between child and carers, which will ensure all their needs are met, is described by Sobsey (1994) in relation to the earliest contacts between professionals and parents:

> Sadly information given to parents by professionals at the time disability is diagnosed often implicitly or explicitly contains the message – 'don't get too attached to this child'. (p.162)

The importance of attachment is now well documented in the child care literature in the UK. The link between attachment difficulties and neglect has also been explored (Howe *et al.* 1999; Turney and Tanner 2001). However, there is little in the literature that furthers our understanding of the way in which attachment patterns may be affected between a disabled child and their parents.

For instance, what do we know about attachment of blind children who cannot see their parents, or of deaf children who cannot hear their parents? What do we know about the disruption of early years hospitalization for disabled children, and absence of parents during this time? (Although there are hospitals which have residential units for parents, this does tend to apply for only very seriously ill or dying children in many places.) What do we know about repeat respite care and the effects of parental separation on a monthly basis, or even weekly basis? What do we know about how residential school provision for disabled children, sometimes for very young disabled children, impacts on attachment?

A useful discussion in Morgan (1987) around emotional abuse of disabled children (though some parts of this book need serious challenging) argues that there is a form of emotional abuse called 'escape':

The most obvious form of escape is desertion of the child. Parents can engage in more subtle forms of escape that may not be at a conscious level. They will find ways to be away from the child as much as possible during waking hours. For instance, they may take jobs that require extensive travel or late working hours; they may take frequent weekend trips; they may join social or charitable groups and those activities engage most of their time; and they may place their child in a distant residential facility when there are comparable facilities nearby. (p.61)

We add, or they may ask for repeated respite/shared care. We more readily accept parental/child separation when the child is disabled. Is this because we believe it will not be so harmful for these children? Or are we saying the parent's need for 'a break' over-rides the child's need of attachment? These are complex ethical and child care issues. Are we very clear about the reasons for that separation, and has the separation been part of the assessment of need?

Since research indicates that disabled children are 3.8 times more likely to be neglected than non-disabled children (Sullivan and Knutson 1998), it is vital that we begin to explore the nature of the relationship between disabled children, neglect and disruption to patterns of attachment.

Any assessment of emotional warmth must ask some fundamental questions.

- How were parents first informed about their child's impairment and how has this affected their relationship with the child?

- Are parents misreading the signals of disabled children who are experiencing anxiety? Certain impairments may mean that the child might not communicate anxiety in the same way as their non-disabled peers.

- If signals are being misread, does this lead to the child internalizing a view of the world where they do not believe their needs will be met?

- Could such insecure attachment patterns be at the root of the 'challenging behaviour' which is so often seen as a consequence of the impairment, rather than a result of relationship difficulties?

- Is the response to 'challenging behaviours', such as increased institutional care, exacerbating the problem and becoming a form of emotional neglect?

- Are services focused on practical solutions, rather than on the relationship between parents and children?

Stimulation

Parents are required to promote the child's learning and intellectual development through encouragement and cognitive stimulation. This includes facilitating the child's cognitive development and potential through interaction, communication, talking. It includes ensuring the child's school attendance or
equivalent opportunity. Important parental concerns should be about facilitating the child's development of happiness and success. This may be assessed in
looking at the parent's expectations of their disabled child. All parents have
expectations, and many parents skilfully encourage children in favoured areas
without significant harm, such as nurturing sporting success. Children receive
the message that the parents are truly interested in what they are doing and
achieving; this fosters self-esteem. Some, however, put too much pressure on
the child, such that the child feels they are only accepted as far as they meet the
parents' expectations: conditional love. As well as expectations, pride in our
children is one of the markers of emotional warmth.

Parents of disabled children are no different, and the same dangers are
present. Morgan (1987, p.61) is again helpful when she highlights two
concerns:

> *Strong under-expectations of achievement:* The parents devalue the child's abilities;
> when they set goals they set them too low. The child becomes aware, at some
> level, of the parents' attitudes, begins to believe them, and behaves accord-
> ingly – creating a self-fulfilling prophecy.

It should be added that professionals do this also!

> *Setting unrealistic goals:* In this case the parents set goals that are too high. When
> the child cannot live up to these established goals, and fails, then the parents
> feel justified in their negative attitudes toward their child.

And professionals do this too! This negative attitude can lead to neglect. The
neglect of this aspect of the child's life can lead to severe loneliness, depression,
or lack of self-esteem in later years. For disabled children this needs to be realistic. What counts as 'realistic' is often difficult to assess, but the dangers above
should be factored in.

For disabled children communication is the cornerstone of stimulation,
and where this is neglected the child's development will be impaired. The
parent–child communication, the child–peer, and child–'other' communication all need to be promoted. If a parent is engaged in encouraging a whole
range of situations where their child will be stimulated in interaction with a
range of people, they may well be hampered in doing this if the child does not
have a sufficient and efficient communication method. Conversely, parents may
not be 'interested' in exploring communication issues. There are a number of
reasons why this may happen:

- The educational services fail to supply a computer-aided system or other technological communication aid due to budget constraints. We argue that this may infringe human rights under the Universal Declaration of Human Rights, Article 19, 'Freedom of expression'. The child must cope with a poor substitute (Disabling Barrier).

- The educational services *do* buy expensive communication equipment but this is not allowed outside the classroom. This leaves the disabled child unable to communicate effectively with peers in the playground, parents and siblings at home, or to participate in any social activities with other children.

- Parents may be reluctant, or outright resistant, to learning the communication system the child needs, such as British Sign Language or Makaton or other augmentative systems.

- Some deaf parents resist hearing aids, as they argue the child will use Sign Language.

- The parent may not allow their child to use an alternative or augmentative system and may insist on an oral only approach on the grounds that it is more 'normal'.

- There may be a lack of interpreters or communication facilitators to help a child engage in a stimulating environment, such as Scouts or clubs (Disabling Barrier).

- There are 'low expectations' of the child's ability to communicate, therefore specialized equipment is not advised or even tested with the child.

Whilst having a child who needs an alternative or additional communication system complicates the dimension of 'stimulation', it is not insurmountable. For example, the National Deaf Children's Society has a 'Family Communication Service' which helps new parents learn Sign Language. A parent describes how it helped:

> We both remember the first time Joanne walked through the door. Yes, she was here to teach us sign language, but more than that we had never met a 'real deaf person' before. For the last year, Joanne has come nearly every Tuesday evening for an hour. It is great to think that as Daniel grows up, and as the vocab changes from 'pooey nappies' to 'football' to 'science GCSE coursework' – and who knows what then, that we have the support of a language to help. BSL (British Sign Language) courses are great but they don't supply the subject-specific vocab you need as parents at various life stages. (*Talk* July/August 2003)

Communication aids such as computers, or communication aides such as inter-preters, facilitators and communication teachers, are *not a luxury* but an essential ingredient in helping a child develop his or her involvement in life. Too often service providers or parents pay scant regard to these needs. If parents resist in this area, it should be a cause of great concern.

Guidance and boundaries

How far parents and others are able to maintain appropriate guidance and boundaries for some disabled children might be an area that needs exploration. The dangers of over-protection and unrealistic goal setting have been outlined above. Additionally, the child might experience the imposition of rigid bound-aries based on a stereotypical view of the child's impairment. This might mean that individual needs are neglected.

In a Canadian video on emotional abuse and neglect (BC Institute Against Family Violence 1999), a mother describes how her daughter was prevented from going on school outings based on the view that autistic children do not like change. Her daughter loved change, and the imposition of such a boundary was preventing her daughter from accessing experiences which could have enhanced her life.

Conversely, neglect of disabled children's needs for boundaries in some areas of their lives may leave them wide open to other abuses. For example, failing to impose boundaries around such behaviour as masturbation might increase vulnerability to sexual abuse. An already perceived 'sexualized' child may be a target of a sex offender.

Failing to help a disabled child understand such concepts as 'privacy' may also leave a child without safety resources. The public toileting, dressing and other hygienic and care tasks make a child believe their body is a commodity of the caregivers, not their own. It is essential that disabled children learn 'body-ownership'. Their body only belongs to them. They must learn to *direct caregivers* themselves as to their own needs – a task which will be needed in later life should they utilize personal carers and have a Direct Payment benefit.

Caregivers, as well as parents, need the skills to hand over *power* to the growing disabled child. Too often caregivers assume power and this leads to infantilization and lack of control.

Another area under this dimension is the whole concept of 'confidential-ity'. Disabled children, teenagers and adults are used to having every aspect of their lives discussed by myriad professionals. Great attention must be given to the need to discuss with disabled children which aspects of their lives *they want* in the public-professional realm. Parents and caregivers have a duty to guard against privacy and confidentiality breaches.

Stability

Many disabled children experience much less stability in their lives than do non-disabled children. They may regularly be sent away from home for short breaks, be looked after by a number of different caregivers and even experience 52-week placements in residential school (see the discussion on 'escape' above).

One recent example described on a training course was a one-year-old girl who spent every day of the week at a different day placement (hospital playgroup/childminder/family centre, etc.) whilst her mother had a break. At the weekends, her father cared for the child. The statutory services had fed this situation by the plans they had in place, and in their desire to support the parent had set up a situation whereby the child had very little sense of stability, or who her main caregiver might be. It would hardly be surprising if this little girl went on to display some 'challenging behaviour' as a result of this situation. Should such a situation be identified as neglect?

Not only might disabled children experience a lack of stability, but also the use of institutional care might well lay them open to a range of abuse, including neglect. Some practices in institutions have been outlined above, and in addition there is the concern that however good the caregiving, the fact that they will come into contact with a large number of caregivers means that their emotional needs are being neglected.

MacNamara (1992 cited in Sobsey 1994) described different types of abusive caregivers based on his extensive experience working in institutions: a salutary reminder that where there are large groups of caregivers there also may be abusers. Nevertheless, because disabled children are perceived as 'difficult' to care for, or because parents are perceived as 'stressed', such environments or caregivers are not challenged. Neither parent nor professional wants to lose this service. A less than satisfactory placement is accepted.

Whilst research on the neglect of disabled children is limited, we would argue that there is sufficient practice-based evidence to guide us in developing more protective models of practice.

Messages for practice

- Practice should be based on a positive attitude towards disabled children, their lives and achievements.

- The question should always be asked, 'Would this situation be acceptable for a non-disabled child?'

- There is an essential need to focus more on the relationships between disabled children, their peers and adults around them.

- The emotional and psychological needs of disabled children should be a priority, and could be neglected by a heavy focus on their bodies and physical development and care.

- Practitioners should not fall into the trap of assuming severely disabled children will not be able to conceptualize the experience of neglect.

- Basic care needs such as food/feeding should not be medicalized, and care needs to focus on sufficient nutrition for quality of life and development.

- Basic health care needs, such as dentistry and immunization, require closer monitoring by professionals.

- Practitioners should not assume that adequate care of the disabled child means that all other emotional and psychological needs are being met.

- Care and love may mask a general incompetency of practice by caregivers.

- Families with disabled children are often struggling financially and practically. The lack of provision of care may be related to this. Assessments must attempt to differentiate between neglect caused by poverty and neglect caused by lack of emotional resources of caregivers.

- Where children are receiving consistent messages that they are not wanted, and despite well-planned intervention change does not occur, the same processes and procedures should be used as for non-disabled children.

- Plans and interventions for disabled children suffering neglect should be time-limited, with a focus on measuring whether sufficient change has occurred to secure the safety and well-being of the child.

- The lack of placement possibilities should not determine whether a neglected disabled child is removed from home.

- Practitioners should be aware that parents 'doing their best' may not be the same as 'good enough' parents.

Chapter 14

Who Cares?

The Role of Mothers in Cases of Child Neglect

Danielle Turney

Introduction

Neglect is notoriously difficult to define. However, one feature that seems to thread through different definitions is an acknowledgement that it involves the breakdown or absence of a relationship of care (Turney 2000). So an understanding of the nature of care may therefore be important for those working with neglect. But care is a heavily gendered concept, closely associated with women or femininity – and this, in turn, has significant implications for the way professionals make sense of and work with families where child neglect is a concern.

The first part of this chapter explores how neglect is constructed as a problem for and about women. I consider the relationship between care and neglect and highlight the gendered nature of care in western social/political thought, looking particularly at motherhood as the 'ideal' caring relationship.

But the close connection between women and caring can be challenged on both practice and broader ethical grounds. So the second part of the chapter briefly considers some of the negative consequences of adopting a heavily gendered view of care, and proposes a repositioning of the idea of care that allows us to see it as a 'universal aspect of human life' (Tronto 1993, p.110) rather than as simply something women do. This opens up a broader debate about both who can and who should care, and may lead to a way of understanding relationships of care that better serves both children and their mothers. It also invites consideration of the ways in which social workers and others can intervene to ensure that children experience the relationships of care that they need for healthy development. The latter part of the chapter identifies some of the practice issues that arise as a result of the earlier analysis, using an ecological perspective to consider different levels of intervention – intra-personal, interpersonal, and social/community-based.

Caring and gender: how neglect is feminized

The focus on women/mothers in child care and child protection work has been noted by a number of writers (for example Farmer and Owen 1995; Milner 1993; O'Hagan and Dillenberger 1995), and is particularly pertinent in relation to neglect. The way we understand neglect – and mothers – reflects various assumptions about the different roles of women and men in relation to the care and nurture of children and it is these assumptions that are explored in the first half of this chapter. My focus on the role of women/mothers does not imply that the role of men/fathers is unimportant or that it should not be subject to the same level of analysis. As Chapter Fifteen shows (and see also Featherstone 2003), there are equally significant issues to consider in relation to working with men.

The importance of care

The need for care at certain points in the life course is universal. For babies and young children in particular, it is crucial for survival and the very possibility of healthy development. 'Care is a multi-dimensional concept that includes within it an attitude of sympathy and compassion as well as the discharge of specific duties' (Clark 2000, p.41). Using this definition, we can see that care consists of the performance of certain tasks – in relation to young children, for example, these may include the provision by the carer of adequate food, in a form that the child is able to manage; warmth; shelter; safety etc. An inability or unwillingness to carry out these duties could certainly be seen to constitute neglect. But, as the quotation above suggests, a full understanding of 'care' includes the idea that it is more than just the provision of these basics (necessary though they are): it involves a particular emotional input from the carer, too. Children who do not experience this emotional engagement with a primary carer may not be in danger of physical neglect, but may well suffer from emotional neglect.

The importance of a secure emotional base has been noted by a number of authors (see, for example, Holden and Nabors 1999; Howe 1996b, 2001).

> Care giving responses are generally triggered when adults are faced with infant attachment behaviors. More generally, it is now recognised that even very young babies show a remarkable range of 'prosocial' behaviours, many of which are highly effective in engaging parents and carers. Children's interest in others, indicated by smiles, vocalisation, looks of concentration and overall excitement, normally encourages adults to maintain contact. It is within these

interactions that young children learn about themselves and others as emotional, psychological and interpersonal beings. However, if caregivers' interest in their children is either absent or hostile, this has been shown to have damaging developmental consequences. (Howe 2001, p.153)

Attachment as one key aspect of a care-giving relationship

Consideration of the quality and nature of the attachments between a child and their caregivers forms part of the assessment of parenting capacity, one of the three 'domains' of the 'assessment triangle' (Department of Health 2000). Howe, Dooley and Hinings (2000) show how an attachment perspective can usefully inform assessment and decision-making in situations where abuse or neglect occur, and it is clear that a child's ability to form secure attachments may be severely jeopardized by inadequate or neglectful parenting. It may also be the case that if parents' ability to cope is compromised by external events (for example, the difficulties of caring for a baby with very low birth weight) this will impact on the nature and quality of their attachment relationships (see Chapter Eleven in this volume) with possible implications for the child's healthy development.

Care and women / mothers

Care has traditionally been seen as 'women's work' and it is fair to say that much of the day-to-day work of caring – for children, for older people and those with disabilities – is still done by a female workforce (both paid and unpaid). Care ethics is an area of study that has given serious consideration to the meaning and importance of care, particularly for women. Margaret Walker, for example, a writer on feminist ethics, says that care ethics has:

> the power to foreground, dramatically and satisfyingly to many women, the ways responsibilities are gendered, and the arbitrary or exploitative fit between social contributions and recognition. Care ethics provides a conceptual framework that makes vast amounts of care taking and care giving activity appear in theory as they are in life – central and indispensable to the continuance, and many goods, of human societies. (Walker 1998, pp.77–78)

A range of positions, some explicitly from a feminist perspective, have been elaborated, giving different analyses of the role and significance of care in the lives of women. Some women writers have endorsed the care perspective and prized women's connection with caring. For example, in the early 1980s, Carol Gilligan put forward the idea that women speak 'in a different voice' to men – a care voice rather than a justice voice (Gilligan 1982). Her work was significant in that it challenged the prevailing view of moral development that saw girls as morally less developed than boys. By identifying a care voice – a form of moral reasoning that valued 'connectedness', caring and a concern with the needs of others – Gilligan gave serious recognition to the centrality of caring in the lives of many women. Others, such as Noddings (1984) Manning (1992) and Ruddick (1989), have developed positions that value and celebrate women's involvement in caring.

However, these accounts have been criticized for not addressing the social context of care and the unequal power relations that structure women's involvement in relationships of care. A number of writers have suggested that care relations reflect not only oppressive gender relations but also other aspects of oppression, notably race and class (Bubeck 1998; Hoagland 1991; Walker 1998; Wong 1994).

> The lens of 'care' magnifies questions about the distribution and recognition of this vital labor: Who cares? The distribution of caring labors disproportionately to women in our society, more disproportionately still to women who are relatively poor and nonwhite, and the low(er) social status of care giving activities and caregivers, are no longer hidden but in plain sight. (Tronto 1993)

> If gender is a feature of status revealed in who gets to do what to whom, it also shows in who is expected or permitted to do what for whom. (Walker 1998, p.78)

In the West, the association between women and caring is most clearly expressed in a range of academic and popular discourses about mothering, which present the relationship between mother and child as the epitome of caring. As Bowden (1997) says, 'The very nature of caring seems to be produced in the connection between the apparently ultimate vulnerability of early childhood and the potentially perfect responsiveness of mothers' (p.21). Even the more overtly woman-focused analyses mentioned earlier – for example, those of Noddings (1984) and Ruddick (1989) – confirm the link between care and the 'natural' mother and proceed from the asumption that maternal love is a given. The bond between mother and child is both natural and, apparently, non-negotiable; Noddings puts it succinctly: 'Mothers quite naturally feel with their infants' (p.31).

Mothers, then, are portrayed as the very model of caring, and a powerful ideology is built up around the 'ever-bountiful, ever-giving, self-sacrificing mother…[who] finds fulfilment and satisfaction in caring for her offspring. This is the mother who "loves to let herself be the baby's whole world"' (Winnicott 1973, p.83 cited in Bassin, Honey and Kaplan 1994, p.3). But the idealization of mothers and mothering is contradicted, for some, by the reality of maternal caring (Bassin et al. 1994; Glenn, Chang and Forcey 1994; Parker 1995, 1997; Romero 1997). For many women, becoming a mother is a hugely satisfying and important part of their lives. But this is not always the case, and mothering needs to be seen in the light of the real social, economic and emotional costs to women in fulfilling the role.

It is important to note that the way motherhood has been conceptualized and understood has not necessarily been the same for all women. In particular, a number of writers have commented that the woman at the centre of the picture of idealized motherhood is invariably white. They acknowledge that motherhood may carry different meanings for black women and women from minority ethnic groups (Collins and Hill 2000; James 1993) and that there are also differences in the ways that black and white women are perceived in relation to roles of wife and mother.

However, at a 'common sense' level, there is a powerful myth that presents the (white, heterosexual, middle-class) mother as the epitome of selfless carer. And while the myth remains, there are consequences for any woman who 'falls short' of the ideal, for whatever reason – the woman who cannot or will not care in the right way. Bowden (1997) sums this up:

> Coloured by links to the biological dimensions of mothering, caring comes to be perceived as an innate characteristic of women and therefore a natural determinant of women's possibilities and roles. Correlatively, the absence of caring attitudes is used to castigate and denigrate women. (p.8)

Mothers and neglect

Is neglect, then, a problem for and about women? As the previous section has shown, there is an abiding connection between women/mothers and care. While this can be seen positively (as a number of writers within the field of care ethics have proposed) or negatively, the connection nonetheless remains strong. So who is likely to be implicated if, for some reason, adequate care is not provided for a child? As things stand, I think that it is likely to be a woman – and, more specifically, the child's mother. This is borne out by an examination of the literature on family functioning and neglect where discussion of the role and contribution (or not) of mothers is predominant and the equivalent role of fathers is conspicuously less fully documented (see for example Baker and Carson 1999; Coohey 1998; Crittenden 1988; Crittenden 1996; Gaudin *et al.* 1996; Polansky *et al.* 1981; Polansky, 1985 As Dubowitz and Black (1996) comment: 'Most of the research on child neglect and high-risk families focuses on mothers and ignores fathers. This bias probably reflects the greater accessibility of mothers…' (p.232).

In some of the literature, discussion is framed in terms of 'parents', but this does not ensure that women and men are subject to the same level of scrutiny. In practice, the research is dealing almost exclusively (though not always explicitly) with mothers. For example a study carried out by Polansky and colleagues (Polansky *et al.* 1981) has the title *Damaged Parents: An Anatomy of Child Neglect.*

But despite the title of the work, the discussion relates primarily to mothers and their failings. According to Polansky *et al.* 'chronically neglectful mothers are very likely to be character-disordered' (1981, p.37), and the traits they are likely to display include 'apathy-futility syndrome' (p.39), that is a sense of powerlessness and lack of agency, and lack of emotional maturity. Crittenden (1988) comes to a similar conclusion with her description of neglecting mothers:

> [They] appear to conceive of relationships as empty. The key to their representational models is their belief that everyone is helpless; some people have more, some less, but no one has control. It is this which leads to their frightening lack of effort to improve their situation or their children's. It is not surprising that it was these mothers who were most often found to be mentally retarded. (p.195)

And it is not just the academic literature that makes the link between women and neglect – news media, for example, are quick to make the connection. 'Home alone' stories find their way into the papers on a regular basis and typically take the format shown in Box 14.1.

Box 14.1 Headlines

'Mother jailed for abandoning sons to go on holiday'
(26 May 2001, *The Guardian*)

'Home alone mother found'
(23 December 2002, *The Telegraph*)

'Missing mother went on skiing trip'
(24 December 2002, *The Guardian*)

'Home alone mum is arrested at airport'
(4 March 2003, *The Mirror*)

These headlines all refer to stories where children have been left without adult supervision – sometimes for extended periods of time.

While this is not to condone the abondonment of children, it is interesting to note that it is the mother specifically who comes in for criticism in these stories. As Parker (1995) observes, with reference to an earlier story of a woman who reportedly left her 11-year-old daughter to go on holiday (see Box 14.2): 'no one seemed to notice that the father was signally absent from the family altogether and had clearly abandoned his daughter for far longer than the length of a holiday on the Costa del Sol' (p.123).

Box 14.2 Headlines

'Truant mum freed from jail'
The story following this headline was about a 'negligent mother' who had been jailed for 'letting her tearaway kids play truant'.
 Underneath a photo of the woman, the caption read: 'GUILTY: Patricia Amos was sent down for neglecting her children's interests.' (22 May 2002, *The Mirror*)

'Is this really our most wanted woman?'
This headline preceded a story about the Metropolitan police publishing a list of its '10 most wanted fugitives. On the list were men suspected of murder, sex attacks and gun running – and a woman accused of neglecting her children.' (18 April 2003, *The Guardian*)

Headlines and stories such as these, reflecting cases that have been reported in national newspapers in recent years, suggest that, in the public's perception at least, neglect is still something that is firmly located with mothers. So in the next section, we will look at some of the implications for practice of the continuing connection between women and neglect.

Messages from research

- Many writers have noted the difficulty in defining neglect. The definition proposed in this chapter involves understanding chronic neglect as the breakdown or absence of a relationship of care.

- Research highlights the importance of attachment as one element of care giving – for example, Howe comments on the role of 'caregiver as attachment figure' (Howe 2001).

- The need for care is universal: care is necessary for survival and healthy development, but the way that care is expressed and organized is not the same everywhere.

- In the West, care is a gendered concept and is primarily associated with women, with mothering seen as the archetypal caring relationship.

- Relationships of care are not only gendered but are also mediated by factors such as race and class.

- The close association between care and 'the feminine' has been promoted by some as a positive identity for women.

- However, there is a danger that this can also have negative consequences for women who do not conform to the idealized view of mothering (for example, women who neglect their children).

- Literature on neglect has tended to focus on the role and perceived inadequacies of women/mothers and to pay less attention to the role and importance of fathers in families where neglect occurs.

Working with neglect: implications for health and social care practice

The feminizing of care and therefore neglect has implications for thinking and practice in health and social care. In this section, I look in more detail at the possible consequences of a gender-biased understanding of neglect and offer some suggestions for practice.

Women and neglect: why does it matter?

I noted in the first section that one consequence of the feminization of care is that it reinforces an existing tendency within social work to focus on women at the expense of men and that this is particularly pertinent in relation to neglect. I suggest here that this can lead to practice that is potentially oppressive to women and unhelpful to vulnerable children. The question I am trying to address here is why it matters if work around neglect focuses on women, particularly mothers. Clearly, while care is still mainly the province of women, it may seem inevitable that they will be the focus of attention when care 'goes wrong'. But I think that three points can be put forward to challenge this:

1. It leads to the personalizing or individualizing of the very complex problem of neglect and to the pathologizing of women. The assumption that 'mothers care' can leave the worker with few ways of thinking about or relating to a woman who apparently cannot or will not care. If we start with the view that all mothers automatically and naturally care for their children then it is easy to slip into a mother-blaming approach towards women who do not fulfil that role, and for

professionals to respond as if the 'problem' lies solely with the individual woman rather, perhaps, than the context within which she is being asked to provide care.

2. A gender-biased approach runs the risk of producing only partial assessments. If social workers, health visitors and other professionals see provision of care as solely the responsibility of the mother, then they are potentially only seeing part of the picture. Men can and do make significant contributions to the care of their children and their role and level of involvement needs to be carefully assessed in each case.

3. It reflects a failure to recognize the complexity of caring/mothering and the relational basis of neglect. Again, accepting the 'natural' equation of women with caring may make it harder to understand the complexity of different mother–child relationships and to analyse the 'meaning of the child' in particular cases (Reder and Duncan 1999; Reder *et al.* 1993). Accurate assessment requires the worker to think carefully about the meaning of each relationship they encounter; appropriate intervention can then be planned, based on the characteristics of that particular relationship.

I am not suggesting that we should now ignore women or stop trying to work effectively with them in cases of child neglect. However, I think that we need a rather different understanding of the nature of care and relationships of care in order to avoid the shortcomings noted above.

Rethinking care

It is probably uncontentious to state that all human infants need a degree of care in order to survive, even if the way that care is provided differs within and between cultures. But care needs are not limited only to infancy: care is a 'universal aspect of human life' (Tronto 1993, p.110). An ecological approach that recognizes interdependency – of people with one another and with their environment – and maintains a relational understanding, suggests that we could all be in situations where we give and receive care throughout our lives. As Tronto says, 'All humans have needs that others must help them meet' (p.110). Yet care remains in the social shadows, 'devalued for its assumed connection with the privacy, emotion and with the "needy"' (Parton 2003, p.10). It is generally low-status work that is carried on out of sight, away from the public gaze.

Writers such as Tronto point out that there is nothing particularly 'natural' about the way in which care roles are assigned. Rather, she suggests that there are political reasons for the prevailing distribution of caring responsibilities, and that care is depoliticized if we see it as 'just' something women do.

Rethinking the place and meaning of care in a broader social and political context – that is, grounding care in the public as well as the private domain – acknowledges the central role it plays in human life and allows us to think more broadly about not only who does care but also who can or should care. Is it all down to individual mothers? Parents? Is there a broader social responsibility – and if so, how can this be met?

Implications for practice

This broader understanding of the place of care in our lives could lead to a range of responses, addressing different levels of concern – intra-personal, interpersonal or family, and social/community-based.

The intra-personal level

In the context of work with mothers, at the intra-personal level this perhaps means starting with the mother as an individual and trying to assess the meaning for her of the relationship between herself and each of the children in the family. It may be that one child is treated conspicuously differently from the others because that child carries 'a particular psychological significance' for her (Reder and Duncan 1999, p.71) or that all the children experience the same (unsatisfactory) level of care or psychological unavailability. In the first part of the chapter, I referred to the attachment needs of children and noted that the experience of neglect can disrupt the child's ability to form secure attachments. Accurate assessment of attachment relationships is crucial if the worker is going to be able to offer appropriate and constructive intervention, and this will entail a thorough understanding of how different parenting styles (themselves, to some extent, a response to the parent's own attachment history) affect the way in which children's attachment needs are or are not met (Turney and Tanner 2001). But this approach invites the worker to hold off from making assumptions about the relationships and to explore each one in its own right.

Effectively, this asks the practitioner to be open to the idea that some women cannot or will not care. This may be very challenging and require a deal of heart-searching on the part of the worker. Taking time to be aware of and reflect on one's own values and assumptions here may be instructive. Ideas about appropriate care for children, who delivers it and how, are emotive topics and it is unwise to suppose that practitioners are somehow 'outside' or unaffected by the prevailing discourses about mothering and caring. Featherstone draws out some of the 'complex emotional dynamics' (Featherstone 1999, p.50) that may be operating, particularly between female workers and service users when issues of mothering are being considered. She raises some potentially difficult questions for these practitioners to address: 'Are they able to hear a range of stories about mothering? What does it mean for them to take seriously a mother's assertion that she does not want to mother a particular child?', and goes on to comment:

> Such assertions may actually mobilize furious anger towards a woman, anger which may arise from a multiplicity of sources, identification with the vulnerable child, as well as the chords that may be struck for those struggling with motherhood themselves... Raised as 'copers' they may find a woman's neediness difficult to bear and be actually more punitive towards her. (pp.50–51)

To summarize the preceding points, we could perhaps just say: do not idealize *mothering* as this may be at the expense of supporting individual mothers. The myth of perfect motherhood is a powerful regulative ideal and may distract us from the realities of women's day-to-day lives – the pressures, the conflicting feelings and sometimes overwhelming emotions that make up the daily experience of mothering. Rozika Parker (1995, 1997) makes a convincing case for the acknowledgement of ambivalence in the mother–child relationship; that is, she suggests that feelings of love and hate can co-exist at times for mothers, but need not be problematic if they can be held in a creative tension. Awareness of conflicting feelings can prompt the mother to think more carefully about the relationship, something which would not occur if she were entirely in the grip of either 'only hostile feelings or untroubled love' (Featherstone 1999, p.48). Parker (1995) puts this as follows:

> ...mothers are prompted by their ambivalence to think about what children themselves are trying to achieve, why and how it may differ from the mother's own experiences and aspirations. Then we can speak of the creative outcomes of manageable ambivalence.

In this analysis, the difficulty comes not from having negative feelings but from the expectations that are placed on mothers not to acknowledge them. Again, to quote from Parker (1997):

> Women mother within cultures that maintain impossible, contradictory maternal ideals which render the range of feelings considered 'normal' or 'natural' in mothers narrow indeed. Hence maternal ambivalence is viewed askance and defended against by both idealization and denigration of mothers. Ambivalence of itself is not automatically a problem. But the shame that often surrounds it renders it deeply problematic. (p.35)

Perhaps one way of dealing with unmanageable ambivalence is simply to switch off – to protect oneself from the pain of trying to resolve these difficult (and socially unacceptable) feelings. For the practitioner, an understanding of the dynamics that Parker describes may be invaluable in helping a mother to acknowledge the conflicting feelings her child provokes in her and provide a framework for bringing love and hate back into a creative and bearable relationship.

The interpersonal or family level

This chapter has been arguing for an ongoing awareness on the part of practitioners of gender issues, to ensure that assessment and intervention around child neglect is effective in terms of protecting vulnerable children but does not contribute to the oppression of women. In practice, at the interpersonal or family level this requires the practitioner to think about whom he or she is working with in cases of neglect. Who is the focus of attention from social and health services? If it is just the mother, is this the result of a conscious decision by the worker? Has there been any attempt to engage the father in the process of assessment and intervention – and if not, why not? While the continuing centrality of women in the care of young children is not in dispute, it is clear that they are not and need not be the only carers. Involvement of men in both social work practice with families and research studies will highlight what they can and do contribute to the welfare of their children.

In addition, gender awareness involves attention to and reflection on language use. We have noted earlier the way in which much of the literature about neglecting families refers to 'parents' when, in practice, the authors are referring primarily to mothers and that this can obscure the roles of the individuals concerned. So it is important that practitioners do not fall into the same trap and are clear whether they mean 'mother', 'father' or 'parents', using the appropriate words in assessments, reports etc.

The social or community level

The approach to practice discussed here fits with a reframing of the concept of care along the lines proposed by Tronto (1993).

> To recognize the value of care calls into question the structure of values in our society. Care is not a parochial concern of women, a type of secondary moral question, or the work of the least well off in society. Care is a central concern of human life. It is time we began to change our political and social institutions to reflect this truth. (p.180)

As we saw in the first section, her analysis challenges the notion of care as primarily a private and dyadic relationship. She identifies the social and political context within which relationships of care take place and the possibilities for change that emerge if the 'moral boundaries' of care are redrawn. This kind of analysis allows the worker to look beyond the immediate family and to consider the social context of care – and this 'bigger picture' may be particularly pertinent in cases of neglect.

This seems to fit well with the ecological approach endorsed by a number of writers such as Bronfenbrenner (1979), Garbarino (1982, 1995) and Jack (2000). Jack, for example, looks at the concept of resilience but also goes on to consider how the wider community environment can affect children's development. He uses the idea of 'social capital' to look at different forms of social support that can impact on – and improve – individuals' experience of parenting and children's experiences of being parented.

For example, one of the defining features of neglect is the breakdown or absence of a relationship of care. In practice, this means that a neglected child does not experience the sustained, affectionate and engaged interest of their parent(s). Research into factors that promote resilience (Daniel *et al.* 1999; Gilligan 1999; Werner 2000) suggests that children may benefit from relationships outside the home that offer them such an experience. So are there other key adults inside or outside the family who could be involved, to the benefit of the child/ren? Perhaps the child can be supported through the involvement of a particular trusted teacher at school, or be linked with a 'buddy' or 'social aunt/uncle'. Such ideas shift the locus of care and move some of the responsibility for supporting and caring for children to the broader social arena.

In this section, I first looked at the effects on assessment and intervention if practitioners focus solely on women and fail to include men in their work. I have then considered some of the options that become available when care is reframed to include both an acknowledgement of the potential importance of men in caring for their children, and a reappraisal of the broader social contexts within which relationships of care are located and understood. A broadly ecological approach that looks at intra-personal dynamics, interpersonal relationships and issues of social 'connectedness' and inclusion shifts the focus away from a narrow mother-blaming response and allows for more wide-ranging intervention that both supports women and promotes the well-being of vulnerable children.

Messages for practice

- Not only women can care. Assessment needs to consider the nature of care the child receives from each of his/her caregivers. You cannot assume that you know what either parent contributes – or that two parents will share the same values, concerns and interests. As part of the assessment, you will need to test this out.

- Workers should ensure that they use language carefully. Be specific about whom you are referring to – do you mean mother, father, parent or other carer? Just using the term 'parent' can obscure the identity of the individual(s) concerned.

- Not all women *do* care. Practitioners may need to examine their own assumptions about gender and care to ensure that they do not work in ways that oppress women who do not conform to the caring stereotype.

- Workers need to develop ways to work with maternal ambivalence. The experience of ambivalence can be one of creative tension or of unmanageable and paralysing burden.

- There is a risk that focusing solely on women will result in partial and flawed assessment.

- Health and social care practitioners need strategies for engaging and working with men.

- In each family where neglect occurs, there is a need for the worker to understand the particular relationship(s) of care and the meaning of the child in these specific contexts.

- It is possible to 'reframe' the idea of care to move away from the current focus on mothers.

- Within an ecological framework, understanding factors that promote resilience allows for a focus outside the mother–child relationship and locates care within a broader social and political context.

Chapter 15

Do They Care?

The Role of Fathers in Cases of Child Neglect

Brigid Daniel and Julie Taylor

Introduction

There has recently been an explosion of interest in the role of the father in children's lives. This interest has been paralleled by an increased recognition that child care and protection processes tend to focus on mothers whether they are the perpetrators of alleged abuse and neglect or not. In this chapter we will consider the situation of fathers of neglected children within the context of changing social discourses about men and fathers. We will explore the literature indicating that child protection processes are not in step with these broader changes and that they consistently retain a focus on mothers. The focus on mothers can be criticized from different perspectives. Such a focus reinforces a view of the mother as solely responsible for the care, protection and nurture of the child. It also effectively cuts fathers out of the picture. Fathers who are abusive or neglectful are not required to take responsibility for their actions in the way that mothers are and caring fathers are neither recognized nor supported. This lack of attention to fathers of neglected children ignores the potential risks that men can pose to children and also misses the opportunity to build on what fathers and paternal extended families may offer to children.

Social policy context

The circumstances of children who are neglected must be considered within the context of family life for all children. The wider policy context affects how practitioners respond to family circumstances, and affects how families see themselves and are seen in comparison with the rest of society.

As Hobson and Morgan (2002) describe, the increased attention to the role of fathers has come from a number of different directions, including men's movements, organizations campaigning on issues of custody and residence and feminist organizations. There are different thrusts to the range of arguments, and the aspirations differ, for example from the strengthening of marriage through to ensuring that fathers assume their responsibilities. However, the one common emerging theme is that the role of the father should not be ignored. Hobson and Morgan also set out the policy developments in different countries with regard to men. They point to the convergence of social policy in Western Europe and the USA where two-earner families are becoming the norm, but without an equivalent rise in the extent to which men are involved in unpaid care of children. They describe the policies that some countries, for example Sweden and the Netherlands, have introduced to increase fathers' involvement in child care. Studies in Britain suggest that mothers still take the main responsibility for organizing care for children and also still perform the lion's (or lioness') share of the domestic chores (Ferri and Smith 1995). Overall, though, there is more movement towards policies aimed at including fathers in child care, for example allowing for paternal leave.

Another convergence across western nations is of the rise in divorce and lone-parent families. But divorce does not automatically lead to loss of contact between children and fathers. Bradshaw *et al.* for example found that only 3% of separated or divorced fathers were out of contact with their children (Bradshaw *et al.* 1999). At the same time resident and non-resident fathers are increasingly asserting their rights to be involved in the lives of their children.

The circumstances of children involved in child protection processes in Britain are different, though, from the majority of children. Although there is a rise in the number of lone-parent families, abused and neglected children are far more likely to be living with one parent than the norm. So whilst 73% of children in the UK live with both birth parents and 8% in reconstituted families, only 38% of those involved in the child protection process live with both parents (Ryan and Little 2000). These lone parents tend to be mothers but even when fathers are present the circumstances are also different from the norm. Such paternal rights as there are tend to benefit working families, but paternal leave, for example, is irrelevant to fathers who do not have a job: the situation for the majority of men whose children are referred to statutory authorities because of neglect. As is developed in detail in Chapter Two, children who are referred for neglect tend to be living in extremely deprived circumstances and it can be assumed that absent fathers will often also be living in deprived circumstances.

What fathers offer to children

As described in Chapter Fourteen, the language of parenting is laden with assumptions about the relationship of care that is entailed in mothering. The concept of care is bound up with our understandings of attachment. The vast bulk of research about adult–child relationships with their children have concentrated on attachment to the mother. Other significant relationships, including those with fathers, have not been ascribed the same significance nor scrutinized to the same extent. However, what research there is demonstrates that children can, and do, form secure attachments to fathers. Although there tends to be an association between the type of attachment to the main carer and other significant people, 31% of children may show different types of attachment to one parent and the other (Main and Weston 1981). If the father adopts the role of primary caretaker then the young child shows the same kind of attachment behaviours as he or she would to a female primary caretaker (Geiger 1996).

So, it is the case that attachment between men and children can be good, but the evidence about what fathers offer to children is very mixed and difficult to interpret. It is particularly difficult to disentangle whether the presence of a father is beneficial because of the specific male fathering role he plays or because he is another adult and parent who can assist with care of the children. Comparisons between families where fathers are present and lone-mother households are subject to considerable confounding factors, especially those of material circumstances. Therefore it is difficult to gauge the specific impact of the absence of a father in a child's life. Studies of children reared by two women in a relationship, for example, indicate that outcomes are as good as for children reared by a mother and father (Kershaw 2000).

There is, however, a growing body of studies on the positive effects father involvement can have on children. Lamb (1997) provides an overview of the different ways in which fathers can impact on their children's development:

- as the primary breadwinner
- in caring for, playing with and teaching children
- as support for the mother.

He emphasizes the importance of the quality of the relationships between men and their children, which appear to transcend the significance of the gender of the parent. Children themselves say that what they want of fathers is that they be a role model, offer quality time, support them, show love and provide physical contact (Milligan and Dowie 1998). Fathers appear to have the potential to offer a particularly positive impact on children's attitude to school and educational achievement (Coley 1998; Katz 1999).

Flouri and Buchanan (2003) carried out an extensive survey of 2722 British young people aged 14–18 in order to ascertain the role of father and mother involvement on adolescents' psychological well-being, regardless of family composition. The young people were asked to complete a questionnaire which included questions about the extent of each parent's involvement and in which they rated their happiness. Self-report of happiness by adolescents was found to be significantly, and independently, associated with greater involvement of the mother and greater involvement of the father. Indeed, father involvement had the stronger effect, and for both boys and girls. However, the effect was not related to the family structure: a father could still be involved with his offspring and impact upon happiness even if he was not part of the same household. Socioeconomic status was not found to be related to happiness. As the authors conclude, the findings 'generally supported the notion that fathers are salient figures in the lives of their adolescents' (Flouri and Buchanan 2003, p.405). The study did not examine the salience of other potentially significant adult figures in children's lives and so cannot assist with whether there is some specific quality of fathers as *men* that is essential. However, as the work on 'socio-genealogical connectedness' indicates, even if children do not have an emotional connection with an absent parent, they value information that can help them understand their own heritage and culture, and this can be particularly important for children of mixed-race heritage (Owusu-Bempah and Howitt 1997).

Therefore, there is now ample evidence that fathers have potentially much to offer their children. This, of course, must be tempered by the considerable body of evidence about the extent of the risks that can be posed to children by men. Men are responsible for the majority of domestic abuse of their partners, and the direct and indirect effects upon children of domestic abuse are now well delineated (Hester, Pearson and Harwin 2000). Men are also responsible for the majority of the sexual abuse of children, and, when the amount of time with the child is taken into account, for more physical abuse of children. This is why it is as important to assess the potential risk that a man may pose as the potential asset he may be. The extent to which a man may simultaneously be a risk and an asset is a more contentious area (Featherstone 2001).

Naturally, it is vital in child care and protection work that the prime focus is upon protection of children, but adults' relationships with their children can be complex and it is, therefore, also vital that practitioners take account of each child's individual circumstances and emotional ties.

Fathers and child protection

Child protection practice

Within the realm of child care and protection practice, there is a lack of research-based information and of a clear framework for practice with fathers and male figures (Daniel and Taylor 1999). There is literature that criticizes health visitors and social workers for concentrating on the mother, however, given the complexity of the findings about fatherhood in general and the lack of policy guidance it is perhaps not surprising that practitioners are struggling to formulate a coherent approach to men (Daniel and Taylor 2001).

There is considerable evidence that current practice does not take sufficient account of the risks that some men pose towards children, although clearly outcomes will be improved if potential risks from all quarters are properly assessed. Despite the fact that Munro (1998) had highlighted the failure to assess the role of mothers' male partners as a recurrent error in cases that were subject to child protection public enquiries, a subsequent examination of serious case reviews in England and Wales again highlighted the failure to take account of male figures (Sinclair and Bullock 2002). Similarly a review of child protection in Scotland showed that previous convictions committed by male figures could be buried in old case files and not taken account of in current child protection practice (Scottish Executive 2002a). Even when the source of risk is identified as a male figure the focus of intervention is nearly always the mother, who is expected to protect the child (Dempster 1993; Farmer and Owen 1998). As Stanley (1997) describes it, men are rendered 'invisible' in child protection processes.

By the same token the positive role that fathers may play in their children's lives is often ignored in child protection practice. Edwards (1998) suggests that men are viewed by professionals as a 'problem' whether present or absent. If present they are seen as unhelpful, unsupportive and possibly violent, while if absent they are considered irresponsible. A man is only considered to be a 'father' if living in the household with the children. In her observations of social work and health visiting practice she noted that men were frequently in the households visited, but were not engaged with constructively, and were often given subtle messages that caring for children is the mother's domain. Health visitors not only often fail to involve fathers, they may also lack a concept of what role fathers could play. A study of fathers' views indicated that they were marginalized by health visitors and felt ignored or dismissed. They also felt that lower levels of knowledge and skills in child care were expected of them (Williams and Robertson 1999). In a study evaluating a particular Sure Start initiative that aimed to provide support to vulnerable parents Taylor *et al.* (2002) highlighted the lack of any focus on fathers by practitioners involved with vulnerable children.

Child neglect

The neglect literature, in particular, pays scant attention to fathers who seem to make up part of the group of 'invisible' men associated with child protection work. They are described as having a tangential relationship with the family at the very most. This was found to be the case in a recent study carried out by Daniel and Baldwin (2002), that revealed a very complex pattern of family structure in cases of child neglect. It was not uncommon for there to be several children, each with a different father, and perhaps a current partner who acted as a father to the children. Case files contained minimal, if any, information about how the children viewed their fathers and how the adults in the family viewed the parenting role of men.

And yet it is in the area of neglect that the issue of gender is so central. Swift (1995), in her detailed analysis of gender and neglect, vividly portrays the extent to which neglect is constructed as a failure in mothering, as provided by women. It is mothers who are labelled as perpetrators of neglect, not fathers. Scourfield's (2003) recent ethnographic study of a children and families social work team in England showed that neglect and mothering are still intertwined in practitioner discourse. He describes an increase in attention to neglect as a child protection issue in the locality under study and suggests that such an increased focus on neglect will lead inevitably to the increased scrutiny of mothers. Swift found that any child care action by a father tended to be written in case files as positive, whereas partial or total absence was not remarked upon. On the other hand, Scourfield showed that practitioners do seem, now, to be more aware of men but tend to focus on the more negative aspects. He identified five social work discourses that described men as:

- a threat
- no use
- irrelevant
- absent
- no different from women
- better than women.

Significantly, men were really only likely to be described as better than women when it had been decided that the woman was a 'bad mother', so that a 'good' father had to be connected with a 'bad' mother.

The fact that so many children referred because of neglect are living with their mothers may be a significant issue and indeed may have a causal relationship. For example, it may be that father absence increases the risk of neglect, or that father presence protects children from neglect. It may also be that the factors associated with the relationship breakdown are also associated with neglect. Father involvement may be associated with child well-being among children in the general population but there is very little research evidence to help with understanding the possible inter-relationships in cases of neglect. One study that attempts to disentangle this is described in Box 15.1.

Box 15.1 Example of research

Dubowitz *et al.* (2000) carried out research into the relationship between fathers and neglect with 244 five-year-old children as part of a longitudinal study of child health and development among families at risk of abuse and neglect. Mothers were asked if the father was present or there was at least monthly contact with the child's father or 'someone like a father' and, if there was, the fathers were approached for interview. In 68 cases no father was identified, in 59 the father was identified but was not available for interview and in 117 cases fathers were interviewed. Two thirds of the fathers who were interviewed lived with their children. Interviews covered aspects of parenting including satisfaction, involvement with the child and relationship with the mother. Parenting scales and an analysis of video-taped recordings of the fathers playing with their children were also used. All the children were given a rating on a 'neglect index' developed on the basis of scales of neglect, child protection statistics and observations of mother and child interaction. For the total 244 cases there were no significant differences in neglect according to presence or absence of fathers and there was a suggestion that another adult in the household (for example a grandmother) could fulfil the role of 'father'. But for the 117 interview cases neglect was less likely when the father:

- was involved for a longer period
- expressed more parenting effectiveness
- was more involved in household tasks
- was less involved in child care.

They suggest that the latter slightly contradictory finding could be due to the father being forced to take on child care because the mother was relatively unavailable. A number of variables were not associated with neglect, including fathers' financial contributions, whether the man was the biological father or a father-figure and whether the father lived in the household. 'Both the quality of the relationship and the fathers' involvement seem to be more important than the biological relationship of the father or where he resides' (Dubowitz *et al.* 2000, p.140).

It may be that the factors associated with relationship breakdown are separately associated with neglect. Most research about the characteristics of parents whose children are neglected has been carried out with mothers and it tends to catalogue a range of personal and social difficulties that are likely to impede satisfactory relationship-building (see Chapter One).

Two studies have looked specifically at the relationship between mothers whose children had been neglected and their partners. In comparison with mothers whose children had not been referred for neglect the women in Lacharite, Ethier and Couture's (1996) study described their male partners as:

- less adequate marital partners
- less supportive
- more violent.

Interestingly, though, they perceived their partners to be equally adequate as fathers as women whose children were not neglected did. The study does not indicate what standards of fathering were expected by either group of women, but this does reaffirm that even if the parental relationship is not positive the father–child relationship may still be important. In contrast Coohey (1995) found that mothers of neglected children did describe getting emotional support from their male partners, but that the men were less likely to:

- be the biological fathers of the children
- be living with the mother
- have been in the relationship longer than five years.

These findings seem slightly contradictory, but it is interesting that Coohey also found that women whose children are neglected received far less emotional support from their mothers who were not seen as warm and caring. This chimes with much of the research into neglect that shows that the mothers lack social support, and therefore may need to rely to a greater extent on male partners, even if the partnership is not that satisfactory. It also reinforces the idea that it may not be the fact that the man is the biological father that is so important, rather that he is another adult who can help with parenting the child.

When it is decided by the mother or social work department that a child can no longer live with her because of neglect then fathers could be considered as a possible option for placement and a study into paternal placements for neglected children is described in Box 15.2 (Greif and Zuravin 1989).

The research evidence about fathers and neglect is therefore sparse and somewhat confusing. The absence of research about the fathers of neglected children is significant in itself and clearly more information is needed about the complex inter-relationships between factors associated with neglect and the role of fathers.

Box 15.2 Example of research

Drawing from a sample of 518 low-income, urban, single-parent mothers in Baltimore who were part of a study into factors associated with physical abuse and neglect Greif and Zuravin (1989) identified 14 women whose children were living with a total of 17 fathers. Thirteen of the case files provided sufficient information for detailed examination of how and why fathers obtained custody. The researchers compared their circumstances with fathers without custody. They also looked at the circumstances of 47 women whose children were living elsewhere, but not with their fathers. Only two of the fathers had actively sought custody, the rest fell into one of three categories:

1. The mothers told the fathers they wanted to give up custody of the child.

2. Child protective services found the fathers, who had not previously been involved with the children, and encouraged them to assume custody.

3. Children chose to live with their fathers.

Mothers' circumstances did not appear to significantly affect whether children went to fathers: either mothers gave their children up or child protection agencies removed them and the placement decision was secondary. However, fathers' circumstances did affect the likelihood of the children living with them; the most important appeared to be that they were in a relationship with a woman:

> If the father has a stable living arrangement with a woman, shows an interest in having the children, and is not a serious abuser of alcohol or drugs, he has a much better chance of getting custody than if none of these factors are present. (Greif and Zuravin 1989, p.487)

The disappointing aspect of this study was that the picture of the placement with the father was 'neither a flattering nor encouraging one'. Many of the men had histories of violence and drug use and were not co-operative with social workers. The study is limited by the fact that the fathers themselves were not interviewed, nor were the children, so the conclusions about the placements have to be based on inference from case files.

Messages from research

- There is now an accepted rhetoric of father involvement, although the aspirations differ for different organizations.

- Separation of the father from the mother does not necessarily mean that fathers are not salient figures for children.

- Neglected children's fathers are more likely to be living apart from the children's mothers, to be materially deprived and to have emotional difficulties.

- The attachment relationship between fathers and children can be, and often is, significant and secure.

- Fathers potentially have much to offer their children, especially with regard to school performance.

- Current child protection practice tends to ignore the risks some men pose.

- Current child protection practice fails to recognize fathers as a potential asset.

- Neglect is still overwhelmingly constructed as a failure in mothering.

- Father presence may help to reduce the level of neglect, even if just as another adult to offer support.

- The factors associated with poor adult relationships may also be associated with a tendency to neglect children.

Assessing the role of the father

First and foremost social workers, health visitors and other professionals must ensure that they render the men in neglected children's lives visible (Daniel and Taylor 2001). Current social trends are towards the greater recognition of the role of fathers. Practitioners need to ask themselves whether they have lower expectations of fathers they encounter in practice than of fathers in the general population. This may be coupled with significant expectations of mothers to take full responsibility for parenting under very difficult circumstances. Practitioners also need to ask themselves whether they are ignoring men who pose a potential risk.

Comprehensive assessment is essential for effective practice with neglect and being comprehensive entails considering all the significant adults in a child's life. Information must be separately recorded and collated about:

- the mother
- the biological father
- the mother's current partner/s or other father figure/s
- the nature of the relationship of each of these people with the child
- the nature of their relationships with each other.

It is, of course, important to ask children about their relationships with, and perceptions of, significant adults. Flouri and Buchanan's (2003) scale of father involvement used in the study described above could be useful for assessing the extent of father involvement; it asks children about the extent to which a father or father figure:

- spends time with them
- talks through their worries with them
- takes an interest in their school work
- helps with their plans for the future.

Men as risks

To ignore fathers and father figures is to ignore the possible risks that men can pose to children. Fathers may be exacerbating the likelihood of neglect, for example if they use household income to finance substance misuse. It is important to know who spends the money and on what. It may be the case that fathers are undermining the confidence of their partners and therefore contributing to their sense of powerlessness. They may be overly critical, exacting or demanding and may encourage the children to see their mother in a negative light. Practitioners must be alert to the possibility of domestic abuse and be prepared to broach the subject with women who appear to be suffering physical harm. If they do encounter domestic abuse they should offer practical and emotional support to women and be aware of the significant dangers that women face if they choose to leave violent partners (Hester and Radford 1996). Midwives should be aware that domestic abuse can escalate during pregnancy (Mezey and Bewley 1997).

Fathers and father figures may also pose a sexual risk to children. Because neglect can be associated with chaos, crisis and chronic need it is very easy for practitioner energies to be consumed in trying to tackle it. Sexual abuse may be masked and overlooked. Indeed, men who want to sexually abuse children will often seek out such families and target them because they provide easy access to children. Children who are neglected are more likely to have a low sense of self-efficacy and therefore to find it difficult to seek help. Many women whose children are neglected have low self-esteem and self-efficacy themselves and may form a series of superficial relationships. They often find it difficult to stop dangerous men from moving into the household. Some men may also bring other people into the house who pose a sexual risk to children, or take the children to households where they are abused. And because a series of men in these transient relationships may be encountered it is easy for practitioners to fail to take them into account in their assessments. It may seem pointless to try to engage with them and they may very skilfully avoid contact with professionals. However, it is essential to be alert to these men and to ask questions of them and about them. It is not sufficient to rely on maternal report because men may go to great lengths to conceal past offences, or to convince women that they have changed. It is important to look at historical information that may be held within probation or criminal justice files as men may have previous convictions of abuse.

The art of assessment, which transcends data collection, is the analysis of the information about the child's needs and strengths and about each adult in a way that allows a purposeful intervention plan to be developed and monitored. Sophisticated analysis is essential if the complexity of human characteristics is to be captured. The capacity of each significant, or potentially significant, person to meet the child's needs should be assessed as well as the kind of supports and intervention that might enhance that capacity. The risks and benefits posed by each significant adult, male or female, should also be delineated. That is, practitioners need to entertain the possibility that the same person can be risky in some respects whilst simultaneously having something to offer the child. For example, a mother may offer the benefits of attachment, but the risks related to bouts of excessive drinking. A father may offer the benefit of taking an interest in the child's schooling but the risks related to aggressive behaviour towards the mother. Such assessment takes time, and it is essential that practitioners make a strong case for sufficient time to carry out such assessments.

Practice with fathers

One of the findings of Dubowitz *et al.*'s (2000) study was that fathers' sense of parenting effectiveness was associated with lower neglect ratings, therefore fathers may need help to develop a sense of competence and efficacy as a father. The scale they used included items such as:

- Considering how long I've been a father, I feel thoroughly familiar with the role.

- I honestly believe I have all the skills necessary to be a good father to my child.

- I meet my own personal expectations for expertise in caring for my child.

During assessment, therefore, it may be helpful to discuss separately with the father how confident and competent he feels as a parent and to provide support and advice about areas where perceived competence is lower. It would be important to discover what aspects of being a father are important to the man himself.

In addition to specific aspects of parenting there may be other aspects of the father's life that require attention; fathers may need help with:

- violent behaviour
- alcohol or drug problems
- finances
- housing
- mental health problems
- relationships
- childhood experiences of abuse and neglect.

Dubowitz *et al.* also found that lower levels of neglect were associated with longer relationships. It is well known that disruptive relationships and household conflict are highly corrosive for children's emotional well-being. Therefore, it may be that fathers would benefit from help with relationships with:

- the child's mother
- their partner, if different
- the child.

Dubowitz *et al.* suggest that fathers should be encouraged to be more involved with their children in ways that are 'optimally nurturing'. Health care workers should include fathers and there should be more programmes for fathers. They should facilitate fathers' emotional and material support to mothers and encourage mothers to allow father involvement. It is essential to be alert to the fact that a father can be a salient figure to the child, even if he is not in the same household. Therefore it may be necessary to facilitate direct or indirect contact by offering practical and emotional support on a sustained basis to enable the relationship to be beneficial to the child.

Schooling is so often a problem for neglected children. The evidence from the general population suggests that father involvement can enhance school performance and interest in school. However, many fathers of neglected children are likely to have had difficult experiences of school themselves and may well have left school with no qualifications. It may be necessary, therefore, to carry out considerable groundwork with a father to help him to appreciate the importance of education and to explain to him the benefits of father involvement with schooling. It will be helpful, therefore, to consider ways in which the father could be engaged to help with school issues. The school records may not hold accurate information about both parents, about who should receive information, about how to involve both, and about circumstances that may pose a risk to children. Fathers may need considerable support to take part in school meetings, go to parents' evenings and so on.

As described in Chapter Twelve family centres can be the sites of effective provision for family support in cases of child neglect. Family centres can provide combinations of groupwork, individual work and fun activities for adults and children. It is now recognized by staff in many family centres that their provision has tended to be mother-oriented and attempts are being made to involve fathers more. Ghate *et al.* (2000) found that centres could encourage father involvement if they adopted deliberate policies of engagement with men. Centres were equally successful whether they adopted a 'gender-blind' approach that assumed that men and women's needs were similar, or a 'gender-differentiated' approach that organized different activities for men. Centres without any clear strategy for involving men were far less successful in encouraging fathers to come to the centre. Factors associated with encouraging fathers to attend centres are identified by Ewart (2003) and are shown in Box 15.3.

Box 15.3 Suggestions for practice

Ewart (2003) carried out a study of father's involvement in family centres in Northern Ireland. In 15 child protection cases she interviewed mothers, fathers and social workers. Several deterrents to father involvement were identified. Some fathers said they would prefer to talk to a male social worker, but were not offered the choice. All the fathers stated that most fathers, if given the choice, would choose not to attend. Some found it difficult to accept the severity of the problem or they could not see their role in improving the situation. The use of authority in requiring attendance of fathers contributed to reluctance to attend. Some were fearful of involvement and were especially apprehensive if renewing contact with children they had not seen for a long time. The main deterrent, though, was the perception that mothers were central to child care and therefore the primary clients of the centres. Social workers and mothers either directly, or indirectly, contributed to the exclusion of fathers.

Father attendance was promoted positively by a number of factors. Social workers could engage with fathers if they used the core skills of showing respect, listening, making fathers feel comfortable, working at the pace of the individual, avoiding technical and jargonized language and maintaining objectivity when working with couples. Ewart makes several suggestions for the promotion of father-inclusive social work policy and practice:

- comprehensive regional strategies and policy initiatives focused on paternal involvement
- systematic attention to the covert feminization of family centres
- training to assist practitioners to identify how their attitudes may deter father involvement
- an expectation of father involvement as the norm rather than an option
- more male staff
- multi-agency policies and procedures to address the issue of male violence
- specific training on how to work with fathers
- the development of more groupwork provision for fathers.

Fathers who pose risks because of factors such as difficult relationships with the mother, irresponsible use of money, lack of interest in the household and so on should not be avoided. Just as practitioners are prepared to confront and challenge mothers about what is an acceptable level of care for children and an acceptable environment for them, so they must apply the same standards to fathers. The message has to be conveyed that the children are a joint responsibility.

When a father appears to pose a more serious threat to either the mother or the child then this must not be ignored. It is not reasonable to place all the responsibility upon the mother to end the relationship or to protect the child. Again practitioners must be prepared to work directly with men. This does not mean that they must place themselves in risky situations, but perhaps they can seek advice, or work jointly with, a social worker who is skilled in working with offenders, for example. If a man is not prepared to acknowledge that his behaviour is damaging to the child and will not change, then the child must be protected from that behaviour, preferably by removal of the man from the household, not the child.

Messages for practice

In conclusion, therefore, it is clear from the evidence that fathers are not given due attention in child care and protection processes and that especially in cases of neglect their potential is often ignored. It would be unrealistic to provide a rosy picture of fatherhood in this context. The fathers of children who are neglected may have significant personal problems and exhibit difficult or violent behaviour towards children and women. However, no assessment or intervention plan can be considered complete if the parenting roles of men, both positive and negative, are not addressed.

- Fathers must be rendered visible.

- Comprehensive assessment includes attention to all significant or potentially significant adults, male or female.

- Children's own views about who is important to them must be ascertained.

- The complexity of relationships must be recognized.

- The potential for a father to pose a risk to children must be considered and assessed for carefully.

- It may be helpful to look at the father's sense of efficacy as a parent.

- Children may benefit if fathers are offered support with other problematic areas of their lives.

- Fathers can be encouraged to develop nurturing relationships with their children.

- Fathers may have an important role in encouraging school performance and enjoyment.

- Family centres should ensure that they work effectively with mothers as well as fathers.

Chapter 16

Intervening with Neglect

Geraldine Macdonald

'What works' credentials

Evidence-based decision-making is a demanding task, requiring much more than simply knowledge about which interventions are effective and which are not. The other chapters in this book highlight the importance of a sound knowledge of the factors contributing to neglect, the importance of high quality assessments, maintaining a child-focused approach. That said, knowing what works, and if so in what timescale, with what demands on resources, and with what chances of success in a particular set of circumstances, is essential. For the reader familiar with the literature, this chapter may appear to ignore a number of studies purporting to address effective interventions in the field. For practitioners, it may at first sight offer less than was hoped for in terms of answers to the important question 'what works?' This is because in order to be included in this summary account of 'what works?', only certain kinds of evidence have been deemed acceptable. They are, in order of evidential weight:

1. Systematic reviews, that is, reviews in which all the primary studies have been systematically identified, appraised and summarized according to an explicit and reproducible methodology (see Chapter Three).

2. Randomized controlled trial, that is, studies in which participants have been randomly allocated to receive either the intervention being evaluated or to be in a control group. The control group may have received an alternative intervention, usual services, or no services, that is, be on a waiting list.

3. Two-group studies, that is, studies in which one group of participants received the intervention being evaluated and another group (possibly matched on important characteristics such as age, gender, ethnicity, type or history of neglect) received one of the alternatives described in Point 2 above.

4. Studies which do not enjoy high quality evidential credentials (that is, do not meet the above criteria) but which themselves do not make claims beyond the evidence, and which – in the author's judgement – merit consideration as 'promising approaches'.

Problems in the evidence base

When the above threshold criteria are applied, one inevitably finds oneself with a preponderance of US studies, and a paucity of UK studies. Some consider that there can be little generalizability of results to a UK context, and in some areas this may be so, for example when the policy context determines the intervention and is quite different from our own. The principle adopted here is that if a study concerns participants who are similar to those we work with, the workers are similarly qualified, and the interventions in principle deployable, then they merit serious consideration – if effective. More problematic is that few studies employ explicit and/or consistent definitions of neglect, fewer still focus only on neglect, or differentiate the results relating to neglect from those relating to physical abuse, and in general there is a dearth of good quality studies (Macdonald 2001).

It is also easy to forget that few studies demonstrate efficacy for all participants in a study. The best evidence suggests only that one intervention outperforms an alternative. Perhaps 'what works best' would be a better term. Knowing 'what works' is only a component of evidence-based decision-making. Professional judgement, information about why and how things work, and what service users feel about being on the receiving end of such endeavours are also essential. Knowing that something is effective may not be the most important factor in decision-making if the timescale necessary to change something is such that the child cannot wait, or if the resources required are not available. Knowing what works does not guarantee that it will work with any particular family. Careful monitoring and evaluation are essential when pursuing a course of action that appears, on the basis of the research evidence, to be optimum.

Interventions not included here

Not covered in this chapter are interventions designed to improve overall standards of parenting, or to prevent the likelihood of neglect at the level of the community or neighbourhood. Thus, interventions such as Sure Start are not included, nor are community-based parenting classes. This is not because such interventions are not important (see Chapter Two), but because the families that cause professionals most concern are not those for whom the causes of neglect are predominantly socioeconomic, even though these may be important (see Chapter Nine).

One of the features of most outcome research to date is its focus on mothers (see Chapter Fourteen). As a research-based chapter, this bias is mirrored here. It would be a serious error, though, to dismiss the findings of studies on the grounds that they have not included fathers, unless there are sound reasons for thinking that their exclusion (or lack of presence) invalidates the results. What is needed is astuteness in using these data when developing practice.

Interventions directed at carers

Before considering programmes directed at parents who have already formed neglectful patterns of behaving, it is worth highlighting one group of interventions targeted at groups of parents considered 'high risk' – so-called 'home visiting' programmes.

Home visiting programmes

There have been a number of reviews of the effectiveness of these interventions, but methodologically the most secure review remains that conducted by MacMillan and her colleagues (MacMillan *et al.* 1994). They conclude that the only effective programmes were those delivered to families with 'one or more of single parenthood, poverty, and teenage parent status' (p.852), over a lengthy period. One of these was the Hardy and Streett study, which was designed as a prevention study (Hardy and Streett 1989). The other was a randomized controlled trial conducted by David Olds and colleagues (Olds, Henderson and Kitzman 1994), targeted at high risk first-time mothers. This long-term programme of visiting by trained nurses begun *during* pregnancy and was designed to address a number of aspects of maternal and child functioning, viz:

- outcomes of pregnancy for mother and child

- the qualities of caregiving (including associated child health and developmental problems)

- maternal life-course development (helping mothers return to education, or work, and plan future pregnancies)

- the prevention of child maltreatment.

(Olds 1997, p.133)

The programme conceptualized the adequacy of care provided by parents as a function of other relationships, and the wider social context. Home visitors therefore focused attention on the social and material environment of families. They sought to promote informal networks of friends and family members who could provide reliable sources of material and emotional support. As it has developed, the programme has paid more attention to theories of human attachment, and to the perceived importance of self-efficacy theory, that is, that human behaviour is partly a function of how effective people perceive themselves to be. The latter resulted in an emphasis on behaviour rehearsal, reinforcement and problem-solving, rather than a reliance on information and insight. The former has had particular relevance to the *process* of helping, stressing the importance of:

- establishing an empathic relationship between mother and home visitor

- reviewing with caregivers their own child-rearing histories

- an explicit focus on promoting a sensitive, responsive, and engaged caregiving in the early years of a child's life.

Visiting begins during pregnancy because this is conceptualized as a window of 'motivational opportunity'. The authors theorize that at no other time are women quite as engaged and concerned about their own health and that of their unborn child. Mothers received an average of nine visits during their pregnancy and 23 visits (SD = 15) from birth through the second year of the child's life. The results showed that of those who received home visiting, only 4% abused or neglected their children, compared with 19% of those who did not receive this service. Between their twenty-fourth and forty-eighth month of life, children of home-visited women were 40% less likely to visit a physician for an injury or ingestion (poisoning) than those in the comparison group, they lived in homes with fewer safety hazards, and which were deemed more conducive to their intellectual and emotional development (Olds *et al.* 1995). However, there were no differences noted in referrals for child maltreatment during this period. The authors point out that child maltreatment in the comparison group is likely to be under-detected, and over-detected in the experimental group due to the increased surveillance of child abuse and neglect which the project effected, but this 'wash out' effect should not be minimized.

Since this first study was completed, subsequent replications have had less striking results in respect of child maltreatment (Olds *et al.* 1998; Olds *et al.* 1999) The authors speculate that perhaps even longer periods of visits are required in order to make a serious impact. Given (i) the need to acquire new, age-appropriate knowledge and parenting skills as children grow, and (ii) the long-standing nature of many of the problems faced by vulnerable families, it may well be that longer-term interventions merit serious consideration. There is much in this programme that targets factors that lead to neglect, including poor attachment, social isolation, poverty and the needs of carers, and these themes recur in most of the literature on what works in dealing with neglect (see also Holden and Nabors 1999; Singer, Minnes and Arendt 1999).

Cognitive-behavioural programmes

These are based on the premise that many of the difficulties we encounter or present are the result of learning, and that unhelpful or dangerous ways of behaving are learned in the same way as other kinds of behaviour. This holds out the possibility that undesirable or undesired ways of behaving can be unlearned and more desirable ones learned. Assessment includes a functional analysis (e.g. examining what people do, what triggers their behaviour and what maintains it, how it has been learned or shaped, what obstacles prevent alternate strategies being adopted). Interventions are derived from learning theory and include modelling, instruction, practice feedback and positive reinforcement. Enhancing self-efficacy or 'can do' (Bandura 1977) is a key feature of cognitive-behavioural programmes, and provides a concrete example of empowerment. Few studies of the effectiveness of cognitive-behavioural therapy (CBT) have focused particularly on helping families where serious neglect is the main problem.

Knowing how a variety of factors (social, psychological, cognitive) from a range of arenas (interpersonal, intra-personal, familial and social) contribute to the development and maintenance of problems has influenced the development of broad-based approaches to cognitive-behavioural assessment and intervention (Patterson 1982). The term often used to describe these interventions is eco-behavioural (see Donohue and Van Hasselt 1999). This rather cumbersome term denotes the application of behavioural principles and interventions across the variety of sources of influence on families. Referring to earlier work, Lutzker *et al.* (1998) describe it as follows:

> By ecobehavioural, they meant that assessment and treatment were conducted within the families' social ecologies such as homes, schools, foster care, preschool and other settings within the natural community. Treatment strategies combined direct observation, behavior assessment, behavior analysis and therapeutic procedures, and humanistic counselling procedures. Further, within this ecobehavioral context, active attempts were made to program for generalization of newly learned skills across settings, behaviors and time. (p.164)

In other words, eco-behavioural programmes target identified problems in a range of settings including, but not restricted to, the family. Project 12-Ways is amongst the best known and best evaluated of these. It derives its name from the 12 core services described in the original programme: parent–child training, stress reduction for parents, basic skill training for the children, money management training, social support, home safety training, multiple-setting behaviour management *in situ*, health and nutrition, problem-solving, couples counselling, alcohol abuse referral, and single mother services (see Lutzker *et al.* 1998).

Single case experimental designs have demonstrated the programme's effectiveness in dealing with a range of problems assessed as contributing to child abuse and neglect (see Macdonald 2001). A series of matched comparison studies provide evidence of the effectiveness of the programme overall, and in a five-year follow-up of more than 700 families Project 12-Ways families had consistently lower rates of abuse across all years. The authors note that over time, the incidence of reported abuse increases for both groups, and the gap between them, whilst still statistically significant, looks 'clinically' less impressive. In other words, there seems to be a 'wash out' effect over time, perhaps pointing to a need for 'booster services' or additional support to these families, in order to maintain the early differences between the group. Lutzker and his colleagues are developing and evaluating a modified version of this programme which tackles three key areas of particular relevance to young parents at risk of neglecting their children: home safety, infant and child health care, bonding and stimulation (Lutzker et al. 1998). This programme, known as Project Safe Care, comprises 15 weeks of intervention divided equally across the three areas. This is a one-to-one intervention provided by either social workers or nurses, and using modelling (sometimes by video), behaviour rehearsal and feedback. The results of single case studies are promising (Bigelow, Kessler and Lutzker 1995; Cordon et al. 1998; Lutzker et al. 1998), but no data from more robust evaluations have yet been published. Consumer feedback suggests it is well received by parents (Taban and Lutzker 2001).

Family therapy

Despite its popularity family therapy is rarely subjected to rigorous evaluation. Here too, the evidence favours an approach to family therapy that is inclusive of the other systems in which the child and family are nested, and which addresses the role of cognitive and extra-familial variables in maintaining problem behaviour, such as multisystemic family therapy (MST). MST comprises a pragmatic amalgam of intervention strategies, including interventions based on strategic family therapy, structural family therapy, and cognitive-behavioural therapy (Henggeler and Borduin 1995). Most studies have focused on children deemed delinquent or anti-social, and to date, only one study of good methodological quality has been published where the focus is explicitly on child abuse and neglect (Brunk, Henggeler and Whelan 1987). This small, randomized controlled trial compared group-based parent training (learning-theory based) with MST (conducted in the home). Both interventions appeared to bring about statistically significant improvements in parental psychiatric symptomatology, overall levels of parental stress, and in the severity of identified problems. Pre-post-test comparisons suggested that parent training was most effective in reducing identified social problems such as social isolation (perhaps because of the group format). MST did better in terms of restructuring parent–child relationships, and facilitating positive change in those behaviour problems that differentiate maltreating families from non-problem families (Crittenden 1981). In the case of the neglectful families, this meant that they were more responsive to their children's behaviour. This study did not include subsequent incidents of child abuse or neglect amongst its outcomes, and had no follow-up. It therefore provides rather precarious evidence of the effectiveness of MST in addressing serious child neglect and is, at best, a promising approach. A systematic review being conducted by Littell and colleagues may provide clearer evidence of the effectiveness of MST for a range of problems.

Social network interventions

Social network interventions explicitly aim to address the problems of neglect by increasing the amount and quality of social support available to needy and socially isolated parents. Only one controlled study has been conducted to date, but it is one of the few studies primarily to target the needs of neglectful parents (Gaudin *et al.* 1990–1991; Gaudin 1993). Intervention begins with a careful assessment of existing community supports, and an individual assessment of a family's informal support network, covering size, composition and supportiveness. This is followed by a psychosocial assessment aimed at identifying the range of problems facing a family, across a range of settings (school, home, housing, substance misuse, debt etc.). Significant material and psychosocial barriers to the development of supportive networks are identified (e.g. lack of telephone, poor verbal and social skills, poor self-esteem, unresolved conflicts with family members or neighbours) and goals for intervention are agreed with the family. Given the impact of these factors on parenting, there is therefore a tight 'logical fit' between the strategies proposed and the analysis of the contributing problems.

The workers use five designated social network interventions, together with professional case work/case management activities that include extensive advocacy and brokering of formal services. The social network interventions are as follows:

- *Personal networking.* These are direct interventions aimed at promoting family members' existing or potential relationships with other family members, friends, neighbours or work associates.

- *Establishing mutual aid groups.* These focus on teaching parenting and more broadly based social skills, to develop mutual problem-sharing and problem-solving and to enhance self-esteem.

- *Volunteer linking.* Recruiting and training volunteers to do tasks similar to those undertaken by 'family aides' in the UK.

- *Recruiting neighbours as informal helpers.* These people were paid a small sum, and received support and weekly guidance from the social workers.

- *Social skills training.* This is designed to help overcome those skill deficits which might account for a paucity of enduring socially supportive relationships.

Given the recognized difficulties in intervening effectively with neglectful families, the results of this study are particularly encouraging. Eighty per cent of those receiving nine months or more of this intervention improved their parenting from neglectful or severely neglectful to marginally adequate parenting (on the standardized parenting measures used in the study). Almost 60% of cases were closed because of improved parenting. However, as the authors themselves point out, certain weaknesses in the study make it difficult to draw firm conclusions about its likely effectiveness in mainstream work. First, all the participants were voluntary, so it is questionable whether these results would generalize to reluctant or resistant parents. Second, there was a high drop-out rate due to the extreme mobility of the families involved. This is a characteristic of many neglectful families, but presents a particular challenge to this way of working. Implications for mainstream practice within the UK are (i) that this intervention requires frequent, consistent professional consultation for problem-solving and support; (ii) successful implementation depends on manageable case loads of 20 or less; and (iii) this intervention also requires well-trained social workers with a combination of knowledge and skills that include case management, individual case work/counselling, group leadership, advocacy, mediation, supervision and consultation with volunteers, and community relations skills.

Problems that impact upon parenting

A variety of circumstances can undermine a parent's capacity adequately to care for a child, leading sometimes to serious neglect. Three of the most commonly occurring problems are learning disability (Feldman 1998), substance misuse (Barnard and McKeganey forthcoming) and mental illness, particularly maternal depression (Bellis *et al.* 2001; Radke-Yarrow and Klimes-Dougan 1997). One can do little more here than flag up trends in effectiveness research in each of these areas, but it is important to include them in the 'what works' discussion. If substance misuse or severe, chronic depression are major causes for concern, then decision-makers need to take into account what is known about the relative effectiveness of different treatment options, and how long such interventions might take to bring about stable change. Similar consider-ations apply when working with parents with learning disabilities.

Learning disabled parents

It is generally recognized that learning disabled parents face particular problems in providing the kind of care that will ensure a child's optimum development. A lack of adequate physical care and appropriate stimulation can lead to developmental delay, behaviour problems and injury (Feldman, Leger and Walton-Allen 1997; Reed and Reed 1965; Tymchuk and Feldman 1991). Learning disabled parents are more likely to have their children removed from their care than other parents. This reflects prejudice and discrimination, but also indicates the parenting difficulties that learning disabled people encounter in the absence of appropriate support from informal and formal networks (Feldman 1998). Learning disabled parents can experience high levels of stress and depression, which may contribute to their parenting difficulties (Feldman *et al.* 2002). These may arise, in part, from the adverse social circumstances in which they often live. Children of learning disabled parents may need compensatory social and educational experiences, in addition to interventions aimed at improving their general level of care and stimulation, as well as interventions of the kind described below.

In one intervention, trained parent education therapists visit participants' homes twice weekly (more often if necessary, and for newborns). In addition to parenting skills training, the staff provide ongoing counselling, stress management, community living and social skills training. The programme is sensitively and carefully structured, and makes use of direct observation, modelling, instruction and reinforcement. Training is pitched at the skills required for caring for a child at the age relevant to the family. Trainers see their work as an essential component of a multi-agency approach.

The results of various evaluations testify to the promise of these programmes (see Feldman *et al.* 1992a, 1992b, 1993, 1989), but Feldman and his colleagues observe that such interventions are not a panacea, and that other interventions, such as specialized pre-school programmes, may have more to offer *some* children whose parents are learning disabled. Parents with learning disabilities will need long-term help and support that is shaped by the developmental needs of the child. Departments taking decisions to support parents must take in principle decisions for the long term, with the associated resource implications.

Parents who misuse drugs and/or alcohol

The literature on substance misuse is large, reflecting the complexity of the subject matter, and it is difficult to find unequivocal messages regarding 'what works'. Nowhere is this more so than in relation to women who misuse legal or illegal substances, where researchers have done more to document the failure of professionals to tailor interventions to their particular needs than to develop effective interventions for this group (Finkelstein 1994; Howell, Heiser and Harrington 1999). To some extent this is reflected in policy guidance, where there is more information available regarding the prevalence and incidence of substance misuse, its impact on children and how to go about assessing this, than on effective treatment options (Royal College of Psychiatrists 2002). Robust outcome studies are few, and often fail to differentiate between different kinds of substance misuse.

Most evaluative work has focused on the use of drugs, such as imipramine or naltrexone. Few psychological interventions have been rigorously evaluated and no high quality systematic reviews could be identified at the time of writing. A review conducted in Sweden suggests that psychosocial treatment methods with a clear structure and well-defined intervention have favourable effects on alcohol dependence. These include cognitive-behavioural therapy and the 12-step treatment (Berglund et al. 2001). This review also concluded that relearning therapies (cognitive-behavioural therapy) targeted at the behaviour of drug abusers are the most effective among the psychosocial methods for treating heroin and cocaine dependence. The authors conclude that psychosocial therapies used to address other drug addictions have no proven effect or are insufficiently studied. This was not an international systematic review, so the results must be treated with some caution (see also Kownacki and Shadish 1999).

We urgently need to understand better what factors encourage or inhibit people from entering into, or remaining in, treatment programmes, if we are to provide services that are acceptable as well as effective (Nelson-Zlupco, Kaufmann and Dore 1995; Tracey and Farkas 1994; Tsogia, Copello and Orford 2001). In a review of the literature on substance abuse treatment for pregnant women, Howell et al. conclude that there is no clear evidence that one form of provision is better than another (e.g. residential versus outpatient) but that retention within programmes is an essential prerequisite to good outcomes (Howell et al. 1999; Plasse 2000). Factors that might be regarded as qualitative in their dimension are therefore centre stage: if we need parents to address their substance misuse we must take steps to facilitate this. This means ensuring that programmes are culturally and ideologically acceptable to potential users, that practical obstacles are removed (for example, child care, financial concerns, transport), that anxieties and fears are minimized and that other problems are addressed. For example, alcohol misuse may be co-terminous with, or mask, other deficits in parenting, or other relationship problems. Unless tackled, relapse is likely, even if the programme is initially successful. Though not of optimal quality, one review suggests that family or couples-based treatment is more effective for drug abuse than other kinds of intervention, both psychosocial and pharmacotherapeutic (Stanton and Shadish 1997). Given the role that partners and others can play in relapse, this is likely. Reviewing the evidence from four studies, three of which used experimental methodology (family-based training and home visiting), Barnard and McKeganey conclude that there is a lack of a secure evidence base to direct the strategic development of effective interventions (Barnard and McKeganey forthcoming). Their review suggests that effective interventions are likely to be resource intensive, relatively long-term, and need to intervene on a variety of fronts, including extended families and partners with drug problems.

Parents with mental illness

Many parents will suffer from mental illness at some time in their lives, and for most their children will be protected from any adverse fall-out by the temporary nature of the illness, and the presence of significant others – another parent, extended family, neighbours, friends, schools, to name but a few. For some children, however, serious mental illness in a parent can pose a significant threat to their well-being and, for a few, their safety. Such threatening circumstances include those children whose only carer is seriously depressed and socially isolated, and who perhaps has other problems such as substance misuse. Infants and young children are particularly vulnerable to the adverse effects of carers who are emotionally unavailable to them. It is important when drawing up plans to help such families that due regard is given to providing effective help to the parents, as well as taking steps to safeguard the welfare of the children concerned. As with substance misuse the field of mental health is large, and one would be ill-advised to produce simple messages. However, there is a growing body of evidence that, alongside pharmacotherapeutic interventions, cognitive-behavioural interventions have much to offer when compared with other psychosocial interventions, and – on occasion – when compared with drug treatments (Churchill et al. 2001). Workers will need to ensure that supportive networks are in place and working, and help to establish these when they are not.

Helping children who have suffered neglect

Apathy, passivity and social withdrawal are amongst the documented effects of child physical neglect, along with behaviour problems and academic delay (Crittenden 1981; Egeland, Sroufe and Erickson 1983; Wodarski et al. 1980). Clearly this provides some indication of where we might usefully expend our energies in helping children who have suffered neglect. Providing compensatory experiences is probably fairly straightforward, but when seeking to deal with the cumulative impact of neglect, the evidence base is almost non-existent.

Some of the work discussed above included interventions aimed at helping neglected children (see Project 12-Ways). Otherwise, only a very few studies have focused specifically on the needs of neglected children, or identified neglected children as a sub-sample of those for whom services were provided. A series of studies by Fantuzzo and colleagues (Fantuzzo 1990; Fantuzzo *et al.* 1987, 1988) evaluated a range of interventions designed to develop social interaction skills in withdrawn, maltreated pre-school children. One study explored a variety of attempts to engage socially withdrawn children attending a day centre, first using specially trained 'peers', then comparing this to interaction initiated by adults. Children responded best to peer-initiated interactions, which resulted in significant increases in positive social behaviour across a range of settings. In contrast, children who received adult-initiated interactions displayed a significant decrease in social behaviour after treatment. Puzzlingly perhaps, a moderate increase in the negative behaviour of withdrawn children occurred alongside increases in positive interactions.

In another study, Fantuzzo and colleagues randomly allocated 46 socially withdrawn Head Start children, of whom 22 had been physically abused or neglected, to two groups. In the experimental group, children were paired with 'resilient' peers who, under the supervision of the classroom teacher, initiated play. Results show that these children demonstrated significant increases in positive interaction and peer play, and a decrease in solitary play for all withdrawn children, both those who had been maltreated, and those who had not. These improvements were maintained at two months follow-up (Fantuzzo *et al.* 1996). Other studies are not sufficiently robust to allow us to draw upon them as a sound basis for decision-making, and the Fantuzzo studies are very limited in scope. As Fantuzzo stated in 1990:

> This is clearly a case of *child neglect*. To date, behavioral and social scientists have neglected to provide child victims with empirically tested treatment strategies based on scientific assessment of their unique needs. (p.317)

Sadly, in 2004, the picture is little different (Gershater-Molko, Ronit and Sherman 2002). The message therefore is that we should be very cautious in our dealings with children who have suffered neglect, particularly neglect over a long period, and that we should seek to remedy this most serious gap in our knowledge base.

Messages for practice

- Comprehensive assessment is essential for planning effective intervention.
- Multifaceted approaches are required.
- There must be planning for long-term approaches.
- Brave decisions need to be taken about children's future well-being at points when intervention can improve outcomes, rather than intervening too late.

Chapter 17

Neglect in Theory and Practice
The Messages for Health and Social Care

Julie Taylor and Brigid Daniel

Introduction

Embarking on this book we wanted to provide practitioners with some solid, evidence-based practice guidance in working effectively with children who are (or may be potentially) neglected. As a by-product we hoped that we would also be able to identify where there are gaps in our knowledge, or in current research and theory, and as a consequence be able to point to those areas where we have less confidence in our practice guidance. The chapter contributors have skilfully woven a number of arguments about this form of child maltreatment; raised numerous questions; debated a diversity of definitional issues; suggested improvements to practice; summarized current research and highlighted its gaps and limitations; proposed parallels with other health or social situations; made some stark pronouncements and at times have made some extremely disturbing statements. This should not have been a comfortable read, nor did we ever intend it to be so, as we have not yet 'got it right' in terms of our research and practice in this field. And whilst one single child is ever in need or at risk it is still one too many.

The range of topics covered, the focus of each chapter, the stylistic differences, do raise some tensions and we had an early worry that there would be stark differences of opinion or that contributors would draw different conclusions from the research. In fact, though, there is little that has been posited in opposition. Neglected children face the duality of being both in need and at risk simultaneously and every single chapter has emphasized this in a variety of ways. In this final chapter the messages from research and practice have been collated into a number of themes. We provide a summary (with pointers to indicative chapters) of what we see as the emergent issues for development, for research, and for guiding effective practice in this field.

Neglect is a serious concern

If there has ever been any doubt at all that child neglect is something we should be extremely concerned with, then the contributors of these chapters have totally disabused us of such a notion. Whilst of serious concern, neglect is still sometimes difficult to define, entangled as it so often is with other aspects of maltreatment. Many writers have noted the difficulty in defining neglect, but we understand chronic neglect as the breakdown or absence of a relationship of care. The contributors here have defined well what child neglect is and can mean, and in some instances have taken these definitions further. There can be no doubt that neglect has serious consequences for children, physically, developmentally, socially, emotionally, psychologically and child neglect (both physical and emotional) often co-exists with other forms of maltreatment. Whilst some neglected children die, the majority live, but they live dreadful lives. Whilst we know that protective factors can be helpful, the longer a child has to live in a neglecting environment the more irreversible are the long-term effects. There are some subtle differences, too, between different forms of neglect, so whilst the provision of finance and services will improve the situation of children in need and who are perhaps materially neglected it will not necessarily improve the situation of those children maltreated through emotional neglect. Further, emotional neglect is not usually a specific event, or series of events, but the daily atmosphere in which neglected children have to live, the very 'air that they breathe'.

Despite its appalling legacy neglect is often a somewhat hidden phenomenon. The majority of referrals of suspected child abuse to statutory agencies concern neglect, and the majority of these are filtered out at an early stage. Child neglect is traditionally accorded low priority in the continuum of child abuse – many reasons are given to explain this phenomenon, mainly attributing the trend to a combination of the complexity of neglect and pessimism of practitioners. Many are concerned that social services, in particular, lack sufficient resources to offer an appropriate response to the range of referrals of children in need. The concept of neglect is problematic and any research, policy or practice on neglect needs to be understood within a stated definition of harm, scope of responsibility and interpretation of responsibility.

We suggest that practitioners should not be deflected by the apparent lack of any one agreed definition of neglect. Instead they should concentrate on carefully describing the day-to-day lived experience of the individual child and delineating the impact of this experience upon current development and the developmental trajectory. Further, practitioners should not be sidetracked by conflicts of understanding about what conditions are harmful to children. Each practitioner must respect the expertise that other disciplines contribute and be prepared to hear their views both on aspects of harm and on potential protective factors.

Care and commitment

A major theme arising from the chapters concerned the care and commitment required, compromised or missing in the lives of children. How that care is conceptualized and structured, by society as well as by parents, is mediated by a range of ecological factors, professional input being an important component. The need for care is universal: care is necessary for survival and healthy development, but the way that care is expressed and organized is not the same everywhere. Moreover, 'caregiving' does not necessarily mean the same as 'caring for'. Emotional neglect, for example, 'implies indifference to the child's basic emotional needs – to his or her distress and achievements and needs for control, guidance, security, protection, praise and affection'. So whilst families that need support must be supported, those that lack commitment to care must be recognized, their ability or otherwise to change assessed and the child protected from harm.

Parental deficits of commitment can be compounded by child health deficits and whilst neglect is rarely the outcome for such children, we should not ignore its potential. In the case of very preterm, very low birth weight infants for example, there may be special needs in relation to feeding or oxygen therapy that take extra parental commitment. We also recognize that there is a tendency to allow a standard of care for disabled children that would not be acceptable for a non-disabled child. 'Level of commitment to care' may therefore serve as a proxy for recognition of parenting deficit.

However much parents may care, though, there may be circumstances where the stresses of caring for children combined with a lack of material or social resource will be enough to affect the care, and the commitment, that parents can provide. Within a wider ecological perspective therefore the extent to which society protects families from economic or material adversity is likely to exert a direct effect on parenting capacity.

Embedded within this theme of care and commitment is the attachment process. Providing the conditions that enable the child to develop secure attachments is an extremely important element of caregiving because attachment is a fundamental aspect of child development. Attachment to fathers can be as significant and as secure as with mothers and should not be overlooked as a protective factor. Sometimes health deficits can compromise the attachment relationship and this is an important consideration in many instances, although we only highlight a few. Where children have been ill at birth for example, parents may take longer to get to know their infants, with a potential impact on the attachment process. Institutional arrangements can in themselves be considered neglectful, reducing infant and parental proximity and affecting the attachment process.

Finally within this theme emerges the concept of blame. Blame is a somewhat pejorative word yet nonetheless is highlighted because when the care relationship is compromised, the direction (real or perceived) of blame can strongly affect the focus of intervention. If practitioners, and indeed society, concentrate their efforts on where suspected causative agents may be located, there is the potential to be blinded to holistic patterns of intervention. In child neglect this 'blame' is generally gendered and is overwhelmingly constructed as a failure in mothering. The focus of assessment and intervention tend therefore to be on the mother. Furthermore, social workers can display a diverse range of individual assumptions about parenting and the needs of the children that are likely to influence attitudes towards neglect.

Again, therefore, it is essential that practitioners consider the situation from the child's perspective. Whatever the reason for a child not having a meal at night the subsequent hunger will exert a powerful physical and emotional effect on the child. Practitioners must ensure that somehow or other the layers of assessment must work up from the building blocks of the child's essential needs, not work down from the parent's motivation. In other words, the process must start with, and be rooted in:

- a careful description of the child's actual lived experience
- a consideration of the impact of the child's experience upon their developmental trajectory
- an analysis of the extent to which development is compromised by unmet needs.

Once this is clear there can be conceptual progression towards:

- a careful description of parental caregiving behaviour
- an analysis of the extent to which parental capacity is undermined by social and economic factors
- an analysis of the parent's motivation and ability to change with appropriate support.

Antecedents and associations

One of the most striking themes, and possibly the one that makes neglect so difficult to define and assess, concerns the potential of, and the parallels with, other factors and situations. In the majority of cases these factors would neither lead to neglect nor be a result of neglect. But sometimes they would. Whilst we do not advocate crude checklists of risk factors, we acknowledge that awareness and therefore thorough assessment of associated factors is crucial.

Social and material circumstances in particular need to be considered. There is an association between cognitive developmental delay and neglect in extremely low birth weight infants whose parents are socially and economically disadvantaged and indeed this would often tend to be the case in many potentially vulnerable groups. Families of disabled children for example are more likely than those of non-disabled children to live in poverty, experiencing lower incomes at the same time as accruing costs.

The factors associated with poor adult relationships may also be associated with a tendency to neglect children. Emotional neglect seems to occur particularly in situations where the parents are preoccupied with other concerns, for example, situations of marital violence, social isolation and where marriages end in increased bitterness. It is also frequently found in situations where parents are dependent on alcohol or drugs, or suffer from parental mental illness, and disorder. Neglected children's fathers are more likely to be living apart from the children's mothers, to be materially deprived and to have emotional difficulties.

There is also a strong case to be made for very early assessment and identification of risk factors, even in the ante-natal period. And whilst most children meeting the definition of failure to thrive (for example) do not show evidence of abuse and neglect, such children are still at increased risk of abuse and neglect.

There is an association between neglect and children with disabilities which can further be linked to the fact that a substantial number of very low birth weight infants (as one example) experience some residual disability. Often such children may find themselves in a doubly vulnerable situation. Disabled children, for example, face coping with an impairment and may also experience oppression, prejudice, discrimination and abuse. Further, disabled children are more likely than non-disabled children to find themselves in potentially vulnerable situations, for example, on short breaks, in respite care and at residential schools. Similarly, children with severe health deficits may find themselves at potential risk of institutional, programme or system abuse. Whilst the impact of neglect on such children may be no different than on other children, this impact may not be as visible and signs of the neglect may be masked by factors associated with their disability or health care need.

Assessment

It is interesting in pulling the chapters together to note how much emphasis has been placed on assessment and a number of assessment models have been described. We do not advocate a particular one, indeed their strengths and weaknesses have been debated throughout the book. The Assessment Framework is probably the most familiar in England but there are a number of others presented here that readers may find useful. What is clear, however, is that thorough, reliable and consistent assessment is essential. It also seems apparent, though, that we have not quite cracked the assessment nut just yet.

Practice wisdom is always important but standardized tools can enable workers to obtain a more objective view of difficulties within a particular family. If practitioners are to be open-minded when assessing cases of child neglect they may benefit from an 'aide memoire'. The assessment framework emphasizes that standardized practice is most likely to occur if the use of professional judgement is informed by an evidence-based approach to care. However, even when we know the 'what' we may miss out on the 'why' and it is such aspects that need probing most in effective assessment.

We know, too, that neglect requires a multi-agency response. Often one agency can have information of which another agency is not aware. Pulling together pieces of the multi-agency 'jigsaw' can change professional perceptions, depending on the information available. As well as co-operation it also needs a practitioner to take control and to co-ordinate activities. Sometimes people are so busy trying to work with each other that individual cases do not progress. This control needs to be at a level where appropriate authority can be exercised.

However, child protection guidelines and frameworks for assessment tend to be social work driven and are built on the presumption that social workers can elicit the required amount of co-operation from relevant disciplines. This is a huge presumption and we need to be proactive in converting such rhetoric into a working reality, a theme we will return to shortly. We also know that there are regional variations in the way neglect is defined and this in turn can affect the assessment process. Current child protection practice is not always as full as it might be, for example by tending to ignore the risks (and also the assets) some men pose. Assessment therefore needs to consider the nature of care the child receives from each of his/her caregivers.

The assessment process does not always account fully for the voice of the child. This is crucial in order to set realistic targets and as a constant check on harm (real and potential) to the child. Children's own views about who is important to them must be ascertained. Also crucially, assessment and intervention should be focused on the needs of children and their caregivers. In each family where neglect occurs, there is a need for the worker to understand the particular relationship(s) of care and the meaning of the child in these specific contexts.

Professional roles

How professionals understand and work with each other and with families, the assumptions they bring to practice, the effects of that practice, and how each professional role can be used to best effect are still not fully determined. Providers of services need to ensure that they do not do more harm than good and that the services they provide do not have unknown negative consequences. And whilst we tend to rehearse the phrase that multi-agency work 'is a good thing', multidisciplinary involvement in child neglect is a concept laced with assumptions and is open to many interpretations. There should therefore be a familiarity with the roles and responsibilities of other professionals. Even within particular single disciplines there can be a lack of shared understanding. In one study for example social workers differed in their understanding of 'good enough parenting'. Between groups this can be even more challenging: whilst community-based nurses are ideally placed to intervene with vulnerable children and families nurses can be reluctant to refer cases of neglect to social work because of anticipated lack of response. On the other hand social services have been given a clear lead in completing assessments and co-ordinating information from other services. This inherent tension need to be disentangled.

There are some core skills that all practitioners require when dealing with neglected children and their families. Recognition of emotional neglect often depends on careful observation and listening. Practitioners need to have a repertoire of questions that elucidate the extent to which parents appear to be adequately and sensitively involved in caring for and controlling their children. Skills are needed in involving the parents in the decision-making process, particularly when a family is hostile. Practitioners need to work with parents to take bullying of children seriously, and it is important to plan the work in advance and with the child as much as possible so they know what to expect. It is also important to recognize that practitioners can also be distracted, for example when they feel so sympathetic to parents that the focus on the child is lost. In summary, advanced interpersonal and communication skills are absolutely crucial particularly in trying to find productive strategies for engaging with more difficult parents.

The evidence base

The evidence base for neglect is still woefully lacking, but we know what works methodologically, and we are beginning to know what works in practice for neglected children. We also know the limitations of the research. Given the gaps in current knowledge it seems that rather than asking what works for neglected children, we need at this point to be asking what works best according to our knowledge so far.

Much research in the social sciences does not provide much benefit because of weaknesses in the choice of design, execution or reporting of studies, generalizability, sampling error, reliability and validity, accessibility of studies, and lack of cumulative focus of research. Literature reviews and academic expert opinion can provide useful summaries of findings in a research area, but unless there is explicit information that systematic methods were used then it is not possible to know whether the results are trustworthy.

Despite the explosion in evidence-practice debates and the central rhetoric in emphasizing interventions based only on good quality research there are still anomalies. Social workers can be 'shy' about drawing explicitly on theory, whereas their counterparts in other professions operate a more empiricist style of assessment drawing on quantifiable evidence.

There are also huge gaps in what we know. Almost all UK research on child abuse fails to address the experience of disabled children. Likewise few studies have examined the effects of intervention for growth faltering, although it appears that community-based intervention has a significant effect. The links between neglect and preterm births are largely based on conjecture.

We would propose, therefore, a research agenda focusing specifically on neglect that would address a range of questions such as:

- What interventions work best for neglected children: in the home, in school, in hospital?

- Where neglect may be masked by other factors, how can we best evaluate the effectiveness of (a) assessment and (b) intervention?

- What might be the relative benefits and disadvantages for neglected children of universal or targeted approaches?

- What are the most effective methods of ensuring children's voices are heard and incorporated throughout the process?

- Which assessment tools, in which circumstances, and administered by which people, are the most comprehensive and most user-friendly?

- Should standardized instruments be used for assessment (as in growth charts for example)?

- What specific protective factors could be enhanced in children's lives that would make a significant difference in both proximal and distal outcomes for potentially neglected children?

- What intra- and interagency arrangements lead to the best organizational environment within which to provide an effective response to neglect?

Such questions are hard questions, but must be answered if we are to move forward.

Protective factors

Protective factors did not in fact really arise as a theme in the chapters, more as an omission. It is very easy to assume that because we know what does not help in cases of neglect, or what might tip the scales towards neglect, then the opposite situation must be therefore protective. However, there is not always the evidence for such assumptions, even if practice wisdom suggests this is probably the case. Whilst parents and carers can be mediators of wider economic and societal influences we do not yet know exactly how to capture this in meaningful interventions for neglected children. In particular, little is known about how best to compensate the child for what they have missed. As we know, neglect is likely to undermine the characteristics associated with long-term emotional and physical health. Therefore we need to draw on our extensive knowledge of children's developmental needs to craft interventions that provide children with what they have missed and may continue to miss.

Conclusion

There is no doubt that social work alone cannot meet the needs of all neglected children, and this is not merely a matter of lack of resources. Even with considerable increases in resources it would not be possible, or indeed appropriate, for all children whose needs are being neglected to be referred to statutory social services.

When it comes to recognition of neglect, then anyone who has any contact with children must be able to 'see' neglect. This would include doctors, dentists, teachers, speech therapists, educational psychologists, accident and emergency staff, housing officers, probation workers and so on.

The professional context of child protection is changing and in particular, all agencies are facing fundamental questions about what constitutes child protection. It can no longer be solely defined by the essential protective activities carried out by the agencies with statutory protective duties (social services, police, legal system). Increasingly the definition of protection is broadening out to incorporate the wider roles of universal agencies in:

- preventing abuse
- promoting the welfare of children
- ensuring that their services reach all children, regardless of their family circumstances
- providing a responsive and trustworthy environment that will enable children to share their concerns
- making appropriate and effective referrals to the police and social work.

Agencies, therefore, need to find ways to form a protective network around all children.

If one of the manifestations of the neglect is that the child's access to a universal service is impeded then that agency has to consider whether they can find a way to deliver their service to the child. This may not necessarily entail a referral to statutory child protection systems. For example, some schools have home liaison workers, or some doctors will provide treatment within schools. The role of health visitors, until now a universal service to all children up to age five, is changing as we write. If developed with care the role of the targeted community public health facilitator offers great potential as a key part of the protective network.

All professionals must also consider whether the issues they are identifying are an indication of more entrenched problems and whether the expertise of other agencies is required. In many cases the expertise of social workers will be needed for assessment, but not necessarily delivery of services. The key expertise of social workers, whether located in statutory or voluntary agencies, is in holistic assessment of children's needs, parenting capacity, potential for change and planning therapeutic intervention. However, a range of disciplines have expertise that can be harnessed on behalf of neglected children and all can play their part in the planned intervention.

Many parents of neglected children are prepared to acknowledge that they are struggling and indeed will often have asked for help in various ways. They will often be willing to accept help on a voluntary basis. In some cases, though, the parents are unwilling or unable to change and this is where there is a need for the investigative system, to establish that there is a case for compulsory intervention on behalf of a child. However, it is a very complex matter to assess whether a parent is able or willing to change and at this stage of the process it may be necessary to combine the skills of different disciplines, for example of health visitors and social workers, sometimes within the context of child protection investigation. The difficulty for other disciplines, though, is that they often feel that the assessment skills of social workers are denied them. It is essential, therefore, to agree local arrangements and protocols for handling the concerns of health, education, other practitioners, parents and the general public that incorporate mutual trust and allow for discussions about the best way to proceed. As Cooper suggests, there needs to be a 'space for negotiation' within the system (Cooper 2002).

We opened the book by arguing that the child protection system struggles to find an appropriate response to neglect. Whilst there are numerous reasons for this (and the debates are tackled with energy in many chapters) the debate that tries to separate need from risk can limit appropriate, timely, proactive and sufficiently robust support and intervention for families where neglect may be a concern. In true ecological style we have travelled from the macro to the micro and back again. Some issues have received considerable attention and have numerous messages from theory and for practice. The amount of space given to assessment is a good example of this, representing perhaps a turn in the tide towards a more consistent approach in the way we 'judge' and intervene in the lives of families and children. It is also refreshing to see how seriously multidisciplinarity is taken, with understanding of each other's roles and actually working together being a major priority. And we are glad too to see how much emphasis and debate has been focused on the requirement for rigorous research that not only asks the right questions but uses the right methods to answer these as well.

Reflecting on some of the missing pieces in the jigsaw it is clear that so very often neglect is a neglected issue and we therefore just do not have sufficient available evidence or knowledge about how best we can respond to this child protection issue. So for example, we know instinctively, and to some extent theoretically, that we need to reinforce protective factors in neglected children and their families, yet we are still somewhat foggy about exactly which protective factors work best, in which situations and delivered by whom. Further, we can sometimes then feel constrained in how far we can push for protective factors that in many cases involve socio-political intervention and seem far removed from the real-world coalface of health and social care.

There is, however, hope for theory and practice in neglect. In fact it is more than hope because there is a demonstrable commitment across a range of practices, disciplines, institutions and political affiliates that suggests that the messages for child neglect at least are being heard. We need now to adhere to those messages and develop our theory and most especially our practice so that effective interventions are found and used for neglected children. We have thought about neglect for long enough, it is time to apply those thoughts more productively.

Outline Format for Comprehensive Assessment

Brigid Daniel and Norma Baldwin

This format was developed in conjunction with a number of local authority social work departments in Scotland as part of the 'Assessment into Action' project part-funded by the Scottish Executive.

1. Basis of report

2. Current family composition

3. Current family circumstances

4. Chronology of family events, causes for concern, observations and so on

5. Chronology of social work and other involvement

6. Cause for concern

7. Profile of all key adults and their relationships

8. Assessment of parenting

9. Profile Of Child

   - Health

   - Education

   - Identity

   - Family and social relationships

   - Social presentation

   - Emotional and behavioural development

   - Self-care skills

   - Material and social circumstances

10. Evaluation of parents' co-operation and potential for change

11. Parents' views of professional concern

12. Child's views

13. Professionals' assessment of current situation

   • Risks (adversity/hazards)

   • Needs (vulnerabilities)

   • Resilience (strengths)

   • Protective factors

14. Plan for intervention

15. Plan for monitoring outcome

Guidance Notes

1. Basis of report

This section should detail the number of visits to the family and who was involved in the process of assessment. It should also detail the contribution of other agencies and whether their views have been incorporated or whether a separate report has been submitted. Any tools or assessment checklists used should be detailed and referenced.

2. Current family composition

MOTHER'S DETAILS

Basic details about the mother's name, age, marital status and so on.

FATHER'S DETAILS

Basic details about the father's name, age, marital status and so on.

ANY OTHER ADULT IN THE HOUSEHOLD'S DETAILS

Basic details about other adults e.g. mother's partner, adult offspring, lodgers and so on.

ALL CHILDREN

Basic details about any siblings and half-siblings whether they live in the household or elsewhere. All existing details such as DOB must be verified with the source and confirmed.

3. Current family circumstances

FINANCIAL CIRCUMSTANCES

Information about current income and outgoings, including any outstanding debts. An assessment of whether the income is sufficient to allow the family to meet the child's needs.

HOUSING CIRCUMSTANCES

A description of the housing situation, linked with the housing provider's responsibility. A detailed assessment would include attention to such issues as the stability of the housing situation, whether housing benefit forms have been appropriately completed and so on.

The internal state of the house should be described, with a fair assessment of factors that are the responsibility of the householder and those that are the responsibility of the landlord (if rented). Record the state of furnishing, level of cleanliness and hygiene in as much factual detail as possible.

4. Chronology of family events, causes for concern, observations and so on

Detailed family history to provide a context for the current concerns.

5. Chronology of social work and other involvement

Detailed history of all other professional and voluntary agencies' involvement. Information about what intervention strategies have been attempted, by whom and for how long.

6. Cause for concern

Outline of the reason for referral and the evidence for concern. If there is an allegation that the young person is sexually abusing other children then refer to local assessment frameworks for those circumstances.

7. Profile of all key adults and their relationships

MOTHER'S HEALTH

Assessment of the physical health of the mother and whether there are any health issues that may impact upon her parenting including issues of medical treatment or management of illness.

FATHER'S (AND/OR PARTNER'S) HEALTH

Whether the father is resident in the household or not every effort must be made to assess the father's circumstances. Any man resident in the household, even if not the biological father, should be assessed.

MOTHER'S EMOTIONAL NEEDS

Attention to the emotional needs of the mother in detail, for example with an assessment of level of self-esteem or emotional well-being.

FATHER'S (AND/OR PARTNER'S) EMOTIONAL NEEDS

As above

LEARNING DISABILITY ISSUES

Assessment of the mother and/or father's/partner's level of intellectual capacity. Attention to whether the parents have general or specific learning disabilities.

MENTAL HEALTH ISSUES

Attention to the mental health of the mother and/or father/partner, if possible and where appropriate, backed up by psychiatric assessment.

SUBSTANCE ABUSE ISSUES

Consideration of any drink or drug issues and their direct impact upon parenting.

PARENTAL RELATIONSHIP AND PARENTING ENVIRONMENT/ATMOSPHERE

Consideration of issues of accord or discord in the household. For example, assessment of whether there is marital/partner discord or violence between partners. This could also include attempts to assess whether the overall parenting environment is warm or critical.

SOCIAL SUPPORT

An assessment of the social network of either or both parents. This should include the views of the parents themselves about whether they have people they can turn to as well as a more objective assessment of who appears to be available.

8. Assessment of parenting

Specific details of the areas of parenting that are causing concern. Several checklists for the formal assessment of the level of neglect and emotional abuse exist and may be useful. The central area for consideration has to be the actual and potential impact upon the child.

9. Profile of child, taking account of developmental stage

To aid compatibility with the Looking After Children materials it is advisable to consider the child's development using the following headings when carrying out an assessment of the child.

HEALTH

Attention to the child's physical and mental health, including attention to whether there are any special needs. Detailed assessment would include any formal assessments by a health visitor or GP etc.

EDUCATION

Attention to the child's current educational status and educational needs. Examples of detailed assessment would be a record of a formal educational assessment, a list of educational achievements, a consideration of the type of most appropriate school placement, a record of detailed discussions with a teacher and/or educational psychologist and so on.

IDENTITY

Consideration of cultural and ethnic issues, for all children, not just those of an ethnic minority. Geographical identity and attachment is also important for many children.

FAMILY AND SOCIAL RELATIONSHIPS

Attention to the child's attachments to parent/s, other significant adults and siblings. More detailed assessment would include examples of observations of attachment behaviour with significant adults, discussion of ability to make attachments to others, for example, daycare staff and description of whether attachment appears secure or insecure.

SOCIAL PRESENTATION

Taking into account the child's level of development, an assessment of their social skills, which is likely to have a direct impact upon their level of social isolation.

EMOTIONAL AND BEHAVIOURAL DEVELOPMENT

Assessment of whether the child's behaviour is appropriate for their age. If the child is seen to have behaviour problems attempt to assess the level of difficulty and to consider the reasons for the problem. In particular it is important to consider the child's levels of self-esteem, perhaps by using self-esteem scales.

SELF-CARE SKILLS

Taking account of developmental stage.

MATERIAL AND SOCIAL CIRCUMSTANCES

Assessment of the impact of material and social circumstances upon the child, for example, does the child lack resources to take part in activities that his or her peers do, does he or she have an adequately furnished bedroom?

10. Evaluation of parents' co-operation and potential for change

ABILITY OF PARENT/S TO MAKE USE OF HELP ON OFFER

There needs to be explicit consideration of whether previous help has been offered and whether the parents were able to make use of such support, with attempts to analyse why help was not used. If there have been a number of referrals regarding similar concerns, then this will be an indication that previous responses have not been effective.

11. Parents' views of professional concern

Record the parent's response to the concern, their account of the situation and their view of what would help. If possible there should be a verbatim statement from the parent/s expressing their views on their needs and the plan for intervention. This could be in the form of a written statement by the parent/s or a transcription of their recorded view. Any differences of opinion should be noted down in specific detail.

12. Child's views

Record of direct contact with the child and detail about any kind of communication with the child whether verbal or through play and drawings. Attempts to ascertain the child's views should also be noted, if possible in their words either written or recorded and transcribed.

13. Professionals' assessment of current situation

- Risks (adversity/hazards)
- Needs (vulnerabilities)
- Resilience (strengths)
- Protective factors

A systematic assessment of risks, needs, strengths and protective factors is required. Risks may be described as hazards. However, unmet needs can also be described as hazards. If a parent has unmet needs their ability to parent may be undermined, whilst if a child has unmet needs they may be more vulnerable to the effects of neglect and their developmental potential may be undermined.

Resilience and protective factors are not simply the absence of risk and need and indeed can co-exist with them. There is now good evidence about the factors associated with resilience in children and young people and areas of actual and potential resilience within the child need to be assessed. Protective factors may exist both within the parent and within the wider environment. A full assessment is not complete without comprehensive attention to all actual and potential protective factors.

RISKS

In summary the following factors are associated with continued neglect:

- previous referrals for neglect
- number of out-of-home placements
- caretaker neglected as a child
- single caretaker in home at time of referral
- caretaker history of drug/alcohol abuse

- age of youngest caretaker at time of referral
- number of children in home
- caretaker involved in primarily negative social relationships
- motivation for change on part of caretaker

NEEDS OF CHILD/REN AND OF PARENT/S

- Material
- Emotional
- Educational
- Developmental
- Social

RESILIENCE

Resilience can be identified at the internal, family and community level. Three building blocks of resilience in a child are:

- Secure base
- Self-esteem
- Self-efficacy

PROTECTIVE FACTORS

- Child (flow from areas of resilience)
- Parental
- Internal characteristics
- Extended family support
- Community resources
- Material resources

14. Plan for intervention

PLAN FOR PURPOSEFUL INTERVENTION

All the information to be drawn together in ways which indicate how components of the assessment are linked to specific plans. Each specific concern should be addressed, with a clear plan for how it is to be tackled. Clear information about who will be responsible for which aspects should be included.

IDENTIFICATION OF RESOURCES NEEDED

Consideration of the available resources that might meet the assessed need. For a detailed assessment this should include notes about the waiting time to access resources, whether there are places available and so on. Also detail what resources that do not currently exist might have been helpful.

CONSIDERATION OF THE LENGTH OF TIME SUPPORT MAY BE NEEDED

Assessment of whether this family needs short-term help during a crisis or whether they are likely to need ongoing support. A more detailed assessment would include an assessment of whether the child could be sustained at home with structured long-term support.

15. Plan for monitoring outcome

Explicit note of what the outcome should be and how this outcome will be measured, how it will be known that outcome has been achieved and what the timescales are. Outcomes should be broken down into outcomes for the child and outcomes for each parent and should be set out in a way that will be clear to the parents.

Worksheets

Moira Walker and Mary Glasgow

The following example worksheets provide some simple ideas about how to structure work with families and record your discussions and progress. You can make worksheets to suit the individual needs of the child and his or her family and deal with pertinent issues for them. This can be a useful way to review work with families and present evidence of strengths and difficulties to other professionals.

Where families need support because of literacy issues you can use the information verbally and record the words while the children draw or paint to illustrate the point. Families can personalise their work by putting a folder or file together which can include photos, drawings or other art work. This means that they can refer to the work when at home and add to it when they are able.

Contract between Mum/Dad and Me

This is an agreement between
me _____ (child's name) and
my mum/dad _____
(parent's name) to make clear rules which we all
have to stick to. These rules, if kept, will make us
all happier and help us to get on better.

1. _____

2. _____

3. _____

4. _____

5. _____

6. _____

Date _____

Parent's signature _____

Child's signature _____

Witness's (worker's)
signature _____

Plan of work for _____ (child's name)

Wednesday 26th March

- Snack
- Play game for 10 minutes
- Calendars

Wednesday 2nd April

- Snack
- Play game for 10 minutes
- Finish off feelings
- Talk about future, what does it mean

Wednesday 9th April

- Snack
- Play game for 10 minutes
- My future: hopes/fears

Wednesday 16th April

- Outing for my birthday treat

Wednesday 23rd April

- Snack
- Play game for 10 minutes
- My future: when I grow up I want to be...
- Story book

Wednesday 30th April

- Snack
- Play game for 10 minutes
- My future
- Story book

Wednesday 7th May

- Snack
- Ready, steady, cook

Wednesday 14th May

- Snack
- Play game for 10 minutes
- My future
- Finish

Wednesday 21st May

- Snack
- Play game for 10 minutes
- Finish off story book
- Look back on what we've worked on
- Preparation for next week: final session

Wednesday 28th May

- Finish with outing: ten pin bowling

Worksheet for Children

My worst memory of you is...

My worst day was when we...

My favourite memory of you is...

My best day was when we...

Homework Task for Parents

To be brought to the next session:_____ (time of session)

Spend ten minutes thinking about your child:

How did you feel when s/he was born?

Describe what s/he was like as a small child.

How do you feel about him/her now?

Worksheet for parents

What is your best memory of something your mum or dad did or said?

How would you like your kids to remember you?

What do you think they would say if we asked them today?

Worksheet for sessions with children and parents

In the box below draw how you feel about each other...

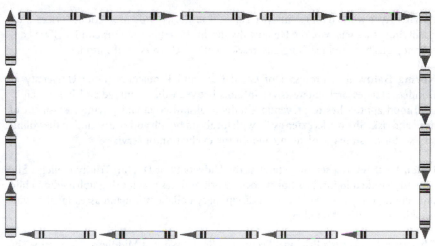

I love you because... (please write reason below)

♥ _____

♥ _____

♥ _____

Sometimes I get annoyed with you because...

☹ _____

☹ _____

☹ _____

The Contributors

Patrick Ayre worked for twenty years in local authority child protection services, after qualifying as a social worker. He now divides his time between his child welfare consultancy business and teaching and research at the University of Luton.

Norma Baldwin is Professor of Child Care and Protection at the Univeristy of Dundee. Her research interests are in links between disadvantage and harm; neighbourhood approaches to prevention; individual and community-wide assessment of need and risk. She works extensively with local and health authorities and in the voluntary sector on strategic planning and on the evaluation of services.

Helen Buckley is a senior lecturer at the University of Dublin, Trinity College. She formerly worked in local authority social work and has previously published on child protection policy and practice, multidisciplinary collaboration and assessment of vulnerable children and families.

Christine Cocker is a Principal Lecturer of Social Work at Middlesex University. She has considerable experience working in the fields of child protection and looked-after children in both the statutory and voluntary sector. Her most recent research has been on the mental health needs of looked-after children. Christine is also a social work consultant for NCH – The Bridge Childcare Development Service, having worked there previously as Service Development Director.

Brigid Daniel is Professor of Child Care and Protection in the Department of Social Work at the University of Dundee. She is a qualified social worker and has worked in local authority children and families social work. She was a member of the multidisciplinary team that carried out a Ministerial national audit and review of child protection in Scotland. She is co-author of books on child development, working with fathers and on the promotion of resilience, all published by Jessica Kingsley Publishers.

Renuka Jeyarajah Dent is an educational psychologist and Director of NCH – The Bridge. NCH – The Bridge has a respected reputation for undertaking serious case reviews and to date has completed more than 50 of these.

Richard Fountain is the service manager for Family Support and Child Protection with Luton Social Services. During thirty years of service he has constantly sought to improve services in relation to neglect. He helped establish GCP as a multi-agency tool.

Mary Glasgow is a service manager within a large Scottish voluntary organization. She has been in social work practice since qualifying in 1991. She has held a number of posts working with children and their families as a practitioner and manager and latterly developed and managed a Family Resource Centre in Easterhouse, Glasgow. Mary has a particular interest in the values and attitudes which underpin work with disadvantaged families.

David Gough is Deputy Director of the Social Science Research Unit and its EPPI-Centre at the Institute of Education, University of London. He is co-editor of *Child Abuse Review* and on the National Executive and wider advisory board respectively of the British and Japanese national child abuse societies, BASPCAN and JaSPCAN. He was previously Secretary of ISPCAN. www.ioe.ac.uk/ssru

Jan Horwarth is a senior lecturer in social work studies at the University of Sheffield. She has a social work background and has worked as a manager and practitioner in a range of social work settings. Jan's research interests include child welfare systems, assessment processes and child neglect. She has published widely on these topics.

Margaret Kennedy is an independent trainer and consultant on disability and abuse. She has spent 18 years pressing for better protection for disabled children nationally and internationally. She has written and lectures extensively on these issues. She was co-editor and co-author of the Department of Health funded training and resource pack 'Abuse and Children who are Disabled' (1993). She is disabled herself. She is also a specialist on 'Clergy Abuse of Adult Women' and her present PhD research is on this topic.

Geraldine Macdonald was Professor of Social Work at the University of Bristol from 1997 until 2004 when she was appointed Director of Information and Knowledge Management at the Commission for Social Care Inspection. Her interests include evidence-based decision-making in child protection.

Brian Minty was for many years a joint appointee with the University of Manchester, Salford Social Services and the Royal Manchester Children's Hospital. His interests include child and family mental health, and outcomes for children in care and therapy.

Nick Spencer is Professor Emeritus of Child Health in the School of Health and Social Studies and Warwick Medical School, University of Warwick. He was until recently a practising community paediatrician. His research interests are effects of social circumstances and poverty on child health.

O. Prakash Srivastava is a consultant community paediatrician and has special interest in the effect of environment and care on child development. He has researched on this subject and reviewed both literature and actual practice, which spans over thirty years.

Olive Stevenson is Professor Emeritus of Social Work Studies at the University of Nottingham. She has researched and published widely in child welfare with particular interest in neglected children and in interdisciplinary work in child protection. She has chaired five area child protection committees and various serious case reviews.

Janice Stewart is the Designated Nurse for Child Protection for Luton and Bedfordshire and honorary lecturer at the University of Luton. She introduced GCP to child health nurses because of her keen interest in child care and supported its use after a pilot.

Julie Taylor is Director of Postgraduate Studies at the School of Nursing and Midwifery, University of Dundee. Julie's substantive research programme is centred around vulnerablility and violence in protecting children, particularly at the interface between health and social care. She also has a keen interest in developing theoretical and methodological issues in this area. She and Brigid Daniel have worked together for many years, and co-authored *Engaging with Fathers: Practice Issues for Health and Social Care*, published by Jessica Kingsley Publishers.

Danielle Turney is a qualified social worker and has worked in local authority children and families teams. She has been involved in social work education since 1994 and currently teaches at the Open University. Recent publications address different aspects of social work practice with child neglect.

Moira Walker is a senior research fellow at the Social Work Research Centre, University of Stirling. Her current research includes a study of the use and effectiveness of secure accomodation for young people in Scotland and evaluating the 'Fast Track' Children's Hearings pilot. Her other research interests centre around parenting and ways of effectively supporting parents living in stressful environments. These include evaluation of a parenting education programme, a family centre and two broader studies of coping strategies adopted by parents and children. Prior to becoming a researcher she worked as a social worker with children and families.

Jane Wonnacott is a social worker who works as an independent trainer and consultant. Her main interests are assessment, supervision, the positive use of serious case reviews and the way in which child protection knowledge can be applied to work with disabled children.

Gill Watson is a lecturer in the School of Nursing and Midwifery, University of Dundee. Previously, she has worked in a variety of health visiting posts. Prior to this, she worked within neonatal intensive services in Scotland and the Middle East.

Charlotte M. Wright is a senior lecturer at the University of Glasgow and Consultant in Community Child Health at Yorkhill Children's Hospital. She has been researching the causes, diagnosis and management of weight faltering (failure to thrive) for the past 15 years. She has a strong background in child protection and her clinical work is mainly with children with under-nutrition or complex feeding problems.

References

Adcock, M. (1985) 'Assessing parenting: the context.' In M. Adcock and R. White (eds) *'Good-Enough Parenting': A Framework for Assessment.* London: British Agency for Adoption and Fostering.

Adcock, M. (2001) 'The core assessment: how to synthesise information and make judgements.' In J. Horwath (ed) *The Child's World: Assessing Children in Need.* London: Jessica Kingsley Publishers.

Ainsworth, M., Blehar, M., Waters, E. and Wall, S. (1978) *Patterns of Attachment: A Psychological Study of the Strange Situation.* London: John Wiley and Sons.

Alison, L. (2000) 'What are the risks to children of parental substance misuse?' In F. Harbin and M. Murphy (eds) *Substance Misuse and Child Care.* Lyme Regis: Russell House.

Alison, L. and Wyatt, S. (1999) *Outcomes of Infants of Drug Addicts.* Paper presented at the Abstract from Proceedings of Royal College of Paediatrics and Child Health Annual Meeting, York.

Atkar, S., Baldwin, N., Ghataora, R. and Thanki, V. (2000) ' Promoting effective family support and child protection for Asian children.' In N. Baldwin (ed) *Protecting Children: Promoting Their Rights.* London: Whiting and Birch.

Avent, M., Coile, D. and Mathai, L. (2001) 'Neonatal chronic lung disease.' *Journal of Pharmacy Practice, 14,* 3, 181–206.

Ayre, P. (1998) 'Significant harm: making professional judgements.' *Child Abuse Review, 7,* 330–342.

Baginsky, M. (2000) *Child Protection and Education.* Leicester: NSPCC.

Baker, P. and Carson, A. (1999) '"I take care of my kids": Mothering practices of substance-abusing women.' *Gender and Society, 13,* 3, 347–363.

Bakwin, H. (1949) 'Emotional deprivation in infants.' *Journal of Pediatrics, 85,* 512–521.

Baladerian, N. (1991) *Abuse Causes Disabilities: Disability and the Family.* Culver City, CA: Spectrum Institute.

Baldwin, N. (2001) *West Lothian Children and Families: Audit of Sample of 30 Cases.* Dundee: University of Dundee.

Baldwin, N. (2002) *West Lothian: Placement of Children Away from Home.* Dundee: University of Dundee.

Baldwin, N. and Spencer, N. (1993) 'Deprivation and child abuse: implications for strategic planning in children's services.' *Children and Society, 7,* 4, 357–375.

Bandura, A. (1977) *Social Learning Theory.* Englewood Cliffs, NY: Prentice Hall.

Barbero, G.J. and Shaheen, E. (1967) 'Environmental FTT: a clinical view.' *Journal of Pediatrics, 71,* 639–645.

Barnard, M. (1999) 'Forbidden questions: drug dependent parents and the welfare of their children.' *Addiction, 94,* 8, 1109–1111.

Barnard, M. (2003) 'Between a rock and a hard place: the role of relatives in protecting children from the effects of parental drug problems.' *Child and Family Social Work, 8,* 4.

Barnard, M. and Barlow, J. (2003b) 'Discovering parental drug dependence: silence and disclosure.' *Children and Society, 17,* 1, 45–56.

Barnard, M. and McKeganey, N. (forthcoming) 'The impact of parental problem drug use on children: what is the problem and what can be done to help?' *Addiction.*

Bassin, D., Honey, M. and Kaplan, M.M. (eds) (1994) *Representations of Motherhood.* New Haven, CT and London: Yale University Press.

Batchelor, J. and Kerslake, A. (1990) *Failure to Find Failure to Thrive.* London: Whiting and Bush.

Bates, T., Buchanan, J., Corby, B. and Young, L. (1999) *Drug Use, Parenting and Child Protection: Towards an Effective Interagency Response.* University of Liverpool: University of Central Lancashire.

BC Institute Against Family Violence (1999) *The Person Within: Strategies for Recognising and Preventing Abuse of Children with Disabilities.* Vancouver: BC Institute Against Family Violence.

Beck, U. (1992) *Risk Society: Towards a New Modernity.* London: Sage.

Bellis, M.D.D., Brousaard, E.R., Herring, S.W., Maritz, G. and Benitez, J.G. (2001) 'Psychiatric co-morbidity in caretakers and children involved in maltreatment: a pilot research study with policy implications.' *Child Abuse and Neglect, 25,* 923–944.

Belsky, J. (1984) 'The determinants of parenting: a process model.' *Child Development, 55,* 83–96.

Bentovim, R. and Bingley, L. (1985) 'Parenting and parenting failure: some guidelines for the assessment of the child, his parents and the family.' In M. Adcock and R. White (eds) *Good-Enough Parenting': A Framework for Assessment.* London: British Agency for Adoption and Fostering.

Beresford, B. (1995) *Expert Opinions: A National Survey of Parents Caring for a Severely Disabled Child.* York: Joseph Rowntree Foundation.

Berglund, M., Andreasson, S., Franck, J., Fridell, M., Hakanson, I. and Johansson, B.A. (2001) *Treatment of Alcohol and Drug Abuse - an Evidence-Based Review, Report No. 156/1 (Vol I); 156/2 (Vol II).* Sweden: Swedish Council on Technology Assessment in Health Care.

Berry, E. (2003) *At the Chalkface of Child Protection: How Teachers View their Role in Relation to Child Protection.* Dublin: University of Dublin, Trinity College.

Berry, M., Charlston, R. and Dawson, K. (2003) 'Promising practices in understanding and treating child neglect.' *Child and Family Social Work, 8,* 1, 13–24.

Berwick, D.M., Levy, J.C. and Kleinerman, R. (1982) 'Failure to thrive: diagnostic yield of hospitalization.' *Archives of Disease in Childhood, 57,* 5, 347–351.

Bhui, K. and Olajide, D. (1999) *Mental Health Service Provision.* London: Saunders.

Bialoskurski, M., Cox, C. and Wiggins, R. (2002) 'The relationship between maternal needs and priorities in a neonatal intensive care environment.' *Journal of Advanced Nursing, 37,* 1, 62–69.

Bifulco, A., Brown, G.W. and Harris, T.O. (1994) 'Childhood experience of care and abuse (CECA), a retrospective interview model.' *Journal of Child Psychology and Psychiatry, 35,* 8, 1345–1419.

Bifulco, A. and Moran, P. (1998) *Wednesday's Child: Research into Women's Experience of Neglect and Abuse in Childhood and Adult Depression.* London and New York: Routledge.

Bifulco, A., Moran, P.M., Baines, R., Bunn, A. and Stanford, K. (2002) 'Exploring psychological abuse in childhood, II: Association with other abuse and adult clinical depression.' *Bulletin of the Menninger Clinic, 66,* 3, 241–258.

Bigelow, K.M., Kessler, K.L. and Lutzker, J.R.I.I. (Chair) (1995) *Improving the parent–child relationship in abusive and neglectful families.* Paper presented at the Third National APSAP Colloquium: Four Approaches, Tuscon, AZ.

Birch, E. and O'Connor, A. (2001) 'Preterm birth and visual development.' *Seminars in Neonatology, 6,* 487–497.

Birchall, E. and Hallett, C. (1995) *Working Together in Child Protection.* London: HMSO.

Black, M.M., Dubowitz, H., Hutcheson, J., Berenson Howard, J. and Starr, R.H., Jr. (1995) 'A randomized clinical trial of home intervention for children with failure to thrive.' *Pediatrics, 95,* 6, 807–814.

Black, R. and Mayer, J. (1980) 'Parents with special problems: alcoholism and opiate addiction.' *Child Abuse and Neglect, 4,* 45–54.

Blom-Cooper, L. (1985) *A Child in Trust.* London: HMSO.

Bonner, B., Crow, S. and Logue, M. (1999) 'Fatal child neglect.' In H. Dubowitz (ed) *Neglected Children: Research, Practice and Policy.* Thousand Oaks, CA: Sage.

Bowden, P. (1997) *Caring: Gender-Sensitive Ethics.* London and New York: Routledge.

Bowlby, J. (1969) *Attachment and Loss (Vol. 1).* London: Hogarth Press.

Bowlby, J. (1973) 'Maternal deprivation.' In S. Hutt and C. Hutt (eds) *Early Human Development.* London: OUP.

Bowlby, J. (1988) *A Secure Base: Clinical Applications of Attachment Theory.* London: Routledge.

Bradbury, B. and Jantti, M. (1999) *Child Poverty Across Industrialized Nations, Innocenti Occasional Papers (Vol. 71).* Florence: UNICEF Innocenti Research Centre.

Bradshaw, J., Stimson, C., Skinner, C. and Williams, J. (1999) *Absent Fathers?* London: Routledge.

Bradshaw, T. (2000) *The Role of Secondary Schools in Supporting Students who are Recovering from Sexual Abuse, MSc Thesis.* Dublin: University of Dublin, Trinity College.

Brandon, M. and Lewis, A. (1996) 'Significant harm and children's experience of domestic violence.' *Child and Family Social Work, 1,* 1, 33–42.

Bridge Childcare Consultancy (1995) *Paul: Death Through Neglect.* London: Bridge Consultancy Services.

Bridge Childcare Development Service (1999) *Neglect and Developmental: Part 8 Case Review Overview Report Re: Case 1/99 in Caerphilly.* Newbury: Bridge Publishing House.

Bridge Childcare Development Service (2001) *Childhood Lost: Part 8 Case Review Overview Report D M.* Newbury: Bridge Publishing House.

Briggs, F. (1997) 'The importance of schools and early childhood centres in childhood protection.' *Journal of Child Centered Practice, 4,* 11–21.

Bronfenbrenner, U. (1979) *The Ecology of Human Development: Experiments with Nature and Design.* Cambridge: Harvard University Press.

Bross, D. (2001) 'Protecting children from maltreatment in a hospital setting.' *Child Abuse and Neglect, 25*, 1551–1553.

Brown, R. (1996) *Group Processes: Dynamics Within and Between Groups*. Oxford: Blackwells.

Browne, K. and Saqui, S. (2002) 'Approaches to screening for child abuse and neglect.' In K. Browne, H. Hanks, P. Stratton and C. Hamilton (eds) *Early Prediction and Prevention of Child Abuse*. Chichester: Wiley.

Brunk, M., Henggeler, S.W. and Whelan, J.P. (1987) 'Comparison of multisystemic therapy and parent training in the brief treatment of child abuse and neglect.' *Journal of Consulting and Clinical Psychology, 55*, 2, 171–178.

Brunssen, S. and Miles, M. (1996) 'Sources of environmental stress experienced by mothers of hospitalised medically fragile infants.' *Neonatal Network, 15*, 3, 88–89.

Bubeck, D. (1998) 'Ethic of care and feminist ethics: a review essay.' *Women's Philosophy Review, 18*, 22–45.

Buckley, H. (2002) *Child Protection and Welfare: Innovations and Interventions*. Dublin: Institute of Public Administration.

Buckley, H. (2003a) *Child Protection Work: Beyond the Rhetoric*. London: Jessica Kingsley Publishers.

Buckley, H. (2003b) *Working Together – Training Together: An Evaluation of the North Tipperary Pilot Inter-Agency Training Programme*. Limerick: Mid-Western Health Board.

Buckley, H., Skehill, C. and O'Sullivan, E. (1997) *Child Protection Practices in Ireland: A Case Study*. Dublin: Oak Tree Press.

Bullard, D.M., Glaser, H.H., Heagarty, M.C. and Pivchik, E.C. (1967) 'Failure to thrive in the neglected child.' *American Journal of Orthopsychiatry, 37*, 680–690.

Callaghan, L., Cartwright, D., O'Rourke, P. and Davies, M. (2003) 'Infant to staff ratios and risk of mortality in very low birth weight infants.' *Archives of Disease in Childhood, 88*, F94–F97.

Campbell, H., Hotchkiss, R., Bradshaw, N. and Porteous, M. (1998) 'Integrated care pathways.' *BMJ, 316*, 133–137.

Carroll, L. (1872) *Through the Looking Glass and What Alice Found There*. London: Macmillian & co.

Cattell, V. (2001) 'Poor people, poor places, and poor health: the mediating role of social networks and social capital.' *Social Science and Medicine, 52*, 1501–1516.

Cawson, P., Wattam, C., Booker, S. and Kelly, G. (2000) *Child Maltreatment in the United Kingdom: a Study of the Prevalence of Child Abuse and Neglect*. London: NSPCC.

Chalmers, I. (2003) 'Trying to do more good than harm in policy and practice: the role of rigorous, transparent, up to date, replicable evaluation.' *Annals of the American Academy of Political and Social Science, 589*, 22–40.

Chamba, R., Ahmad, W., Hirst, M., Lawton, D. and Beresford, B. (1999) *On the Edge: Minority Ethnic Families Caring for a Severely Disabled Child*. Bristol: Policy Press.

Chapin, H. (1915) 'Are institutions for infants necessary?' *JAMA, 64*, 1–3.

Chapman, T. (2002) 'Safeguarding the welfare of children: 1.' *British Journal of Midwifery, 10*, 9, 569–572.

Charles, M. and Hendry, E. (2001) *Training Together To Safeguard Children: Guidance on Inter-Agency Training*. Leicester: NSPCC.

Chief Secretary to the Treasury (2003) *Every Child Matters*. London: The Stationery Office.

Children are Unbeatable (2002) *Why Smacking Babies, Toddlers and Children Should be Banned*. London: Children are Unbeatable.

Churchill, R., Hunot, V., Corney, R., Knapp, M., McGuire, H., Tylee, A. and Wessely, S. (2001) 'A systematic review of controlled trials of the effectiveness and cost- effectiveness of brief psychological treatments for depression.' *Health Technology Assessment, 5*, 35.

Clark, C.L. (2000) *Social Work Ethics: Politics, Principles and Practice*. Basingstoke: Macmillan.

Clausen, A. and Crittenden, P. (1991) 'Physical and psychological maltreatment: relations among types of maltreatment.' *Child Abuse and Neglect, 15*, 5, 5–18.

Cleaver, H., Unell, I. and Aldgate, J. (1999) *Children's Needs – Parenting Capacity: The Impact of Parental Mental Illness, Problem Alcohol and Drugs Use, and Domestic Violence on the Development of Children*. London: The Stationery Office.

Cohen, R., Coxall, J., Graig, G. and Sadiq-Sangster, A. (1992) *Hardship Britain: Being Poor in the 1990s*. London: Child Poverty Action Group.

Cole, E., Leavey, G. and King, M. (1995) 'Pathways to care for patients with first episode of psychosis: a comparison of ethnic groups.' *British Journal of Psychiatry, 167*, 770–776.

Cole, T.J., Freeman, J.V. and Preece, M.A. (1995) 'Body mass index reference curves for the UK, 1990.' *Archives of Disease in Childhood, 73*, 25–29.

Coleman, R.W. and Provence, S. (1957) 'Environmental retardation (Hospitalism) in infants living in families.' *Pediatrics, 19*, 285–292.

Coley, R.L. (1998) 'Children's socialization experiences and functioning in single-mother households: the importance of fathers and other men.' *Child Development, 69*, 1, 219–230.

Collins, P. and Hill, A. (2000) *Black Feminist Thought: Knowledge, Consciousness and the Politics of Empowerment.* (Second edition) New York: Routledge.

Coohey, C. (1995) 'Neglectful mothers, their mothers, and partners: the significance of mutual aid.' *Child Abuse and Neglect, 19*, 8, 885–895.

Coohey, C. (1998) 'Home alone and other inadequately supervised children.' *Child Welfare, 77*, 3, 291–310.

Cooke, P. (2000) *Final Report on Disabled Children and Abuse.* Nottingham: Ann Craft Trust (funded by BBC Children in Need).

Cooper, A. (2002) *International perspectives on child protection.* Paper presented at the Seminar held as part of the Scottish Executive Child Protection Review, Edinburgh.

Cooper, C. (1983) *'Good-enough', Border-Line and 'Bad-Enough' Parenting.* London: BAAF.

Cooper, H., Arber, S., Fee, L. and Ginn, J. (1999) *The Influence of Social Support and Social Capital on Health: a Review and Analysis of British Data.* London: Health Education Authority.

Cordon, I.M., Lutzker, J.R., Bigelow, K.M. and Doctor, R.M. (1998) 'Evaluating Spanish protocols for teaching bonding, home safety and health care skills to a mother reported for child abuse.' *Journal of Behavior Therapy and Experimental Psychiatry, 29*, 1, 41–51.

Coyle, J. (1999) 'Understanding dissatisfied users: developing a framework for comprehending criticisms of health care work.' *Journal of Advanced Nursing, 30*, 3, 723–731.

Creighton, S. (1992) *Child Abuse Trends in England and Wales, 1988–1990: an Overview from 1973–1990.* London: NSPCC.

Crittenden, P. (1988) 'Distorted patterns of relationship in maltreating families: the role of internal representation models.' *Journal of Infant and Reproductive Psychology, 6*, 183– 199.

Crittenden, P.M. (1981) 'Abusing, neglecting, problematic, and adequate dyads: Differentiating by patterns of interaction.' *Merrill-Palmer Quarterly, 27*, 201–208.

Crittenden, P.M. (1996) 'Research on maltreating families: Implications for intervention.' In J. Briere, L. Berliner, J.A. Bulkley, C. Jenny and T. Reid (eds) *The APSAC Handbook on Child Maltreament.* Newbury Park, London, New Delhi: Sage.

Crittenden, P.M. (1999) 'Child neglect: causes and contribution.' In H. Dubowitz (ed) *Neglected Children: Research, Practice and Policy.* London: Sage.

Curran, A., Brighton, J. and Murphy, V. (1997) 'Psychoemotional care of parents of children in a Neonatal Intensive Care Unit: results of a questionnaire.' *Journal of Neonatal Nursing 3*, 1, 25–29.

Daley, B.J. (1999) 'Novice to expert: an exploration of how professionals learn.' *Adult Education Quarterly, 49*, 133–147.

Daniel, B. (1999) 'A picture of powerlessness: an exploration of child neglect and ways in which social workers and parents can be empowered towards efficacy.' *International Journal of Child and Family Welfare, 4*, 3, 209–220.

Daniel, B. (2000) 'Judgements about parenting: what do social workers think they are doing?' *Child Abuse Review, 9*, 2, 91–107.

Daniel, B. (2002) 'Assessment practice in cases of child neglect: a developmental project.' *Practice, 13*, 4, 21–38.

Daniel, B.M. (2004) 'An overview of the Scottish Multidisciplinary Child Protection Review.' *Child and Family Social Work 9*, 247–257.

Daniel, B.M. and Baldwin, N. (2002) 'Assessment practice in cases of child neglect: a developmental project.' *Practice, 13*, 4, 21–38.

Daniel, B.M. and Taylor, J. (1999) 'The rhetoric versus the reality: a critical perspective on practice with fathers in child care and protection work.' *Child and Family Social Work, 4*, 3, 209–220.

Daniel, B.M. and Taylor, J. (2001) *Engaging with Fathers: Practice Issues for Health and Social Care.* London: Jessica Kingsley Publishers.

Daniel, B.M. and Wassell, S. (2002a) *The Early Years: Assessing and Promoting Resilience in Vulnerable Children I.* London: Jessica Kingsley Publishers.

Daniel, B.M. and Wassell, S. (2002b) *The School Years: Assessing and Promoting Resilience in Vulnerable Children II.* London: Jessica Kingsley Publishers.

Daniel, B.M. and Wassell, S. (2002c) *Adolescence: Assessing and Promoting Resilience in Vulnerable Children III.* London: Jessica Kingsley Publishers.

Daniel, B.M., Wassell, S. and Gilligan, R. (1999) *Child Development for Child Care and Protection Workers.* London: Jessica Kingsley Publishers.

Darlow, B., Harwood, L., Mogridge, N. and Clemett, R. (1997) 'Prospective study of New Zealand very low birthweight infants: Outcome at 7–8 years.' *Journal of Paediatric Child Health, 33*, 47–51.

Daycare Trust (2002) *Raising Expectations: Delivering Childcare for All.* London: Daycare Trust.

Dempster, H. (1993) 'The aftermath of child sexual abuse: women's perspectives.' In L. Waterhouse (ed) *Child Abuse and Child Abusers: Protection and Prevention.* London: Jessica Kingsley Publishers.

Department of Child Youth and Family (2002) *Evaluation of the Social Workers in Schools Programme.* New Zealand: CYF.

Department of Health (1995) *Messages from Research: Studies in Child Protection.* London: HMSO.

Department of Health (2000) *Framework for the Assessment of Children in Need and their Families.* London: The Stationery Office.

Department of Health (2001) *Children and Young People on Child Protection Registers: Year Ending 31 March 2001.* London: Department of Health.

Department of Health (2002) *Safeguarding Children: A Joint Chief Inspectors' Report on Arrangements to Safeguard Children.* London: Department of Health.

Department of Health (2003) *Review Standards for Training on Inter Agency Working.* London: Department of Health.

Department of Health and Children (Ireland) (1999) *Children First: National Guidelines for the Protection and Welfare of Children.* Dublin: Government Publications.

Department of Health and Social Security (1974) *Committee of Inquiry into the Care and Supervision Provided in Relation to Maria Colwell.* London: HMSO.

Department of Health Committee on the Medical Aspects of Food Policy (1991) *Dietary Reference Values for Food Energy and Nutrients for the UK.* London: HMSO.

Department of Health Committee on Medical Aspects of Food Policy (2002) *Scientific Review of the Welfare Foods Scheme.* London: The Stationery Office.

Department of Health, Home Office and Department for Education and Employment (2000) *Working Together to Safeguard Children: a Guide to Inter-Agency Working to Safeguard and Promote the Welfare of Children.* London: The Stationery Office.

Dignan, K. (2000) 'Teenage pregnancy.' In J. Kerr (ed) *Community Health Promotion.* London: Harcourt Publishers Limited.

Dingwall, R., Eekelaar, J. and Murray, T. (1983) *The Protection of Children.* Oxford: Blackwell.

Dingwall, R., Eekelaar, J. and Murray, T. (1995) *The Protection of Children: State Intervention and Family Life* (Second edition). Oxford: Blackwell.

Disability Awareness in Action (2003) *Report of the Review of Evidence on Infringements of Human Rights of Disabled People.* London: DAA.

Dominelli, L. (1986) 'Father–daughter incest: patriarchy's shameful secret.' *Critical Social Policy, 16*, 8–22.

Donohue, B. and Van Hasselt, V.B. (1999) 'Development and description of an empirically based ecobehavioural treatment program for child maltreatment.' *Behavioral Interventions, 14*, 55–82.

Dowler, E., Turner, S. and Dobson, B. (2001) *Poverty Bites: Food, Health and Poor Families.* London: Child Poverty Action Group.

Drewett, R.F., Corbett, S.S. and Wright, C.M. (1999) 'Cognitive and educational attainments at school age of children who failed to thrive in infancy: a population-based study.' *Journal of Child Psychology and Psychiatry and Allied Disciplines, 40*, 4, 551–561.

Drotar, D. (1985) 'Summary of discussion at NIMH Conference 1984: New developments in failure to thrive.' In D. Drotar (ed) *New Directions in Failure to Thrive.* New York: Plenum Press.

Drotar, D. and Sturm, L. (1988) 'Prediction of intellectual development in young children with early histories of nonorganic failure-to-thrive.' *Journal of Pediatric Psychology, 13*, 2, 281–296.

Dubowitz, H. (ed) (1999) *Neglected Children: Research, Practice and Policy.* Thousand Oaks, CA: Sage.

Dubowitz, H. and Black, M.M. (1996) 'Medical neglect.' In J. Briere & L. Berliner, J.A. Bulkley, C. Jenny and T. Reid (eds.) *The APSAC Handbook on Child Maltreament.* Newbury Park, CA, London, New Delhi: Sage.

Dubowitz, H., Black, M.M., Kerr, M.A., Starr, R.H. and Harrington, D. (2000) 'Fathers and child neglect.' *Archives of Pediatric and Adolescent Medicine, 154*, 135–141.

Dubowitz, H., Black, M.M., Starr, R.H. and Zuravin, S. (1993) 'A conceptual definition of child neglect.' *Criminal Justice and Behavior, 20*, 1, 8–26.

Dubowitz, H., Zuckerman, D.M., Bithoney, W.G. and Newberger, E.H. (1989) 'Child abuse and failure to thrive: individual familial and envionmental characteristics.' *Violence and Victims, 4*, 3, 191–201.

Dulude, D., Belanger, C., Wright, J. and Sabourin, S. (2002) 'High-risk pregnancies, psychological distress and dyadic adjustment.' *Journal of Reproductive and Infant Psychology, 20*, 2, 101–123.

Edwards, J. (1998) 'Screening out men: or "Has mum changed her washing powder recently?"' In J. Popay, J. Hearn and J. Edwards (eds) *Men, Gender Divisions and Welfare.* London: Routledge.

Egeland, B., Sroufe, L.A. and Erickson, M. (1983) 'The developmental consequences of different patterns of maltreatment.' *Child Abuse and Neglect, 7,* 459–469.

Elliot, E. and Watson, A. (2000) 'Responsible carers, problem drug takers or both?' In F. Harbin and M. Murphy (eds) *Substance Misuse and Child Care.* Lyme Regis: Russell House.

Elliott, L., Crombie, I., Irvine, L., Cantrell, J. and Taylor, J. (2001) *Nursing for Health. The Effectiveness of Public Health Nursing: A Review of Systematic Reviews.* Edinburgh: NHS Scotland.

Elmer, E. (1960) 'Failure to thrive: role of the mother.' *Pediatrics, 25,* 717–725.

Ennew, J. (1986) *The Sexual Exploitation of Children.* Cambridge: Polity Press.

Escobar, G., Littenberg, B. and Petitti, D. (1991) 'Outcome among surviving very low birth weight infants: a meta-analysis.' *Archives of Disease in Childhood, 66,* 204–211.

Evans, S.L., Reinhart, J.B. and Succop, R.A. (1972) 'Failure to thrive: A study of 45 children and their families.' *Journal of the American Academy of Child Psychiatry, 11,* 440–457.

Ewart, S. (2003) *An Investigation into the Involvement of Fathers in Family Centre Social Work in Northern Ireland.* Ulster: University of Ulster, Magee.

Falkov, A. (1996) *A Study of Working Together Part 8 Reports: Fatal Child Abuse and Parental Psychiatric Disorder.* London: Department of Health.

Famularo, R., Kinscherff, R. and Fenton, T. (1992) 'Parental substance abuse and the nature of child maltreatment.' *Child Abuse and Neglect, 16,* 475–483.

Fanaroff, A., Kennell, J. and Klaus, M. (1972) 'Follow-up of low birthweight infants: the predictive value of maternal visiting patterns.' *Pediatrics, 49,* 287–290.

Fantuzzo, J.W. (1990) 'Behavioral treatment of the victims of child abuse and neglect.' *Behavior Modification, 14,* 316–339.

Fantuzzo, J.W., Jurecic, L., Stovall, A., Hightower, A.D., Goins, C. and Schachtel, D. (1988) 'Effects of adult and peer social initiations on the social behavior of withdrawn, maltreated preschool children.' *Journal of Consulting and Clinical Psychology, 56,* 34–39.

Fantuzzo, J.W., Stovall, A., Schachtel, D., Coins, C. and Hall, R. (1987) 'The effects of peer social initiations on the social behavior of withdrawn maltreated preschool children.' *Journal of Behavior Therapy and Experimental Psychology, 18,* 357–363.

Fantuzzo, J.N., Sutton-Smith, B., Meyers, R., Atkins, M., Stevenson, H., Cooolahan, K., Weiss, A. and Manz, P. (1996) 'Community based resilient peer treatment of withdrawn maltreated preschool children.' *Journal of Consulting and Clinical Psychology, 64,* 6, 1377–1386.

Farmer, E. and Owen, M. (1995) *Child Protection Practice: Private Risks and Public Remedies – Decision-Making, Intervention and Outcome in Child Protection Work.* London: HMSO.

Farmer, E. and Owen, M. (1998) 'Gender and the child protection process.' *British Journal of Social Work, 28,* 545–564.

Faughey, M. (1996) *A case study of a special intervention into non-organic failure to thrive.* Unpublished Dissertation, Trinity College, Dublin.

Faughey, M. (1997) *Public Health Nurses and Child Neglect.* Unpublished MSc, Trinity College, Dublin.

Fazil, Q., Bywarters, P., Ali, Z., Wallace, L. and Singh, G. (2002) 'Disadvantage and discrimination compounded: the experience of Pakistani and Bangladeshi parents of disabled children in the UK.' *Disability and Society, 17,* 3, 237–253.

Featherstone, B. (1999) 'Taking mothering seriously: implications for child protection.' *Child and Family Social Work, 4,* 43–53.

Featherstone, B. (2001) 'Research review: putting fathers on the child welfare agenda.' *Child and Family Social Work, 6,* 2, 179–186.

Featherstone, B. (2003) 'Taking fathers seriously.' *British Journal of Social Work, 33,* 2, 239–254.

Feldman, M.A. (1998) 'Parents with intellectual disabilities: implications and interventions.' In J.R. Lutzker (ed) *Handbook of Child Abuse Research and Treatment.* New York: Plenum Press.

Feldman, M.A., Case, L., Garrick, M., MacIntyre-Grande, W., Carnwell, J. and Sparks, B. (1992a) 'Teaching child care skills to parents with developmental disabilities.' *Journal of Applied Behavior Analysis, 25,* 205–215.

Feldman, M.A., Case, L., Rincover, A., Towns, F. and Betel, J. (1989) 'Parent education project 111. Increasing affection and responsivity in developmentally handicapped mothers: Component analysis, generalisation, and effects on child language.' *Journal of Applied Behavior Analysis, 22,* 211–222.

Feldman, M.A., Case, L. and Sparks, B. (1992b) 'Effectiveness of a child-care training program for parents at-risk for child neglect.' *Canadian Journal of Behavioral Science 24,* 14–28.

Feldman, M.A., Leger, M. and Walton-Allen, N. (1997) 'Stress in mothers with intellectual disabilities.' *Journal of Child and Family Studies, 6*, 4, 471–485.

Feldman, M.A., Sparks, B., and Case, L. (1993) 'Effectiveness of home-based early intervention on the language development of children of mothers with mental retardation.' *Research in Developmental Disabilities, 14*, 387–408.

Feldman, M.A., Varghese, J., Ramsay, J. and Rajska, D. (2002) 'Relationships between social support, stress and mother–child interactions in mothers with intellectual disabilities.' *Journal of Applied Research in Intellectual Disabilities, 15*, 314–323.

Feldman, R., Weller, A., Leckman, J., Kuint, J. and Eidelman, A.I. (1999) 'The nature of the mother's tie to her infant: maternal bonding under conditions of proximity, separation, and potential loss.' *Journal of Child Psychology and Psychiatry, 40*, 6, 929–939.

Fenwick, J., Barclay, L. and Schmied, V. (2001) '"Chatting": An important clinical tool in facilitating mothering in neonatal nurseries.' *Journal of Advanced Nursing, 33*, 5, 583–593.

Ferguson, H. and O'Reilly, M. (2001) *Keeping Children Safe: Child Abuse, Child Protection and the Promotion of Welfare.* Dublin: A & A Farmar.

Ferri, E. and Smith, K. (1995) *Parenting in the 1990s.* London: Family Policy Studies Centre/ Joseph Rowntree Foundation.

Finkelstein, N. (1994) 'Treatment issues for alcohol- and drug-dependent pregnant and parenting women.' *Health and Social Work, 19*, 7–15.

Fitzgerald, J. (1998) 'Policy and practice in child protection: its relationship to dangerousness.' In J. Dent (ed) *Dangerous Care: Working to Protect Children.* London: Bridge Childcare Development Service.

Fitzpatrick, G. (1995) 'Assessing treatability.' In P. Reder and C. Lucey (eds) *Assessment of Parenting: Psychiatric and Psychological Contributions.* London: Routledge.

Flouri, E. and Buchanan, A. (2003) 'The role of father involvement in children's later mental health.' *Journal of Adolescence, 26*, 1, 63–78.

Forbat, L. (2002) 'Tinged with bitterness: re-presenting stress in family care.' *Disability and Society, 17*, 7, 759–768.

Forrester, D. (2000) 'Parental substance misuse and child protection in a British sample: a survey of children on the child protection register in an inner London district office.' *Child Abuse Review, 9*, 235–246.

Foulder-Hughes, L. and Cooke, R. (2003) 'Motor, cognitive, and behavioural disorders in children born very preterm.' *Developmental Medicine and Child Neurology, 45*, 97–103.

Franck, L., Bernal, H. and Gale, G. (2002) 'Infant holding policies and practices in neonatal units.' *Neonatal Network, 21*, 2, 13–20.

Fraser, A.C. and Cavanagh, S. (1991) 'Pregnancy and drug addiction: long term consequences.' *Journal of the Royal Society of Medicine, 84*, 530–532.

Fraser Askin, D. (2001) 'Complications in the transition from fetal to neonatal life.' *Journal of Obstetrical Gynaecological and Neonatal Nursing, 31*, 3, 318–327.

Freeman, J.V., Cole, T.J., Chinn, S., Jones, P.R.M., White, E.M. and Preece, M.A. (1995) 'Cross sectional stature and weight reference curves for the UK, 1990.' *Archives of Disease in Childhood, 73*, 17–24.

Garbarino, J. (1982) *Children and Families in the Social Environment.* New York: Aldine.

Garbarino, J. (1995) *Raising Children in a Socially Toxic Environment.* San Francisco, CA: Jossey Bass.

Garbarino, J., Gutteman, C. and Seeley, J. (1986) *The Psychologically Battered Child.* San Francisco, CA: Jossey Bass.

Garbarino, J. and Kostelny, K. (1994) 'Neighbourhood based programs.' In G.B. Melton and F.D. Barry (eds) *Protecting Children from Abuse and Neglect.* New York: Guilford.

Garbarino, J. and Sherman, S. (1980) 'High risk neighbourhoods and high-risk families: the human ecology of child maltreatment.' *Child Development, 51*, 188–198.

Gaudin, J.M. (1993) *Child Neglect: A Guide for Intervention.* National Center on Child Abuse and Neglect (US Department of Health and Human Services).

Gaudin, J.M., Polansky, N.A., Kilpatrick, A.C. and Shilton, P. (1996) 'Family functioning in neglectful families.' *Child Abuse and Neglect, 20*, 363–377.

Gaudin, J.M., Wodarski, J.S., Arkinson, M.K. and Avery, L.S. (1990–1991) 'Remedying child neglect: effectiveness of social network interventions.' *Journal of Applied Social Sciences, 15*, 97–123.

Geiger, B. (1996) *Fathers as Primary Caregivers.* Westport, CT: Greenwood Press.

Gershater-Molko, R.M., Ronit, M., Lutzker, J.R. and Sherman, J.A. (2002) 'Intervention in child neglect: an applied behavioral perspective.' *Aggression and Violent Behavior, 7*, 103–124.

Ghate, D., Shaw, C. and Hazel, N. (2000) *Fathers and Family Centres: Engaging Fathers in Preventive Services.* York: Joseph Rowntree Foundation.

Gibbons, J., Conroy, S. and Bell, C. (1995) *Operating the Child Protection System.* London: HMSO.

Giddens, A. (1994) 'Living in post industrialist society.' In U. Beck, A. Giddens and S. Lash (eds) *Reflexive Modernisation Politics, Tradition and Aesthetics in the Modern Social Order.* Cambridge: Polity Press.

Gil, D.G. (1979) 'Confronting societal violence by recreating communal institutions.' *Child Abuse and Neglect, 3,* 1–7.

Gil, E. (1982) 'Institutional abuse of children in out-of-home care.' *Child and Youth Services, 4,* 7–13.

Gilligan, C. (1982) *In a Different Voice: Psychological Theory and Women's Development.* Cambridge, MA: Harvard University Press.

Gilligan, R. (1998) 'The importance of schools and teachers in child welfare.' *Child and Family Social Work, 3,* 1, 13–25.

Gilligan, R. (1999) 'Enhancing the resilience of children and young people in public care by mentoring their talents and interests.' *Child and Family Social Work 4,* 3, 187–196.

Giovannoni, J.M. and Becerra, R.M. (1979) *Defining Child Abuse.* New York: The Free Press.

Glaser, D. (2002) 'Emotional abuse and neglect (psychological maltreatment): a conceptual framework.' *Child Abuse and Neglect, 26,* 697–714.

Glaser, D. and Prior, V. (1997) 'Is the term child protection applicable to emotional abuse?' *Child Abuse Review, 6,* 315–329.

Glaser, D. and Prior, V. (2002) 'Predicting emotional abuse and neglect.' In K. Browne, H. Hanks, P. Stratton and C. Hamilton (eds) *Early Prediction and Prevention of Child Abuse: A Handbook.* Chichester: John Wiley and Sons.

Glenn, E.N., Chang, G. and Forcey, R. (eds) (1994) *Mothering: Ideology, Experience and Agency.* London and New York: Routledge.

Glennie, S., Cruden, B. and Thorn, J. (1988) *Neglected Children: Maintaining Hope, Optimism and Direction.* Nottinghamshire and City Area: Child Protection Committee.

Goldberg, S. (1988) 'Risk factors in infant–mother attachment.' *Canadian Journal of Psychology, 42,* 2, 173–188.

Goldberg, S. and Di Vitto, B. (2002) 'Parenting children born preterm.' In M. Bronstein (ed) *Handbook of Parenting* (Second edition, Vol. 1, pp.329–354). London: Lawrence Erlbaum Associates.

Goldberg, S., Perrotta, M., Minde, K. and Corter, C. (1986) 'Maternal behaviour and attachment in low birth weight twins and singletons.' *Child Development, 57,* 34–46.

Golden, M.H., Samuels, M.P. and Southall, D.P. (2003) 'How to distinguish between neglect and deprivational abuse.' *Archives of Disease in Childhood, 88,* 105–107.

Gonzalvo, G. (2002) 'Maltreatment of children with disabilities: characteristics and risk factors.' *Anales Espanoles de Pediatria, 56,* 3, 219–223.

Goodinge, S. (1999) *NCH Fact File.* London: NCH.

Gordon, D. (2000) 'Measuring absolute and overall poverty.' In D. Gordon and P. Townsend (eds) *Breadline Europe: The Measurement of Poverty.* Bristol: The Policy Press.

Gordon, D., Parker, R. and Loughran, F. (2000) *Disabled Children in Britain.* London: The Stationary Office.

Gottesman, M. (1999) 'Enabling parents to "read" their baby.' *Journal of Pediatric Health Care, 13,* May/June, 148–151.

Gough, D.A. (1996) 'Defining the problem.' *Child Abuse and Neglect, 20,* 993–1002.

Gough, D.A. (2004) 'Systematic research synthesis.' In R. Pring and G. Thomas (eds) *Evidence-based Practice.* Buckingham: Open University Press.

Gough, D.A. and Elbourne, D. (2002) 'Systematic research synthesis to inform policy, practice and democratic debate.' *Social Policy and Society, 1,* 1–12.

Graham, B. (1998) *Overwhelmed or Underwhelmed? The Response of an Area Social Work Team to Neglect.* Unpublished dissertation, Trinity College, Dublin.

Greif, G.L. and Zuravin, S.J. (1989) 'Fathers: a placement resource for abused and neglected children?' *Child Welfare League of America, 68,* 479–490.

Griffin, J. and Tyrrell, I. (2002) *Psychotherapy and the Human Givens* (Second edition). Chalvington: HG Publishing.

The Guardian (2003) 'New Laws Urged Over Child Killers.' 15 April.

Gustavsson, N. and Segal, E. (1994) *Critical Issues in Child Welfare.* Thousand Oaks, CA: Sage Publications.

Hack, M., Wilson-Costello, D., Friedman, H., Taylor, G., Schluchter, M. and Fanaroff, A. (2000) 'Neurodevelopment and predictors of outcomes of children with birth weights of less than 1000g 1992–1995.' *Archives of Pediatric Adolescent Medicine, 154,* 725–731.

Hackett, S. (2003) *A Framework for Assessing Parenting Capacity.* London: Russell House Publishing.

Hall, D.M.B. and Elliman, D. (2002) *Health For All Children.* Milton Keynes: OUP.

Hall, D.M.B. and Elliman, D. (2003) 'Child health promotion: focus on parent.' In D.M.B. Hall and D. Elliman (eds) *Health for all Children*. Oxford: Oxford University Press.

Hallett, C. (1995) *Interagency Coordination in Child Protection*. London: HMSO.

Hallett, C. and Birchall, E. (1992) *Coordination and Child Protection: A Review of the Literature*. Edinburgh: HMSO.

Hamilton, C. and Browne, K. (2002) 'Predicting physical maltreatment.' In K. Browne, H. Hanks, P. Stratton and C. Hamilton (eds) *Early Prediction and Prevention of Child Abuse*. Chichester: Wiley.

Hampton, D., Batchelor, J., Birks, E., Bowers, L., Buswell, C., Coulter, P., Harris, G., Rudolf, M., Underdown, A. and Wright, C.M. (2002) *Recommendations for Best Practice for Weight and Growth Faltering in Young Children*. London: Children's Society.

Hanafin, S. (1998) 'Deconstructing the role of the public health nurse in child protection.' *Journal of Advanced Nursing, 28*, 1, 178–184.

Hannah, V. (2000) 'Social workers criticised after girl left in cast for 10 months.' *The Herald*.

Harbin, F. (2000) 'Therapeutic work with children of substance misusing parents.' In F. Harbin and M. Murphy (eds) *Substance Misuse and Child Care*. Lyme Regis: Russell House.

Hardy, J.B. and Streett, R. (1989) 'Family support and parenting education in the home: an effective extension of clinic-based preventive health care services for poor children.' *Journal of Pediatrics, 115*, 927–931.

Hargreaves, D. (1996) *Teaching as a Research-based Profession: Possibilities and Prospects*. London: TTA.

Hart, S. and Brassard, M. (1991) 'Psychological maltreatment: progress achieved.' *Development and Psychopathology, 3*, 61–70.

Hart, T. (1971) 'The inverse care law.' *Lancet, 1*, 405–412.

Henggeler, S.W. and Borduin, C.M. (1995) 'Multisystemic treatment of serious juvenile offenders and their families.' In I.M. Schwartz and P. AuClaire (eds) *Home-based Services for Troubled Children*. Lincoln, NE: University of Nebraska Press.

Heptinstall, E., Puckering, C., Skuse, D., Start, K., Zur-Spiro, S. and Dowdney, L. (1987) 'Nutrition and mealtime behaviour in families of growth retarded children.' *Human Nutrition: Applied Nutrition, 41a*, 390–402.

Hester, M., Pearson, C. and Harwin, N. (2000) *Making an Impact: Children and Domestic Violence*. London: Jessica Kingsley Publishers.

Hester, M. and Radford, L. (1996) *Domestic Violence and Child Contact Arrangements in England and Denmark*. Bristol: The Policy Press.

Hill, M. (1990) 'The manifest and latent lessons of child abuse inquiries.' *British Journal of Social Work, 20*, 197–213.

Hoagland, S. (1991) 'Some thoughts about "caring".' In C. Card (ed) *Feminist Ethics*. Lawrence, KS: Kansas University Press.

Hobcraft, J. (1998) *Intergenerational and Lifecourse Transmission of Social Exclusion: Influences of Childhood Poverty, Family Disruption and Contact with the Police*. London: Centre for Analysis of Social Exclusion, London School of Economics.

Hobcraft, J. (2003) *Continuity and Change in Pathways to Young Adult Disadvantage: Results from a British Birth Cohort*. London: Centre for Analysis of Social Exclusion, London School of Economics.

Hobson, B. and Morgan, D. (2002) 'Introduction: making men into fathers.' In B. Hobson (ed) *Making Men Into Fathers*. Cambridge: Cambridge University Press.

Hogan, D. and Park, J. (2000) 'Family factors and social support in the developmental outcomes of very low birth weight children.' *Clinics in Perinatology, 27*, 2, 433–460.

Hoggan, D. (2003) 'Parenting beliefs and practices of opiate-addicted parents: concealment and taboo.' *European Addiction Research, 9*, 113–119.

Holden, E.W. and Nabors, L. (1999) 'The prevention of child neglect.' In H. Dubowitz (ed) *Neglected Children: Research, Policy and Practice*. Thousand Oaks, CA: Sage Publications.

Holt, S., Manners, P. and Gilligan, R. (2002) *Family Support in Practice. An Evaluation of the Naas Child and Family Project. A Springboard Initiative*. Naas: Kildare Youth Services and South-Western Area Health Board.

Home Office (2003) *Hidden Harm: Responding to the Needs of Children of Problem Drug Users*. London: Advisory Council on the Misuse of Drugs.

Hong, G.K. and Hong, L.K. (1991) 'Comparative perspectives on child abuse and neglect: Chinese versus hispanics and whites.' *Child Welfare, 70*, 4, 463–475.

Horbar, J., Badger, G., Carpenter, J., Fanaroff, A., Kilpatrick, S., LaCorte, M., Phibbs, R. and Soll, R. (2002) 'Trends in mortality and morbidity for very low birth weight infants, 1991–1999.' *Pediatrics, 110,* 1, 143–151.

Horwath, J. (2002) 'Maintaining a focus on the child?' *Child Abuse Review, 11,* 195–213.

Horwath, J. and Bishop, B. (2001) *Child Neglect: Is My View Your View?* Dunshaghlin: North Eastern Health Board.

Horwath, J. and Morrison, T. (1999) *Effective Training in Social Care.* London: Routledge.

Horwath, J. and Morrison, T. (2001) 'Assessment of parental motivation to change.' In J. Horwath (ed) *The Child's World: Assessing Children in Need.* London: Jessica Kingsley Publishers.

Horwath, J. and Sanders, T. (2003) *Child Neglect: Professional Perspectives in the North Eastern Health Board Region.* Sheffield: University of Sheffield.

Howard, M., Garnham, A., Fimister, G. and Veit-Wilson, J. (2001) *Poverty: The Facts.* London: Child Poverty Action Group.

Howe, D. (1996a) 'Surface and depth in social work practice.' In N. Parton (ed) *Social Theory, Social Change and Social Work.* (pp.77–97). London: Routledge.

Howe, D. (ed) (1996b) *Attachment and Loss in Child and Family Social Work.* Aldershot: Avebury.

Howe, D. (2001) 'Attachment.' In J. Horwath (ed) *The Child's World: Assessing Children in Need.* London: Jessica Kingsley Publishers.

Howe, D., Brandon, M., Hinings, D. and Schofield, G. (1999) *Attachment Theory, Child Maltreatment and Family Support.* London: MacMillan Press.

Howe, D., Dooley, T. and Hinings, D. (2000) 'Assessment and decision-making in a case of child neglect and abuse using an attachment perspective.' *Child and Family Social Work, 5,* 143–155.

Howell, E.M., Heiser, N. and Harrington, M. (1999) 'A review of recent findings on substance abuse treatment for pregnant women.' *Journal of Substance Misuse Treatment, 16,* 3, 195–219.

Hufton, I.W. and Oates, R.K. (1977) 'Nonorganic failure to thrive: a long-term follow-up.' *Pediatrics, 59,* 1, 73–77.

Iverson, T.J. and Segal, M. (1990) *Child Abuse and Neglect: An Information and Reference Guide.* London: Garland.

Iwaniec, D. (1995) *The Emotionally Abused and Neglected Child: Identification, Assessment and Intervention.* Chichester: John Wiley and Sons.

Jack, G. (2000) 'Ecological influences on parenting and child development.' *British Journal of Social Work, 30,* 703–720.

Jaffe, P.G., Wolfe, D.A. and Wilson, K.A. (1990) *Children of Battered Women.* Newbury Park, CA: Sage Publications.

James, G. (1994) *Study of Working Together Part 8 Reports.* London: Department of Health.

James, S.M. (1993) 'Mothering: a possible Black feminist link to social transformation?' In S.M. James and A.P.A. Busia (eds) *Theorizing Black Feminisms: The Visionary Pragmatism of Black Women.* London: Routledge.

Janis, I.L. (1972) *Victims of Group Think.* Boston, MA: Houghton Mifflin.

Jaudes, P., Ekwo, E. and VanVoorhis, J. (1995) 'Association of drug abuse and child abuse.' *Child Abuse and Neglect, 19,* 1065–1075.

Jenkins, A. (1996) 'NEWPIN: a creative mental health resource for parents and children.' In M. Goepfert, J. Webster and M.V. Seemen (eds) *Parental Psychiatric Disorder: Distressed Parents and their Families.* Cambridge: Cambridge University Press.

Johnson, C.F. (1999) 'Child abuse as a stressor of pediatricians.' *Pediatric Emergency Care, 15,* 84–89.

Johnson, M. and Webb, C. (1995) 'Rediscovering unpopular patients: the concept of social judgement.' *Journal of Advanced Nursing, 21,* 3, 466–475.

Johnson, Z., Molloy, B., Scallon, E., Fitzpatrick, P., Rooney, B.N., Keegan, T. and Byrne, P. (2000) 'Community Mothers Programme: Seven year follow-up of a randomised controlled trial of non-professional intervention in parenting.' *Journal of Public Health Medicine, 22,* 337–342.

Jones, C. (2001a) 'Voices from the front line: state social workers and new labour.' *British Journal of Social Work, 31,* 547–562.

Jones, D. (2001b) 'The assessment of parental capacity.' In J. Horwath (ed) *The Child's World: Assessing Children in Need.* London: Jessica Kingsley Publishers.

Jones, L. (1993) 'Decision Making in Child Welfare: a Critical Review of the Literature.' *Social Work Journal, 10,* 3, 241–262.

Jowitt, S. (2003) *Child Neglect: Contemporary Themes and Issues.* London: Bridge Publishing House.

Kahneman, D., Slovic, P. and Tversky, A. (1990) *Judgement under Uncertainty: Heuristics and Biases.* Cambridge: Cambridge University Press.

Kasese-Hara, M., Wright, C. and Drewett, R. (2002) 'Energy compensation in young children who fail to thrive.' *Journal of Child Psychology and Child Psychiatry, 43,* 449–456.

Katz, A. (1999) *Leading Lads.* Oxford: Oxford University, sponsored by Topman.

Keeling, J., Bryan, E. and Fearne, J. (1999) 'Iatrogenic disease.' In G. Levitt , D. Harvey and R. Cooke (eds) *Practical Perinatal Care. The Baby Under 1000g.* Oxford: Butterworth Heinemann.

Kelley, S.J. (1992) 'Parenting stress and child maltreatment in drug exposed children.' *Child Abuse and Neglect, 16,* 317–328.

Kelly, J. (1997) 'What do teachers do with child protection and child welfare concerns which they encounter in their classrooms?' *Irish Journal of Social Work Research, 1,* 23–35.

Kelly, J. and Milner, J. (1996) 'Child protection decision making.' *Child Abuse Review, 5,* 2, 91–102.

Kelly, J. and Milner, J. (2000) 'Child protection decision making: the efficacy of the case conference.' *Child Centered Practice, 7,* 1, 71–96.

Kennedy, M. (1995) *Euthanasia and Disabled Children (Vol. 119).* London: Children's Legal Centre.

Keown, J. (2002) 'The Tony Bland case.' In J. Keown (ed) *Euthanasia, Ethics and Public Policy.* Cambridge: Cambridge University Press.

Kerr, M.A. and Black, M.M. (2000) 'Failure-to-thrive, maltreatment and the behavior and development of 6-year-old children from low-income, urban families: a cumulative risk model.' *Child Abuse and Neglect, 24,* 5, 587–596.

Kershaw, S. (2000) 'Living in a lesbian household: the effects on children.' *Child and Family Social Work, 5,* 4, 365–371.

King, J.M. and Taitz, L.S. (1985) 'Catch up growth following abuse.' *Archives of Disease in Childhood, 60,* 1152–1154.

Kirkham, M. (1989) 'Midwives and information-giving during labour.' In S. Robinson and A. Thomson (eds) *Midwives, Research and Childbirth* (Vol. 2, pp.117–138). London: Chapman and Hall.

Kirkham, M., Stapleton, H., Curtis, P. and Thomas, G. (2002) 'The inverse care law in antenatal care.' *British Journal of Midwifery, 10,* 8, 509–513.

Koel, B.S. (1969) 'Failure to thrive and fatal injury as a continuum.' *American Journal of Diseases in Childhood, 118,* 565–567.

Kownacki, R.J. and Shadish, W.R. (1999) 'Does Alcoholics Anonymous work: the results from a meta-analysis of controlled experiments.' *Substance Use and Misuse, 34,* 13, 1897–1916.

Kramer, M., Goulet, L., Lyndon, J., Seguin, L. and McNamara, H. (2001) 'Socio-economic disparities in preterm birth: causal pathways and mechanisms.' *Paediatric and Perinatal Epidemiology, 15,* (Suppl. 2), 104–123.

Kramer, M., Seguin, L., Lydon, J. and Goulet, L. (2000) 'Socio-economic disparaties in pregnancy outcome: why do the poor fare so poorly?' *Paediatric and Perinatal Epidemiology 14,* 194–210.

Krieger, N., Rowley, D., Hermann, A.A., Avery, B. and Phillips, M.T. (1993) 'Racism, sexism, and social class: implications for studies of health, disease and well-being.' *American Journal of Preventive Medicine, 9* (Suppl. 2), 82–122.

Kristiansson, B. and Fallstrom, S.P. (1987) 'Growth at age of 4 years subsequent to early failure to thrive.' *Child Abuse and Neglect, 11,* 35–40.

Kroll, B. (2003) *Parental Substance Misuse and Child Welfare.* London: Jessica Kingsley Publishers.

Kroll, B. and Taylor, A. (2000) 'Invisible children? Parental substance misuse and child protection: dilemmas for practice.' *Probation Journal, 47,* 2, 91–100.

Lacharite, C., Ethier, L. and Couture, G. (1996) 'The influence of partners on parental stress of neglectful mothers.' *Child Abuse Review, 5,* 1, 18–33.

Lally, J.R. (1984) 'Three views of child neglect: expanding visions of preventative interventions.' *Child Abuse and Neglect, 8,* 243–254.

Lamb, M.E. (1997) 'Fathers and child development: an introductory overview and guide.' In M.E. Lamb (ed) *The Role of the Father in Child Development.* New York: John Wiley and Sons.

Lawhorn, G. (2002) 'Facilitation of parenting the premature infant within the newborn intensive care unit.' *Journal of Perinatal and Neonatal Nursing, 16,* 1, 71–82.

Laybourn, A., Brown, J. and Hill, M. (1997) *Hurting on the Inside: Children's Experiences of Parental Drug Misuse.* Tyne and Wear: Avebury Press.

Lee, K., Kim, B., Khosnood, B., Hsieh, H., Chen, T.-J., Herschel, M. and Mittendorf, R. (1995) 'Outcome of very low birth weight infants in industrialised countries: 1947–1987.' *American Journal of Epidemiology, 141,* 1188–1193.

Leonard, M.F., Rhymes, J.P. and Solnit, A.J. (1966) 'Failure to thrive in infants. A family problem.' *American Journal of Diseases in Childhood, 111*, 600–612.

London Borough of Brent (1985) *A Child in Trust: Report of the Panel of Inquiry into the Circumstances Surrounding the Death of Jasmine Beckford.* London: Borough of Brent.

Lord Laming (2003) *The Victoria Climbié Inquiry.* London: HMSO.

Lupton, C., North, N. and Khan, P. (2001) *Working Together or Pulling Apart? The National Health Service and Child Protection Networks.* Bristol: The Policy Press.

Luthar, S.S., D'Avanzo, K. and Hites, S. (2003) 'Maternal drug abuse versus other psychological disturbances.' In S. Luther (ed) *Resilience and Vulnerability: Adaptation in the Context of Childhood Adversities.* (pp.104–129). Cambridge: Cambridge University Press.

Lutzker, J.R., Bigelow, K.M., Doctor, R.M. and Kessler, M.L. (1998) 'Safety, health care, and bonding within an ecobehavioral approach to treating and preventing child abuse and neglect.' *Journal of Family Violence, 13*, 2, 163–185.

Lynch, M. and Stevenson, O. (1990) *Fox, Stephanie: Report of the Practice Review.* London: Wandsworth Child Protection Committee.

Macdonald, G. (2001) *Effective Interventions for Child Abuse and Neglect: An Evidence-Based Approach to Planning and Evaluating Interventions.* Chichester: John Wiley.

Mackey, M., Williams, C. and Tiller, C. (2000) 'Stress, preterm labour and birth outcomes.' *Journal of Advanced Nursing, 32*, 3, 666–674.

MacMillan, H.L., MacMillan, J.H., Offord, D.R., Griffith, L. and MacMillan, A. (1994) 'Primary prevention of child physical abuse and neglect: a critical review. Part 1.' *Journal of Child Psychology and Psychiatry and Allied Professions, 35*, 5, 835–856.

MacNamara, R.D. (1992) *Creating Abuse Free Environments for Children, the Disabled and Elderly: Preparing, Supervising and Managing Caregivers for the Emotional Impact of Their Responsibilities.* Springfield, IL: Charles C Thomas.

Main, M. and Weston, D.R. (1981) 'The quality of the toddler's relationship to mother and to father: related to conflict behaviour and the readiness to establish new relationships.' *Child Development, 52*, 932–994.

Manning, R. (1992) *Speaking from the Heart: A Feminist Perspective on Ethics.* Lanham, MD: Rowan and Littlefield.

Marks, D. (1999) *Disability: Controversial Debates and Psychosocial Perspectives.* London: Routledge.

Maslow, A.H. (1954) *Motivation and Personality.* New York: Harper and Row.

Maternity Alliance (2001) *Tackling health inequalities, consultation on plan for delivery – response from the Maternity Alliance.* London: Maternity Alliance. Retrieved 16 December 2003 from www.maternity alliance.org.uk

Maternity Alliance (2003) *Details of new parental leave rights.* London: Maternity Alliance. Retrieved 16 December 2003, from www.maternityalliance.org.uk

Mayall, P.D. and Norgard, K.E. (1983) *Child Abuse and Neglect: Sharing Responsibility.* Chichester: John Wiley and Sons.

McCarrick, C., Over, A. and Wood, P. (2001) 'Towards user friendly assessment.' In N. Baldwin (ed) *Protecting Children: Promoting Their Rights?* London: Whiting and Birch.

McCreadie, C. (1996) *Elder Abuse: Update on Research.* London: Age Concern Institute of Gerontology, Kings College.

McHaffie, H. (1990) 'Mothers of very low birth weight babies: how do they adjust?' *Journal of Advanced Nursing, 15*, 6–11.

McKeown, K. (2000) *A Guide to What Works in Family Support Services for Vulnerable Families.* Dublin: Government Information Services.

McLean, A., Townsend, A., Clark, J., Sawyer, M., Baghurst, P., Haslam, R. and Whaites, L. (2000) 'Quality of life of mothers and families caring for preterm infants requiring home oxygen therapy: a brief report.' *Journal of Paediatric Child Health, 36*, 440–444.

McMunn, A.M., Nazroo, J.Y., Marmot, M.G., Boreham, R. and Goodman, R. (2001) 'Children's emotional and behavioural well-being and the family environment: findings from the Health Survey for England.' *Social Science and Medicine, 53*, 423–440.

Mezey, G.C. and Bewley, S. (1997) 'Domestic violence and pregnancy.' *BMJ, 314*, 1295.

Middleton, L. (1998) 'Services for disabled children: integrating the perspective of social workers.' *Child and Family Social Work, 3*, 4, 239–246.

Middleton, L. (1999) *Disabled Children: Challenging Social Exclusion.* London: Blackwell Science.

Miller, F.J.W., Court, S.D.M. and Knox, E.G. (1960) *Growing up in Newcastle Upon Tyne. The Nuffield Foundation.* London: Oxford University Press.

Miller, F.J.W., Court, S.D.M. and Knox, E.G. (1974) *The School Years in Newcastle Upon Tyne.* London: Oxford University Press.

Milligan, C. and Dowie, A. (1998) *What Do Children Need From Their Fathers?* Edinburgh: Centre for Theology and Public Issues.

Milner, J. (1993) 'A disappearing act: the differing career paths of fathers and mothers in child protection investigations.' *Critical Social Policy, 38,* 48–63.

Minde, K. (2000) 'Prematurity and serious medical conditions in infancy: implications for development, behaviour, and intervention.' In J.C.H. Zeanah (ed) *Handbook of Infant Mental Health* (Second edition). London: The Guilford Press.

Minty, B. and Pattinson, G. (1994) 'The nature of child neglect.' *British Journal of Social Work, 24,* 733–747.

Mires, G. and Patel, N. (1999) 'Aetiology and incidence.' In G. Levitt, D. Harvey and R. Cooke (eds) *Practical Perinatal Care. The Baby Under 1000g.* Oxford: Butterworth Heinemann.

Moffitt, T.E. and Caspi, A. (1998) 'Annotation: the implications of violence between intimate partners for child psychologists and psychiatrists.' *Journal of Child Psychology and Psychiatry, 39,* 2, 137–144.

Molloy, B. (2002) *Still Going Strong: A Tracer Study of the Community Mothers Programme, Dublin, Ireland.* The Hague: Bernard Van Leer Foundation.

Money, J., Anecillo, C. and Kelley, J. (1983) 'Growth of intelligence : failure and catch-up associated respectively with abuse and rescue in the syndrome of abuse dwarfism.' *Psychoneuroendocrinology, 8,* 309–319.

Moore, M. (2000) 'Perinatal Nursing Research: A 25-Year Review –1976–2000.' *Maternal and Child Nursing, 25,* 6, 305–309.

Morbey, H. (2002) 'Older women's understanding of elder abuse: quality relationships and the "stresses of caregiving".' *The Journal of Adult Protection, 4,* 3, 4–13.

Morgan, S. (1987) *Abuse and Neglect of Handicapped Children.* Boston, MA: College-Hill.

Morley, R. and Mullender, A. (1994) 'Domestic violence and children: what do we know from research?' In A. Mullender and R. Morley (eds) *Children Living with Domestic Violence: Putting Men's Abuse of Women on the Child Care Agenda.* London: Whiting and Birch Ltd.

Morris, J. (1991) *Pride Against Prejudice.* London: Women's Press.

Morris, J. (1998a) *Accessing Human Rights: Disabled Children and The Children Act.* London: Barnardo's.

Morris, J. (1998b) *Still Missing Vol. 1.* London: Who Cares Trust.

Moss, P. (2002) *The UK at the Crossroads: Towards an Early Years European Partnership.* London: Daycare Trust.

Mrazeck, D. (1995) 'Clinical assessment of parenting.' *Journal of the American Academy of Child and Adolescent Psychiatry, 34,* 3, 272–282.

Mullender, A., Kelly, L., Hague, G., Malos, E. and Imam, U. (2000) *Children's Needs, Coping Strategies and Understandings of Woman Abuse, Research Report.* London: ESRC.

Munro, E. (1996) 'Avoidable and unavoidable mistakes in child protection work.' *British Journal of Social Work, 26,* 6, 793–808.

Munro, E. (1998) 'Improving social workers' knowledge base in child protection work.' *British Journal of Social Work, 28,* 1, 89–105.

Munro, E. (1999) 'Common errors of reasoning in child protection work.' *Child Abuse and Neglect, 23,* 8, 745–758.

Munro, E. (2002) *Effective Child Protection.* London: Sage.

Muntaner, C., Lynch, J.W., Hillemeier, M., Lee, J.H., David, R., Benach, J. and Borrell, C. (2002) 'Economic inequality, working class power, social capital, and cause-specific mortality in wealthy countries.' *International Journal of Health Services, 32,* 629–656.

Muraskas, J., Marshall, P., Tomich, P., Myers, T., Gianopoulos, J. and Thomasma, D. (1999) 'Neonatal viability in the 1990s: held hostage by technology.' *Cambridge Quarterly of Healthcare Ethics, 8,* 160–172.

Murray, C., Field, F., Brown, J.C., Walker, A. and Deakin, N. (1990) *The Emerging British Underclass.* London: Institute of Economic Affairs, Health and Welfare Unit.

Murray, L., Hipwell, A., Hooper, R., Sein, A. and Cooper, P. (1996) 'The cognitive development of 5-year-old children of post-natally depressed mothers.' *Journal of Child Psychology and Psychiatry, 37,* 8, 927–935.

Nadya, R. (2002) 'Nurses' decisions in cases of child abuse.' *Child Abuse Review, 11,* 168–178.

NCH Action for Children (2000) *NCH Action for Children Factfile 2000.* London: NCH Action for Children.

Nelson-Zlupco, I., Kaufmann, E. and Dore, M.M. (1995) 'Gender differences in drug addiction and treatment: implications for social work intervention with drug abusing women.' *Social Work and Social Sciences Review, 40,* 45–54.

Newcombe, M.D. and Locke, T.F. (2001) 'Intergenerational cycle of maltreatment: a popular concept obscured by methodological limitations.' *Child Abuse and Neglect, 25*, 9, 1219–1240.

Newham Area Child Protection Committee (2002) *Ainlee: Chapter 8 Review.* London: Newham Area Child Protection Committee.

Noddings, N. (1984) *Caring: A Feminine Approach to Ethics and Moral Education.* Berkley and Los Angeles, CA: University of California Press.

NSPCC (2001) *Out of Sight: Report on Children Deaths from Abuse 1973–2000.* London: NSPCC.

O'Hagan, K. and Dillenberger, K. (1995) *The Abuse of Women Within Child Care Work.* Buckingham: OUP.

Oakley, A. (2000) *Experiments in Knowing: Gender and Method in the Social Sciences.* Cambridge: Polity Press.

Oates, R.K. (1984) 'Child abuse and non-organic failure to thrive: similarities and differences in the parents.' *Journal of Australian Paediatrics, 20*, 177–180.

OECD and Statistics Canada (2000) *Literacy in the Information Age – Final Report of the International Adult Literacy Survey.* Paris: OECD.

Ogden, S. and Baldwin, N. (2001) *Audit of Child Protection Cases.* Dundee: University of Dundee.

Olds, D.L. (1997) 'The Prenatal Early Infancy Project: preventing child abuse and neglect in the context of promoting child and maternal health.' In D.A. Wolfe, R.J. McMahon and R.D. Peters (eds) *Child Abuse: New Directions in Prevention and Treatment Across the Lifespan.* Thousand Oaks, CA: Sage.

Olds, D.L., Henderson, Jr, C.R., Chamberlain, P., Kitzman, H., Eckenrode, J., Cole, R.C. and Tatelbaum, R. (1999) 'Prenatal and infancy home visitation by nurses: recent findings.' *The Future of Children, 9*, 1, 44–65.

Olds, D.L., Henderson, J.C.R. and Eckenrode, J. (2002) 'Preventing child abuse and neglect with prenatal and infancy home visiting by nurses.' In K. Browne, H. Hanks, P. Stratton and C. Hamilton (eds) *Early Prediction and Prevention of Child Abuse* (Second edition). London: Wiley.

Olds, D.L., Henderson, J.C.R. and Kitzman, H. (1994) 'Does prenatal and infancy nurse home visitation have enduring effects on qualities of parental caregiving and child health at 25 to 50 months of life?' *Pediatrics, 93*, 89–98.

Olds, D.L., Henderson, J.C.R., Kitzman, H. and Cole, R. (1995) 'Effects of prenatal and infancy nurse home visitation on surveillance of child maltreatment.' *Pediatrics, 95*, 365–372.

Olds, D.L., Henderson, Jr., C.R., Kitzman, H., Eckenrode, J., Cole, R. and Tatelbaum, R. (1998) 'The promise of home visitation: research from two randomized trials.' *Journal of Community Psychology, 26*, 1, 5–21.

Oliver, M. (1999a) *Understanding Disability: From Theory to Practice.* London: Macmillan.

Oliver, S. (1999b) 'Users of health services: following their agenda.' In S. Hood, B. Mayall and S. Oliver (eds) *Critical Issues in Social Research: Power and Prejudice.* Buckingham: Open University Press.

Owusu-Bempah, J. and Howitt, D. (1997) 'Socio-genealogical connectedness, attachment theory, and childcare practice.' *Child and Family Social Work, 2*, 199–207.

Parker, R. (1995) *Torn in Two: The Experience of Maternal Ambivalence.* London: Virago.

Parker, R. (1997) 'The production and purposes of maternal ambivalence.' In W. Hollway and B. Featherstone (eds) *Mothering and Ambivalence.* London: Routledge.

Parton, N. (1995) 'Neglect as child protection: the political context and the practical outcomes.' *Children and Society, 9*, 1, 67–89.

Parton, N. (1996) 'Social work, risk and the "blaming system".' In N. Parton (ed) *Social Theory, Social Change and Social Work.* (pp.98–114). London: Routledge.

Parton, N. (2003) 'Rethinking professional practice: the contribution of social constructionism and the feminist "ethics of care".' *British Journal of Social Work, 33*, 1, 1–16.

Parton, N., Thorpe, D. and Wattam, C. (1997) *Child Protection, Risk and the Moral Order.* Basingstoke: Macmillan.

Patterson, G.R. (1982) *A Social Learning Approach to Family Intervention: 111 Coercive Family Process.* Eugene, OR: Castalia Publishing.

Patton, R.G. and Gardner, L.I. (1962) 'Influences of family environment on growth: the syndrome of maternal deprivation.' *Pediatrics, 30*, 957–962.

Paul, A. and Cawson, P. (2002) 'Safeguarding disabled children in residential settings: what we know and what we don't know.' *Child Abuse Review, 11*, 262–281.

Payne, H. (2000) 'The health of children in public care.' *Current Opinion in Psychiatry, 13*, 381–388.

Pearson, J. and Anderson, K. (2001) 'Evaluation of a program to promote positive parenting in the neonatal unit.' *Neonatal Network, 20*, 4, 43–48.

Pelton, A. (1992) 'The role of material factors in child abuse and neglect.' In G.B. Melton and F.D. Barry (eds) *Protecting Children from Child Abuse and Neglect.* New York: Guilford Press.

Petit, M. and Curtis, P. (1997) *Child Abuse and Neglect: a Look at the States.* Washington, DC: Child Welfare League of America.

Piecuch, P., Leonard, C. and Cooper, B. (1998) 'Infants with birth weight 1000–1499 grams born in three time periods: has outcome changed over time?' *Clinical Pediatrics, 37,* 537–546.

Plasse, B.R. (2000) 'Components of engagement: women in a psychoeducational parenting skills group in substance abuse treatment.' *Social Work with Groups, 22,* 4, 33–50.

Platt, L. (2002) *Parallel Lives? Poverty Among Ethnic Minority Groups in Britain.* London: Child Poverty Action Group.

Polansky, N.A., Chalmers, M.A., Buttenwieser, E. and Williams, D.P. (1981) *Damaged Parents: An Anatomy of Child Neglect.* Chicago, IL: University of Chicago Press.

Polansky, N.A., Gaudin, J.M., Ammons, P.W. and Davis, K.B. (1985) 'The psychological ecology of the neglectful mother.' *Child Abuse and Neglect, 9,* 265–275.

Pollitt, E. and Leibel, R. (1980) 'Biological and social correlates of failure to thrive.' *Social and Biological Predictors of Nutritional Status, Physical Growth and Neurological Development.* Orlando, FL: Academic Press.

Portwood, S.G. (1998) 'The impact of individuals' characteristics and experiences on their definitions of child maltreatment.' *Child Abuse and Neglect, 22,* 5, 437–452.

Powell, G., Brasel, J. and Blizzard, R. (1967) 'Emotional deprivation and growth deprivation simulating idiopathic hypopituitarism II endocrinological evaluation of the syndrome.' *NEJM, 276,* 1279–1283.

Pugh, G., De'Ath, E. and Smith, C. (1994) *Confident Parents, Confident Children: Policy and Practice in Parent Education and Support.* London: National Children's Bureau.

Radke-Yarrow, M. and Klimes-Dougan, B. (1997) 'Children of depressed mothers: A developmental and interactional perspective.' In S.S. Luthar, J.A. Burack, D. Cicchetti and J.R. Weisz (eds) *Developmental Psychopathology: Perspectives on Adjustment, Risk and Disorder.* New York: Cambridge University Press.

Randall, P. (1997) *Adult Bullying: Perpetrators and Victims.* London: Routledge.

Raynor, P., Rudolf, M.C.J., Cooper, K., Marchant, P. and Cottrell, D. (1999) 'A randomised controlled trial of specialist health visitor intervention for failure to thrive.' *Archives of Disease in Childhood, 80,* 6, 500–505.

Reading, R. and Reynolds, S. (2001) 'Debt, social disadvantage and maternal depression.' *Social Science and Medicine, 53,* 441–453.

Reder, P. and Duncan, S. (1999) *Lost Innocents: A Follow-Up Study of Fatal Child Abuse.* London and New York: Routledge.

Reder, P. and Duncan, S. (2003) 'Understanding communication in child protection networks.' *Child Abuse Review, 12,* 2.

Reder, P., Duncan, S. and Gray, M. (1993) *Beyond Blame: Child Abuse Tragedies Revisited.* London and New York: Routledge.

Reder, P. and Lucey, C. (1995) *Significant Issues in the Assessment of Parenting.* London and New York: Routledge.

Reed, R. and Reed, S. (1965) *Mental Retardation: A Family Study.* New York: Saunders.

Reid, W. and Epstein, L. (1972) *Task Centred Casework.* New York: Columbia University Press.

Reid, W. and Shyne, A. (1969) *Brief and Extended Casework.* New York: Columbia University Press.

Riley, J. (2000) *Communication in Nursing.* St Louis, MO: Mosby.

Ringwalt, C. and Caye, J. (1989) 'The effect of demographic factors on perceptions of child neglect.' *Children and Youth Services Review, 11,* 133–144.

Rivers, K., Aggleton, P., Chaise, E., Downie, A., Mulvihall, C., Sinkler, P., Tyrer, P. and Warwick, I. (1999) *Learning Lessons: A Report on Two Research Studies Informing The National Healthy School Standard (NHSS).* London: Department of Health and the Department for Education and Employment.

Romero, M. (1997) 'Who takes care of the maid's children? Exploring the costs of domestic service.' In H.L. Nelson (ed) *Feminism and Families.* New York and London: Routledge.

Rose, G. (1992) *The Strategy of Preventive Medicine.* Oxford: Oxford Medical Publications.

Rose, W. (2001) 'Assessing children in need and their families: an overview of the framework.' In J. Horwath (ed) *The Child's World. Assessing Children in Need.* London: Jessica Kingsley Publishers.

Rosenberg, D. and Cantwell, H. (1993) 'The consequences of neglect – individual and societal.' In S.J. Hobbs and J.M. Wynne (eds) *Child Abuse.* London: Bailliere Tindall.

Ross, D., Scott, K. and Kelly, M. (1996) *Child Poverty: What Are The Consequences?* Ottawa, Canada: Centre for International Statistics, Canadian Council on Social Development.

Royal College of Psychiatrists (2002) *Advice to Commissioners and Purchasers of Modern Substance Misuse Services, Council Report CR100.* London: Royal College of Psychiatrists.

Ruddick, S. (1989) *Maternal Thinking: Towards a Politics of Peace.* London: The Women's Press.

Ruhm, C.J. (2000) 'Parental leave and child health.' *Journal of Health Economics 19*, 931–960.

Runyan, D.K., Hunter, W.M., Socolar, R.S., Amaya-Jackson, I., English, D., Lasverk, J., Dubowitz, H., Browne, D.H., Bangdiwala, S.I. and Mathew, R.M. (1998) 'Children who prosper in unfavorable environments: the relationship to social capital.' *Pediatrics, 101*, 12–18.

Ryan, M. and Little, M. (2000) *Working with Fathers.* London: HMSO.

Sacker, A., Schoon, I. and Bartley, M. (2002) 'Social inequality in educational achievement and psychosocial adjustment throughout childhood: magnitude and mechanisms.' *Social Science and Medicine, 55*, 863–880.

Sanders, R., Colton, M. and Roberts, S. (1999) 'Child abuse fatalities and cases of extreme concern: lessons from reviews.' *Child Abuse and Neglect, 23*, 3, 257–268.

Sandford Zeskind, P. and Iacino, R. (1984) 'Effects of maternal visitation to preterm infants in the neonatal intensive care unit.' *Child Development, 55*, 1887–1893.

Schweinhart, L.J., Barnes, H.V. and Weikart, D.P. (1993) *Significant Benefits: The High/Scope Perry Preschool Study Through Age 27.* Ypsilanti, MI: High/Scope Press.

Scottish Children's Reporter Administration (2003) *Study on Youth Offending in Glasgow.* Stirling: SCRA.

Scottish Executive (2000) *Protecting Children – A Shared Responsibility: Guidance for Health Professionals in Scotland.* Edinburgh: The Stationery Office.

Scottish Executive (2001) *For Scotland's Children: Better Integrated Children's Services.* Edinburgh: Scottish Executive.

Scottish Executive (2002a) *'It's Everyone's Job to Make Sure I'm Alright' Report of the Child Protection Audit and Review.* Edinburgh: The Scottish Executive.

Scottish Executive (2002b) *An Analysis of Calls to Childline on the Subject of Child Abuse and Neglect.* Edinburgh: Scottish Executive. www.scotland.gov.uk/childprotection/

Scottish Women's Aid (1999) *Young People Speak Out About Domestic Violence.* Edinburgh: Scottish Women's Aid.

Scourfield, J. (2000) 'The rediscovery of child neglect.' *The Sociological Review, 68*, 3, 365–382.

Scourfield, J. (2003) *Gender and Child Protection.* Houndsmills: Palgrave MacMillan.

Seale, A. and Mkandla, M. (2000) 'Work partnerships with Black communities: issues and principles for social work education, training and service delivery.' In N. Baldwin (ed) *Protecting Children: Promoting their Rights.* London: Whiting and Birch.

Sedlack, A.J. and Broadhurst, D.D. (1996) *The Third National Incidence Study of Child Abuse and Neglect.* Washington, DC: US Department of Health and Human Services.

Seebohm Report (1968) *Committee on Local Authority and Allied Personal Social Services.* London: HMSO.

Shakespeare, T. (2000) *Help.* Birmingham: Venture Press.

Shandor Miles, M., Holditch-Davis, D., Burchinal, P. and Nelson, D. (1999) 'Distress and growth outcomes in mothers of medically fragile infants.' *Nursing Research, 48*, 3, 129–140.

Shaw, B. (1999) 'Chronic lung disease of prematurity.' In G. Levitt, D. Harvey and R. Cooke (eds) *Practical Perinatal Care. The Baby Under 1000g.* (pp.64–72). Oxford: Butterworth Heinemann.

Sheldon, B. (1987) 'The Psychology of Incompetence.' In the Department of Social Policy and Social Science, Royal Holloway and Bedford New College and the University of London. *Essays on Themes Related to Child Abuse.*

Sheldon, B. and Chivers, R. (2000) *Evidence-Based Social Care: A Study of Prospects and Problems.* Lyme Regis: Russell House Publishing.

Sherrod, K.B., O'Connor, S., Altemeier, W. and Vietze, P. (1985) 'Toward a semi-specific multi-dimensional threshold model of maltreatment.' In D. Drotar (ed) *New Directions in Failure to Thrive.* (pp.89–106). New York: Plenum Press.

Shields, L., Kistensson-Hallsrom, I., Kristjansdottir, G. and Hunter, J. (2003) 'Who owns the child in hospital? A preliminary discussion.' *Journal of Advanced Nursing, 41*, 3, 213–222.

Shropshire, J. and Middleton, S. (1999) *Small Expectations: Learning to be Poor?* York: Joseph Rowntree Foundation.

Sidebotham, P., Golding, J. and The ALSPAC Study Team (2001) 'Child maltreatment in the "Children of the Nineties": a longitudinal study of parental risk factors.' *Child Abuse and Neglect, 25*, 1177–1200.

Sidebotham, P., Heron, J., Golding, J. and The ALSPAC Study Team (2002) 'Child maltreatment in the "Children of the Nineties": deprivation, class, and social networks in a UK sample.' *Child Abuse and Neglect, 26*, 12, 1243–1259.

Sidebotham, P.D. and The ALSPAC Study Team (2000) 'Patterns of child abuse in early childhood: a cohort study of the "Children of the Nineties".' *Child Abuse Review, 9*, 311–320.

Sidebotham, P.D., Heron, J. and The ALSPAC Study Team (2003) 'Child maltreatment in the "Children of the Nineties": the role of the child.' *Child Abuse and Neglect, 27*, 337–352.

Sills, R.H. (1978) 'Failure to thrive: the role of clinical and laboratory evaluation.' *American Journal of Diseases in Children, 132*, 967–969.

Sinclair, R. and Bullock, R. (2002) *Learning from Past Experience: a Review of Serious Case Reviews.* London: Department of Health HMSO.

Singer, L., Minnes, S. and Arendt, R.E. (1999) 'Innovations for high-risk infants.' In P. Biegal and A. Blum (eds) *Innovations in Practice and Service Delivery across the Lifespan.* New York: Oxford University Press.

Skeels, H.M. (1966) 'Adult status of chidren with contrasting early life experiences: a follow up study.' *Monographs of Research in Child Development, 31.*

Skinner, C. (2002) '"Under Siege." Professional Social Work 6 February 2002.' *Archives of Disease in Childhood, 88*, 101–104.

Skuse, D., Gill, D.G., Lynch, M. and Wolke, D. (1995) 'Failure to thrive and the risk of child abuse: a prospective population survey.' *Journal of Medical Screening, 2*, 145–149.

Skuse, D., Wolke, D. and Reilly, S. (1992) 'Failure to thrive: clinical and developmental aspects.' In H. Remschmidt and M.H. Schmidt (eds) *Child and Youth Psychiatry. European Perspectives, Vol 2. Developmental Psychopathology.* (pp.46–71). Lewiston, NY: Hogrefe and Huber.

Smyth, M. (1998) *Half the Battle: Understanding the Effects of 'The Troubles' on Children and Young People in Ireland.* Londonderry: INCORE (University of Ulster and the United Nations University).

Sobsey, D. (1994) *Violence and Abuse in the Lives of People with Disabilities: The End of Silent Acceptance.* Baltimore, MA: Paul Brookes Publishing.

Spencer, N.J. (1994) 'Teenage mothers.' *Current Paediatrics, 4*, 48–51.

Spencer, N.J. (2002) 'Reducing unintended pregnancy among adolescents: changes in social, economic and educational policy need to be taken into account [letter].' *BMJ, 325*, 777.

Spencer, N.J., Taylor, J., Baldwin, N. and Read, J. (2001) 'The impact of poverty and deprivation on caring for infants and children.' *Reader for 'Fragile: handle with care: protecting babies from harm' training pack.* London: NSPCC.

Spitz, R.A. (1945) 'Hospitalism: an enquiry into the genesis of psychiatric conditions in early childhood.' *The Psychoanalytic Study of the Child, 1*, 53–74.

Spratt, T. (2001) 'The influence of child protection practice orientation on child welfare practice.' *British Journal of Social Work, 31*, 933–954.

Srivastava, O.P., Fountain, R., Ayre, P. and Stewart , J. (2003) 'The Graded Care Profile: a measure of care.' In M.C. Calder and S. Hackett (eds) *Assessment in Child Care.* Lynne Regis, Dorset: Russell House Publishing.

Srivastava, O.P. and Polnay, L. (1997) 'Field trial of Graded Care Profile (GCP) scale: a new measure of care.' *Archives of Diseases in Childhood, 63*, 337–340.

Sroufe, L.A. (1983) 'Infant–caregiver attachment and patterns of adaptation in pre-school: the roots of maladaption and competence.' In L. Perlmutter (ed.), *Minnesota Symposium on Child Psychology* (Vol. 16). Hillsdale, NJ: Erlbaum.

Stanley, N. (1997) 'Domestic violence and child abuse: developing social work practice.' *Child and Family Social Work, 2*, 135–145.

Stanley, S. and Goddard, C. (2002) *In the Firing Line: Violence and Power in Child Protection Work.* Chichester: Wiley.

Stanton, M.D. and Shadish, W.R. (1997) 'Outcome, attrition, and family-couples treatment for drug abuse: a meta-analysis and review of the controlled, comparative studies.' *Psychological Bulletin, 122*, 2, 170–191.

Steer, P. and Flint, C. (1999) 'Preterm labour and premature rupture of membranes.' *BMJ, 318*, 1059–1062.

Stevenson, J. and Bailey, V. (1998) *A controlled trial of post natal mothers' groups as psychosocial primary prevention. II: Evaluation of outcome.* Surrey: University of Surrey.

Stevenson, O. (1981) *Specialisation in Social Service Teams.* London: Allen and Unwin.

Stevenson, O. (1989) 'Multi disciplinary work in child protection.' *Public Policy and Professional Practice.* London: Harvester Wheatsheaf.

Stevenson, O. (1996) 'Emotional abuse and neglect: a time for reappraisal.' *British Journal of Social Work, 1*, 1, 13–18.

Stevenson, O. (1998a) *Neglected Children: Issues and Dilemmas.* Oxford: Blackwell Science.

Stevenson, O. (1998b) *Children in Need and Abused: Interprofessional and Interagency Responses.* Oxford: Blackwell Science.

Stevenson, O. (1998c) 'Neglect: where now? Some reflections.' *Child Abuse Review, 7*, 111–115.

Stone, B. (1998) 'Child neglect: practitioners' perspectives.' *Child Abuse Review, 7*, 87–96.

Stone, B. (2003) *A Framework for Assessing Neglect*. Lyme Regis: Russell House Publishing.

Stone, M. (1993) *Child Protection: A Model for Risk Assessment in Physical Abuse/Neglect*. Thomas Ditton/Surrey Social Services Department.

Strathearn, L., Gray, P., O'Callaghan, M. and Wood, D. (2001) 'Childhood neglect and cognitive development in extremely low birth weight infants: a prospective study.' *Pediatrics, 108*, 1, 142–151.

Straus, M.A. and Kantor, G.F. (2003) *Definition and measurement of neglect: some general principles and their application to self report measures*. Family Research Laboratory, University of New Hampshire. Retrieved 22 January 2004, from: http://pubpages. unh.edu/~mas2/NS2H-ss.pdf

Sullivan, M. and McGrath, M. (2003) 'Perinatal morbidity, mild motor delay, and later school outcomes.' *Developmental Medicine and Child Neurology, 45*, 104–112.

Sullivan, P.M. and Knutson, J.F. (1998) 'The association between child maltreatment and disabilities in a hospital-based epidemiological study.' *Child Abuse and Neglect, 22*, 271–288.

Sullivan, S. (2000) *Child Neglect: Current Definitions and Model. A Review of Child Neglect Literature*. Canada: Family Violence Unit.

Srivastava, O.P., Fountain, R., Ayre, P. and Stewart, J. (2003) 'The Graded Care Profile: a measure of care.' In M. Calder and S. Hackett (eds) *Assessment in Child Care*. Dorset: Russell House Publishing.

Swift, K.J. (1994) 'An outrage to common decency: historical perspectives on child neglect.' *Child Welfare, 74*, 1, 71–91.

Swift, K.J. (1995) *Manufacturing 'Bad Mothers': A Critical Perspective on Child Neglect*. Canada: University of Toronto Press Inc.

Szatmari, P., Saigal, S., Rosenbaum, P. and Campbell, D. (1993) 'Psychopathology and adaptive functioning among extremely low birth weight children at eight years of age.' *Development and Psychopathology, 8*, 345–357.

Taban, N. and Lutzker, J.R. (2001) 'Consumer evaluation of an ecobehavioral program for prevention and intervention of child maltreatment.' *Journal of Family Violence, 16*, 3, 323–330.

Talbot, N.B., Sobel, E.H., Burke, E.S., Lindeman, E. and Kaufman, S.B. (1947) 'Dwarfism in healthy children: its possible relation to emotional, nutritional and endocrine disturbances.' *New England Journal of Medicine, 263*, 783–793.

Talk (2003) 'A language for Daniel.' *Talk* 193, July–August, 19.

Tanner, K. and Turney, D. (2003) 'What do we know about child neglect? A critical review of the literature and its application to social work practice.' *Child and Family Social Work, 8*, 1, 25–35.

Taylor, A. (1993) *Women and Drug Use: An Ethnography of a Female Injecting Community*. Oxford: Clarendon Press.

Taylor, J., Spencer, N.J. and Baldwin, N. (2000) 'The social, economic and political context of parenting.' *Archives of Diseases in Childhood, 82*, 113–120.

Taylor, J., Watson, G. and Cable, S. (2002) *An Evaluation of the Camelon, Larbert and Grangemouth Support for Parents (CLASP) Initiative*. University of Dundee and Aberlour Child Care Trust.

Thoburn, J. (1996) 'Psychological parenting and child placement: "But we want to have our cake and eat it".' In D. Howe (ed) *Attachment and Loss in Child and Family Social Work*. Aldershot: Avebury.

Thoburn, J., Wilding, J. and Watson, J. (2000) *Family Support in Cases of Emotional Maltreatment and Neglect*. London: The Stationery Office.

Thompson, R.A. (1995) *Preventing Child Maltreatment Through Social Support*. Thousand Oaks, CA, London, New Dehli: Sage.

Thorpe, D. (1994) *Evaluating Child Protection*. Milton Keynes: Open University Press.

Thorpe, D. (1997) 'Regulating late modern childrearing in Ireland.' *Economic and Social Review, 28*, 63–84.

Tozer, R. (1999) *At the Double: Supporting Families with Two or More Severely Disabled Children*. York: Joseph Rowntree Foundation.

Tracey, E.M. and Farkas, K.J. (1994) 'Preparing practitioners for child welfare practice with substance-abusing families.' *Child Welfare, 75*, 57–68.

Tresider, J., Jones, J. and Glennie, S. (2003) *Report of multi-agency action research to improve service delivery to families with complex needs*. Nottingham: University of Nottingham.

Tronto, J. (1993) *Moral Boundaries: A Political Argument for an Ethic of Care*. New York and London: Routledge.

Tsogia, D., Copello, A. and Orford, J. (2001) 'Entering treatment for substance misuse: a review of the literature.' *Journal of Mental Health, 10*, 5, 481–499.

Tuck, V. (2000) 'Links between social deprivation and harm to children.' In N. Baldwin (ed) *Protecting Children: Promoting their Rights*. London: Whiting and Birch.

Turney, D. (2000) 'The feminizing of neglect.' *Child and Family Social Work, 5*, 1, 47–56.

Turney, D. and Tanner, K. (2001) 'Working with neglected children and their families.' *Journal of Social Work Practice, 15,* 2, 193–204.

Tymchuk, A.J. and Feldman, M.A. (1991) 'Parents with mental retardation and their children: Review of research relevant to professional practice.' *Canadian Psychology, 32,* 433–440.

Underdown, A. and Birks, E. (1999) *Faltering Growth – Taking the Failure out of Failure to Thrive.* London: The Children's Society and CPHVA.

UNICEF (2000) *A League Table of Child Poverty in Rich Nations, Innocenti Research Report No 2.* Florence: UNICEF Innocenti Research Centre.

UNICEF (2002) *A League Table of Educational Disadvantage in Rich Nations, Innocenti Report No 4.* Florence: Innocenti Research Centre.

United Nations (1989) *United Nations Convention on the Rights of the Child.* New York: General Assembly of the United Nations.

US Department of Health and Human Services, A.o.C., Youth and Families (1999) *Child Maltreatment 1997.* Washington, DC: US Department of Health and Human Services.

Utting, W., Baines, C., Stuart, M., Rowlands, J. and Vialva, R. (1997) *People Like Us.* London: The Stationery Office.

Valkama, M. (2000) *Prediction of Neurosensory Disability in Very Low Birth Weight Preterm Infants. Structural and Functional Brain Imaging and Hearing Screening at Term Age and Follow-up of Infants to a Corrected Age of 18 Months [Online].* Access Date: 1 July 2003. Available: http://herkules.oulu.fi/isbn9514259157/html/index.html

Velleman, R. (1993) 'Parental alcohol abuse – children's experience, children's response.' *Childright, 99,* 11–14.

Velleman, R. and Orford, J. (1999) *Risk and Resilience: Adults Who Were the Children of Problem Drinkers.* Amsterdam: Harwood Academic Publishers.

Vohr, B. and Wright, L. (2000) 'Neurodevelopmental and functional outcomes of extremely low birth weight infants in the national institute of child health and human development neonatal research network.' *Pediatrics, 105,* 6, 1216–1226.

Wakschlag, L.S. and Hans, S.L. (1999) 'Relation of maternal responsiveness during infancy to the development of behavior problems in high risk youth.' *Developmental Psychology, 35,* 2, 569–579.

Walker, M.U. (1998) *Moral Understandings: A Feminist Study in Ethics.* London and New York: Routledge.

Walker, S. (2002) 'Culturally competent protection of children's mental health.' *Child Abuse Review, 11,* 380–393.

Walter, I., Nutley, S. and Davies, H. (2003) *Research Impact: A Cross Sector Review Literature Review.* St Andrews: Research Unit for Research Utilisation.

Ward, H. (1995) *Looking after Children: Research into Practice.* London: HMSO.

Waugh, J., O'Callaghan, M., Tudehope, D., Mohay, H., Burns, Y., Gray, P. and Rogers, Y. (1996) 'Prevalence and aetiology of neurological impairment in extremely low birth weight infants.' *Journal of Paediatric Child Health, 32,* 120–124.

Weiss, C.H. (1979) 'The many meanings of research utilization.' *Public Administration Review, 39,* 426–431.

Werner, E. (2000) 'Protective factors and individual resilience.' In J. Schonkoff and S. Meisels (eds.), *The Handbook of Childhood Intervention.* Cambridge, MA: Cambridge University Press.

Western Health Board (1996) *Kelly: A Child is Dead. Report of the Committee of Enquiry.* Dublin: Western Health Board.

Whitten, C.F., Pettit, M.G. and Fischhoff, J. (1969) 'Evidence that growth failure from maternal deprivation is secondary to undereating.' *JAMA, 209,* 1675–1682.

Widdowson, E.M. (1951) 'Mental contentment and physical growth.' *Lancet, 1,* 1316–1318.

Wiggins, M., Oakley, A., Roberts, I., Turner, H., Rajan, L., Austerberry, H., Mujica, R. and Mugford, M. (2003) *Postnatal support for mothers living in disadvantaged areas: a randomised controlled trial and economic evaluation: Report to HTA.* London: Social Science Research Unit, Institute of Education.

Wilcox, A. (2001) 'On the importance – and the unimportance – of birth weight.' *International Journal of Epidemiology, 30,* 1233–1241.

Wilcox, W.D., Nieburg, P. and Miller, D.S. (1989) 'Failure to thrive: a continuing problem of definition.' *Clinical Pediatrics, 28,* 391–394.

Wilding, J. and Thoburn, J. (1997) 'Family support plans for neglected and emotionally maltreated children.' *Child Abuse Review, 6,* 343–356.

Wilensky, D.S., Ginsberg, G., Altman, M., Tulchinsky, T.H., Ben Yishay, F. and Auerbach, J. (1996) 'A community based study of failure to thrive in Israel.' *Archives of Disease in Childhood, 75,* 2, 145–148.

Williams, R. and Robertson, S. (1999) 'Fathers and health visitors: "it's a secret agent thing".' *Community Practitioner, 72,* 3, 56–58.

Wilson Schaef, A. (1992) *Women's Reality: An Emerging Female System in a White Male Society.* London: HarperCollins.

Winnicott, D.W. (1957) *The Child and the Family.* London: Tavistock.

Winnicott, D.W. (1964) *The Child, the Family, and the Outside World.* Harmondsworth: Penguin.

Wodarski, J.S., Howing, P.T., Kurthz, P.D. and Gaudin, J.M. (1980) 'Maltreatment and the school-age child: major academic, socio-emotional and adaptive outcomes.' *Social Work and Social Sciences Review, 35,* 506–513.

Wolfe, D.A., Wekerle, C. and Scott, K. (1997) *Alternatives to Violence: Empowering Youth to Develop Healthy Relationships.* Thousand Oaks, CA: Sage.

Wong, S.C. (1994) 'Diverted mothering: representations of caregivers of color in the age of "multi-culturalism." In E.N. Glenn, G. Chang and R. Forcey (eds) *Mothering: Ideology, Experience and Agency.* London: Routledge.

World Health Organization (2003) *International Classification of Diseases – 10 Volume 2 Perinatal [Online].* Access Date: 10 February 2003.

Wright, C.M., Avery, A., Epstein, M., Birks, E. and Croft, D. (1998) 'A new chart to evaluate weight faltering.' *Archives of Disease in Childhood, 78,* 40–43.

Wright, C.M., Booth, I., Buckler, J., Cameron, N., Cole, T., Healy, M., Hulse, A., Preece, M., Reilly, J. and Williams, A. (2002) 'Growth reference charts for use in the United Kingdom.' *Archives of Disease in Childhood, 86,* 11–14.

Wright, C.M., Callum, J., Birks, E. and Jarvis, S. (1998) 'Effect of community based management of failure to thrive: a randomised controlled trial.' *BMJ, 317,* 571–574.

Wright, C.M., Loughridge, J. and Moore, J. (2000) 'Failure to thrive in a population context: two contrasting case control studies of feeding and nutritional status.' *Pediatric Nutritional Society, 59,* 37–45.

Wright, C.M. and Parker, L. (2004) 'Forty years on: the effect of deprivation on growth in two Newcastle birth cohorts.' *International Journal of Epidemiology 33,* 147–152.

Wright, C.M. and Talbot, E. (1996) 'Screening for failure to thrive – what are we looking for?' *Child: Care, Health and Development, 22,* 4, 223–234.

Wright, C.M., Waterston, A. and Aynsley-Green, A. (1994a) 'Effect of deprivation on weight gain in infancy.' *Acta Paediatrica, 83,* 4, 357–359.

Wright, C.M., Waterston, A. and Aynsley-Green, A. (1994b) 'What is a normal rate of weight gain in infancy?' *Acta Paeditrica, 83,* 351–356.

Zero Tolerance Charitable Trust (1998) *Young People's Attitudes Towards Violence, Sex and Relationships.* Edinburgh: Zero Tolerance Charitable Trust.

Subject Index

Page numbers in italics refer to tables and diagrams

Author Index